OPPORTUNITY 08

MICHAEL E. O'HANLON
EDITOR

Independent Ideas for
America's Next President

Second Edition

BROOKINGS INSTITUTION PRESS
Washington, D.C.

Opportunity 08: Independent Ideas for America's Next President
may be ordered from Brookings Institution Press, c/o HFS, P.O. Box 50370,
Baltimore, MD 21211-4370; Tel. 800/537-5487, 410/516-6956; Fax 410/516-6998;
Internet: www.brookings.edu

Library of Congress Cataloging-in-Publication Data

Opportunity 08 : independent ideas for America's next president / Michael E.
O'Hanlon, editor. — 2nd ed.
    p.   cm.
    Includes bibliographical references and index.
    Summary: "Answers the call for nonpartisan discussion on challenges that matter
most to the future of our society, our prosperity, and our world, including Iran and
Iraq, China's rise, poverty and equality, health care reform, and retirement security.
New topics added include homeland security, foreign aid, and relations with
Pakistan"—Provided by publisher.
    ISBN 978-0-8157-6471-7 (pbk. : alk. paper)
    1. Presidents—United States—Election—2008. 2. Presidential candidates—
United States. 3. United States—Politics and government—2001– 4. United
States—Economic policy—2001– 5. United States—Social policy—1993– I. Title:
Independent ideas for America's next president.
    JK5262008 .O77 2008
    320.60973—dc22   2008029339

9 8 7 6 5 4 3 2 1

Typeset in Sabon with Gotham display

Composition by Cynthia Stock
Silver Spring, Maryland

Printed by R. R. Donnelley
Harrisonburg, Virginia

This book is dedicated to
the memory of our Brookings colleague
PETER RODMAN
(1943–2008)

Contents

PART II **Our Society**

Foreword

American presidential election years are always important, but this year's is remarkably so, given the magnitude and complexity of the challenges facing the nation and the world. The 2008 race is unusual in another respect: despite the differences among them, the nineteen candidates who sought the Democratic and Republican nominations had one thing in common: none was an incumbent president or vice president. That meant they were likely to be more open to fresh ideas on how to deal with the challenges facing the nation and the world.

Moreover, voters have made clear that in the course of this unusually long, crowded, and expensive campaign, they want to hear more from candidates about the issues and less of intense, destructive partisan politics. Ideas on how better to govern the country and lead the world are what Brookings is all about. So is civility of political discourse. Therefore, 2008 is a special year—carrying with it a special opportunity—for Brookings, just as it is for America. Hence this book and the work that is represented in the pages that follow. And now that we are on the eve of the presidential election, we thought it important not only to update the book where events demand, but also to present further new analysis of issues that are of supreme importance as November beckons. Publishing a second edition of *Opportunity 08* gives us another chance to put this important work in front of voters, media, and the candidates in advance of the election, and it hopefully will help guide November's winner through the early days of the new administration.

THE RELEVANT HISTORY

The last time we had open primaries in both parties was eighty years ago. In 1928 President Calvin Coolidge chose not to enter the race, saying that "Ten years in Washington is longer than any other man has had it—too long!" Coolidge's vice president, Charles Dawes, also declined to throw his hat in the ring, since he and Coolidge had feuded since nearly the beginning of their term in office. As a result, neither the sitting president nor his vice president sought the White House, though both were eligible to run.

The Republican nomination went to Herbert Hoover, who had been a member of the Coolidge cabinet but someone the president barely tolerated. (Coolidge famously quipped: "For six years that man has given me unsolicited advice—all of it bad.") The Democrats nominated New York's popular governor, Al Smith, the first Roman Catholic nominated for the presidency by either party. That year the nation was enjoying enormous prosperity; the newsreel was just emerging as a force in American political life, which brought into American movie theaters the jubilation at Le Bourget Airfield in France when Charles Lindbergh completed his first transatlantic flight.

Brookings itself had just turned twelve, having already helped the government adopt a modern accounting and budgeting system.

With both Hoover and Smith favoring corporate-led economic growth, the central issue in the election was the Volstead Act, prohibiting alcohol, which Hoover supported and Al Smith opposed. Often considered the first modern presidential election, it was won by Hoover in a landslide, claiming nearly 60 percent of the votes and carrying all but eight states.

In the eight decades since, wide-open primaries in both parties have not happened again. The closest to an open election was in 1952. While U.S. troops under UN command were mired in an unpopular conflict in Korea, President Harry Truman lost the New Hampshire primary and decided not to run for another term. His vice president, Alben Barkley, took a stab at the nomination and lost. Governor Adlai Stevenson won the Democratic nomination and was crushed in the national contest by the soldier-statesman Dwight D. Eisenhower.

Both the '28 and '52 campaigns were more about the future and less about policies of the incumbent administration than has been the case when at least one ticket is heavily invested in defending a record and continuing a legacy. Now we have that dynamic again—and the opportunity that comes with it.

A SIGNATURE BROOKINGS PROJECT

We launched Opportunity 08 in February 2007, in partnership with ABC News, to help the public and presidential candidates focus on critical issues facing the nation and to produce ideas, information, and policy forums on a broad range of domestic and foreign policy questions. The principal product of the project is represented in these pages: concise yet substantive research papers on topics worthy of presidential focus and intended to spark discussions based more on policy than ideology. While candidates in both parties certainly have demonstrated that they are loyal to core beliefs within their parties, they also have been looking for ways to distinguish themselves by their ability to set a new course for the country. This election has already stimulated a more forward-looking, open-minded debate within—as well as between—the two major parties. Indeed, this has been especially the case as the primary season has given way to the general election, and both Senators McCain and Obama have increasingly been highlighting efforts to break with their respective party's mainstream on crossover issues such as the environment for Senator McCain and faith-based initiatives for Senator Obama.

Our goal in this effort was also to help elevate the debate, in part by showing that specialists with different political orientations and backgrounds can put their heads together and come up with bold yet practical ways of addressing the toughest, most important problems.

We are holding everything we do under the banner of Opportunity 08 to three standards represented by our motto: quality, independence, impact. We are commissioning high-quality research, ensuring that the work reflects a variety of perspectives, and using our convening ability, our new website (www.opportunity08.org/), our partnership with ABC and others, and every other means at our disposal to maximize impact.

The topics for this volume were selected by the Opportunity 08 leadership team, headed by Senior Fellow Michael O'Hanlon, who has worked closely with an advisory council led by Ken Duberstein, a former chief of staff to Ronald Reagan, and Tom Donilon, a former chief of staff to Secretary of State Warren Christopher, and with Melissa Skolfield, our vice president and director for communications. For each topic, we asked our top specialists to draw from the best of their research and put forward the most compelling ideas that the next president should address. Where we felt our work could be complemented by others, we also asked a small circle of friends of Brookings to contribute. From the war in Iraq; to policy toward China; to health care, budget, tax, and energy policy, the chapters in this volume provide some of the best policy analysis available. This second edition contains revised as well as several new articles—including new ones on Pakistan, Iraq, foreign aid, and homeland security—keeping pace with current political and policy developments.

The work in this volume is also unequivocally independent. First, I should explain why we use that word rather than "bipartisan." Bipartisanship implies cooperation between Republicans and Democrats (which—don't get me wrong—we're all for). A truly independent institution respectfully rejects the notion that truth and wisdom are necessarily to be found in one major party or the other. Independence means that the public policy scholars most worth listening to—however they might register and whomever they might vote for—develop their ideas independently of any platform, agenda, or party line. They find solutions to today's most pressing and—by definition, complex—problems, as opposed to finding a rationale for their own established views. Or, to put it differently, independence is a state of mind, one that was captured by Daniel Patrick Moynihan—a Democrat with a Ph.D. who worked for Richard Nixon. "We're all entitled to our own opinions," said Professor/Ambassador/Senator Moynihan, "but we're not entitled to our own facts." That frame of mind prospers inside the walls of Brookings and throughout the activities undertaken by Opportunity 08.

Note that earlier I said "intense, destructive" partisanship. Partisanship is not only, in and of itself, a natural and healthy part of our political system—it's institutionalized in the two-party system. The same could be said of polarization. Barry Goldwater had a valid point when he said that our elections should offer the American people "a choice, not an echo." As you will see in this volume, Brookings and Opportunity 08 emphatically resist the notion that to be nonpartisan means that we've always got to reflect both sides of a contested issue. We have not seen it as our job to forge compromises or to aim for the middle (which, by the way, is a moving target in the American political spectrum). That said, we also have tried to put forward innovative solutions and fresh ideas that we think are capable of gaining broad-based public support. In the process, we have tried to create and sustain an atmosphere that actively—indeed, *pro*actively—encourages collaboration on projects without regard to party lines, which brings people of different backgrounds and perspectives together.

Last, this project has been designed from the start to have maximum impact. Being independent doesn't mean being "policy neutral"—a phrase, and a concept, that is anathema to our goal of being policy relevant. Once our scholars have completed their research, we have encouraged them to help move the public debate. Indeed, the Opportunity 08 project itself has been Brookings's most important institutionwide attempt to engage the public debate, using the 2008 presidential elections as an opportunity to seek a wider and more influential audience for our work.

To that end, the scope of Opportunity 08 is represented by more than simply the chapters in this volume. Over the past eighteen months, the scholars involved in this project have offered to brief all the candidates and staffs from both parties. Not only have they done so, but already several of these ideas have become part of the core platforms of candidates. We have already hosted a series of events around the country—in early primary states of Iowa, New Hampshire, Nevada, and South Carolina, and in battleground states such as Ohio and Florida. We have worked closely with partner institutions and a wide range of Americans in the effort. We also have featured speeches by the presidential candidates from both parties, as well as policy discussions that include scholars, journalists, and political experts, structured around the ideas in this collection. These forums, like this volume, aimed to present the presidential candidates and, just as important, the American people, with fresh policy ideas on a range of topics. To help broaden the discussion of America's policy challenges, policy forums and information will be featured on the ABC News website, which provides live 24/7 news coverage online, on television, and on mobile devices. In addition to being available on our website, www.brookings.edu, the material has been featured on the project's interactive website, www.opportunity08.org.

On behalf of all of Brookings, I want to thank Mike, Melissa, Ken, Tom, and the entire advisory council, which has provided invaluable guidance and support.

Finally, thanks to you, our readers. Being a think tank entails more than thinking, writing—and talking: it also entails listening and reflecting on what we hear. You, the readers of this book in its two editions, have your own vital role to play in shaping how this election is conducted—and those that lie ahead of us as well. We hope this book along with its predecessor—as well as the project of which it is a part—will be of some use to you in that respect, and we hope to hear back from you on your own views about how to take maximum advantage of America's opportunity in 2008.

STROBE TALBOTT
President

Washington, D.C.
August 2008

OPPORTUNITY 08

1 ❱

Big Ideas for the 2008 Race

MICHAEL E. O'HANLON

With the 2008 general election campaign fully upon us, and a new administration getting ready to start its first 100 days in office shortly thereafter, Brookings is happy to offer this new and updated version of *Opportunity 08: Independent Ideas for America's Next President.* Among other things this version includes new chapters on Pakistan by Bruce Riedel, homeland security by Jeremy Shapiro, and foreign assistance by Ken Dam.

Since August 2007, the Opportunity 08 project has been to Nevada, New Hampshire, Iowa, South Carolina, Florida, and Ohio, teaming up with ABC News and regional organizations such as the University of Nevada at Las Vegas, St. Anselm College, the University of Iowa, the Charleston Chamber of Commerce, the University of Miami, and the Cleveland Clinic, in the process. We have shared ideas, listened to other authors and institutional voices, received feedback from the public, watched the candidates, and updated our chapters for developments at home and abroad over the last year. This book is a key result of our efforts.

Our project is explicitly bipartisan, with an advisory council including former Reagan chief of staff Ken Duberstein, along with Tom Donilon, A. B. Culvahouse, Fred Malek, former representative John Porter, former senator and ambassador Jack Danforth, Mack McLarty, Mickey Kantor, Judith McHale, and Casey Wasserman.

Our chapter writers include our own scholars, former Bush National Security Council official Michael Green, former senator Warren B. Rudman, and former representative Charles W. Stenholm. The reader can go to the Brookings website (www.brookings.edu) and that of the Opportunity 08 project (www.opportunity08.org) to read updates of some of these chapters as well as to access other papers within the three subject areas: Our World, Our Society, and Our Prosperity.

Some ideas coming out of the project are quite provocative. A simple and elegant place to start is with economist Bill Gale's proposal for how to begin to address our anemic personal savings rates. Today, if you want a 401(k), you have to sign up for one—and that simple fact discourages many people from creating this savings-inducing financial vehicle. Why not automatically enroll them when they take a new job? If they wish to opt out, fine—but doesn't it make sense to take advantage of human inertia to a good end?

In another paper, David Sandalow argues the near-total dependence of our cars and trucks on oil is a more fundamental problem than oil imports per se. If drivers had a choice between oil and other fuels, Sandalow argues, many of the national security, environmental, and economic problems often associated with oil could be mitigated. He calls for measures to transform both the auto fleet with "plug-in hybrids" and the fuel supply with new forms of ethanol. His core proposals remain relevant even in light of the fact that corn-based ethanol, which Sandalow never overemphasized, has partly fallen from grace since the publication of the first edition of this book (because of its effects on rising world food prices).

He would use federal vehicle purchases and tax incentives to accelerate development of such technologies, and increase the ethanol production subsidy for so-called cellulosic ethanol (made from various grasses and trees). Even for those not using ethanol, plug-in hybrids would help reduce energy consumption and oil imports—as well as global warming—because electricity plants are far more efficient than internal combustion engines.

Bill Frenzel, Charles Stenholm, Bill Hoagland, and Belle Sawhill lay out a serious bipartisan plan for eliminating the fiscal deficit. Their approach would cut spending and increase revenues in roughly equal proportion. For example, they would limit total itemized income tax deductions to 15 percent of income and would cap the exclusion on employer-paid health insurance.

Speaking of taxes, in another paper, Bill Gale proposes revenue-neutral changes to the law that would tax new corporate investment income once and only once, and introduce return-free filing for many taxpayers (an idea since espoused by John Edwards as well). Controversially, he would change the mortgage interest deduction to a one-time homebuyers' tax credit, focusing this tax break on those who most need the help.

Former Bush administration official Ron Haskins and Belle Sawhill propose an ambitious, if moderately expensive, plan to tackle poverty. They would expand the Earned Income Tax Credit, increase further the minimum wage, subsidize child care for low-wage workers, invest more in high-quality early childhood education, and use some noneconomic tools, such as teaching relationship skills to individuals getting married.

Bruce Katz and Margery Austin Turner present a plan for revamping federal housing policy. Designed partly to avoid building houses in inner cities, it would engage metropolitan planning organizations in creating regional housing concepts linked to regional transportation and job creation strategies.

Peter Berkowitz of the Hoover Institution suggests new policies for higher education in the United States. My favorite is the dramatic expansion of fellowship programs to support the study of critical foreign languages.

Hady Amr and Peter Singer also call for major improvements in America's foreign language capacities in their paper on engaging the Muslim world—in which they further suggest the next president include stops in major Islamic countries on his first overseas trip.

In a separate education paper, INTEL executives Sean Maloney and Christopher Thomas develop a policy agenda to enhance America's future prospects for a robust Internet economy, including much greater federal support for technical education and IT research and development. And in yet another paper with implications for education policy, Hugh Price, Amy Liu, and Rebecca Sohmer propose more college aid for students attending school part time, a large group that has grown over the years, yet has never been the main focus of aid and scholarship programs. They also favor creating special short courses to help disadvantaged students prepare college applications and raising Pell Grant levels.

The 2008 election represents the first time since 1952 that neither party has an incumbent president or vice president as its nominee. It also represents one of the most momentous elections in our nation's history. Our collective national goal should be to encourage and assist Senator McCain and Senator Obama in providing fresh ideas that meet the huge challenges of the day. And our role as a nonpartisan think tank with an explicitly bipartisan approach to Opportunity 08, as unusual as that may be in these times, will I hope allow us to do so.

OUR WORLD

2

Expand the U.S. Agenda toward Pakistan

Prospects for Peace and Stability Can Brighten

BRUCE RIEDEL

SUMMARY ❙ Pakistan is the most dangerous country in today's world. There, the forces that threaten global peace and security all come together: proliferation of weapons of mass destruction, the risk of nuclear war, terrorism, poverty, dictatorship, radical Islam, and narcotics.

Pakistan's fragile politics reflect a history of alternating military dictatorships with periods of weak elected civilian rule. Recently, violence has become a dominant feature of the political landscape—most notably in the assassination of Benazir Bhutto in December 2007. But, following the February 2008 elections, Pakistan may have embarked on a tortuous path toward democracy.

The United States has failed democratic forces in Pakistan. With some history of democratic traditions and a predominantly Muslim population of almost 170 million, Pakistan would appear to be the perfect candidate for the declared U.S. strategy, proclaimed by President Bush in his second inaugural address, "to seek and support the growth of democratic movements and institutions in every nation and culture." Instead, the Bush administration chose to continue the fifty-year tradition of the United States' befriending Pakistani dictators.

In most respects, the administration's policy has not paid off. Polls now show Pakistani approval of America at all-time lows. Many, if not

most, Pakistanis, see the war against jihadis in the nation's western badlands as Mr. Bush's war, not their own.

The next president must change the agenda with Pakistan and seek to
alter the mood by revamping Pakistani visions of America. He must work
to persuade the Pakistani people that the United States supports democracy in their country, that we can be a long-term and reliable ally, and that
the struggle against al Qaeda and its allies is their war as well as ours.

The immediate and urgent requirement is to eliminate al Qaeda's safe
haven in Pakistan before the terrorists use it to attack us again here at
home—perhaps around our presidential election or shortly after inauguration day. This effort requires substantially greater Pakistani cooperation
in the war against al Qaeda and its allies in the badlands near the Afghan
border.

The next U.S. administration should engage in a new public diplomacy
and launch new aid programs, both economic and military. It should support fully Pakistan's democratically elected leadership, even if the United
States and Pakistan disagree on some key issues, ranging from how to
prevent nuclear proliferation to how to contain terrorist threats.

Reordering our aid, we should initiate a multibillion and multiyear
effort to improve Pakistan's educational and transportation infrastructure. This initiative should include a "democracy bonus," as proposed by
Senator Joe Biden, which would increase the aid level automatically every
year the president certifies that Pakistan is a democracy. It also should
include the convening of a donors' conference.

Increased military aid should be directed to the development of a counterinsurgency and counterterrorism approach. The increase should be
conditioned on an end to military interference in politics and the consort-
ing with terrorist elements by Pakistan's intelligence apparatus, the Inter-
Services Intelligence, or ISI.

The next president also should take advantage of opportunities to
improve the security situation in South Asia by

—working with Kabul and Islamabad to gain a public agreement,
guaranteed by the United States, that the Durand Line, which is the dis-
puted border between Afghanistan and Pakistan, can be altered only with
the consent of both governments;

—quietly seeking an agreement between New Delhi and Islamabad on
Kashmir, probably based on a formula that would make the Line of Control between Indian and Pakistani authority in Kashmir a permanent and

normal international border (perhaps with minor modifications) and render it a permeable frontier, so that the Kashmiri people can live more normal lives;

—pursuing a special agreement allowing India and Pakistan to cooperate on social and economic issues in Kashmir;

—greatly intensifying efforts to ensure the security of Pakistan's weapons arsenal, while avoiding reckless talk about using unilateral means to secure the Pakistani systems.

In dealing with Pakistan, the next president must go beyond threats and sanctions, beyond commando raids and halfhearted intelligence cooperation, beyond poorly directed aid and aircraft sales. It is time to come to grips with the ideals and interests motivating Pakistan's behavior and to help Islamabad make peace with itself and its neighbors. ❯

CONTEXT ❯ Today Pakistan is in the midst of a complicated transition from military rule, which is taking place in an environment where violence has become a dominant feature, as evidenced by the recent bombing of the Danish embassy in June. ❯

THE MOST DANGEROUS COUNTRY

Pakistan is the most dangerous country in today's world. Many forces combine in Pakistan to threaten global peace and security: proliferation of weapons of mass destruction, terrorism, poverty, dictatorship, radical Islam, and narcotics.

In recent years the dangers have taken many forms:

—*Potential war of mass destruction.* Nowhere is the risk of nuclear war higher than in South Asia, where Pakistan and India already have fought four wars.

—*Nuclear proliferation.* Pakistan has sold nuclear technology to North Korea, Iran, and Libya and acquired it partly by theft in the Netherlands.

—*Organizing acts of terrorism.* The September 11 plot against America was planned and carried out from Pakistan's neighbor, Afghanistan, and the alleged tactical mastermind of the plot, Khalid Sheikh Mohammed, was arrested in Pakistan.

—*Haven for terrorists.* The top leaders of al Qaeda, Osama bin Laden and Ayman al-Zawahiri, fled to Pakistan after the collapse of Afghanistan's

Taliban regime in 2001, along with Taliban leader Mullah Omar. All three scoundrels are believed to be still hiding somewhere in the borderland between the two countries.

—*Drug trafficking.* The country is a pathway for opium from Afghanistan to the world market.

THE PATH TO DEMOCRACY

Pakistan's internal politics are brittle. The lack of stability reflects the nation's underdeveloped conditions, as more than half of Pakistanis live in grinding poverty and most women are illiterate.

The first country created after World War II and the first created as a Muslim state, Pakistan has alternated between weak elected civilian regimes and military dictatorships. In many frontier areas, its central government exercises only nominal authority. Furthermore, resource-rich Baluchistan has been in a state of revolt since 2000; Karachi, the largest city, has been plagued by intense gang warfare for years; and the civilian institutions of the state—the judiciary, parliamentary processes, law enforcement authorities, regulatory agencies, financial controls, and other mechanisms for assuring civil order—are all weak.

Until the elections in February 2008, Islamist political parties had steadily gained strength. Violence and terrorism have emerged as familiar features of the current landscape: there were fifty-six suicide bombing attacks in 2007, culminating in the shocking public assassination of former prime minister Benazir Bhutto on the streets of Rawalpindi on December 27.

Today Pakistan is in the midst of a complicated transition from the military rule of Pervez Musharraf, who as chief of staff of the army took power in a bloodless coup in 1999, to what many Pakistanis *hope* will be democracy. This process is extremely fragile, and the future of Pakistan's government—perhaps along with the very survival of the state—is uncertain. Pakistan has already fought one civil war when Bangladesh seceded in 1971.

THE U.S. ROLE TO DATE

The United States has largely failed democratic forces in Pakistan. As a nation with impressive democratic traditions and a predominantly Muslim population of 170 million, Pakistan would appear to be the perfect candidate for the declared U.S. strategy, proclaimed by President George W. Bush in his second inaugural address, "to seek and support the growth of democratic movements and institutions in every nation and culture." Unlike Saudi Arabia or many other Muslim states, Pakistan offers a history of elections to political parties that have strong voter support (although all have been riddled with controversy) and a tradition of functioning secular institutions and society.

Unfortunately, instead of supporting these democratic initiatives, the United States historically has backed Pakistan's military dictators. This is a bipartisan history. On the first U.S. presidential visit to South Asia, Dwight Eisenhower praised Pakistan's first military ruler, Ayub Khan. John Kennedy went Eisenhower one better, hosting a lavish state dinner for Khan at Mount Vernon—the first use of George Washington's mansion to entertain a foreign leader. Lyndon Johnson continued the conspicuous support for Ayub Khan. Richard Nixon then went so far as to endorse the brutal and unsuccessful war in Bangladesh initiated under Ayub Khan's successor, Yahya Khan. Jimmy Carter and Ronald Reagan both supported another dictator, Muhammad Zia-ul-Haq, because of his participation in Afghanistan's war against the Soviet Union. (Carter, however, was deeply angered by Zia's execution, also in Rawalpindi, of the democratically elected prime minister Zulfikar Ali Bhutto, father of Benazir Bhutto.)

When Musharraf seized power, Bill Clinton imposed sanctions and pressed for an early end to military control. He worked to ensure that ousted prime minister Mian Muhammad Nawaz Sharif would not suffer the same fate as Ali Bhutto. But Clinton also became the first head of state to visit Pakistan after the 1999 coup, thus providing Musharraf with his first measure of international legitimacy.

George W. Bush went much further to support Musharraf. His administration acted to repeal all sanctions and provide $11 billion in aid, more than half through direct funding to the Pakistani army with little or no accounting. When Musharraf staged phony elections in 2002 and 2007, Bush did not object. When he sacked the head of Pakistan's Supreme Court and the nation's lawyers went into the streets to protest, the Bush team backed the general. Even while Musharraf was clearly losing popular support in the run-up to the February 2008 elections, the administration still touted him as "the indispensible man" of Pakistan.

CHANGE THE AGENDA AND THE MOOD

The cost of the Bush administration's policy has been the alienation of most Pakistanis from the United States and our interests. Polls now show Pakistani approval of the United States at record lows. In the eyes of too many Pakistanis, the war against jihadis in the nation's western badlands is Bush's war, not their own.

The next president has to change the agenda with Pakistan and recast Pakistani visions of this country. He must work to persuade the Pakistani people that the United States supports democracy in their country, that the United States can be a long-term and reliable ally, and that the struggle against al Qaeda and its allies is their war as well as ours.

GAIN SUPPORT FOR FIGHTING TERRORISTS ALONG THE BORDER

Pakistan is a safe haven for al Qaeda, and the safe haven has grown steadily larger under a military dictatorship in the last few years and now poses the number one threat to the United States.

The Need Is Urgent

The immediate and urgent requirement is to eliminate al Qaeda's safe haven in Pakistan before the terrorists use it to attack America again in the region or here at home. Eighty percent of the suicide bombers attacking U.S. and NATO forces in Afghanistan are trained in Pakistan by the Taliban or al Qaeda, and Pakistan has done far too little to prevent this cross-border carnage.

For a dramatic illustration of how dangerous the al Qaeda network remains, consider this summer's London trial of al Qaeda members charged with plotting to blow up ten jumbo jets en route from Heathrow Airport to Chicago, Montreal, New York, Washington, San Francisco, and Toronto. Had the British not foiled the plot at the last minute, in August 2006, it would have killed hundreds, if not thousands.

The British trial has shown that the explosives worked, that the martyrs were already selected and had made their obligatory martyr videos, and that the plot was linked directly to the al Qaeda leadership in Pakistan. The plotters also calculated that they could conduct the same operation repeatedly, because all the forensic evidence would lie at the bottom of the Atlantic.

The masterminds got away in Pakistan. Only one person, Rashid Rauf, was arrested, and he escaped custody while being transferred from one jail to another by Pakistan's Inter-Services Intelligence (ISI). This unimpressive performance illustrates the problem in a nutshell. Pakistan is only a halfhearted ally in the war against al Qaeda and is even less committed to the struggle against the Taliban and Kashmiri groups.

Initiate a New Diplomacy

Just targeting al Qaeda is a strategy that has proved a failure. Within Pakistan, al Qaeda swims in a sea of jihadis—Kashmiri groups like Lashkar-e-Tayyiba, anti-Shi'a groups like Sipah-e Sahaba, the Taliban, and others. The ISI itself created much of this nexus of terror, either to fight the Soviet Union in Afghanistan (to increase Pakistani influence there) or to fight India in Kashmir. The local ties to al Qaeda are deep. Every major al Qaeda figure arrested in Pakistan since 9/11 has been caught in a safe house operated by one of these groups.

But, while the need is pressing and al Qaeda may well plan to strike either before the November elections in the United States or shortly after the inauguration of a new U.S. president, there is no quick fix or unilateral option available. *We need substantially greater Pakistani cooperation in the war against al Qaeda and its allies in the badlands of South Asia.* There is no alternative. Predator strikes or commando missions into the badlands cannot eliminate the safe haven. Even a full-scale U.S. invasion and occupation (which is beyond our military's reach and could provoke a nuclear war) would only spread the virus more deeply into Pakistan.

We must find a way to embrace the new Pakistani leadership and persuade it to work with us. This will be a difficult undertaking, given the bad blood the Bush team has created and the legacy of the last half century. It requires, in sports terms, a full-court press. The next administration should engage in a new public diplomacy and launch new aid programs, both economic and military. Finally, it should vigorously undertake an altogether new diplomatic approach.

Our public posture should be one of full support for the democratically elected leadership. We should embrace the Pakistani people's choices, despite the shortcomings of some of the new leaders (actually, many are not new at all, which is why their defects are known). Accordingly, we should no longer stand by Musharraf. His fate should be decided in Pakistan by Pakistanis without our meddling and commentary.

On many issues, the new democratic government in Pakistan will not back our positions enthusiastically. We will differ over how to deal with Islamism, over the idea of negotiating with the Taliban, over nuclear weapons development, over the fate of the nuclear pirate (and Pakistani national hero) A. Q. Khan, and other issues.

In this context, we must disagree without being disagreeable. We need to take our differences to the elected leadership, not to the army leadership or the ISI director, to get results. To go to the army on political issues is to undermine the rule of law and proper civil-military relations once again, repeating and solidifying the errors of the past.

INCREASE ECONOMIC AID— AND RECHANNEL MILITARY AID

Behind a new public posture should emerge a vast expansion in our aid relationship and a qualitative change in its nature. Of the $11 billion dollars in aid since 9/11, very little has gone to meet Pakistan's desperate need for economic help.

We should provide a multibillion and multiyear commitment to help rebuild Pakistan's deteriorating educational system and to construct new highways and other modern transportation infrastructure. Senate Foreign Relations Committee Chairman Joe Biden (D-Del.) has proposed several useful ideas, including a "democracy bonus" that would increase the aid level automatically every year the president certifies that Pakistan is a democracy. Besides implementing a democracy bonus, the next president should organize a donors' conference to obtain help from other key friends of Pakistan, including Saudi Arabia, the EU, and China.

Increased assistance to the Pakistani military and security forces also makes sense. The forces need to refocus their orientation and infrastructure. Instead of concentrating on fighting a war with India, along the lines of the last four wars, they should work toward becoming an effective counterinsurgency and counterterrorism force. This will be expensive and difficult; it means changing doctrine and thought processes, not just equipment, but clearly such change falls within our mutual national interests.

In practical terms, more worthwhile military aid means fewer F-16 fighter jets and more helicopters, fewer tanks and more night vision devices. Increased aid to the Pakistani army should be conditioned on two premises. First, the army needs to stay in the barracks and out of politics. Civil-military relations need to change forever. The second condition is that the ISI needs to be entirely on the side of fighting terror, not working both sides of the fence at the same time. In conversations with the author early this year, senior Afghan and senior Indian officials both stressed an ISI committed to fighting terror, not sponsoring it, is the sine qua non of real change in Pakistan. Congress should require an annual secret certification from the CIA that ISI is on one side only: ours.

HELP ISLAMABAD DEAL WITH KABUL AND KASHMIR

Joint U.S. and Pakistani diplomacy should focus on two critical issues: Pakistan's relations with Afghanistan and with India.

Toward a Stable Border with Afghanistan

The Afghan-Pakistan border region, 1,610 miles long, is the heart of al Qaeda's sanctuary in South Asia. The border recognized by Pakistan has never been accepted by any Afghan government, largely because it was unilaterally imposed by the British colonial government in 1893. This so-called Durand Line divides both the Pashtun and Baluchi peoples and has never been popular in Afghanistan. Kabul governments have always been unwilling to forfeit their claim to a larger "Pashtunistan."

Former U.S. ambassador to Afghanistan Ronald Neuman rightly characterizes the current situation as "borderline insanity" and suggests that resolving its ambiguity is part of the required "big think" solution to the threat posed from the badlands. It is unlikely that the government of President Hamid Karzai could accept the Durand Line formally and finally any more than its predecessors could. But the United States should work with Kabul and Islamabad to gain a public agreement that the line can be altered only with the consent of both governments.

Such an acceptance of the de facto permanence of the border also should set the stage for greater willingness on both sides to police the line and to regard it as a real international frontier. Improved policing would not immediately stop smuggling and infiltration, but it would provide a basis for long-term cooperation between Kabul and Islamabad—a critical ingredient for progress against al Qaeda and something seriously lacking in the past.

Because we have so much at stake in the stabilization of this border and the end to the al Qaeda safe haven that exists along it, the United States should be prepared to endorse an agreement and guarantee the integrity of the border. Pakistan, for its part, would need to treat its badlands region as part of its national domain, policing and administering it like any other region.

Toward a Negotiated Agreement with India

The other critical issue for American diplomacy is the underlying problem that drives Pakistan's relationship with terror: India and Kashmir. The Pakistani state and army have been obsessed with confronting India since the two nations achieved independence in 1947. It is to fight India asymmetrically that ISI created much of the modern jihadi infrastructure in South Asia, both in Kashmir and in Afghanistan.

Pakistan's Position

In the best case, the international community, led by the United States, would disrupt Pakistan's preoccupation with India by resolving the two countries' underlying dispute over Kashmir. From the Pakistani perspective, an optimal resolution of Kashmir would lead to the unification with Pakistan of the entire province, or at least the Muslim-dominated Valley of Kashmir including the scenic city of Srinagar, currently the capital of the Indian state of Jammu and Kashmir.

With Kashmir reunited with Pakistan, the motivation to have nuclear weapons would be reduced, if not removed, and the need for a jihadi option to compel India to withdraw from the valley would disappear. This is precisely the outcome that Pakistani leaders have in mind when they urge U.S. leaders to devote diplomatic and political energy to the Kashmir issue.

India's Position

Pakistan's preferred scenario is completely unrealistic. India has made it clear it will not withdraw from Kashmir. On the contrary, India argues it has already made a major concession by accepting the de facto partition of the province among itself, Pakistan, and China. India is probably prepared to accept the Line of Control, in effect the cease-fire line of 1948, as the ultimate border with Pakistan. But it is not prepared for a fundamental redrawing of borders to put the valley under Pakistan's sovereignty.

Still, India's position does not preclude a subtle effort to resolve the Kashmir problem on a realistic basis, complementing the ongoing Indo-Pakistani bilateral dialogue. Already that dialogue has produced a series of confidence-building measures between the two countries, including reopening transportation links, setting up hotlines between military commands, and holding periodic discussions at the foreign minister level on issues that divide the two nations.

U.S. Noninvolvement

Unfortunately, the current Indo-Pakistani dialogue has not seriously addressed the Kashmir issue because of the wide gulf between the two parties and India's refusal to negotiate while still a target of terrorist attacks planned and organized in Pakistan. Meanwhile, the United States has been reluctant to engage more actively in the Kashmir dispute in light of India's position that outside intervention is unwarranted and that Kashmir is a purely bilateral issue. Faced with the likelihood of India's rejection of U.S. involvement, U.S. diplomacy relegated the Kashmir problem to the "too hard" pot and left it to simmer.

The results have been all too predictable. The Kashmir issue periodically boils over, forcing the United States and the international community to step in to prevent a full-scale war. This was the case during the Kargil crisis in 1999, after the terrorist attack on the Indian parliament in December 2001, and again in 2002, when India mobilized on the Pakistani border.

Opportunity for Progress

A unique opportunity for quiet American diplomacy to help advance the Kashmir issue to a stable solution may occur in 2009. The U.S.-India nuclear deal, agreed to during President Bush's July 2005 visit to South Asia, should create a more solid and enduring basis for U.S.-Indian relations than ever before existed.

The deal (if implemented) removes the central obstacle to closer strategic ties between Washington and New Delhi—the nuclear proliferation problem, which has held back the development of the relationship for two decades. The deal should be implemented once India concludes its arrangements with the International Atomic Energy Agency (IAEA) and the Nuclear Suppliers Group.

In the new era of U.S.-Indian strategic partnership, Washington should work with India on many issues in the subcontinent and be able to help New Delhi to be more flexible on Kashmir. It is clearly in the U.S. interest to defuse a lingering conflict that has generated global terrorism and repeatedly threatened to create a full-scale military confrontation engulfing the subcontinent. Similarly, it is in India's interest to find a solution to a conflict that has gone on far too long. And since the Kargil War in 1999, India has been a bit more open to a U.S. role in Kashmir because they sense Washington leans toward a resolution on the basis of the status quo, which favors India.

The United States currently enjoys better relations with India than at any time in the last several decades and is in a position to gain the confidence of Pakistan as well. The rapprochement with India, begun by President Clinton and advanced by President Bush, is now supported by an almost uniquely bipartisan consensus in the U.S. foreign policy establishment and in Congress. At the same time, the sanctions that poisoned U.S.-Pakistani ties for decades have been removed by legislation supported by both Republicans and Democrats. This is a unique moment.

Possible Formula

A Kashmir solution would have to be based around a formula that would accomplish two things at once: make the Line of Control between Indian and Pakistani authority in Kashmir a permanent and normal international border (perhaps with minor modifications) and render it a permeable frontier so that the Kashmiri people could live more normal lives.

In addition, a special condominium might be created to allow the two countries to work together on issues that are internal to Kashmir, such as transportation, the environment, sports, and tourism. For example, the two currencies of India and Pakistan could become legal tender on both sides of the border, an idea recently floated in India.

It is unlikely the two states will be able to reach an agreement on their own, given the history of mistrust that pervades both sides. A quiet U.S. effort, led by the next president, is probably essential to any timely effort to move the parties toward a solution. This should not be a formal, public initiative; discretion and privacy are essential.

FRUITS OF AN AGREEMENT

Resolution of the Kashmiri issue would go a long way toward making Pakistan a more normal state, less preoccupied with hostility toward India. It would remove a major rationale for the army's disproportionate role in Pakistani governance and would facilitate genuine civilian democratic rule in the country. A resolution of the major outstanding issue between Islamabad and New Delhi would reduce the arms race and the risk of nuclear conflict. And it would defuse Pakistan's desire to find allies to fight asymmetric warfare against India—allies that could include the Taliban, Lashkar-e-Tayyiba, and al Qaeda.

Of course, it would not resolve all the tensions between the two neighbors or dissolve the threat of the Taliban in Afghanistan. But, more than anything else that realistically could be achieved, it would set the stage for a different era in the subcontinent and for more productive interactions between the international community and Pakistan.

The alternative to diplomatic engagement is to let Kashmir simmer. In the long run, this approach is virtually certain to lead to another crisis. Sooner or later, the two countries will again find themselves on the precipice of war. In a worst-case scenario, a terrorist incident like the July 2006 metro bombings in Mumbai or the December 1999 hijacking of Indian Airlines flight 814—both linked to ISI—could spark an Indian military response against targets in Pakistan suspected of planning and orchestrating terrorism. And that could lead to nuclear war.

MAKE NUCLEAR WEAPONS MORE SECURE

For 25 years the United States sought to keep Pakistan from becoming a nuclear weapons state. Ultimately, that effort failed. We now have a strong interest in ensuring the security of the weapons stockpile Pakistan is developing—somewhere between 50 and 200 bombs.

On paper Pakistan has an impressive national command structure to ensure that the weapons are kept under its control, a system designed in part with U.S. help. But civil unrest, extremism within the army or ISI, or international conflict could lead to a diversion of part of the nuclear arsenal. Even the theft of one weapon could be a disaster. One area for progress would be to account for so-called orphan material, items that Khan and his ilk may have kept off-line in the past.

Former director of Central Intelligence George Tenet describes in his memoirs the intense efforts of al Qaeda to get its hands on a nuclear weapon. Pakistan's arsenal is its most likely target, due to geographic proximity and al Qaeda's penetration of the Pakistani security services.

The next president of the United States should greatly intensify efforts to ensure the security of Pakistan's weapons arsenal. To this end, he should avoid reckless talk about using unilateral means to secure the Pakistani systems. We in America do not know where all the warheads are stored, so we cannot "seize" them. Any attempt to do so will be resisted by the Pakistani armed forces, steadfastly committed to keeping the nation's nuclear deterrent (their crown jewel of defense) out of foreign hands. Talking about such contingency options only reinforces the suspicion of many Pakistanis, including vocal elements of the officer corps, that we have an ulterior motive for cooperating on nuclear security issues.

In this, as in other policy areas, the next president must adopt a more sophisticated approach to Pakistan and its terror nexus that goes beyond threats and sanctions, beyond commando raids and intelligence cooperation, beyond aid and aircraft sales. It is time to come to grips with what motivates Pakistan's behavior and to help Islamabad make peace with itself and its neighbors.

CONCLUDING OBSERVATIONS

In the final analysis, Pakistanis should determine the fate of their country. But Americans should assist the forces of democracy, not resist them. We have a common interest with Pakistanis in helping their country move from being a dangerous state that breeds terror at home and abroad to a healthy, stable, and free country. Afghans and Indians share that interest as well. American leadership needs to make a difference in Pakistan before it is too late.

Countering Iran's Revolutionary Challenge

A Strategy for the Next Phase

PETER W. RODMAN

SUMMARY ❱ Iran is a revolutionary power, still in an exuberant phase of its revolution. Geopolitically it seeks to dominate the Gulf; ideologically it challenges the legitimacy of moderate governments in the region. Indeed, Iran aspires to be the leader of Islamist radicalism in the Muslim world as a whole. Iran's conventional military buildup, its pursuit of nuclear weapons in defiance of the UN Security Council, and its interventions in Lebanon and Iraq not only reflect its ambitions but also explain its current self-confidence.

The nature of the regime is at the core of the challenge it poses, but the starting point of a counterstrategy is containment—that is, George Kennan's classic vision of bringing countervailing pressures to bear against a revolutionary power's external expansion until the structural contradictions within the system begin to weaken it internally.

Iran is not mainly a U.S. problem; it is a threat in the first instance to all our allies and friends in the Middle East. Thus the first stage in a counterstrategy is to bolster Arab allies and friends as counterweights to Iranian power. While military cooperation with some Gulf Arab states, especially Saudi Arabia, is controversial at home, tightening U.S. links with these allies is logically the core of such a strategy. A wider strategic consensus may be emerging that would join the United States, key Arab states, and Israel against the Iranian threat. This should be nurtured.

Arab countries have other options, including their own nuclear development or appeasement of Iran. It is far preferable that they retain confidence in us as a reliable friend and protector.

One element of U.S. policy should be to update the Nixon and Carter doctrines, to declare the U.S. stake in shielding the security of our friends in the Middle East against nuclear blackmail. This would strengthen deterrence and possibly deny Iran much of the benefit of pursuing nuclear weapons by nullifying the blackmail potential it seeks to gain.

Proposals have been made for bilateral political engagement with Iran, but there would be serious costs and no benefits to such engagement in the present context. Our Arab friends (and Israel) would be shaken by what they would see as a major reversal, if not collapse, of long-standing U.S. policy. It would have not only procedural but substantive significance, representing final U.S. acceptance of the Iranian Revolution—a card we should not play without some significant change in Iranian policy in return. We need to achieve a much better geopolitical and psychological balance—a significant deflation of the Iranians' self-confidence and bolstering of our friends' confidence in us—before such diplomacy would have any hope of serving U.S. interests. Achieving balance requires

—further success in stabilizing Iraq,

—much broader use of economic pressures (as opposed to the narrowly targeted sanctions employed thus far),

—more aggressive support for civil society in Iran, including by improving the quality of U.S. official broadcasting into Iran.

How we conduct ourselves in Iraq is crucial. Our friends in the Middle East will view our policy in Iraq in a broader context, as a test of the credibility of the reassurances we are trying to give them over Iran. There is no way for the United States to be strong against Iran if we are weak in Iraq. ❱

CONTEXT ❱ During the Iran-Contra scandal of the mid-1980s, editorial cartoonist Mike Luckovich produced a cartoon on the then-popular theme of how to distinguish between "radicals" and "moderates" in the Iranian regime. It depicts two mullahs carrying placards. The mullah on the left carries a placard that reads "Death to America." The other mullah carries a placard that reads "Serious Injury to America." A bystander says to a companion: "I think the one on the right's a moderate."

At various periods since the Iranian revolution, Americans have nursed the hope that we could influence Iran's internal politics in favor of more moderate forces. Alas, the Iranian radicals have demonstrated over and over again that they play that game far better than we can. Arguably, it really is the pivotal issue confronting American policymakers—how to understand, and influence, the internal dynamics of regime policy. Sadly, there is no indication that we have yet broken the code. ❯

HOW TO HELP IRANIAN MODERATES

A new approach to this problem would begin with two key propositions. The first point is to acknowledge that there are undoubtedly differences of opinion within any regime. However, the way to help "moderates" is not to sneak them TOW missiles that they can show off at a staff meeting (as the Reagan administration attempted) but rather to shape their environment at a more macropolitical level. Any government surely includes individuals who are more risk-averse than others—who might be prepared in a crisis to argue that continuation of provocative policies risks harm to the country and to the regime. We can strengthen their arguments by actually posing such risks. The strenuous exertion of U.S. goodwill is less likely to be persuasive in the inner sanctums of the regime than visible demonstrations of such costs. Conversely, weakness in the face of Iranian provocation only strengthens radicals, who can show that no price is being paid—indeed, that their policies are paying off.

The second point has to do with differences, not within the regime, but within the country. During the last few years, the regime's hard-liners have effectively atomized or crushed reformist elements in the intelligentsia and in political life. The replacement of Mohammed Khatami by Mahmoud Ahmadinejad in 2005 completed the process. Yet many observers believe the regime's popular support is less solid than it appears. It is a political system rent by many internal divisions and burdened by severe economic problems. There are signs of the regime's nervousness about international pressures and of a ferment that has never been completely suppressed. How do we influence *that*?

THE CHALLENGE: IRAN IS A REVOLUTIONARY POWER

The Iranian challenge is not hard to define. Iran is a revolutionary power, still in an exuberant phase of its revolution; it combines a geopolitical and an ideological thrust.

Geopolitically, Iran seeks to dominate the Gulf (the "Persian" Gulf, as it would say) and become the leader of the Middle East and the Muslim world. Iran urges on its neighbors a concept of Gulf security that excludes all outside powers and leaves it to "us Gulf countries" to run things; that would leave its weaker Arab neighbors without their traditional recourse to an outside protecting power (once Britain, now the United States) to counterbalance a would-be regional hegemon. Iran's buildup of naval, air, and missile forces testifies to that ambition, as does its pursuit of nuclear weapons. There can be no doubt that Iran is keeping its nuclear weapon option open and will not relinquish it unless significant costs are imposed.

The ideological thrust is Iran's radical Islamism, which is a challenge to the legitimacy of the domestic structures of all its moderate neighbors. This thrust is in part channeled through its Shi'a brethren in Iraq, Saudi Arabia, Lebanon, Bahrain, and other nearby Arab countries. But one can detect Iran's ambition to be the leader of the Islamist movement as a whole. Ahmadinejad's open letter to President Bush of May 2006 reflected this aspiration. In that letter he presented himself as President Bush's moral counterpart and equal, and he wrote as if he were the spokesman of the Muslim world. That claim is hardly accepted in the Arab world, but it is being asserted nonetheless.

Iran's is a militant and activist foreign policy. As U.S. General David Petraeus testified to the Senate on May 22, 2008, "Tehran has, to varying degrees, fueled proxy wars in an effort to increase its influence and pursue its regional ambitions."

For a few years after the fall of the shah in 1979, there were fears that Iran's revolutionary Islamist ideology would spread in the Middle East. But it did not spread then—because of an Arab allergy to things Persian and the Sunni-Shi'a divide. The Muslim Brotherhood had been brutally suppressed in most Sunni countries throughout the long ascendancy of the secular, nationalist "Arab socialism" of Nasser and his heirs. After the fall of the Soviet Union, however, the radical Left was weakened globally. Secular, "socialist" radicalism was discredited; legitimacy now came from a different ideological direction. Sunni Islamists were emboldened also by their triumph against the Soviets in Afghanistan. In this new post–cold war ideological vacuum, then, Islamist movements gained traction in many places at the expense of old-line secular forces—in Egypt, Algeria, Palestine, Lebanon, and Iraq. During the Lebanon War in the summer of

2006, we saw the broader crossover appeal in the Sunni Arab world of the Shi'a Hezbollah's struggle against Israel.

That is not to say that Iran's pretensions to leadership of the Islamic world will ever be willingly accepted by Arabs and others; most likely the rich diversity of the Muslim world will prove resistant to Iran's charms. But Iran is building its power and pressing its claim, and its successful defiance of the West over nuclear and other matters is boosting its status—and its self-confidence.

Iran also has sought to exploit the weakness of Iraq. One of the geopolitical objectives of the U.S. intervention in Iraq in 2003 was not only to remove a regime that was seen as a looming threat, but also to help put in its place a moderate Iraq that would be a fit partner for us and the Arabs in facing the longer-term problem of Iran. A contest between the United States and Iran for influence in Iraq was inevitable. But we were confident in the Iraqis' natural resistance to Iranian influence once they succeeded in consolidating their own institutions. Iraqi Shi'a leaders insist on their loyalty to Arab Iraq and on their rejection of Iranian dominance or interference.

The temptations of opportunism, however, have proved irresistible in Tehran. When Muqtada al-Sadr appeared on the scene as a radical spoiler, Iran began funneling him support, at the expense (and to the consternation) of rival Iraqi Shi'a groups that had long enjoyed Iranian support. The Iranian Revolutionary Guard Corps (IRGC) Qods Force has been funding Iraqi extremist cells, training them on Iranian soil, arming them with advanced explosive munitions and other weapons, and in some cases providing advice and direction. While Iranian interference is not the main source of Iraq's turmoil, Tehran appears to have made a strategic decision to fuel instability there to weaken the United States. There is no evidence that it has altered that decision, nor can there be serious doubt of the regime's responsibility for these activities. The Qods Force is not a nongovernmental organization; it is an arm of the Iranian regime and reports to the Supreme Leader.

BOLSTER OUR REGIONAL PARTNERS

Iran is not mainly a U.S. problem; it is a threat in the first instance to all our allies and friends in the Middle East. Not only Israel but our Arab friends as well see revolutionary Iran as an existential threat. Thus, 2006 saw the rare spectacle of leading moderates at an Arab League meeting openly rebuking Hezbollah for precipitating the Lebanon crisis. These leaders saw the Hezbollah war as a power play by Iran to extend its influence in the Arab world. Their discomfiture at Hezbollah's seeming success was as real as that of many in the West.

Our first line of defense—and the first stage in constructing a counterstrategy—is to bolster our Arab allies and friends as counterweights to Iranian power. This the United States has been doing. Whatever the prospects for influencing the regime's internal evolution, the starting point is containment—that is, George Kennan's classic vision of bringing countervailing pressures to bear against a revolutionary power's external expansion until the structural contradictions within the system begin to weaken it internally. That is the very least that must be done.

In 2006 the State and Defense departments jointly launched an initiative called the Gulf Security Dialogue. The United States has worked in concert with all of Iran's Arab neighbors on measures to deter Iran, including strengthening air and missile defenses, improving conventional defense capabilities, cooperating on counterproliferation and counterterrorism measures, engaging them in stronger support for Iraq, and other steps. Egypt and Jordan have joined a foreign ministers' forum with the Gulf Arabs and with the United States, with the same strategic purpose.

Most of these countries have traditional ties with Iran, and some are not eager to be drawn into public military or political alignments against their powerful neighbor. The United States has reassured them that it seeks not to provoke a crisis but to prevent one and to reinforce regional defense and deterrence. Privately, the strategic assessments of these countries are strikingly parallel. All of them welcome this U.S. commitment.

This is no small matter. Facing an Iranian threat, these countries have other options. They could seek nuclear weapons themselves, an option that the Gulf Cooperation Council countries may in fact be flirting with. Or appeasement of Iran could be their default position. The far preferable course is that they retain confidence in the United States as a reliable friend and protector.

These measures deserve bipartisan support.

The Role of Saudi Arabia

The key principle here is the recognition that our Gulf Arab friends are our partners and are on the front line. But implementing such a strategy is inevitably controversial here at home. The strategy involves weapons supply, training, exercises, and other military cooperation with Gulf Arab countries such as Saudi Arabia. Unfortunately, Saudi Arabia does not tap into a great reservoir of goodwill among the U.S. Congress or public; however, if Iran is our focus, then we need the Saudis as a partner. They are the leading power of the Arab Gulf. On many strategic issues (for example, Lebanon-Syria and Iran) they have lately been unusually clear-headed and assertive. One does not have to agree with every Saudi initiative to recognize that objectively, they are one of the most important partners we could have.

Our Israeli friends need to be assured that the United States is committed to ensuring Israel's qualitative military edge. At the same time, solidifying U.S.-Arab ties is in the common interest of Israel and the United States. This is a delicate balance to strike, and the United States needs some flexibility to do so. Israelis need to assess their risks in a different way, weighing their worst-case fears of the capability of certain hardware in Arab hands against the real-world strategic benefit of having Arab countries linked more tightly to the United States and trusting more in the objective strategic context that governs the region today. The extraordinary strategic fact is that preoccupation with Iran is uniting us all—the United States, the Arabs, and Israel. There were rumors of Saudi-Israeli contacts, and there are open links between Israel and other Gulf countries. This emerging strategic consensus is one of the positive developments of this era. It is real, and it needs to be nurtured.

DECLARE THE U.S. COMMITMENT

One piece that is missing so far in the Gulf Security Dialogue is what is called declaratory policy: a public U.S. commitment to provide an umbrella over countries in the region threatened by Iran's pursuit or acquisition of nuclear weapons. That would be a logical extension of what is already implicit in the Gulf Security Dialogue and in other recent steps, such as deploying a second U.S. carrier strike group in the Gulf.

The time has come to update the Carter Doctrine (which declared America's vital interest in the Gulf) and the Nixon Doctrine (which offered an American shield for allies and friends threatened by nuclear blackmail). Like those two famous pronouncements, it would not be a formal defense commitment but a statement of policy; it would articulate the U.S. interest in maintaining the security of the Gulf and the Middle East against major threats that the countries of the region could not reasonably be expected to meet by themselves. Such a declaration today would strengthen deterrence. Arguably, it might deny Iran much of the benefit of pursuing nuclear weapons by nullifying the blackmail potential it seeks to gain.

EXHAUSTING OUR POLITICAL AND ECONOMIC TOOLS

It is time for the United States and its European partners to come to terms with the fact that the UN nuclear diplomacy has failed. The next president will face tougher choices than George W. Bush faced.

Military options are not attractive, especially with the United States engaged in Iraq and Afghanistan. Any person of goodwill will surely prefer that political and economic tools of leverage be exhausted first. Furthermore, economic sanctions in this case could have a significant political effect. But to "exhaust" these tools means to use them, not to exhaust ourselves in debating them for three years, doling them out in small increments, and then wondering why the Iranians have not been intimidated.

Use Our Economic Leverage

There is reason to believe that the Iranian regime fears economic sanctions, worrying that its weak economic performance is a domestic political vulnerability. The Treasury Department has influenced many foreign private banks to cut ties with major Iranian banks on the grounds of their links to terrorism and proliferation. That is a significant financial blow. The UN Security Council resolutions have strengthened the legal and political framework for these actions. Yet the substance of the UN resolutions has focused on narrowly "targeted" sanctions aimed at specific individuals and entities in Iran directly connected to proliferation. Obviously much of this self-denial is due to the lack of consensus on the Security Council for stronger measures. But it has also been explained on the U.S. side as a way to "target the regime while sparing the Iranian people." This concept is quite wrong and should be abandoned. If the strategic goal of economic pressures is to impose costs on Iran that will discredit the radical policies that cause them, then "targeted" sanctions miss the point. It is essential that the next administration pursue a much more comprehensive sanctions policy, outside the UN Security Council, mobilizing all possible economic and financial pressures in a "coalition of the willing" (with Europe, Japan, and others) as long as serious action continues to be blocked at the United Nations. Reluctance to pursue these economic pressures to the fullest will only bring other, more drastic, options back into the discussion.

Should We Engage Iran Diplomatically?

Direct diplomatic engagement with Iran also has been proposed, including by the Baker-Hamilton Iraq Study Group. A number of arguments have been advanced for it:

—The United States had diplomatic relations with the Soviet Union from 1934 onward, which did not prevent us from pursuing containment or whatever other firm strategy we wished to pursue. We have nothing to lose by talking.

—Diplomatic contact should thus be treated as an instrumental, not a substantive, matter. Any initial shock to our allies should wear off if our substantive policy remains as firm as before. (Our Arab allies, after all, all have their own political and economic relations with Iran.) So we should just get it over with.

—It can also be argued that the passage of time works against us, so that waiting in the hope of building up greater bargaining strength may only leave us worse off as Iran pursues its nuclear project.

—A U.S. political overture might even have a usefully subversive effect in Tehran, where hard-liners who resist it (using arguments that mirror arguments used in Washington) would see it as a collapse of revolutionary purity.

In fact, there are serious costs to pursuing this diplomatic course in the present context, and no foreseeable benefits:

—If there is anything our Arab friends fear more than Iran, it is the United States and Iran cutting a deal. Past rumors of U.S.-Iranian political contacts have caused a degree of panic in the Arab world. In the context of Iran's continued defiance on the nuclear issue and aggressiveness in Iraq and Lebanon, a U.S. political overture to Tehran would be understood as a major reversal, if not collapse, of a long-standing U.S. policy. (Indeed, some would hail it for that very reason.)

—The fact that the Arabs have their own ties with Iran does not alter that calculus. We are not in the same position as they are. They are counting on us to hold the line against Iran to ensure their survival.

—In addition to unnerving the Arabs, a U.S. overture to Iran could also unhinge the Israelis, who so far have been relying on a firm U.S. policy to prevent Iran from developing or obtaining nuclear weapons. If this is perceived as a significant weakening of the U.S. posture toward Iran, it could be the factor that tips Israel in the direction of unilateral action.

—What Tehran would gain from the fact of such a political engagement is the final step in its quest for international legitimacy—that is, acceptance by the United States of the finality of the Iranian Revolution. That would be a huge *substantive* step for us, which would reverberate loudly in the region—demoralize opposition forces inside Iran. This is a card we should not play without some significant benefit in return. And what would that be? In the absence of a significant change in Iranian policies, this is a large, unreciprocated, and unjustified concession.

—For the record, U.S. diplomatic relations with the USSR began after Hitler came to power, when Stalin feared German as well as Japanese belligerence. Similarly, the U.S.-Chinese rapprochement of the 1970s was driven by the Soviet threat. Thus, geopolitical forces brought these parties together, not a reflexive hunger for "engagement." Today, the main geopolitical force at work with respect to Iran is the rise of *its* power and the weakness of international counterweights to it. Many invocations of U.S.-Soviet diplomacy and the U.S.-China rapprochement in this context misunderstand their historical and geopolitical basis.

We must achieve a better military, geopolitical, and psychological balance—a significant deflation of the Iranians' self-confidence and bolstering of our friends' confidence in us—before exploring bilateral diplomacy. Otherwise we are merely a supplicant to a radical regime that will conclude that it is winning. Restoring this balance is *the* imperative—and would remain so whether we were talking to Iran or not. A bipartisan consensus on measures to strengthen the U.S. position in the Gulf would be a contribution to an Iran strategy.

This bolstering must include further success in stabilizing Iraq. The Baker-Hamilton report argued that this argument has it backward—that we need to engage Iran if we are to succeed at all in Iraq. On the contrary, unless we and the Iraqis restore the balance of forces by our own efforts, we simply would be begging Iran to stop tormenting us; Iran's price would go way up. The goal is not to concede Iran's dominance in Iraq but to block it.

The fact is, there is already a track record of U.S. diplomacy with Iran, which presents a mixed picture overall. We have dealt with Iran at a practical level when this promised to be useful, especially in a multilateral framework. U.S. and Iranian diplomats have met in the context of the UN "6+2" meetings in 2001–02 in support of post-Taliban Afghanistan and more recently in the context of the "neighbors' conferences" intended to garner international support for Iraq. And the United States has promised to join the multilateral nuclear diplomacy with Iran if Iran halts uranium enrichment and reprocessing.

Bilaterally, our ambassador in Baghdad, Ryan Crocker, held a brief series of meetings with his Iranian counterpart. These were a serious disappointment. Iran assured the United States that it shared the objective of a stable, moderate Iraq—an assurance brazenly belied by the military and political actions being taken by Tehran to destabilize Iraq and bleed the United States. The limits of diplomatic "engagement" with a revolutionary regime could not have been revealed more clearly.

Our problem with the Iranian regime is not, and has never been, a communications problem. Even if our leaders or diplomats do not meet, we understand each other all too well. Iran's ambitions are driven by ideology, by the deeply held convictions of its leaders, and those ambitions are, on their face, incompatible with fundamental interests of the United States. We only insult these leaders—and delude ourselves—if we imagine that it is just a misunderstanding or that some conversation will affect the reality. In present conditions the benefits to us of pursuing a political dialogue with Iran are not evident, and the negatives are foreseeable. We should not sell ourselves cheaply.

THE ISRAELI-PALESTINIAN CONFLICT IN PERSPECTIVE

The United States has resumed its engagement in Israeli-Palestinian diplomacy. Our Arab friends constantly tell us that this diplomatic commitment should always be at the heart of our Middle East strategy. But, as we pursue this, we should do so with our eyes open.

It is best to dispense, first of all, with the cliché that the Israeli-Palestinian conflict is the core of all the problems in the Middle East. The generation of turmoil in the Gulf encompassing the Iranian Revolution, the Iran-Iraq War, the Gulf War, and the Iraq War has very little to do with the Palestinian problem. A more precise way to characterize the U.S. strategic interest in a Palestinian solution is that prolongation of the conflict, especially in the age of Al Jazeera, is a source of radical pressure on moderate Arab governments, complicating their ability to cooperate strategically with us. The author heard a wise Gulf leader say that the best reason to solve the Israeli-Palestinian conflict is to shut down the problem on that front and free all of us—meaning Arabs, Americans, and Israelis—to unite in confronting the real problem, Iran.

The Israelis, for their part, are quite conscious that progress on the Palestinian issue, if attainable, would yield a significant strategic payoff for them in their regional relations. The obstacle to progress has been that, while the Israeli political consensus has continued to move toward acceptance of a Palestinian state and flexibility on borders, the Palestinians elected a Hamas government that does not want Israel to exist on any borders. This is yet another self-inflicted wound on the part of the Palestinians.

The Bush administration should be supported in its final effort to broker an agreement between Israel and the Palestinian moderates.

THE LEBANON CRISIS

The Lebanon crisis has even more strategic significance at this stage. The Arab world has correctly viewed Hezbollah's attempt to subvert the Lebanese government as an Iranian power play, and the strategic setback for the United States and the Arab world would be enormous if Hezbollah and Iran were to succeed. The courage of the Lebanese government deserves to be matched by bolder actions by the international community to support it.

The weak link in the Iran-Hezbollah-Syria axis is Syria—a weak country playing a dangerous game by aligning itself with Iran. The next administration should seek to mobilize pressures—Arab, Israeli, European—against the Syrian-Iranian alliance, which is a strategic threat to all our friends in the region.

INFLUENCING IRAN'S INTERNAL EVOLUTION

Influencing Iran's internal evolution is a more difficult challenge. It was George Kennan's insight, in the Soviet case, that maintaining external pressure to block expansion was an indirect way of fostering internal pressure as well. But it was Ronald Reagan's insight that such regimes' internal conditions are susceptible to more direct influence. The Islamic republic is a regime with many vulnerabilities, including ethnic divisions, economic mismanagement, and disaffection among both the intelligentsia and the broader population.

Economic sanctions have already been discussed in the context of nuclear diplomacy. The weakness of the sanctions so far imposed is a missed opportunity not only to discredit radical policies but also to exacerbate fissures within the system.

The U.S. government has initiated a number of programs to aid or encourage civil society in Iran in the hope of enabling pluralism to survive. The United States has never explicitly adopted regime change as a policy objective in Iran, nor does it have to. There can be no doubt that the nature of this regime and its ideological thrust are the core of the problem it poses. However, in the real world the most immediate task is to mobilize leverage; we can err on the side of understating what may be the result rather than overstating it.

The quality of U.S. official broadcasting into Iran has been poor. There is a tension between our broadcasters' aspiration to balanced journalism and our policy imperative to get a message out. The current structure of all our international broadcasting—which deliberately raises barriers to U.S. policy influence over broadcast content—should be reviewed by the next administration. It may not be consistent with our strategic necessities during a period of intense ideological competition.

The time may soon be at hand when we will have to play offense against Iran and not only defense—pressing harder against the regime's internal vulnerabilities across the board.

CONCLUDING OBSERVATIONS

Finally, a further word must be said about Iraq. Our goal must continue to be that Iraq become a stable, moderate country that is a fit partner for us and the Arabs in the new strategic environment in which Iran looms so large. After almost three decades of facing two hostile powers in the Gulf, it will be a stark relief to have an Iraq that is a partner, rather than an erratic, truculent, disruptive danger in its own right.

U.S. Steadfastness in Iraq

Iran has sought to exploit the vulnerability of an Iraq in turmoil. The Bush administration's decision in early 2007 to crack down on IRGC subversive activities on Iraqi soil was long overdue. More broadly, the Iraqi people still hold in their own hands the power to consolidate their national institutions, and as these national institutions are consolidated, the structure will regain its resistance to outside interference. This is part of the struggle that is now under way. During 2008, one of the most encouraging signs has been the new confidence and political will of the entire Iraqi political establishment in standing up to Iranian pressures.

A pivotal element here is U.S. policy. Our Gulf Arab friends, whom we are seeking to reassure regarding Iran, respond by referring to Iraq: "Don't abandon us," they implore. They are viewing Iraq in the context of Iran. We Americans are understandably preoccupied with Iraq. But there is a broader region out there, a vitally important one, that is the strategic context of our current debate. To many in the Middle East, our steadfastness in Iraq will be a test of U.S. credibility, which will affect their confidence in whatever assurances we are trying to give and their willingness to go along with U.S. initiatives.

There is no way for the United States to be strong against Iran if we are weak in Iraq. Some may be tempted by the idea of "cutting our losses" in Iraq while compensating for that by appearing strong in the region in other ways. But there is no way to square this circle.

Organizing a Counterstrategy

We know from the Soviet case that revolutionary ideologies can be defeated—they can be discredited by failure. The renewed militancy of Iran's clerical rulers in recent years may mask a deepening uncertainty about whether their people support them. Those who want change, who were many in number a few years ago, may have been cowed into silence, but they have not gone away. Thus in the longer run we deal from strength, even if we are scrambling in the short run for an effective international counterstrategy.

Organizing such a counterstrategy will be one of the most important tasks on the next administration's agenda. It will be able to build on the policies of its predecessors. Iran's nuclear challenge may prove to be the forcing event; if Iran continues its defiance, then the international community will need to find ways to increase pressure on the regime's internal structure.

The alternative—a nuclear-armed, militant, aggressive Iran, with its neighbors and the world bowing to it—will mean a strategic nightmare for the next generation.

Engaging the Muslim World

A Communication Strategy to Win the War of Ideas

HADY AMR AND P. W. SINGER

SUMMARY ❱ A critical pillar of success in the war on terrorism is restoring the world's trust in America's word. Fortifying this pillar should be a top priority of the next president, with a special focus on relations with the Muslim world. To win the war of ideas with those advocating violence against America, we must act quickly to rebuild the shattered foundations of understanding between the United States and predominantly Muslim states and communities.

For its efforts at public diplomacy and strategic communications to be effective, the U.S. government must move beyond understanding the problem as simply a global popularity contest. The very success of U.S. foreign policy depends on how the United States can engage with, and help shape the views and attitudes held by, foreign populations. Both how and with whom the United States speaks create the environment in which our policies either sink or swim. Today, unfortunately, they are sinking.

Quickly upon taking office, the next president should initiate a strategic planning process leading to a National Security Presidential Directive for improving our relationship with the Muslim world. The president should also take personal steps to use a limited window of opportunity to "reboot" that relationship, such as taking an early presidential trip to Muslim nations, meeting with reporters from Arabic-language media, and clearly condemning anti-Islamic bias. The strategy should then be institutionalized, backed by specific policy initiatives, including

—creating an America's Voice Corps;

—establishing American Centers in predominantly Muslim countries and implementing an American Knowledge Library initiative;

—privatizing Alhurra television and Radio Sawa and launching "C-SPANs" for the Muslim world;

—bolstering cultural exchange programs, while fixing problems with the visa process;

—harnessing America's diversity by engaging Arab and Muslim Americans;

—involving the whole federal bureaucracy in public diplomacy;

—developing military exchange networks and incorporating public diplomacy into the Pentagon budget. ❭

CONTEXT ❭ The current *National Security Strategy of the United States of America,* issued by President Bush in March 2006, states that winning the war of ideas is the key to long-term success in the war on terrorism. Unfortunately, we are losing that war.

During the past few years, America's standing in the Muslim world has sustained a deep and rapid deterioration. According to the Pew Global Attitudes survey, 80 percent of citizens of predominantly Muslim countries have solidly negative views of the United States. Importantly, the anger is not with American values; rather, U.S. foreign policy is identified as the main cause of the negative sentiments—ranging from the war in Iraq, to abandoning the Israeli-Palestinian peace process, to the perceived abandoning of civil liberties values in our detention centers in Guantánamo Bay and Abu Ghraib.[1] Negative ratings are even higher in the key moderate and allied countries of Jordan, Morocco, and Turkey.[2] Yet, inexplicably, out of an already small federal budget of about $1.5 billion for core public diplomacy, only about 9.5 percent ($140 million) is devoted to the Near East and South Asia, core areas of the Muslim world.[3] Meanwhile, 16 percent ($240 million) was spent on the U.S. mouthpiece television and radio stations, Alhurra and Radio Sawa, respectively, which have limited followings and limited impact.[4]

By any measure, U.S. attempts at communicating with Muslim-majority nations since 9/11 have not been successful. The efforts have lacked energy, focus, and an overarching, integrated strategy. Instead, the efforts have relied on informational programming that has lacked priority or been misdirected, lacked nuance in dealing with diverse and sensitive issues, and not reached out to the key swing audiences necessary to marginalize and root out violent extremists.

Getting Our Communications Right

Analysts on both sides of the political aisle often describe the current challenge to the United States as a long-term conflict, akin to the cold war between the United States and the Soviet Union. That conflict, like the current one, was waged both in the realm of ideas and in the realm of national security.[5] If this is a valid comparison, then, at best, we are no further along than where we were before the Truman Doctrine and Marshall Plan in 1947, when we were still wrestling with the fundamental questions of who and what confronts us and what the nature of our long-term response should be. At worst, we may be standing on the wrong side of such a historic comparison, as we are now the ones struggling with credibility and image problems similar to those of the former Soviet Union, so memorably characterized by President Reagan as "the Evil Empire."

American efforts to defeat the Soviet Union and the broader Communist Bloc in the war of ideas during the cold war were also aided by our domestic efforts to confront racism at home.[6] A series of U.S. presidents realized that this transformation in our domestic policy at home greatly contributed to our foreign policy successes overseas, particularly the defeat of communism.[7] In 1958, for example, when an African American handyman, Jimmy Wilson, was sentenced to die in Alabama for stealing $1.95 in change, the Soviets quickly seized on this story to tarnish our good name in the cold war battlegrounds in Africa, Asia, and Latin America, in turn making it harder to effectively conduct our foreign policy.[8] With the story spreading, aided by the then-new technology called television, President Dwight Eisenhower's secretary of state, John Foster Dulles, engaged Alabama governor James Folsom to commute the sentence—which Governor Folsom did, having already received hundreds of letters from around the world asking him to do so. However, our image was already tarnished, the damage was done. But America responded. The 1960s civil rights movement, ultimately embraced by the presidency, cleansed America's image in the world, and we emerged on the other side, increasingly equipped to be the beacon of hope, freedom, and justice to the world, particularly in Eastern Europe on the other side of the Iron Curtain.

In today's digitally interconnected world, when our behavior within the United States is more closely monitored by citizens around the globe, we are not faring so well. Many of those in the Muslim world are unsure whether to love us for our ideals of equality and freedom or loathe us for our practices (which contradict these ideals) in Guantánamo Bay and Abu Ghraib. They are watching carefully, and in years to come, they could move to being tacit supporters of either those who target the United States in the form of terrorism or those who embrace the United States in free trade and political cooperation.

We occupy a crucial period, when enduring attitudes are being formed. Getting our communications right is critical to overall national security now and will continue to be critical in decades to come. Much of the threat we face comes from terrorists around the globe, often acting in a decentralized, self-inspired fashion. However, our security concerns extend beyond terrorism and suggest a longer-term need for a grand strategy to prevent or wage a wider conflict in the future. The United States— and the world—may be standing on the brink of a "clash of civilizations," as Samuel Huntington once warned.[9] The view, widely held among Muslims, that the U.S. war on terrorism is a "war on Islam" illustrates the vast gulf in understanding and perceptions.

The prevailing view in the Muslim world of a war on Islam impedes our success not only in mounting a viable grand strategy in our overall foreign policy but also in confronting localized terrorist threats. The global war on terrorism, after all, is not a traditional military conflict made up of set-piece battles; it is a series of relatively small wars and insurgencies in places like Iraq, Afghanistan, Pakistan, Egypt—and even neighborhoods in Britain. In each case, the United States must sway a population from hostility to support to oust terror cells and shut down recruiting pipelines. As the U.S. Marine Corps *Small Wars* manual famously notes, such ". . . wars are battles of ideas and battles for the perceptions and attitudes of target populations."[10] ❱

CREATING THE STRATEGY

More than merely a lost popularity contest, then, the deepening divide between the United States and Muslim nations and communities around the world poses a huge barrier to our success on a breadth of vital issues, from running down terrorist groups to expanding economic development and political freedom. Progress on these issues will steer the next generation of Muslims toward or against militant radicalism.

Key Principles

For the last seven years, the United States has all but conceded the field in the war of ideas to the radicals. To win this war, the next president must clearly recognize the importance of America's voice and good standing as elements of its power and influence in the world. As a matter of the highest national security importance, the next president should undertake a major, integrative initiative in public diplomacy and strategic communications to reach Muslim states and communities from Morocco to Indonesia, including Muslim minority communities in Europe and India.

Winning the war of ideas and creating better relations with the Muslim world require more than tired tactics, immobility, and budgetary pocket change (the current cost is less than 1/1,000th of our Iraq-related expenditures). The next president should designate this effort as a matter of the highest national security importance. The campaign as a whole should be self-critical, regularly evaluating its own performance, and ready and willing to change in response to evaluation results.

Six broad principles must guide our strategy to influence foreign publics and broaden and deepen relationships between U.S. citizens and institutions and their counterparts abroad:

—*Confronting our civil liberties concerns:* The United States must clearly confront its civil liberties concerns at home and in operations abroad—if we are to be able to inspire the Muslim world to support our

---

Public diplomacy—promoting the national interest and national security through understanding, informing, and influencing foreign publics and broadening dialogue between American citizens and institutions and their counterparts abroad

Strategic communications—communications initiatives that strengthen relationships, enhance influence with key groups, and manage popular perceptions

vision of "liberty and justice for all." Additionally, we must take a zero-tolerance stand against public slurs and biases. When statements of bigotry are made by figures in government or among our political elite, they help only those who claim that we are undertaking a "war on Islam" instead of a "war on terror," thereby aiding the recruiting and propaganda efforts of our foes.

—*Dialogue:* Instead of just producing propaganda, the effort should be audience-centered and designed to build dialogue, ensure mutual respect, forge partnerships, and place a premium on joint participation and planning. This is the only way to restore and secure damaged credibility. It should be two-way—emphasizing "listening" as much as "talking."

—*Outreach:* Rather than merely "preaching to the choir," the United States should engage a varied set of regional players and constituencies, including Islamists and other social conservatives who may sometimes be controversial but carry the greatest influence within the target populations. Beyond traditional vehicles for discussion, which target government counterparts and standard news media, the communications should engage opinion leaders in a variety of forums, including universities, the arts, business and professional associations, labor groups, and non-governmental organizations.

—*Integration:* Diverse U.S. agencies should develop a coordinated, goal-oriented communications approach to maximize effectiveness and resources and to speak with a credible voice.

—*Nimble response:* Strategies and programs should be flexible and responsive to changing events, findings, and trends and should use new technologies and tactics.

—*Investment:* The investment should reflect the very high strategic priority of the war of ideas to ensuring American security.

Initial Steps

The success of any program begins with a central vision. Within the first 100 days in office, the new president should order a reexamination of public diplomacy and strategic communications goals and programs to be carried out at the senior levels of the National Security Council and affected departments and agencies, especially the State Department. This effort should include seeking and integrating input from legislative bodies, universities, think tanks, and friends in the Muslim world. Good advice should be welcomed, not cast aside. (In the past, policymakers

have ignored reports on the issue from groups as varied as the congressionally mandated Advisory Group on Public Diplomacy for the Arab
and Muslim World, the Council on Foreign Relations, and the Center for
the Study of the Presidency.) To ensure both high-level support and durability, the main findings and recommended core strategy should be
embodied in a National Security Presidential Directive, presenting an
agenda for building positive relations with Muslim countries and communities, using public diplomacy and strategic communications.[11]

With the strategic goals established, policymakers could then develop
a more systematic approach to ascertain how far short the United States
now falls from this target state and what exactly is required to attain it.
This analytical and planning process will also identify tangible courses of
action in the most important issue areas (for example, alleviating the
intensity of anti-Americanism in key countries, increasing levels of cooperation on antiterrorist activity, and so on). The objective is to create not
merely a methodological approach to evaluating our successes and failures but also a guide to steer the right course in the future.

As important as the substance of the strategy is in rebuilding the shattered foundations of trust, it is time to get back our style as well. Many
Muslims say they find the style and tone of communication often used by
senior U.S. officials arrogant, patronizing, and needlessly confrontational.
Unfortunately, they are right. Simply returning the *art* of diplomacy to our
public diplomacy could have an immediate impact. Within this, it is
important to demonstrate respect: the empathic and measured tone that
Secretary of State Rice used after the alleged Koran desecration incident in
2005 was all too rare and should serve as a model. Cultural insensitivity,
boasting, and finger wagging, displayed by other senior leaders on countless occasions, need to be avoided. Similarly, U.S. leaders should avoid dis-
playing an openly hostile attitude toward the major Arab media outlets;
like it or not, these channels are the means of conveying our message to
the broader community, and attacking them only undermines our efforts.

SPECIFIC WAYS TO STRENGTHEN RELATIONS
WITH THE MUSLIM WORLD

Applying the quintet of principles presented above, the next president can
improve U.S.-Islamic relations through many interrelated initiatives.
Eleven suggestions follow:

—Exerting presidential leadership in public diplomacy

—Creating an America's Voice Corps

—Establishing American Centers across the region

—Implementing an American Knowledge Library initiative

—Privatizing Alhurra and Radio Sawa

—Launching "C-SPANs" for the Muslim world

—Bolstering cultural exchange programs while improving the visa process

—Harnessing America's diversity, by engaging Arab and Muslim Americans

—Involving the whole federal bureaucracy in public diplomacy

—Developing military exchange networks

—Incorporating public diplomacy into the Pentagon budget

Exert Presidential Leadership in Public Diplomacy

Much of the United States' recent crash in credibility and standing in the Muslim world has been the result of the actions of the current administration, with President Bush cited by name in various regional public polls as well as in conversations with key leaders. Fair or not, this focus on President Bush does present a limited window for his successor. The next president will have a unique opportunity to personally "reboot" the relationship between the United States and Muslim populations. And the president should seize it.

As a sign of the importance of relations with the Muslim world to our long-term security, full consideration should be given to including stops in Muslim states in the new president's first international trip. There, the president could deliver a major policy address outlining goals and revealing a vision of future relations between the United States and the Muslim world, and the president could meet with forward-looking leaders, civil society reformers, and youth.

After the new administration's initial weeks and months, continual presidential effort will be needed. According to the Pentagon's Defense Science Board, "only White House leadership . . . can bring about the sweeping [communications] reforms that are required," and "nothing shapes U.S. policies and global perceptions . . . more than the President's statements."[12] Given the importance of the war of ideas to the battle against terrorism and the risks of a greater, long-term rift between the United States and the Islamic world, efforts should be made to bring the president into personal contact with reform and civil society leaders. These efforts include hosting delegations at the White House to demonstrate respect and to bolster both parties' standing as well as understanding of each other. In addition, the president should schedule time for regular interviews with news media from the Muslim world.

Further, the president should use the bully pulpit of the presidency to condemn hate speech. Shortly after 9/11, President Bush took the compelling personal step of visiting the Islamic Center of Washington, the capital's leading mosque, to show Americans and the world that the administration understood that Islam was not to blame for the attacks. Unfortunately, the clarity of this message was quickly lost. A series of anti-Muslim statements have since been made by various policymakers and close administration supporters.[13] Even though media in the Middle East give extensive coverage to these statements, the administration usually fails to condemn them or separate itself from the speakers. The next president must not repeat this failure of leadership, as it weakens America's moral standing. *Bigotry in our midst is not just distasteful; in the age of globalization, it directly undermines our security.* We live in an era where the world constantly watches to see whether we actually live up to our ideals. At a time when many in the world expect the worst of us, such statements only support the enemy's propaganda and recruiting efforts.

Create and Deploy an America's Voice Corps

Perhaps the most shocking finding of the Advisory Commission on Public Diplomacy's 2005 report was that the State Department had only five Arabic speakers capable of appearing on behalf of the U.S. government on Arabic-language television. Presidential support is needed for the rapid recruitment and training of at least 200 fully fluent Arabic speakers with public diplomacy skills—on average, about ten per Arab country. Constituted as an America's Voice Corps, members of this cadre could become prized guests on Arabic-language talk and news analysis shows. Further, it is equally important to train speakers in other languages—such as Bahasa Melayu, Bahasa Indonesia, Farsi, Urdu, and Turkish—used by some 500 million Muslims in strategically important countries like Indonesia, Iran, Malaysia, Pakistan, and Turkey.

Establish American Centers across the Region

Young people are the most critical audience in a war of ideas that may last for generations. This is all the more important since many of the countries involved have a higher than normal percentage of their population under the age of twenty-five. The frustration that Muslim youth feel with the status quo could be harnessed into a demand for progressive reforms. U.S. foreign policy must be deeply engaged not only in developing a real sociopolitical alternative to offer this next generation but also in articulating this alternative through strategic communications. Otherwise, their pent-up rage will continue to focus on us.

There is a historical model to emulate in reaching foreign youth and, indeed, citizens of all ages. After World War II, the United States launched dozens of "America Houses" across Germany as focal points to build democracy and form a bond with the German people. Located in city and town centers, "America Houses" also served as community hubs. After forty years under U.S. stewardship, many of these centers evolved into German-American institutes under private German control.[14]

Today, American youth centers and libraries are needed throughout the broader Muslim world, with perhaps at least one public American center in every major city. These centers should be staffed partly by members of the America's Voice Corps and should serve as distribution points for translated works from the American Knowledge Library initiative, discussed below. The centers should offer state-of-the-art English-language training programs, seminars, discussions, and a wide selection of current periodicals, newspapers, and literature. They should offer free Internet access and moderated programs that promote direct exchanges with Americans through videoconferencing, webcams, and joint blogs. The centers should not just provide a window into American life but also enable open and critical dialogue on issues of local and international concern explicitly—including dialogue about U.S. policy in the Middle East—and thereby demonstrate the value of free discourse so essential to democracy. Further, the rise of local Indonesian-American, Iraqi-American, or Moroccan-American institutes, if jointly run, would create a community sense of ownership with minimal security risks, in contrast to the U.S. government's current mode of locking its voice behind barbed-wire embassy compounds.[15]

Implement an American Knowledge Library Initiative

The Advisory Commission on Public Diplomacy also pointed out the dearth of Arabic translations of major works of American literature and political theory. While certain U.S. embassies do undertake translations of books into Arabic, the scale of these efforts is minuscule compared with the need. The absence of widely available translations means that many Arabs are cut off from American history, political ideas, literature, and science. An expeditiously run project to translate 1,000 books and journals would soon make such works widely and inexpensively available. Partnerships with Arabic publishers (perhaps through a consortium of Arab and American publishers, with the government paying start-up costs, such as copyright payments) could facilitate public acceptance and help leverage existing distribution channels and marketing capacities. The American centers could also help out by hosting book club groups and discussions of the translated works.

Privatize Alhurra and Radio Sawa

One of the few major U.S. public diplomacy initiatives in the last five years was the launch of U.S. government–organized satellite TV and radio stations, called Alhurra and Radio Sawa, broadcasting in Arabic and intended to supplement or even supplant indigenous media in the region. Despite their massive launch costs, which ate up most of the public diplomacy budget, neither has found its footing, and no credible study has found them to be influential among the populace. Clearly, their problem is not inadequate funding but rather the overt association with the U.S. government, which effectively delegitimizes these media in the eyes of most Arabs. Moreover, Alhurra and Radio Sawa actually undermine broader reform efforts, as the United States is in no position to challenge Arab government control of the media while it runs its own government-funded media there.

Following significant U.S. government investments in these stations' state-of-the-art broadcasting facilities, now is the time to let the stations compete in the Arab media environment on their own. The United States should have a voice in the region, but this voice will more likely be heard, and believed, if people understand that it is being transmitted through a nongovernment source. More collaboration is needed with the private sector, which, as the Defense Science Board has noted, can often be a more credible messenger than the U.S. government. Privatization of Alhurra and Radio Sawa is a good place to start.[16]

Launch "C-SPANs" for the Muslim World

At the same time, there is a need for credible media. Sources of unfiltered information are sorely lacking throughout the Muslim world, even though there is a palpable appetite for them. For example, during the Abu Ghraib crisis, the public in the Middle East watched live coverage of U.S. congressional hearings on Arabic news channels with great interest. Scenes of American policymakers and military leaders directly answering the probing questions of legislators and reporters presented a powerful illustration of democracy in action as well as a sharp contrast to the authoritarian practices predominant in the region.

Seeking to tap this interest, Al Jazeera recently launched a new channel, Al Jazeera Live, which features coverage of events in Arabic. Still, the marketplace for ideas and information in the Middle East and beyond is not saturated by one channel. Just as there are multiple C-SPANs and C-SPAN imitators within the United States, including local cable equivalents that cover state and municipal politics, there can be multiple channels that provide live video of public affairs events across the Arab and Muslim world, ranging from legislatures to local events hosted by nongovernmental organizations to book discussions at the American centers. By being unfiltered and, ideally, coordinated with local organizations, such Arabic channels will leap across the credibility gap that has undermined Radio Sawa and Alhurra. And similar opportunities exist for public affairs channels targeting speakers of other Muslim world languages in Iran, Pakistan, India, Indonesia, Turkey, and elsewhere.

Bolster Exchange Programs and Improve the Visa Process

Very early in the next administration, the new president should ask the secretary of state for recommendations for expanding our people-to-people interaction with the Muslim world. To win the war of ideas, we must enlist all means in the public diplomacy and strategic communications toolbox and provide a role for every American willing to play a part. As in the cold war when U.S. outreach programs created allies around the world, the new administration should enlarge educational and cultural exchange programs, increase exchanges of youth and young professionals, boost incentives for cooperative business and media ventures, and support investments in development, technology, and science initiatives in the Muslim world.

The media in the United States and Islamic countries—television, print, and Internet—can multiply the effects of these exchanges. Not only should exchange initiatives like the Fulbright and Humphrey programs be expanded, but also virtual youth exchanges, harnessing Internet and videoconferencing applications, should be initiated.

The secretary of state's review should include recommendations for fixing a broken visa process that presently undermines national security. Current visa procedures impose onerous requirements and delays that humiliate rather than welcome Arabs and Muslims from abroad; in turn, the cumbersome procedures subvert efforts to reach out to our natural ambassadors—namely, visitors and students who can then attest to the depth and reality of American goodwill.[17]

Special attention should also be given to integrating official visitors' programs across agencies. All too frequently, high-profile visa delays and, in particular, the erroneous detention of officially invited leaders and representatives from the Muslim world have proved embarrassing and detrimental to America's image.[18] Visa denials in high-profile cases should be truly based on security concerns and not, for example, simply due to pressure from interest groups that like or do not like the views of a potential visitor. When the United States hosts Muslim opinion leaders with whom we are not in 100 percent alignment, we have a chance to engage directly with them and their ideas and to prove to the world that we are, as we claim, a tolerant and open society, confident in our beliefs and values in a way that nations that resist open debate are not.

Harness American Diversity: Engage Arab and Muslim Americans

At a time when the U.S. government lacks both credibility abroad and local language speakers to represent our views, the distance between our government and domestic Arab and Muslim communities is stunningly wide. The State Department's office for public diplomacy, for example, did not include a single American Muslim on its staff until 2006. The Departments of Defense, Homeland Security, Justice, and State should all examine how they can better tap the strengths of these communities, both in programming and recruiting, and move beyond symbolic respect for Muslim rituals, such as convening annual Iftar dinners, to real programming. To offer one example, just as political donors and corporate executives often join official travel delegations, Arab Americans and American Muslims could also help brief and even accompany officials when they visit the broader Middle East.

Create Public Diplomacy Expectations in All Agencies

The war of ideas should engage the entire federal bureaucracy. The next president should impart to cabinet- and subcabinet-level officials the priority of improving America's standing in the world. Leaders of the executive branch should conduct regular interviews with the foreign press and engage in genuine dialogue, even with those who hold negative views of our government. In other words, public diplomacy must go beyond "preaching to the converted."

For example, visits by senior U.S. officials to the region should include meetings not merely with government officials, but also with local students, civil society leaders, reformers, and even conservative religious or social leaders. Similar efforts should be made by Department of Defense civilian and military leaders at both the Pentagon and regional command levels. They should follow the cold war model of a wide engagement strategy to expand and deepen relationships with U.S. allies and counterparts in what were then considered "battleground states" in the developing world.

Develop Military Exchange Networks

Foreign military training and exchanges offer another opportunity to greatly expand U.S. relationships and alliances and build up friendly local networks. Although association with the United States is viewed negatively in most social spheres of the Muslim world today, military personnel in most Muslim countries consider military-to-military exchanges and contacts with the United States military as positive and career enhancing. The U.S. military is the most respected in the world, and participants in U.S. military training programs typically advance to more senior levels. Therefore, the full value of such programs—both as vehicles for imparting official U.S. policy and as unofficial channels of communication and influence—should be realized to ensure that the United States develops close working relationships with the Muslim world's next generation of military leaders.

Currently, only about 20 percent of trainees for the International Military Education and Training program come from mostly Muslim countries, and most of these come from just two states, Sierra Leone and Turkey, both of which are outside the Middle East and not at the center of the "war of ideas." Clearly, a far more strategic use of the limited slots can be made in terms of allocation, and there is certainly scope to expand the overall number of students brought to the United States. Just as we increased the number of links with Latin America and Asia during the cold war and with the states of the former Warsaw Pact in the 1990s, we should be strategically building our partnerships with, and the professionalism of, the next generation of young leaders from Muslim states.

The next administration also should expand the structure and funding of the Near East South Asia Center for Strategic Studies (NESA), now located in Washington, D.C. Despite being highly capable, NESA is only about one-fifth the size of the European and the Pacific security centers, which have been located in those regions since the cold war. It's time to reevaluate NESA's size and structure, consider expanding its activities, and explore relocating it to a site in the region.

Formalize Public Diplomacy in the Pentagon Budget

The Defense Department engages, at both the regional and ground levels, in a wide range of civil-military activities that, broadly speaking, could be considered public diplomacy or strategic communications. Too often, though, these activities are an afterthought or undertaken only during emergencies. For example, the Navy sends hospital ships to key zones but only on an ad hoc basis, typically in response to an earthquake or other crisis, and only if the ship is not committed elsewhere. Yet, these visits—most remarkably, the deployment to Southeast Asia after the 2004 tsunami—are powerful examples of American goodwill and demonstrate the U.S. military's professionalism. Indeed, the then-principal deputy under secretary of defense for policy, Ryan Henry, called the tsunami relief effort *the* principal U.S. victory in the war on terrorism to date.

Such strategic and high payoff programs are not included in long-term planning or are supported as separate budget items. Instead, they are seen as an afterthought that takes funds away from operational budgets. The result is that such relief efforts are all too rare and certainly not regularized. Consequently, when in 2005 an earthquake slammed Pakistan—a hub of extremist groups and the only nuclear-armed Muslim state—the initial U.S. response was, at best, meek. Military assets that were already nearby, mostly a small group of helicopters in Afghanistan, were used to move aid but with minimal follow-through. Eventually, the U.S. government pledged $300 million for relief from the earthquake, but the commitment (less than half of what was given to tsunami-affected regions) was slow in coming. By contrast, a relative who's who of al Qaeda–affiliated groups ran a wide range of their own aid efforts in Pakistan. At best, the failure to use such an opening to reset relations in possibly the most important location in the war on terrorism was a missed opportunity. At worst, we ceded key moral ground to radical forces.

In the future, unfortunately, more natural disasters will strike the Muslim world, while populations there will continue to struggle with the day-to-day challenges of development. The next president should make sure that the U.S. government is ready and able to show American goodwill with swift and abundant assistance at any opening that presents itself. The new secretary of defense should investigate how to recognize such activities as part of counterinsurgency and force-protection measures and assess whether they could be regularized in budgeting, perhaps through the humanitarian operations budget. The investment made should at the very least be equal to that of the current psychological operations campaigns organized by the military.[19]

CONCLUDING OBSERVATIONS

In no area could the Bush administration's foreign policy be described as meek, except for its public diplomacy and strategic communications. The administration's combination of an aggressive foreign policy and a feeble effort to maintain our voice and credibility in the world leaves the next president with a historic challenge. The next president will inherit a series of complex and difficult decisions, at the heart of the war on terrorism, about engaging with Muslim states and communities, and will have only a short window of opportunity to "reboot" the relationship.

Simply put, there is a glaring need for the United States to undertake a proactive strategy aimed at restoring long-term security through the presentation of American principles as part of U.S. foreign policy. The tools of public diplomacy and strategic communications can be valuable weapons in the U.S. arsenal. It is not yet too late to wield them.

NOTES

1. Pew Global Attitudes Project, *American Character Gets Mixed Reviews: U.S. Image Up Slightly, but Still Negative* (Washington, June 23, 2005) (http://pewglobal.org/reports/pdf/247.pdf).

2. Shibley Telhami, *2008 Annual Arab Public Opinion Survey* (College Park: University of Maryland, Anwar Sadat Chair for Peace and Development, March 2008); Pew Global Attitudes Project, *America's Image Slips, but Allies Share U.S. Concerns over Iran, Hamas* (Washington, June 13, 2006) (http://pewglobal.org/reports/display.php?ReportID=252).

3. U.S. Government Accountability Office, *U.S. Public Diplomacy: State Department Efforts to Engage Muslim Audiences Lack Certain Communication Elements and Face Significant Challenges* (Washington, May 2006), p. 10 (www.gao.gov/new. items/d06535.pdf).

4. Ibid., p. 7.

5. Eliot A. Cohen, "World War IV," *Wall Street Journal,* November 20, 2001 (http://www.opinionjournal.com/editorial/feature.html?id=95001493); James Woolsey, "At War for Freedom," *Guardian,* July 20, 2003 (http://observer.guardian.co.uk/ comment/story/0,6903,1001642,00.html).

6. For example, in *Mao's Last Dancer,* Chinese dissident Li Cunxin writes of his first trip to America as a Chinese exchange ballet dancer, "For so many years we had been told that the West, especially America, was evil. We'd heard of nothing but the mistreatment of black people, the violence on the streets and the use of firearms." (New York: Berkley Publishing Group, 2003), p. 26.

7. Peter W. Singer, "American Goodwill, in Shackles," *Salon.com,* June 26, 2007 (www.salon.com/opinion/feature/2007/06/26/war_of_ideas).

8. This story is extensively chronicled in Mary L. Dudziak, *Cold War Civil Rights* (Princeton University Press, 2000).

9. Samuel P. Huntington, *The Clash of Civilizations and the Remaking of World Order* (New York: Simon and Schuster, 1998).

10. U.S. Marine Corps Combat Development Command, *Small Wars/21st Century Addendum 2005* (Quantico, Va.: USMC, 2005), p. 79.

11. The focus here is on public diplomacy and strategic communications involving the Muslim world. However, it can serve as a model for broader efforts at restoring the leadership and credibility of the United States on a global basis.

12. U.S. Department of Defense, *Final Report of the Defense Science Board Task Force on Strategic Communication* (Washington: DoD, Office of the Under Secretary of Defense for Acquisition, Technology, and Logistics, September 2004), p. 3.

13. For example, Christian Coalition founder and Bush administration associate Pat Robertson called Islam a "violent religion." Similarly, Franklin Graham called Islam a "very evil and wicked religion." Likewise, Lieutenant General William Boykin set off a firestorm of attention in 2003, when in comparing his faith with a Muslim's he said, "I knew that my God was bigger than his. I knew that my God was a real God and his was an idol." Boykin has since been promoted to deputy under secretary of defense for intelligence, though he recently retired in August 2007.

14. Hady Amr, "American Public Diplomacy: Some Lessons from Germany," *Daily Star,* July 15, 2005 (www.spinwatch.org/content/view/1475/9/).

15. Some may object that the security situation in the Muslim world is simply too volatile and that any American center providing easy access to locals would be an easy target for terrorists. But if we are serious about engaging the terrorists on their turf instead of on ours, we must balance these potential losses against those we would incur if we fail to engage. Additionally, the sense of local ownership of an American center, resulting from joint ownership, planning, and conceptualization, would lead

many residents to interpret any attacks on it as assaults on local interests and citizens, causing the attacks to backfire on the terrorists.

16. Stephen Cook, "Hearts, Minds and Hearings," *New York Times,* July 6, 2004, p. A19 (www.cfr.org/publication/7168/hearts_minds_and_hearings.html).

17. John N. Paden and Peter W. Singer, "America Slams the Door (on Its Foot)," *Foreign Affairs* 82, no. 3 (June 2003) (www.foreignaffairs.org/20030501facomment 11216/john-n-paden-peter-w-singer/america-slams-the-door-on-its-foot-washington-s-destructive-new-visa-policies.html).

18. For example, Ejaz Haider, the editor of one of Pakistan's most moderate newspapers, was arrested in Washington, D.C., in 2003 by Immigration and Naturalization Service agents on visa charges, even though he was in the United States at the direct invitation of the State Department to build goodwill. Those sympathetic to the United States could only charitably conclude that one American hand did not know what the other was doing. Unsurprisingly, those less favorably inclined took a darker view and made sure to publicize their conspiracy theories in regional media.

19. For example, the Joint Psychological Operations (PSYOP) Support Element of the U.S. Special Operations Command has a projected budget of $77.5 million for the coming years to spend on creating TV, radio, and print advertisements to burnish the U.S. image.

5〉

Contending with the Rise of China

Build on Three Decades of Progress

JEFFREY A. BADER AND RICHARD C. BUSH III

SUMMARY 〉 China's rise may pose the most important foreign policy challenge to the United States in the twenty-first century. Chinese economic expansion of 10 percent annually offers exciting export and import opportunities—accompanied by profound economic, military, and political risks. The next president should embrace the strategy of engagement initiated by President Nixon and sustained by all his successors to date. Presidential candidates should avoid tendentious condemnations of China and instead signal their intention to develop a personal relationship of trust with their Chinese counterpart soon after taking office. Specifically, the next president should

—convince Chinese leaders that they can best promote their country's national interests by working in concert with the United States and other great powers to meet challenges to international peace and security, for example, by cooperating to restrain Iranian and North Korean nuclear arms development;

—further China's integration into the network of international organizations and regimes and facilitate China's contribution to their future evolution;

—encourage Chinese economic reforms that will foster a stronger foundation for equitable two-way trade and investment ties with China;

—act to modernize the Asia-Pacific security structure to ensure the United States is not excluded;

—actively promote Chinese cooperation on energy issues;

—lead in building a domestic consensus supporting his China policy.

At the same time, the new president should understand we can best advance the cause of human rights in China by example and discreet encouragement, not by lecturing or unilateral pressures. The next president should reaffirm U.S. commitments to Taiwan and exploit opportunities that have arisen to place relations between the two sides of the Taiwan Strait on a more stable basis. ❚

CONTEXT ❚ China's power is growing rapidly, as its economy expands at about 10 percent annually. Corporations have seen China's cost-effective manufacturing base and massive new consumer market as keys to survival, while countries rich in natural resources see the Chinese market as a key to their competitiveness. China's leaders and diplomats are translating economic clout into global political leverage. And the Chinese military, the People's Liberation Army, is gradually gaining impressive strength.

Since Pearl Harbor, the United States has prevented any rival power from achieving military superiority in the Pacific. America has enforced its military dominance through alliances, bases, and political relationships and has asserted economic leadership through free trade and a network of multilateral institutions, including the International Monetary Fund, the World Bank, and the General Agreement on Tariffs and Trade (now the World Trade Organization). This structure, while fundamentally sound, no longer may suffice. China's rise may pose the most important foreign policy challenge to the United States in the twenty-first century—*if* China surmounts massive internal challenges and becomes a superpower. Although the Communist Party does not enjoy high legitimacy, its mix of promotion of economic growth, selective repression, appeals to nationalism, and management of rapid social change has been successful enough internally to allow it to remain in power and has led the nation to greater international respect. Each leadership cohort has been more capable than the previous one.

The next administration will engage China during a critical phase in that country's power trajectory. Economically, we already share an uneasy codependence. Militarily, the projection of Chinese military power eastward will bump up against existing American deployments. Politically, China's authoritarian system remains at odds with American liberal democratic values. American suspicion that China's rise challenges U.S. leadership in East Asia combines with Chinese concern about U.S. intentions to create a climate of uncertainty. If we treat China as an enemy, we will acquire an enemy; but if we treat China as a potential partner, we will gain in cooperation and support. ❰

FIRST, DO NO HARM

In three election campaigns—in 1980, 1992, and 2000—future U.S. presidents announced their intention to toughen national policy toward China dramatically. In each instance, the United States then endured months or years of costly fumbling before the president decided to return to the path charted by his predecessors:

—In 1980 Ronald Reagan condemned the Carter administration for "abandoning" and derecognizing Taiwan and for terminating the United States–Republic of China Security Treaty. President Reagan suggested he would restore diplomatic relations with Taiwan and sell it advanced fighter aircraft. After he assumed office, eighteen months of tension occurred before he approved the 1982 U.S.-China Communiqué limiting arms sales to Taiwan, and his administration never did sell Taiwan the promised aircraft. The 1982 Communiqué, judged necessary at the time to stabilize a tense relationship, has been a burden on U.S. policy and credibility ever since.

—In 1992 Bill Clinton denounced the Bush administration for "coddling" the "butchers of Beijing" and laid the groundwork for promulgating an executive order that would grant most favored nation (MFN) status for China conditioned on improvements in human rights. China did not satisfy those conditions. In the face of demands from the business community and Asia-Pacific leaders, President Clinton nevertheless abandoned his policy of conditional MFN in 1994—after damaging the credibility of U.S. policy and Sino-American trust. This damage would heighten the 1995–96 tensions over the Taiwan Strait.

—In 2000 George W. Bush criticized the Clinton administration for seeking a "strategic partnership" with China, saying that instead he saw China as a "strategic competitor." In the first several months of his presidency, Bush's national security team signaled a desire to redefine the relationship in more negative terms. Although the president has never repeated his description of China as a "strategic competitor," and even though 9/11 and North Korea's nuclear program have driven Washington and Beijing closer, the campaign slogan has left the Chinese with doubts about U.S. trustworthiness.

Despite these three false starts, all seven presidents since President Nixon's historic visit to China in 1972 have pursued generally similar, reasonably successful policies toward the People's Republic of China (PRC). The logic is simple: China has massive capacity to affect the world for better or worse. We therefore have pursued our interests cooperatively with Beijing whenever possible, even though such cooperation has challenged our values.

DRAW CHINA INTO THE INTERNATIONAL SYSTEM

In driving forward the modernization campaign that Deng Xiaoping began three decades ago, Chinese leaders face staggering problems:

—Per capita GDP that still stands at only $2,500

—An aging population and a high dependent-to-worker ratio

—Inequalities between rich and poor, east and west, and coast and interior

—Water shortages in the north that constrain growth

—Inadequate health care for all but the wealthy

—The world's worst air pollution

—The relocation of 10 million to 13 million people a year from the countryside into the cities

—Corruption that is corroding the capacity of the Chinese state to rule effectively over an increasingly complex society

Recognizing that it cannot resolve these problems in a hostile international environment, China has generally pursued foreign policies designed to promote peace and stability. Its stated policy of "peaceful development" has been matched by actions. It has sought good relations with the United States, understanding it cannot challenge U.S. influence for decades to come (even if it wishes to do so) and accepting that U.S. global leadership need not constrain Chinese development. It has stabilized relations with all its neighbors except Japan and Taiwan and lately has made some progress with Japan. It has not moved aggressively to develop a blue-water navy or the ability to project power beyond its immediate neighborhood. It would be wrong to base U.S. policy on a worst-case perception of Chinese motives.

Even if China wisely has chosen not to challenge the United States for global or regional leadership, the question of how to cope with China's rise poses a test for American foreign policy. Politically, is there a feasible alternative to a competition for power? Militarily, how do we strike the right balance between reasonable adjustments to China's buildup and reckless overreaction? Economically, how do we manage the risks of codependence with the Chinese economy while continuing to reap the benefits? And how do we reconcile the gaps in our political values?

With no coherent vision of China in its first term, the Bush administration adopted a new framework in September 2005. As articulated by then deputy secretary of state Robert Zoellick, the framework calls on China to become a "responsible stakeholder" in international affairs and pledges cooperation toward that end. This policy explicitly and properly rejects the idea that China should be "contained" or that China constitutes an inevitable threat like that posed to the international system by imperial Germany and Japan early in the twentieth century. Zoellick appealed to China to act in concert with the United States and other great powers to address challenges to international peace and security and to strengthen international laws, institutions, organizations, and practices. At the same time, he warned that inevitably countries would "hedge" against the risk that China's rise might turn out to be disruptive.

The current framework is a sound basis for the future. Indeed, the framework would be even more effective if the United States were seen as acting as a responsible stakeholder itself, rather than frequently acting unilaterally. (That would impress upon the Chinese that the concept is not designed to limit them but not us.) Even if the next president avoids the term "responsible stakeholder," the concept should be an important part of our dialogue with the Chinese. We have been most effective with China when we have grounded our diplomacy on recognition of its status as a great power and the expectation that it would adhere to international norms, such as those of the World Trade Organization, the Nuclear Non-Proliferation Treaty, and the Missile Technology Control Regime. When our unilateral concerns are reinforced by international standards, our voice is considerably strengthened in China.

Presidential candidates, even during their campaigns, should send un-ambiguous signals to China's leaders that they highly value a constructive and cooperative relationship with China and would establish working relations with China's leaders soon after assuming office. The new president should make clear the belief that our two nations can work together and should seek to develop a personal relationship of trust with President Hu Jintao. The Chinese will react negatively if a new president throws difficult issues on the table before establishing such trust.

ENSURE THAT CHINA CONTRIBUTES TO A SAFER WORLD

Along with China's dramatic economic rise has come a corresponding increase in political influence. China is now the hub of an integrated East Asian community of nations. It has resolved border disputes with Russia and the states of Central Asia, has established a free-trade zone with the ten-member Association of Southeast Asian Nations (ASEAN), soon will be India's largest trading partner, and is already the largest trading partner of Japan, Korea, and Taiwan. It has coordinated its position on the North Korean nuclear issue with its former adversary, South Korea. And it plays a strong role in the alphabet soup of regional East Asian organizations.

China's military growth has not matched its economic and political rise. But it requires watching, and the United States should make prudent preparations for threats that could emerge (but we hope will not). Military spending has been growing at an official rate of about 12 percent annually for the last decade. Chinese forces are becoming increasingly robust through the development and deployment of intercontinental ballistic missiles (ICBMs), cruise missiles, fighter aircraft, information warfare, and space technologies with military applications. China's destruction of a satellite using one of its missiles during a test in January 2007 signaled its development of the capacity to threaten U.S. communications and surveillance satellites in the event of conflict. Although China has not developed the capacity to take Taiwan by force in the face of U.S. and Taiwan resistance, it can do considerably more damage today than it could have done during the 1996 cross-strait confrontation.

Against this backdrop, Zoellick was right to acknowledge the need to "hedge" against the risk of disruptive Chinese actions. But it would be a mistake to make hedging a rhetorical centerpiece of our policy or to allow it to overpower cooperation. There are risks to excessive hedging. Hostile military, diplomatic, or legal actions will elicit reactions in Beijing and serve the interests of Chinese leaders who might seek confrontation with the United States. Hedging could lead China to cease cooperation with Washington on key international security issues, for which Chinese help could be vital to success, such as North Korea's and Iran's nuclear programs. It could lead to a zero-sum struggle for diplomatic influence in East Asia or even to an arms race.

Instead of focusing narrowly on hedging, the next president should use persuasion. In particular, the president should stress to the Chinese our shared national security interest in preventing North Korea and Iran from becoming nuclear powers. The United States must demonstrate to Beijing that these nuclear programs present a direct threat to U.S. national security and that Chinese cooperation in keeping Korea and Iran free of nuclear arms is a vital component of our mutual confidence and our bilateral relationship.

Meanwhile, the United States should maintain and continue to modernize its security relationships in the Asia-Pacific region, especially with Japan, South Korea, Australia, and the countries of ASEAN. While the Bush administration has been divided on how to handle the North Korean nuclear issue, the relationship with South Korea has suffered, prompting questions about the durability of our alliance. That needs to be corrected by the new president. The United States should continue to restrain the European Union from resuming arms sales to China until the likelihood of conflict in the Taiwan Strait ceases to be a concern. We should control the export of sensitive technologies that could strengthen PRC military capabilities and potentially be used against us in a conflict in the Taiwan Strait.

But we should not accompany such prudent hedging measures with other steps that tilt the balance against broader U.S. interests. We should not, for example, prohibit the export of commercial dual-use technologies to the PRC if such technologies are readily obtainable from other countries or soon can be developed within China itself. To do so would damage our export competitiveness and our relations with China for minimal or no security benefit.

COOPERATE ON ENERGY

As China has grown economically, its demand for energy has mushroomed, far outstripping its supply of domestic oil. Consequently, China has adopted a so-called going-out strategy to achieve energy security, buying energy properties or signing long-term supply contracts with oil-producing countries, including such problematic states as Iran, Sudan, and Burma. China's ravenous energy appetite triggers reasonable U.S. concerns over prices, supplies, international stability, and humanitarian imperatives.

Still, we should not overreact to China's oil consumerism. We have an interest in China's continued economic development, and energy is a foundation of that growth. There is no need to engage in a zero-sum struggle with China for oil supplies around the world. Indeed, as the world's number one and number two users of oil, our two nations have a common interest in ensuring unconstrained access to oil at reasonable prices. The next president should actively encourage energy cooperation with China and between U.S. and Chinese energy companies. We should make clear to China that in the absence of military conflict between our two nations the United States will not pursue a policy aimed at constraining China's access to international oil markets. We also should encourage China's admission to the International Energy Agency, which coordinates the release of oil stockpiles in times of shortage.

At the same time, the next president should make clear to China that its pursuit of oil abroad does not exempt it from international responsibilities. China's oil investments in states that defy international standards should not be permitted to undermine international norms or basic U.S. objectives. The Chinese also should be held to international investment guidelines that forbid or constrain corruption, predatory financing, and foreign aid tied to purchases from the donor country ("soft aid"). China is relatively new to the international investment arena, but with more than a trillion dollars in foreign exchange reserves, it will not remain a novice for long. China's entry into the framework of Organization for Economic Cooperation and Development (OECD) rules is critical.

ACTIVELY MANAGE CROSS-STRAIT RELATIONS

The only issue presenting a clearly discernible risk of armed conflict between the United States and China in the foreseeable future is Taiwan, so the next president must have a clear handle on the complexities of the Taiwan Strait issue. Because crises in other parts of the world, such as the Middle East, are more visible and immediate, U.S. policymakers sometimes pay insufficient attention to this issue, which risks allowing cross-Strait tensions to escalate.

During the past fifteen years, China and Taiwan have each feared that the other side intends to unilaterally change the status quo and challenge its fundamental interests. Each side has crafted policies based on those fears, despite growing economic interdependence. In this environment, the Clinton and Bush administrations have pursued a sound policy of sending clear, cautionary messages to both sides, admonishing China that the use of force will not be tolerated and signaling Taiwan that movement toward de jure independence is equally unacceptable.

The 2008 Taiwan legislative and presidential elections have created a strategic opportunity for transforming cross-Strait relations in a positive direction. Leaders in Beijing and Taipei appear to be prepared to reassure each other about their intentions toward each other and embark on multifaceted cooperation, including, perhaps, in the security arena. If China and Taiwan are indeed willing and able to seize this strategic opportunity (and China as the stronger party should avoid an excess of caution), it will be a net gain for the United States, for we will bear less of the responsibility for preventing a conflict through miscalculation. The next administration should therefore support this process of reconciliation and cooperation. Although it is highly unlikely that U.S. mediation will be needed, Washington should favorably consider requests from the two sides for specific assistance. At the same time, the United States should improve relations with Taipei, which have been in the doldrums since 2006 because of the provocative tactics of President Chen Shui-bian. The next administration can consider resuming arms sales to Taiwan if they are clearly justified as being intended to ameliorate a Taiwan Strait military balance that is shifting sharply in China's favor.

DEFEND U.S. TRADE INTERESTS

The China of 2008 looms spectacularly larger in world trade and investment than did the China of 2000. Newspapers are full of stories about how China's economic achievement challenges U.S. manufacturers and service providers. In 2007 our trade deficit with China reached $232 billion. Many small- and medium-sized enterprises in the United States see Chinese competition as an existential threat. If the next president fails to tell the American people how to respond to the Chinese economic challenge, demagogues and protectionists will have the field to themselves.

The next administration should welcome China's advancing prosperity, building on Treasury Secretary Henry Paulson's assurance that "we wish you success." For sixty years, the United States has promoted global prosperity to undergird our own, engineering an international system of open trade, open investment, and efficient international markets. China's emergence should not persuade us to smash that cornerstone of U.S. policy. In any case, a trade war with China would not be in our interests and would not be containable; it could spark recession throughout East Asia and, in turn, depress our own economy. China is by far our fastest-growing large market, with U.S. exports increasing 240 percent since 2001. That means jobs for Americans. China also is a supplier of low-cost everyday products that Americans purchase to the tune of tens of billions of dollars a year. This helps to keep inflation in check. The People's Republic of China also is a major purchaser of U.S. Treasury instruments, which helps hold down interest rates. Further, access to the Chinese market is fundamental to the global strategy of many American companies.

While we must avoid a trade war, we need to defend our trade and investment interests. The Bush administration is right to place our bilateral economic relationship in the context of broader issues of growth and reform, as Secretary Paulson does in his regular dialogue with Vice Premier Wang Qishan. We should encourage China to move away from an export-driven strategy toward a demand-driven strategy, building a social safety net that will give ordinary Chinese the confidence to consume. Adjusting the yuan to a market-determined level should be part of that strategy, as China more rapidly contributes to global growth by reducing its trade surplus. We need to persuade China's leaders to reinvigorate reform by creating a financial services sector that encourages rational allocation of capital, by eliminating subsidies to bankrupt state-owned enterprises, and by introducing modern standards of corporate governance.

Positive incentives we could offer in return for reform include admitting China to the G-7 Finance Ministers' group, reclassifying China as a market economy under World Trade Organization (WTO) rules, and working toward listing Chinese companies on U.S. stock and commodity exchanges. Negative incentives could include strong antidumping standards, "countervailing" duties on state-subsidized products, and more aggressively using the WTO's dispute settlement mechanism. Certainly, we should vigorously attack unfair trading practices by the Chinese, in particular their woeful enforcement of intellectual property rights. If there is not significant improvement in that arena, the next administration should initiate a complaint within the WTO and pursue it to adjudication.

Being true to our principles may, at times, require the next administration to buck public opinion. For example, we should encourage, not discourage, Chinese investment in the United States. With 1.68 trillion dollars in reserves seeking higher rates of return, the Chinese should be persuaded that investment here, thereby generating U.S. jobs, is a better way of penetrating the U.S. market than relying exclusively on exports. The next president should make that case publicly, so that the next time a major Chinese company seeks to invest in the United States, the decision is not overwhelmed by protectionist and xenophobic fears, as was the Chinese oil company CNOOC's bid for Unocal in 2005.

A truly stable and balanced economic relationship with China should be based not only on a higher level of Chinese consumption but also on achieving higher levels of savings at home, getting the federal budget under control, investing more in education—to strengthen our most important asset, our human capital—and supporting scientific and technological research and development.

Finally, we need to prevent emerging East Asian regional organizations from freezing us out. The Shanghai Cooperation Organization, the proposed East Asian Community, and the ASEAN Plus Three all exclude the United States—despite U.S. leadership in creating a sense of regionalism and several of the leading regional organizations. To ensure that these arrangements do not harm U.S. interests, we should act to improve our relations with Japan, Korea, India, Australia, and ASEAN, so that these friends will block steps contrary to our interests. For example, we could negotiate a free-trade agreement with ASEAN to complement current and pending agreements with Australia, Thailand, Malaysia, Korea, and Singapore.

PROMOTE HUMAN RIGHTS

As the world's largest remaining Communist state, China poses special challenges to the United States in the field of human rights. Democracy and human rights are our defining national values. Beijing's violent repression of the 1989 Tiananmen Square demonstrations destroyed Americans' hope for rapid political liberalization of China. We cannot, simply for the sake of economic gain and greater security, carve out a foreign policy exception for the People's Republic of China and feign indifference to the continuing and massive abuses of human rights that characterize the Chinese system. Recent protests and riots in Tibet demonstrate that Tibetans have simmering grievances that may be masked by repression but have not been addressed.

Our policy on human rights, however, should be tethered firmly to reality and should match action to rhetoric. That is easier said than done. China's human rights record is poor, but its people are much freer than were their parents under Mao. China's spectacular economic growth has produced a leadership and a population that are proud of the country's achievements, wary of risky departures, and resentful of foreign intervention. Outside pressure applied with a heavy hand will not produce positive results and could even impede progress on human rights.

To date, U.S. government actions aimed at improving human rights in China have produced very little impact. We have succeeded in persuading the Chinese to release a number of individual dissidents from prison. But it is hard to point to other significant actions that the Chinese government has taken in response to overt American pressure. In general, we Americans have cause to be modest about our ability to create a free society in a culture steeped in autocracy.

Through nonofficial means, however, the United States has significantly enhanced respect for human rights in China. The most important way lies through force of example. No longer surrounded by the bamboo curtain, China in the twenty-first century is penetrated by the Internet, international media, and a very "open door." Chinese read about the United States and how Americans live. Chinese who travel or study abroad and Chinese Americans who visit the mainland furnish accounts of the American way of life. The effect has transformed Chinese lifestyles and expectations. The emergence of freer lifestyles in China is directly tied to China's opening to the West.

Over time, this process of osmosis will affect political developments as well, although the Communist Party continues periodic crackdowns to send a message that it intends to control the pace of change. But more and more young Chinese accept, and routinely speak about, the inevitability of democracy in China. Chinese central leadership may soon realize that elements of an open political system, such as a free press, can help curtail the regime's most serious political problem—rampant corruption. Thus history is on the side of democracy, not autocracy, in China.

What are the elements of a realistic human rights approach with respect to China?

—Strongly supporting U.S. nongovernmental organizations (NGOs) and academic institutions working with their Chinese counterparts on issues like the rule of law, an independent judiciary, a free and responsible press, local elections, and NGO functions and rights

—Indicating American disapproval of breaches of human rights and raising cases of concern privately with the Chinese government

—Vigorously backing the Dalai Lama's effort to promote, through direct dialogue with the Chinese Government, ways to protect the Tibetan culture, religion, and way of life, as well as discuss his return

—Setting an inspiring example on matters such as treatment of prisoners, due process, minority rights, and torture

—Pressing China to grant safe haven to North Koreans fleeing persecution

—Maintaining a positive overall relationship with China, which will weaken forces of isolation and repression

CONCLUDING OBSERVATIONS

Beyond crafting a complex and effective policy toward China, the next president will have to obtain and sustain domestic support for that policy. Rising polarization between conservatives fearing security threats and liberals fearing economic ones clouds the prospect of widespread public support for a China policy. To maximize support and defuse the extremes, the president should use the bully pulpit of the presidency to make the case for cooperation with China and ease anxieties; rebuild a base of support encompassing the business community, religious leaders, educators and scholars, NGOs, and the science and technology sector; and bring congressional leaders and congressional experts on China into the policy development process.

To date, the performance of the 2008 presidential candidates on issues related to China can best be described as mixed. On the one hand, discussion of China has been seriously unbalanced, with much greater emphasis on the perils rather than on the opportunities brought about by China's rise. In the Democratic primaries, the discussion has been overwhelmingly on the negative impact of Chinese imports on U.S. jobs and food and product safety concerns. On the Republican side, candidates have concentrated on the security threat, with calls for formation of a "concert of democracies" that would exclude China and perhaps be aimed at containing China. Neither of these approaches deals effectively with the complexity of the U.S.-China relationship, nor does either help educate the American public about the importance of the relationship and how to get it right. On the other hand, none of the major candidates has made irreversible commitments to take actions against China that would seriously damage relations, as their predecessors in earlier campaigns did to the detriment of U.S. interests. As such, they have retained the flexibility to deal with China in a pragmatic way. So far, at least, they have lived up to the injunction of Hippocrates, "First, do no harm." That may not point the way to a China policy based on a strategic vision of the future relationship we desire with the world's most populous country, but at least it does not point the way toward disaster either.

Constructing a Successful China Strategy

Promote Balance and Democratic Ideals in Asia

MICHAEL GREEN

SUMMARY ❱ Historians may ultimately judge the next U.S. president more on how his administration managed the rise of China than on how it fought the war on terrorism. The convergence of the Beijing Olympics and the U.S. party conventions in the summer of 2008 will ensure that China policy becomes an issue in the U.S. presidential race. Advocates of containment will call attention to the U.S. trade deficit with China and to the Communist regime's human rights violations, military buildup, repression of Tibet, and expansion of influence throughout Asia. The presidential nominees will feel pressured to demand a tougher stance toward China, a position that the next president is almost certain to abandon after adjusting to the complexities of U.S.-Chinese relations, repeating a pattern of four of the last five administrations.

The rise of China presents a maze of contradictions: the Chinese people are gaining economic freedoms but not political or religious liberties; China is expanding its participation and responsibilities in international organizations and multilateral diplomacy but is using that new influence to put obstacles in the way of international pressures to reform at home; and the greatest contradiction of all is that China holds more U.S. Treasury bonds than does any other nation, yet China continues a focused military buildup to defeat U.S. air and naval power in the Pacific.

The next president would be wise to look at China policy in terms of using a comprehensive toolkit of national power to shape a positive role for Beijing, while hedging against the possibility that China's leaders will ad pursue a negative path.

le first part of this toolkit is bilateral. The next administration will .... to demonstrate a readiness to continue strengthening and expanding ties with China, in spite of domestic pressures, while signaling clearly to Beijing that progress is necessary in all five areas of concern to the American people: economic openness, China's defense posture, human rights, Taiwan, and policy toward dangerous regimes such as Sudan or Iran. Presidents who try to compromise on one of these five areas to make progress on another inevitably harm U.S. interests in Asia and the longer-term prospects for stable U.S.-Chinese relations. The second part of the toolkit is regional. There is no question that China is increasing its influence and soft power in Asia, but there has also been pronounced balancing behavior against China by key states such as Japan, India, Singapore, and Indonesia. No country is interested in joining a united front to contain China, since the Chinese economy is so critical to the success of the entire region, but all seek a strong U.S. presence as well. The next president will need to energize these regional relationships to maintain a strong balance of power in Asia that favors engagement and cooperation with Beijing on terms that reinforce openness and stability. The third part of the toolkit is to mobilize ideas. Although much has been made about a new "Beijing consensus"— that economic development is more important than political liberty—the reality in Asia is that democratic principles have taken strong root in the identity of nations as diverse as Japan, Indonesia, and India. U.S. soft power in Asia should not be measured in the popularity of America alone, but also of American ideals. The key for the next administration will be to support the champions of democracy and good governance within the region, rather than appearing to impose these ideas from outside.

Presidential candidates should be thinking now about a China policy based on hard-headed realism tempered by idealism, rather than waiting until after taking office. We are poised for success in U.S.-Chinese relations, if we understand all the dimensions of the task. ⟩

CONTEXT ⟩ The two most important variables in the future of the international system are the battle for the heart of Islam and the rise of Chinese power and influence. Although the Iraq War now focuses the

United States' attention on the former, future historians may assess the latter as more consequential.

Regardless of its historical import, the China issue will not stay quiet for long. In August 2008—during the run-up to the national party conventions in the United States—world attention will be riveted on the Olympics' host city of Beijing. At that point, if not before, the United States' enormous trade deficit with China, Beijing's backsliding on human rights, and the still-simmering U.S. reaction to China's January 2007 antisatellite test will combine to reignite debate about the U.S. approach to Beijing. If the debate falls along the usual fault lines, we can expect hawks on the right to argue for containing China, the new wave of populists in Congress to demand protectionist barriers, and both the idealistic left and religious right to condemn Chinese human rights abuses and repression of Tibet. Conceivably, these three strands could unite in a grand political coalition against Beijing. In response, supporters of international institutions will argue for sharing power with China through multilateral structures, while business leaders and "neorealists" will make the case for keeping a steady hand on the relationship and rejecting all these impulses for change.

If history is a guide, this debate will intensify friction with Beijing and presage a presidency that—like the Carter, Reagan, Clinton, and current Bush administrations—begins with a hawkish China policy and then falls back into the even-handed mode of its predecessors' policies.[1] ❱

ACCEPT THE CONFLICTING REALITIES

It would be sensible to ground the debate over China policy in recognition that our policy is not a choice of alternative paths but rather a toolkit that helps us to shape a positive role for Beijing while hedging against the possibility that China's leaders will instead pursue a negative path. The reality, after all, is that China's rise presents us with an array of seemingly irreconcilable contradictions:

—The United States has bet that China's entry into the World Trade Organization would change China at a faster rate than China would change the world, but China's growing mercantile clout has allowed Beijing to shape the system in ways that may forestall domestic reforms.

—China's growing integration with the world economy is improving the lives and choices of the average Chinese citizen, but the government is suppressing civil society and religious freedom whenever they might foster alternative power centers to the Chinese Communist Party (CCP).

—China is the largest holder of U.S. Treasury bonds, yet it develops capacities for cyber warfare and submarine and space warfare to defeat the United States in a possible contest over Taiwan.

—Through its campaign of "peaceful development," China is showing new deftness at soft power designed to win over its neighbors, yet it still demonstrates self-destructive nationalism and hubris in territorial and historical disputes.

—China is acutely sensitive to issues of rank and protocol with the United States and seeks to hedge U.S. power and influence, but it refrains from attempts to end the era of global U.S. dominance.

The seeds of these contradictions were planted by Deng Xiaoping three decades ago. Deng's Four Modernizations departed markedly from the Maoist path, but Deng provided no vision of where his path would lead. Subsequently, Jiang Zemin's Three Represents and current President Hu Jintao's Peaceful Development and Harmonious Society are similarly opaque about China's ultimate role in the world. The leadership remains overwhelmingly preoccupied with *internal* challenges to continued economic development and sustained CCP rule.

For the United States, the best policy outcome would be a China that uses its soaring economic clout to bolster the international system while permitting increased political liberty at home—as both South Korea and Taiwan did. In short, the optimal result is a Chinese role as a "responsible stakeholder" (a term used in this context by then deputy secretary of state Robert Zoellick). Chinese leaders, however, may have a different strategy in mind or, perhaps, little more than a coping strategy. Consequently, the United States must avoid placing all bets on any single vision of a future China. Instead, our policy must allow that as China amasses greater power it might become more liberal or more repressive or even a force for destabilization.

To accentuate the positive and hedge against the negative will require a disciplined foreign policy approach on three levels simultaneously: *bilateral, regional,* and *ideational.*

SET A CLEAR BILATERAL AGENDA

The first of these levels (and the one that has preoccupied most U.S. policymakers) is the bilateral agenda. Here it is critical to erect clearly visible guardrails and offer positive rewards to influence Chinese behavior. Although it is a truism that China will do what is in China's interests, it is also clear that ever since the Deng era began in the late 1970s China's modernization strategy has included careful attention to relations with the United States. The U.S. message therefore does carry significant impact.

Often, new U.S. administrations have sent contradictory messages to Beijing and veered from priority to priority. Our next administration should lay out clearly U.S. objectives for relations with China. These objectives should include

—reiterating a commitment to work steadily on improving U.S.-Chinese relations;

—welcoming an expanded partnership with China in international organizations and diplomatic endeavors while Beijing contributes to the maintenance of the current, neoliberal international order;

—paying due attention to issues of "face" in the practice and protocol of diplomacy with China, but being careful not to apply simple labels to the relationship, such as "strategic partnership," that would prematurely imply that China has become a full stakeholder in the system;

—maintaining consistent attention to the five major areas of concern in U.S.-Chinese relations: economic relations, human rights, nuclear proliferation (mainly, Iran and North Korea), Taiwan, and policy toward dangerous and objectionable regimes. This means always refraining from trading progress on one track for concessions on another, as all five are critical to sustaining domestic U.S. support for the relationship.

Although encouraging broader U.S.-Chinese cooperation and a larger role for China in the international system is essential, the bottom line still is that the United States cannot predict whether China will ultimately contribute to maintaining the system or, exploiting its new strength, will game the system to achieve narrow mercantilist or nationalist gains. Both behavior patterns are evident today. For that reason, U.S. strategy should not be simply to participate in an increasingly cacophonous two-voice concert of power with Beijing. Instead, our China strategy must be embedded in a regional strategy.

PURSUE A REGIONAL STRATEGY, AS ASIAN STATES BALANCE THEIR INTERESTS

The prevailing view of U.S. media pundits is that China's expanding economic power and soft power are eclipsing the United States throughout Asia. Granted, the growth of Chinese influence is evident in the Association of Southeast Asian Nations' (ASEAN's) new free trade negotiations with Beijing and the expansion of China's trade with Japan and Korea above the levels of these nations' trade with the United States. In addition, China has moved toward resolving territorial disputes with India, reinvigorated its strategic relationship with Pakistan, and established dominant influence over Cambodia, Laos, and Burma. Meanwhile, close U.S. allies such as Australia and South Korea have publicly resisted Pentagon pressure to take on a more significant role in the defense of Taiwan. At first glance, it does appear that much of the region has boarded the Chinese bandwagon as Beijing gains power.

Upon closer examination, however, it is apparent that most of the region is engaging in pronounced external balancing behavior toward China. The most obvious example is Japan, which agreed in the February 2005 common strategic objectives agreement with the United States that contributing to peace and stability in the Taiwan Strait is a core mission for the U.S.-Japanese alliance. Analysts have focused on China's negative response to this agreement and warned of a defense dilemma. Nevertheless, after the U.S.-Japanese announcement, Beijing's approach to Taiwan shifted from an emphasis on sticks (threats of military coercion, such as the Anti-Secession Law) to an emphasis on carrots (promises of specific economic opportunities if Taipei becomes more compliant).[2]

China's growing clout also has coincided with closer alignment between Washington and New Delhi. Certainly, the Indian political establishment sees enormous economic benefit in maintaining stable relations with Beijing and is not prepared to actively "contain" Chinese power. In addition, the Indian government has none of the Japanese political establishment's neuralgia about China and is more careful to disguise its balancing behavior. Nevertheless, India is not only increasing its defense and foreign policy coordination with the United States, but it also is expanding strategic relations with Japan, including undertaking trilateral U.S.-Japanese-Indian naval maneuvers in March 2007 (India's first multilateral naval exercise).

Singapore, Indonesia, and Vietnam are also implementing balancing strategies. All of Southeast Asia wants to expand political relations and, particularly, trade with China. In 2005 alone Singapore signed a new Strategic Framework Agreement with the United States expanding U.S. military access, Vietnam announced expanded intelligence cooperation and defense exchanges with the United States, and Indonesia took steps to reopen bilateral military ties. All three nations then worked with Japan to invite India, Australia, and New Zealand to join the 2006 East Asia Summit as a counterweight to China's influence. (Beijing has subsequently shifted its attention to the ASEAN Plus Three summit, where it enjoys a larger comparative advantage.) In March 2007 Japan and Australia entered into a new security cooperation agreement, which both nations quickly said was aimed at no third party, but it clearly registered in Beijing.

Seize Opportunity to Strengthen Partnerships

What is striking about this balancing behavior is that most of it was initiated within the region. The next administration will have an enormous opportunity to strengthen diplomatic and security partnerships in Asia. However, one lesson of the past five years should not be forgotten: when the United States pushes for explicit defense commitments, as the Pentagon did with South Korea for "strategic flexibility" on Taiwan, the result will be an embarrassing and strategically damaging no from even our closest allies. As the world's sole superpower and China's largest trading partner, the United States can afford to deepen economic engagement with Beijing while openly discussing the Chinese military threat. For smaller Asian nations, there is no such luxury. We must learn to build our security partnerships in the region on terms that allow our partners to continue their own positive economic and political engagement with Beijing while strengthening cooperation with us as a reassuring hedge.

In this regard, the United States must pay particular attention to South Korea's strategic importance. When Korea becomes an issue in overall East Asian security—as it did in 1894, 1905, and 1950—the result is a much less stable regional order and the prospect of war. Polls indicate that the South Korean people are wary of China's growing influence and consider it a more significant long-term military threat than Japan or even North Korea. Recent polls also suggest that South Korean politics are shifting back to a more conservative, potentially pro-U.S. tilt after a ten-year trend in the reverse direction. However, the country's politics are in flux, and it is critical that the United States restate its commitment to the U.S.-Korean alliance in terms that resonate with Korea's new identity, emphasizing the nation's role as a proactive "balancer" and "hub" in Asia rather than the object of larger powers' competition.

Although not an Asian power, the EU also has important influence on strategic trends in the region—driven by its enormous regional trade and investment and by Chinese fascination with the relationships between European and American power (for example, former French president Jacques Chirac's multipolarity thesis—presented as an alternative to U.S. unipolarity—was particularly unhelpful to U.S. policy toward China). Similar to most Asian countries, the EU is becoming more careful about engaging China, especially after its tentative 2005 decision to lift the arms embargo on China damaged relations with the United States and Japan. The Anti-Secession Law also awakened many European leaders to doubts about China's role. Continuing dialogue with Brussels and EU members on China and Asia strategy will be an important part of our regional strategy for managing China's rise.

Fortunately, Asian balancing behavior has not sparked an arms race. Because the balancing is external, through alignments, rather than internal, through increased military spending, it poses less danger of spiraling military obligations than many experts have predicted. For the past decade, China's defense budget appears to have increased at well over 10 percent per year (China admitted to a 17 percent increase in 2006), while its neighbors' defense spending has been generally flat. The external balancing alone has succeeded in demonstrating to Beijing the consequences of aggressive steps that are dissonant with President Hu's peaceful development theory.

Asian nations' prudent balancing behavior will ensure that the United States has ample opportunity to build stronger partnerships in the region, as long as U.S. policy recognizes that the entire region also wants engagement and economic integration with China.

ENCOURAGE DEMOCRATIC GROWTH: THE IDEATIONAL STRATEGY

The U.S. edge in Asia does not lie in the region's balancing behavior alone, but also in the contest of ideas. While too much can be made of the clash between the "Beijing consensus" (protecting diversity of political systems and noninterference in internal affairs) and the "Washington consensus" (defending human rights, democracy, rule of law, women's empowerment, and good governance), there clearly is an ideational dimension to the balance of power in Asia. Too often scholars have identified soft power in terms of the popularity of the United States itself, missing the significant influence of American ideals in Asia. The norms that underpin the American neoliberal order are spreading across Asia, even if some governments are understandably hesitant to identify them as U.S. norms.

Japanese prime minister Shinzo Abe and Foreign Minister Taro Aso have declared their intention to champion democratic values as a centerpiece of Japanese foreign policy. This posture contrasts with years of value-neutral Japanese diplomacy (and near mercantilism), but it makes sense for a nation seeking new tools to shape its regional environment and ensure a leadership role in regulating economic developments. Some may argue that Tokyo's failure to address issues dating back to World War II and earlier will delegitimize Japan as a standard-bearer for universal values, and indeed, that may be true for China or the Koreas. However, BBC polling has found that Japan was the most respected nation in the world in both 2005 and 2006, while Gallup polling found that Japan is viewed as "positively contributing to Asia's development" by approximately 90 percent of Vietnamese, Indonesians, Malaysians, and Indians.

Under Prime Minister Manmohan Singh, India also has returned to its liberal roots, with a pronounced shift away from nonalignment and toward universal democratic principles as the centerpiece of Indian international identity. Taiwan, too, despite its scandals and literal food fights in the Legislative Yuan, continues to demonstrate the resilience of its governance and rule of law. Even ASEAN, which was built around the principle of noninterference in internal affairs, has produced a new draft charter that highlights "the active strengthening of democratic values, good governance, rejection of unconstitutional and undemocratic changes of government, the rule of law, including international humanitarian law, and respect for human rights and fundamental freedoms."

Present Principles as Asian Norms

The key for the United States is to not claim credit for these evolving norms and standards but rather to acknowledge and encourage their growing adoption by diverse cultures and political systems across Asia. They ultimately must be seen as Asian norms and not ideas imported from the United

States. To that end, the next president should spend more resources on assisting Asian nations in governance and the development of democratic institutions—reversing a slashing of aid for governance and democracy promotion in Asia in fiscal year 2007—and let Asian leaders, like Indonesia's president Yudhoyono, be the face of democratic progress in the region.

So, too, should the architecture of multilateral institutions be treated as an Asian structure, buttressed by U.S. support. The explosion of organizations from the ASEAN Regional Forum to the Asia-Pacific Economic Cooperation (APEC) Summit to the new East Asian Summit will not be rationalized into one simple design. Asian governments themselves seek a variety of institutional options, given their own diversity. It is clear that the United States will not be accepted into all these forums. The next president could attend the East Asia Summit, though, if the administration is willing to sign the largely symbolic Treaty of Amity and Cooperation with ASEAN and send the president out for a second summit after APEC, perhaps suggesting back-to-back summit meetings. The important thing is to ensure that like-minded democracies in the region are coordinating the agenda for all of these institutions and forums so that our common values are being advanced.

While coordinating plans with fellow democracies in the region, the United States should avoid forming an exclusive democratic bloc in Asia that appears aimed at containing China. Many Chinese leaders and citizens recognize the need for better governance and rule of law and more liberal political participation. The regional dialogue on building democratic institutions and rule of law should emanate from the democracies, promoting debate within China about these issues and about the wrenching social and political changes and institutional development that will come with continued economic growth.

ORGANIZE FOR SUCCESS

China escaped careful scrutiny in the last presidential election cycle. That is unlikely to be the case in 2008. China-bashing or protectionist pandering during the campaign will lead some in the bureaucracy to think in January 2009 that they have a mandate for containing China or imposing protectionist policies. Others, inspired by misguided idealism about value-neutral multilateral institutions or hyperrealist notions of offshoring and balancing, could seek to recalibrate U.S. alliances and security partnerships in the region by deemphasizing democratic principles. Judging from history, these extreme views of China strategy will not survive the first year of the new administration but will cause considerable damage in the interim.

The next president ought to avoid the pitfalls of this learning curve by thinking now about a China policy based on hard-headed realism tempered by idealism. That policy advance will require a comprehensive bilateral agenda with Beijing that encourages expanded cooperation but pulls no punches, a strategy for the whole region that shapes China's choices in positive ways and an awareness that ideas in the region matter to China. And it will require a careful and disciplined message about an Asian policy—a goal that has eluded most candidates in the past.

The next administration will need to consolidate our newly strengthened partnerships with Japan, India, and Australia and pay renewed attention to other critical relationships, especially the U.S.-Korean alliance, that have entered a period of drift. The approach in each case must be carefully tailored to avoid forcing nations to choose between China and the United States.

In framing a comprehensive U.S. approach to the region, the new administration should recognize the need for balancing and hedging but should stand confident of the steady pan-Asian spread of universal ideals that reinforce the U.S. edge, shape the regional environment, and encourage positive change in China's attitude toward the rule of law, governance, human rights, and political participation. The next president will need to devote resources to this mission, resources that include both high-level, consistent participation in emerging regional institutions and more support for institution building within fragile and transitional states. We are poised for success, if we understand all the dimensions of the task.

NOTES

1. Another paper in this series notes this same tendency of presidents to argue for a tough stance toward China during their election campaigns, who then adopt a policy of accommodation after taking office. See Jeffrey A. Bader and Richard C. Bush III in chapter 5 of this volume.

2. China's Anti-Secession Law was adopted by the National People's Congress in March 2005, although the law had been announced earlier, to affirm China's opposition to Taiwan independence and, among other things, to preserve China's sovereignty and territorial integrity and safeguard "the fundamental interests of the Chinese nation" (www.china.org.cn/english/2005lh/122724.htm).

7

Ending Oil Dependence

Protecting National Security, the Environment, and the Economy

DAVID SANDALOW

SUMMARY ❯ Plug-in electric vehicles, biofuels, fuel efficiency improvements, and smart growth can help end the United States' oil dependence in a generation. Doing so would provide important national security, environmental, and economic benefits. A broad political consensus and game-changing technological advances create the conditions for dramatic change. Yet presidential leadership and robust policies will be needed. There are no simple or short-term solutions. The next president should

—transform the auto fleet with federal purchases of plug-in electric vehicles, tax incentives for the purchase of plug-in electric vehicles, and a fund to help automakers invest in fuel-saving technologies;

—transform the fuel supply by requiring oil companies to retrofit gas station pumps for ethanol, increasing support for cellulosic ethanol, adjusting the ethanol subsidy as oil prices rise and fall, phasing out the ethanol import tariff for producers that meet social and environmental standards, and establishing a low-carbon fuel standard;

—improve traffic with measures to promote telecommuting and mass transit;

This chapter is based partly upon David Sandalow, *Freedom from Oil* (McGraw-Hill, 2007).

—invest in research on advanced energy technologies;

—transform oil diplomacy by focusing on fuel efficiency in consuming nations, not just on additional supply;

—establish an "oil addiction index" to stimulate and track progress.

Previous efforts to address oil dependence have failed for lack of ambition. The widespread focus on oil imports has obscured a more fundamental problem—the near-total reliance of our transportation sector on oil. To solve the problems created by oil dependence, we must give drivers a choice between oil and other fuels. ❯

CONTEXT ❯ Large majorities of Americans agree that oil dependence is a serious problem. National security hawks raise alarms about vast sums sent to the Persian Gulf. Environmentalists warn about global warming. Farmers see new fortunes in a transition to ethanol. Consumers cry out when oil prices rise. Politicians from across the political spectrum call for an end to Americans' oil addiction.

Yet today, oil provides more than 96 percent of the fuel for our vehicles, barely different from a generation ago. Oil use continues to climb in the United States and around the world. Meanwhile game-changing technologies are moving closer to market, propelled by considerable investor interest. Plug-in electric vehicles and biofuels could reshape the transportation sector. In the years ahead, a confluence of factors—political, technological, and financial—will create an opportunity for transformational change. With sustained commitment, the next president can help end the United States' debilitating dependence on oil. ❯

THE OIL PARADOX

First, a question: How did a product so widely used become so widely resented? Oil is a high-energy-content, easily transportable fuel. Infrastructure worth trillions of dollars is already in place to convert it into services that people want around the world.

Oddly perhaps, this extraordinary success lies at the heart of the problem. Oil's dominance as a transportation fuel is so total, it shapes relations among nation-states. Oil's reward is so rich, it shapes entire economies. Oil's emissions are growing so rapidly, they are warming the planet.

Call it the "oil paradox." Oil's enormous success creates epic problems. Because we depend so completely on oil, we devote extraordinary political and military resources to securing it, at staggering costs. We empower oil-exporting nations that wish us ill. We pour vast quantities of heat-trapping gases into the atmosphere each year.

The solution to these problems would appear straightforward—develop substitutes for oil and use less of it. Yet the challenge is immense. Oil's near-total dominance as a transportation fuel is the result not only of its inherent properties but also of a century of favorable government policies, deeply ingrained cultural patterns, and huge infrastructure investments (in pipelines, service stations, and conventional vehicle manufacturing facilities). Three facts underscore the challenge:

—*Modern vehicles depend almost completely on oil.* If you're thirsty and do not want a soda, you can drink water or orange juice. If you'd like to relax and don't feel like watching a movie, you can watch television or read a book. But if you want to travel any significant distance and don't want to use oil, you're almost certainly out of luck. Perhaps you can buy an alternative fuel, such as E85 (85 percent ethanol, 15 percent gasoline), which is sold at less than 1 percent of U.S. gas stations, or biodiesel (even less available). Perhaps you can bike or ride an electric train. In most situations, though, you will almost certainly need oil.

—*Oil's dominance is deeply entrenched, in part because the vehicle fleet turns over slowly.* It takes roughly fifteen years for the nation's vehicle fleet to turn over. Designing new oil-saving technologies and then retooling production facilities can take several years at least. Policymakers eager to see dramatic reductions in oil consumption—say, within the term of an elected official—will find the pace of change frustratingly slow.

—*Oil's dominance reflects a century of favorable government policies.* Eminent domain authority has been used to build a network of pipelines for moving oil at low cost. Favorable tax treatment has promoted domestic oil drilling. Federal highway funds have vastly exceeded support for mass transit. The U.S. military protects the flow of oil at key locations around the world, providing incalculable benefits to oil markets. Securing diverse and reliable supplies of oil has been a priority of presidents and top government officials for generations.

PROBLEMS

Oil dependence creates national security, environmental, and economic problems.

National Security Threats

The United States is in a long war. Islamic fundamentalists struck our shores and are determined to do so again. Oil dependence is an important cause of this threat. Brent Scowcroft, national security adviser at the time of the first Gulf War, has said that "what gave enormous urgency to [Saddam's invasion of Kuwait] was the issue of oil." After removing Saddam from Kuwait in 1991, U.S. troops remained in Saudi Arabia, where their presence bred great resentment. Osama bin Laden's first fatwa, in 1996, was titled "Declaration of War against the Americans Occupying the Land of the Two Holy Places."

Today, deep resentment of the U.S. role in the Persian Gulf is a powerful recruitment tool for Islamic terrorists. Resentment grows not just because of the war in Iraq but also because of our relationship with the House of Saud, the presence of our forces throughout the region, and more. Yet the United States cannot easily extricate itself from this contentious region. The Persian Gulf has half the world's proven oil reserves, the world's cheapest oil, and the world's only spare production capacity. So long as modern vehicles run only on oil, the Persian Gulf will remain an indispensable region for the global economy.

Furthermore, *the huge flow of oil money into the region helps finance terrorist networks.* Saudi money provides critical support for madrassas promulgating virulent anti-American views. Still worse, diplomatic efforts to enlist the Saudi government's help in choking off such funding, or even to investigate terrorist attacks, are hampered by the priority we attach to preserving Saudi cooperation in managing world oil markets.

This points to a broader problem—*oil dependence reduces the world community's leverage in responding to threats from oil-exporting nations.* Today, the most prominent threat comes from Iran, whose nuclear ambitions could further destabilize the Persian Gulf and put powerful new weapons into the hands of terrorists. Yet efforts to respond to this threat have foundered on fears that Iran would retaliate by withholding oil from world markets. In short, three decades after the first oil shocks—and a quarter century after the humiliating capture of U.S. diplomats in Tehran—we remain hostage to the world's continuing dependence on oil.

Finally, *oil dependence jeopardizes the safety of our men and women in uniform.* Fuel convoys are highly vulnerable to ambush. Diesel generators display an easily detected heat signature. In many Army deployments, oil makes up a staggering 70 percent of the tonnage that must be transported to the front lines. In June 2006, Major General Richard Zilmer, head of the Multi-National Force in Al-Anbar Province, Iraq, made a "Priority 1" request for renewable energy technologies on the front lines. Zilmer's memo declared that without renewable power U.S. forces "will remain unnecessarily exposed" and will "continue to accrue preventable . . . serious and grave casualties."

Environmental Threats

Oil is one of Earth's principal reservoirs of carbon. When oil is burned, this carbon is transformed into carbon dioxide (CO_2), which can stay in the atmosphere—trapping heat—for more than a century. Today, oil accounts for roughly 40 percent of the world's energy-related CO_2 emissions (about the same as coal). Total emissions from oil use are climbing sharply in the United States and around the world. Oil use is also a major cause of urban smog and, as a result, of asthma and heart disease. Furthermore, oil spills have contaminated land and water supplies and damaged marine ecosystems worldwide.

When it comes to fighting global warming, not all ways of reducing oil dependence are created equal. Technologies that improve fuel efficiency are best, since all existing fuels produce at least some heat-trapping gases. Replacing oil with electricity using plug-in electric vehicles is also an improvement. The amount of improvement depends on how the electricity is generated. If the electricity is generated with wind, solar, or nuclear power, emissions are almost nothing. Even when a plug-in vehicle uses electricity from a conventional coal plant, emissions of heat-trapping gases are less than those from a similar vehicle using an internal combustion engine.

There is considerable controversy about the global warming impact of biofuels. Ethanol made from cellulose or sugar is generally considered to be a substantial improvement over oil when it comes to global warming. Ethanol made from corn is generally considered to be a small improvement at best, since growing corn typically involves substantial fossil fuel inputs. Some recent research suggests that growing biofuels feedstocks on arable land could make global warming worse because of indirect impacts such as forest clearing.

The worst fuel from a global warming standpoint—considerably worse than oil—is liquefied coal. Measured on a life-cycle basis, emissions of heat-trapping gases from liquefied coal are roughly twice those from oil. Although the global warming impacts of liquid coal could be partially mitigated if carbon were sequestered at production facilities, the resulting fuel is still rich in carbon. At present there is no way to use liquefied coal so that, on a life-cycle basis, it produces less heat-trapping gases than does oil.

Economic Threats

Oil dependence exposes the U.S. economy to the volatility of world oil markets. Price increases can occur suddenly, and because there are no widely available substitutes for oil in vehicles, consumers and businesses may be unable to respond by changing consumption patterns. Between summer 2003 and summer 2006, world oil prices rose from roughly $25 per barrel to more than $77 per barrel. By July 2008, prices climbed to more than $140 per barrel. Each $10 increase results in roughly $50 billion of additional foreign payments (approximately 0.4 percent of GDP) per year. In 2007 U.S. foreign payments for oil were more than $325 billion.

SOLUTIONS

To solve the problems created by oil dependence, drivers must have a choice between oil and other fuels.

Since the 1970s, "ending dependence on foreign oil" has been a regular applause line in U.S. politics. However, the challenge is more fundamental. Several problems often associated with dependence on *foreign* oil are in fact caused by dependence on oil more broadly:

—Unfortunately, many national security vulnerabilities created by oil would remain even if U.S. oil imports fell. The United States has not purchased a drop of oil from Iran in twenty-five years, but that fact does not prevent Iran from playing its oil card to advance its nuclear ambitions. In an interdependent global economy, in which our prosperity depends on the economic well-being of allies and trading partners, the United States will retain a vital interest in the Persian Gulf so long as global transportation fleets run almost entirely on oil.

—Unfortunately, the global warming impacts of imported and domestic oil are almost exactly the same.

—Unfortunately, American families would remain vulnerable to swings in gasoline prices even if U.S. oil imports dropped dramatically. Oil is a fungible product, traded globally, with prices set on a world market. The percentage of imports has little impact on prices paid by U.S. consumers. (In the United Kingdom in 2000, truck drivers went on strike over rising gas prices. The United Kingdom was a net oil *exporter* at the time, but that did not protect British truckers from rising world oil prices.)

Cutting oil imports can help with some problems, such as the trade deficit. But many of the most important national security, environmental, and economic problems created by oil cannot be solved by cutting imports alone. To solve these problems, we must end oil's near-total dominance of the transportation fuels market. We must give drivers a choice between oil and other fuels. Today several technologies offer the promise of doing just that.

Plug-In Electric Vehicles

To end oil dependence, nothing would do more good more quickly than making cars that connect to the electric grid. The United States has a vast infrastructure for generating electric power. However, that infrastructure is essentially useless in reducing oil dependence, because cars cannot connect to it. If we built cars that ran on electricity, the potential for displacing oil would be enormous. Fortunately, we can.

Historically, electric cars have been limited by several factors, including short range (think golf carts), battery size, and cost. The range problem is solved by hybrid engines that automatically use gasoline when the battery is drained. Up-front costs are still high—roughly $8,000 to $11,000 more than a car with an internal combustion engine—but purchase costs will drop sharply once plug-in vehicles are in mass production.

The potential benefits are enormous. Electric utilities typically have substantial unused capacity each night, when electricity demand is low. Further, utilities maintain reserve generating capacity—known as "peaking power"—for days of unusually high demand. This unused and excess capacity could provide an important cushion for vehicles in case of a sudden disruption in oil supplies or a steep rise in oil prices. Furthermore, driving on electricity is cheap. Even a first-generation plug-in electric car would travel about three to four miles per kilowatt-hour—equivalent to about 75 cents per gallon, based on the national average for electricity prices.

Plug-in electric vehicles (PEVs) would dramatically cut local air pollutants and would be better from a global warming standpoint than cars with standard internal combustion engines. True, the energy to recharge a plug-in vehicle needs to come from somewhere, and in much of the United States, that source would be a coal-fired power plant. However, the thermal efficiency of even an old-fashioned pulverized-coal plant is roughly 33 to 34 percent, while that of an internal combustion engine is roughly 20 percent. In terms of heat-trapping gases emitted, plugging a car with an electric motor directly into a coal-generated electric plant is better than running it on oil with an internal combustion engine.

How much and how quickly could plug-in vehicles displace oil? A lot. Studies have found that gasoline consumption could fall 40 to 60 percent if all cars were plug-in hybrids. According to the Department of Transportation, 40 percent of Americans travel 20 or fewer miles per day, and 60 percent travel 30 or fewer miles.

Finally, tens of millions of PEVs could be added to the fleet without the need for new electric-generating capacity. Even with PEVs making up half the U.S. fleet, electricity demand would increase by only 4 to 7 percent. PEVs could be recharged at night, when electricity demand is low. In fact, PEVs could even sell electricity back to the grid to ease peak loads.

Biofuels

Over the next several decades, biofuels have the potential to replace a significant fraction of U.S. oil use. In 2007 the United States produced roughly 6.5 billion gallons of ethanol (roughly 4.5 percent of gasoline consumption). The Energy Independence and Security Act of 2007 requires fuel producers to use at least 36 billion gallons of ethanol by 2022 A small but growing number of U.S. gas stations are selling E85.

The U.S. ethanol industry has grown rapidly in recent years. Projected capacity of the U.S. industry in 2008–09 is in the range of 11 billion gallons per year. Today, almost all U.S. ethanol is made from corn. In 2007 about 25 percent of the corn crop was used for ethanol production. Many experts believe corn can produce a maximum of roughly 15 billion gallons of ethanol per year. Politicians and the investment community are very interested in ethanol from cellulosic sources, such as switchgrass, corn stalks, and fast-growing trees. However, at present, no U.S. commercial plants produce ethanol from cellulose. The other potential source is sugar. Brazil currently makes ethanol from sugar, and there is considerable potential for Caribbean and Central American nations to do the same. In 2007 U.S. ethanol imports totaled more than 400 million gallons.

As biofuels use has grown in the past several years, food prices have climbed as well. Biofuels have played a role in these price increases, although most of the increases have been due to other factors, such as droughts, crop failures, growing demand, changes in commodity markets, a declining dollar, and increasing energy prices.

Conventional Efficiency Technologies

Many existing technologies can improve fuel efficiency. Most important is the conventional hybrid engine. That hybrid engines can now be considered "conventional" reflects technology's remarkable success in the past few years. The first mass-produced hybrids were introduced into the U.S. market in 1999 amid skepticism that they would find a market. But consumers eagerly accepted them, and the technology is rapidly moving into many new models.

Beyond hybrid engines, many existing or emerging technologies can substantially reduce fuel consumption without sacrificing vehicle performance, safety, or comfort. According to the National Academy of Sciences, "technologies exist that, if applied to passenger cars and light-duty trucks, would significantly reduce fuel consumption within 15 years."

Smart Growth

Americans are driving more and enjoying it less. Between 1993 and 2003, U.S. vehicle miles traveled increased 26 percent. Drivers now spend an average of sixty-two minutes a day in their vehicles, and traffic congestion is a growing frustration for millions. More sensible urban-suburban growth patterns could improve quality of life and reduce oil dependence. *Transit-oriented development*—that is, building mixed-use communities around transit stations—is one increasingly popular approach. According to a study for the American Public Transportation Association, doubling ridership on mass transit nationally could save 1.4 billion gallons of gasoline per year.

Other Technologies

Hydrogen fuels are unlikely to help reduce U.S. oil dependence for at least several decades, because of the cost of separating hydrogen from the compounds in which it occurs naturally and transporting it in usable form.

Liquefied coal faces two significant barriers: high costs and adverse impacts on global warming.

POLICIES

The United States cannot end its dependence on oil without presidential leadership. The next president should develop an aggressive program and build bipartisan support to sustain it. Such a program could include the following principal elements.

Transform the Auto Fleet

Federal Purchases

Each year, the federal government buys more than 65,000 new cars. These purchases should be used to transform the automobile industry. For example, the federal government could issue an open order for 30,000 plug-in hybrid vehicles, offering to pay an $8,000 premium for each one. The federal government should commit to repeating this order each year after the first vehicles are delivered, with the premiums declining over time. *No single step would do more to jump-start the market for PEVs*, finance the conversion of existing production lines, and create economies of scale. The cost of the program would be about $1 billion, spread out over roughly a decade.

A Grand Bargain with Detroit

The financial position of major U.S. automakers has never been worse, with some analysts speculating about impending bankruptcies. One reason is the cost of retiree health care, which averages $680 per vehicle, hurting competitiveness and straining corporate balance sheets. Another reason is the lack of fuel-efficient vehicles in the companies' product lines. For financially weak companies, investments in new fuel-efficiency technologies may be especially difficult.

One solution is a federal trust fund to help defray automakers' retiree health care costs in exchange for investments in fuel-saving technologies. Several structures are possible. The fund could reimburse qualifying expenses involved in retooling production lines, or it could make payments based upon the fuel efficiency of new vehicles sold. Costs could be capped at any level, with funds allocated on the basis of superior performance in terms of oil savings or related factors.

Fiscal Policy

A federal commitment to provide $8,000 of tax credits to purchasers of the first million flex-fuel plug-in hybrids would dramatically accelerate deployment. Similarly, tax credits could help bring down the cost of any vehicle with superior fuel efficiency in its weight class. Credits should be fully refundable, so that all Americans—including those with little or no tax liability—could benefit.

Recent research indicates that sales tax waivers are an especially powerful way to provide incentives for the purchase of alternative fuel vehicles. The federal government could reimburse states that waive sales taxes on the purchase of plug-in electric vehicles.

Fuel Efficiency Standards

Corporate average fuel economy (CAFE) standards helped improve the fuel efficiency of the U.S. auto fleet in the late 1970s and early 1980s. Since then, the fleet's average fuel efficiency has remained roughly flat. The Energy Independence and Security Act of 2007 contained the first significant strengthening of fuel economy standards in more than 25 years. These standards should be fully implemented, with attention paid to further improvements in the years ahead.

Transform the Fuel Supply

E85 Pumps

Less than 1 percent of the nation's roughly 169,000 service stations dispense E85 fuel. Retrofitting costs roughly $4,000 per pump. To address these barriers, major oil companies could be required to retrofit pumps for E85 at half their owned or branded stations. This order would put E85 pumps in almost a quarter of the nation's service stations—enough to give drivers confidence that E85 could be found easily.

Ethanol Subsidies

Currently, ethanol receives a subsidy of 51 cents per gallon, in the form of an excise tax credit to fuel blenders. This subsidy is justified from a public policy standpoint because of the many subsidies received by the oil industry. However, federal ethanol support could be reformed in at least three ways:

—First, the subsidy should vary with the price of oil. If oil prices drop, the subsidy should climb to keep ethanol competitive. Such a mechanism would provide important protection against attempts by OPEC to slow the growth of renewable fuels by manipulating oil prices. Similarly, if oil prices climb, the subsidy should fall to avoid unnecessary federal expenditures at times in which ethanol is fully competitive with gasoline.

—Second, the subsidy should be increased significantly for ethanol made from cellulosic sources.

—Finally, the subsidy should be paid directly to domestic farmers instead of to blenders.

Ethanol Tariff

The United States currently imposes a 54-cents-per-gallon "secondary tariff" on ethanol imports (plus a 2.5 percent tax on the value of each gallon). There is rich irony in taxing ethanol imports but not oil imports. A diverse group of politicians supports ending the tariff. U.S. farm groups are vigorously opposed. The potential for ethanol production in Brazil, the Caribbean, and Central America is considerable. The region could likely supply the United States with 5 billion to 10 billion gallons of ethanol annually within the decade, with more thereafter. Social and environmental impacts of such imports could range from positive to negative, depending on the standards used in overseas production.

One possibility would be to phase out the tariff slowly—perhaps by 10 cents per year—and limit reductions to ethanol from facilities that meet international labor and environmental standards.

Another compromise, proposed by venture capitalist Vinod Khosla, would be to lift the tariff but dye imported ethanol a distinctive color and prohibit it from being used in 90/10 blends (90 percent gasoline, 10 percent ethanol). This would guarantee U.S. corn farmers roughly a 15-billion-gallon market—more than they will be able to produce for years—while allowing imported ethanol to help supply the market for E85.

Low-Carbon Fuel Standard

In 2006 the state of California adopted a low-carbon fuel standard. Under this standard, the carbon content of fuels in the state must decline by 10 percent by 2020. Fuel distributors can meet the standard by replacing petroleum-based fuels with biofuels or electricity from the grid, for example. Measurements are made on a life-cycle basis, so ethanol from cellulose contributes more to meeting the standard than ethanol from corn. When a plug-in car is recharged, electricity from wind power contributes more to meeting the standard than does electricity from coal.

The United States should adopt a similar standard. As noted earlier, from a global warming standpoint, not all oil substitutes are created equal. A low-carbon fuel standard is an excellent tool for ensuring that alternatives to oil help fight global warming.

IMPROVING TRAFFIC

Telecommuting is growing throughout the United States. Many companies report significant improvements in worker productivity and employee job satisfaction as a result. Oil savings can also be substantial. Federal policy should aggressively promote telecommuting, with new measures to overcome barriers among the federal workforce and a major conference on the topic hosted by the president. Congress should pass legislation to prevent double taxation of telecommuters.

In addition, the allocation of federal transportation funding should shift dramatically. The bias toward road construction over mass transit in federal transportation spending is extreme. From the federal gas tax, more than five times as much revenue is dedicated to the Highway Account as the Mass Transit Account. Furthermore, the rules governing federal expenditures for road construction are more generous and lenient than those for mass transit projects. Federal support for repair of roads and bridges is essential, but funding should in general be shifted from new road construction in urban areas to mass transit. In major metropolitan areas, express lanes for the most fuel efficient cars should be a condition for receiving federal highway funds.

INVESTING IN RESEARCH

Many of the technologies we need to end oil dependence are available today. Others are almost ready for widespread commercial use. Yet breakthroughs in nanosciences, biotechnology, genomics, and other disciplines can play an important role in helping end oil dependence more quickly. Much of this research will take place in the private sector, but the federal government should pursue research with strong social benefits or payoffs beyond the time horizons of the private sector. The National

Academy of Sciences, among others, has recommended the creation of a new federal energy research agency, with an initial funding of roughly $300 million annually that will build to roughly $1 billion per year.

TRANSFORMING OIL DIPLOMACY

Traditional oil diplomacy focuses on securing adequate and reliable supplies. This will remain a necessary element of U.S. diplomacy for years to come. But this strategy must be supplemented by another: reducing oil dependence in all consuming nations.

Oil is a fungible product, traded globally. Improvements in fuel efficiency and the use of clean alternative fuels benefit the United States wherever they occur. Improving fuel efficiency in China could do more to protect our national security, fight global warming, and promote economic growth than securing additional supply from the Persian Gulf. (Improving fuel efficiency in the United States could be even better.) To speed the diffusion of oil-saving technologies and promote the rapid transformation of global transportation fleets, the next president should give priority to dialogues that encourage, for example, the global adoption of plug-in hybrid engines and sustainable production of biofuels.

ESTABLISHING AN "OIL ADDICTION INDEX"

In the 1970s, the misery index first emerged in the 1970s as an easily understood summary of macroeconomic problems. Defined as the sum of the inflation and unemployment rates, the index was a somewhat odd apples-and-oranges combination. Yet lowering it was a sensible, easily understood goal.

Today, the United States needs an oil addiction index. One simple measure could be oil's share of the transportation fuels market. In 2007 that share stood at more than 96 percent. Sharply reducing that percentage—by developing alternative fuels and improving fuel efficiency—should be an important goal for policymakers. Of course, this is not the only important goal. Cutting heat-trapping gases from the transportation sector and reducing household fuel costs are also vitally important. But oil's share of the transportation fuels market is a critical indicator. The Department of Energy should calculate and publicize this figure annually.

CONCLUDING OBSERVATIONS

Ending dependence on oil does not mean ending oil use. It means ending our near-total reliance on oil as a transportation fuel. It means giving drivers a choice between oil and other fuels.

If most or all of the proposals outlined above were implemented, the nation could end its dangerous and debilitating dependence on oil in a generation. Under reasonable assumptions, plug-in hybrids could replace 35 billion gallons of gasoline by 2025; biofuels could replace roughly 40 billion gallons more; and efficiency technologies could cut fuel use by a third. Reaching these goals would initially cost the federal government several billion dollars per year, increasing to roughly $10 billion per year and declining thereafter.

The problem of oil dependence cannot be solved by tinkering at the margins. An unusual political consensus and game-changing technologies give the next president a rare opportunity to address several of the nation's most important security, environmental, and economic challenges.

ADDITIONAL RESOURCES

Aspen Institute. 2006. *A High Growth Strategy for Ethanol.* Report of an Aspen Institute Policy Dialogue, Thomas W. Ewing and R. James Woolsey, cochairs. Washington (www.aspeninstitute.org/atf/cf/{DEB6F227-659B-4EC8-8F84-8DF23 CA704F5}/EEEethanol1.pdf).

Bailey, Linda. 2007. *Public Transportation and Petroleum Savings in the U.S.: Reducing Dependence on Oil.* Report prepared for American Public Transport Association. Fairfax, Va.: ICF International (January) (www.apta.com/research/info/ online/documents/apta_public_transportation_fuel_savings_final_010807.pdf).

California Cars Initiative (www.calcars.org).

Deutch, John, and James Schlesinger. 2006. *National Security Consequences of Oil Dependence.* Independent Task Force Report 58. New York: Council on Foreign Relations.

Hendricks, Bracken, and others. *Health Care for Hybrids: Investing in Oil Savings, Retiree Health Care, and a Revitalized Auto Industry for a Stronger America.* Washington: Breakthrough Institute (www.thebreakthrough.org/PDF/HealthCare Hybrids.pdf).

Kalicki, Jan H., and David L. Goldwyn, eds. 2005. *Energy and Security: Toward a New Foreign Policy Strategy.* Washington: Woodrow Wilson Center Press.

Khosla, Vinod. 2006. "Imagining the Future of Gasoline." White Paper (September) (www.khoslaventures.com/presentations/ImaginingTomorrowSept2006a.doc).

Lovins, Amory. 2005. *Winning the Oil Endgame: Innovation for Profit, Jobs and Security.* Old Snowmass, Colo.: Rocky Mountain Institute.

Minsk, Ronald E. 2002. *Ending Oil Dependence as We Know It: The Case for National Action.* Policy Report. Washington: Progressive Policy Institute (January 30) (www.ppionline.org/documents/ending_oil.pdf).

National Research Council, Committee on the Effectiveness and Impact of Corporate Average Fuel Economy (CAFE) Standards. 2002. *Effectiveness and Impact of Corporate Average Fuel Economy (CAFE) Standards.* Washington: National Academies Press (www.nap.edu/catalog/10172.html).

Raskin, Amy, and Saurin Shah. 2006. *The Emergence of Hybrid Vehicles: Ending Oil's Stranglehold on Transportation and the Economy.* New York: Alliance Bernstein (www.calcars.org/alliance-bernstein-hybrids-june06.pdf).

Sandalow, David. 2007. *Freedom from Oil.* New York: McGraw-Hill.

Searchinger, Timothy, and others. 2008. "Use of U.S. Croplands for Biofuels Increases Greenhouse Gases through Emissions from Land-Use Change." *Science* 319, no. 5867 (29 February): 1238–240.

Yergin, Daniel. 2006. "Ensuring Energy Security." *Foreign Affairs* 85, no. 2 (March–April).

8 ▶

Iraq in 2009

How to Give Peace a Chance

CARLOS PASCUAL

SUMMARY ▶ The next president of the United States will inherit 130,000 to 150,000 troops in Iraq amidst a fractured state of Iraqi politics that includes nascent stability in some provinces, militias armed to the gills, and little or no consensus on major national issues that are fundamental to a viable Iraqi state.[1] A precipitous troop withdrawal could unleash an internal conflagration that could increase the threat of transnational terrorism, send oil prices soaring further, and add to the number and anguish of 4.7 million Iraqi refugees and internally displaced people. Yet keeping U.S. troops in Iraq is an unsustainable stopgap in the absence of a political agreement among Iraq's warring factions.

The next U.S. president should seek the help of the United Nations to broker a political settlement in Iraq that breaks through this Gordian knot. Military interventions can help shape the conditions for a political settlement, but without a consensus on peace, military force alone is unsustainable. That has been the case in Bosnia, Kosovo, Haiti, Northern Ireland, South Africa, Sudan, and Liberia, and it will be the case in Iraq. If Iraqis cannot get over their differences to negotiate a political settlement, then U.S. troops cannot resolve their differences for them and should be withdrawn.

A peace initiative must go beyond platitudes about commitments to diplomacy. A central UN role would provide an umbrella to engage Iraq's neighbors and to garner international support from Europe, China, India, and Japan, all of which depend on Middle East energy. The next U.S. president must make it clear that the United States will coordinate military action to support the diplomatic process. A political settlement, if reached, will require international troops, including troops from the United States, to implement it.

The chances for brokering a political settlement are not high. Iraqi factions may still think they can fight and win. Provincial and parliamentary elections are scheduled, respectively, for the fall of 2008 and in 2009. Whether elections will exacerbate political competition among rival factions or inject public accountability remains to be seen. Still, a political settlement is worth pursuing to garner a truce around core issues that divide Iraqis so that a base for sustainable peace is created. The gains from success are huge; the fallout from failure is limited. The process of reviving an international diplomatic process on Iraq could help our friends and allies come to appreciate that they, too, have a stake in ending this war. ❭

CONTEXT ❭ In congressional hearings in early April 2008, General Petraeus and Ambassador Crocker, the top U.S. military and civilian officials in Iraq, presented an impressive array of statistics illustrating reduced violence. "Civilian deaths have decreased . . . to a level not seen since the February 2006 Samarra Mosque bombing," reported Petraeus. The number of deaths due to ethno-sectarian violence has fallen since last September. The U.S. military found more arms caches in 2008 than in all of 2006. "Half of Iraq's 18 provinces are under provincial Iraqi control. Many of these—not just the successful provinces in the Kurdish Regional Government area— . . . have done well."[2] Improved security and rising government expenditures may support 7 percent growth in GDP.[3] ❭

IS RECENT SECURITY PROGRESS SUSTAINABLE?

The question is whether this progress is sustainable. Four factors suggest no—not without a political consensus among Iraq's warring factions. First, cooperation with and among Sunnis depends completely on perceptions of Sunni self-interest. The Sunni insurgency made Iraq ungovernable from 2004 to 2006. By November 2006, before the start of the U.S.

military surge, Sunni tribes in al-Anbar Province and other parts of Iraq decided that they hated al Qaeda in Iraq more than they did the United States and started cooperating with U.S. forces against al Qaeda. Around 85,000–100,000 "Sons of Iraq" now participate in this "Awakening."[4] They are paid by the U.S. military. That puts food on the table. It also provides cash to rearm. For the most part, these Sunni activists have not accepted the authority of a Shi'a-dominated Iraqi government. It is convenient now to coexist, but newly armed and energized, they have not indicated an interest in subjugating themselves to Shi'a majority control.

Second, rivalries among Shi'a militias can erupt at any point and engulf Coalition forces. In August 2007 Moqtada al-Sadr reined in his militia, the Jaysh al-Mahdi (JAM), declaring a cease-fire against U.S. troops. However, this permitted increased intra-Shi'a fighting in Basra, an area void of Coalition troops, to control Iraq's wealthiest region. The cease-fire came apart in March 2008 when Iraqi security forces launched a campaign against "outlaws" in Basra. Some called the campaign an Iraqi government attempt to subdue Moqtada al-Sadr's forces and take sides with the Islamic Supreme Council of Iraq (ISCI), reputed to have strong ties to Iran. The Sadrists associated the United States with the Iraqi campaign since the U.S. supports the Iraqi government. One immediate result was Sadrist retaliation against the U.S. compound in the Green Zone. As of June 2008 the tide has again turned. A sense of hope for greater liberty and reconstruction has emerged in both Basra and Sadr City.[5] Shi'a factions have not settled their differences, none have disarmed, but they have agreed to disengage. As with the Sunnis, progress among the Shi'a is driven by self-interest, but those interests are both diverse and volatile among rival militias.

Third, national Iraqi politics are in shambles. Reduced violence has facilitated incremental progress: an improved 2008 budget, an amnesty law that (unsurprisingly) militia leaders support, some reversal of the de-Baathification laws, legislation to authorize provincial elections in October 2008, and signs of improved governance in some provinces. Yet there is still no understanding on core issues dividing Iraqi society: federal-regional relations, long-term revenue allocation, disarmament and demobilization of militias, the inclusion of former Baathists in senior positions, and protection of minority rights. Turkey has already taken military action in the Kurdish areas. There is no question that Iran can be disruptive when it wants to be. Iraqi security forces have improved, but by and large they cannot carry out operations effectively without Coalition support. The Iraqi police cannot enforce the rule of law.

Fourth, with some security advances, progress in provincial governance has been driven by increased revenues because of rising oil prices. The CIA estimates that GDP has grown from about $38 billion in 2003 to $80 billion to $90 billion in 2007. With triple the revenues to go around, it has been easier for the government to increase resources to provinces without significant compromises among the Sunnis, Shi'a, and Kurds. There is no doubt that provinces are demanding more of their central government. Whether central government factions are willing to compromise to give more to the provinces is another factor.

The overall picture is one of sectarian-based progress built upon a fragile political base. If U.S. forces are taken away from this equation, an upsurge in violence is likely, possibly at even greater levels than seen in the past, given the regrouping and rearming of Sunni militias that have still not accepted a Shi'a-dominated national government. Yet to leave U.S. forces in the midst of this quagmire is also irresponsible if efforts are not made to address the fundamental political issues that drive the Iraqis to war.

A NEW MULTILATERAL STRATEGY

All of these factors make peace in Iraq a long shot. Nevertheless that should not stop serious attempts at brokering a political settlement among Iraqis. Our efforts, however, must match the complexity of the task.

If the path to stability is uncertain, what should be clear is that the current U.S. strategy for reconciliation—setting benchmarks and demanding that a failed Iraqi state achieve them—will not succeed. As of mid-2008, more than one-quarter of Iraq's cabinet seats are vacant or are just nominally filled. The state cannot perform most basic functions, such as maintaining law and order. It is also unrealistic to expect Iraq to fix itself through a sequential process of passing laws and holding elections and referendums. Issues such as oil revenues, federal-regional relations, and the question of de-Baathification are interrelated. We should not expect warring parties to resolve pieces of this equation without understanding the outcomes of related issues. Economic and political progress in some provinces where security has improved is indeed important, but at some point that needs to translate into a willingness to support a national government, which certainly has not yet emerged among Sunni militias.

Diplomatic efforts have not had the strategic focus to advance prospects for a settlement, nor is it likely that they could without massive advance work. Regional meetings in Istanbul, Baghdad, and Sharm el Sheikh, held in the spirit of supporting reconciliation, had neither the necessary preparatory work nor the follow-up to generate momentum. The International Compact with Iraq (ICI) is a framework for assistance conditioned on policy actions by Iraq, similar in spirit to the conditionality packages developed for the former Soviet states in the 1990s. For the short term, the ICI is a self-defining mechanism for stalemate as Iraq cannot realistically meet the conditions. Visits by Secretaries Rice and Gates to encourage the Gulf states to support Iraq have produced little concrete action as long as "support" is perceived as entrenching Shi'a dominance. Moreover, simply convening regional actors without a strategic agenda could complicate negotiations, as each regional player may seek to advance its parochial interests. To advance a realistic agenda for peace in Iraq, regional gatherings would need a clear focus around a defined agenda, which to date is nonexistent.

A new approach is needed. It should be led by the United Nations. The UN has the flexibility to talk to all parties within Iraq and in the surrounding region. All of Iraq's neighbors are members. Even if the UN's image is tarnished in the United States, a UN role will help European, Russian, and Chinese politicians convince their constituents that they should contribute to a political solution and reconstruction in Iraq. Remember that in 2004 when the United States could not get an agreement on a transition government in Iraq, UN special representative Lakhdar Brahimi succeeded, in part because of his direct contacts with all the relevant parties.

For the UN to even consider such a role, the United States must request and welcome UN involvement, and it must coordinate military action to support the diplomatic process. All Iraqi parties that are not associated with al Qaeda in Iraq should be given a voice in the process. To succeed, regional actors would have to endorse a political settlement or agree at a minimum not to undermine it. As seen after virtually every postconflict situation over the last quarter century, international troops would still be required to provide assurances to all the parties that they will have a stable environment in which to implement it.[6] Political agreements to end civil wars require massive preparation and negotiation. They do not spontaneously generate.

To be effective, the UN must recognize its shortcomings, and member states must take seriously that they constitute the UN. Security Council members must place international imperatives over the desire to see the United States mired in this quagmire. Recognizing that, China and Russia could play a constructive role if they could act on their interests in stability in the Middle East and international energy markets to advocate a responsible UN role to seek a viable peace in Iraq. All member states have to put behind them the controversies of the Oil-for-Food Programme, drawing lessons on corruption and transparency from past management mistakes.

UN Security Council Resolution 1770, passed on August 10, 2007, provides the necessary mandate to seek political reconciliation in Iraq. Implementing this mandate will require unequivocal political backing, careful calibration of expectations, and skilled diplomacy. To undertake this task, the UN needs a special team and a flexible mandate. It cannot be business as usual. The lead negotiator should report to the secretary general and must be empowered to engage regional and international actors directly. The team should include individuals who know Iraq and who can liaise effectively and credibly with key external constituencies such as the United States, the European Union, the five permanent members of the Security Council (the P5), and the Gulf states.

TACTICS AND SUBSTANCE MATTER

Running a viable political negotiation is as much art as it is science. We have learned from experience, particularly in Bosnia and Afghanistan, that it will require engaging all key actors in Iraq, the neighboring states, and major external actors (the United States, the EU, the P5, major donors, and potential troop contributors). We have also learned that about half of all political settlements unravel within five years. Strong support for their implementation is just as critical as their negotiation. Following are some key considerations.

—*Core Elements.* Any agreement will likely revolve around a "five plus one" agenda: federal-regional relations; sharing oil revenues; political inclusion (redressing the de-Baathification issue); disarmament, demobilization and reintegration of militias; and minority rights. Even under a minimal-ist federal government arrangement, Sunnis will need assurance of a role in an equitable allocation of oil revenues. Minority rights are key to pro-tecting those who do not succumb to sectarian pressures to move. Demo-bilization of militias will be needed for the state to regain control over the use of force. The Kurds will insist on retaining regional autonomy. The "plus one" is the timing of a referendum on Kirkuk, which is guaranteed by the constitution but could trigger pressures for Kurdish independence and draw Turkey and Iran into the conflict. Because these issues are so interconnected, they should be negotiated as a package rather than sequentially to maximize options for viable compromises.

—*Five-Year Truce.* The focus should be on agreement to a five-year truce—specifically, provisions that can create sufficient confidence to stop the violence—with the option to extend the time frame annually. At this point animosities are too sharp to expect the parties to permanently resolve their grievances. Elections in fall 2008 and in 2009 could also sharpen political competition among competing factions, especially if the Iranian-backed Islamic Supreme Council of Iraq sees itself as losing seats to Sunnis who boycotted previous local elections. Seeking an interim solu-tion could buy time to produce better options than can be developed in just a few months of negotiations.

—*Iraqi Positions.* As a condition for participating in the negotiation process, Iraqi political parties and militia leaders will need to condemn the role of al Qaeda in Iraq and agree to cooperate against al Qaeda. The UN negotiator must have leeway on whom to consult. As seen in the cur-rent U.S. military experience, this consultation may entail talking with militias that once attacked U.S. forces.[7] The UN representative will likely need to meet separately with each Iraqi actor, mapping out their positions against the "five plus one" agenda to determine if there are potential deals to be made that also respect core substantive objectives. In turn, that may lead to small group meetings among parties to test potential alliances.

—*Regional Players.* Similarly, the neighboring states should be sur-veyed on their positions on the core agenda. Again, these meetings should start separately to mitigate the inevitable posturing and gamesmanship that occurs when competing actors are in the same room. From these meetings the UN representative will need to determine which outside actors have useful leverage and with whom and which issues require potential spoilers to be isolated or neutralized.

—*Support Team.* Iraqi and regional consultations will need a dedicated expert support team to provide guidance on issues ranging from the commercial viability of revenue-sharing arrangements on oil to international experience on legal and constitutional arrangements. The UN will need to organize experts to be available in real time to support the negotiation process. It will also need to develop public information strategies, using local and regional television and radio, to explain the UN role and mitigate attempts at disinformation from al Qaeda and other potential spoilers.

—*Brokering an Agreement.* Eventually a judgment will need to be made on whether to try for a major meeting to broker an agreement—like the Bonn Agreement for Afghanistan or the Dayton Agreement for Bosnia. Running such a meeting must be a carefully orchestrated process of negotiating among an inner circle of key Iraqis, while engaging in a more limited way a wider contact group of the neighboring states that is separated from the Iraqis. The United States will need to sustain constant bilateral diplomacy throughout this process, coordinating every step of the way with the UN representative. The Bonn Agreement exemplified such coordination, with the UN special representative (Lakhdar Brahimi) running the core meetings and the U.S. special envoys (Jim Dobbins and Zalmay Khalilzad) engaging with all the external actors.

POLICY AS OPPOSED TO POLITICS

The desire for a political agreement should not result in the acceptance of any settlement. The UN representative, the negotiating team, and key partners in the negotiations will need to determine if the commitments are genuine, adequate, and sufficiently encompassing of the key players to be viable. The initial peace agreement for Darfur in April 2006, for example, was stillborn because it did not involve all the key rebel factions. In 1999 the Rambouillet negotiations on Kosovo were called off because the Serbs would not consider viable compromises on Kosovar autonomy.

Strong coordination is critical between diplomacy and military action to control potential spoilers. During this period U.S. forces must continue to prevent or respond to insurgent attacks. The Iraqi government must say publicly and unequivocally that it supports the peace process. Similar support must be gained from the Sunni, Shi'a, and Kurds for the process, even if they cannot precommit to the outcomes. Every step must be taken to make it as hard as possible for insurgents to find shelter among Iraqis.

For Republicans, the hardest point to accept in this strategy is that given the chance to broker a political settlement, Iraqis could reject it, and that eclipses the rationale to keep U.S. troops in Iraq. U.S. forces cannot fix Iraq for Iraqis. We would need to tell Iraqis clearly that if they do not take this opportunity, we will withdraw and reposition U.S. forces to control the spillover from Iraq.

For Democrats the point of discomfort comes with success. If a settlement can be reached, then Iraqis will need sustained international support to implement it. A UN-brokered settlement increases the prospects to diversify the international military presence, but the core military effort would still have to be borne by the United States.

If attempts at a settlement fail, this diplomatic initiative is still worth the effort. As argued earlier, Europe, China, Japan, Russia, and India all have an incentive to invest in stability in the Middle East and the Gulf. A focused diplomatic effort, led by the UN, could begin the process of reengaging these countries and seeking their support to control the spillover of war into the region and address the plight of refugees. Without such an initiative that can change the diplomatic dynamics around Iraq, the military costs of containment will fall on the United States as well as on the people in the surrounding countries who would suffer the spillover effects of intensified conflict.

PEACE BUILDING IN IRAQ

A political agreement to end the war is not an end point, but a milestone on a course to sustainable peace. From there, the complexity of implementing the agreement takes hold. It will be a long-term proposition. International forces stayed in Bosnia for over a decade, they are still in Kosovo, and even in resource-rich countries such as Russia and Ukraine that went through massive transitions without wars, it took almost a decade to halt their economic declines after the collapse of communism. We must recognize that it will take a decade of sustained peace for Iraq to become stable and prosperous.

That time frame alone underscores why any single nation, even the United States, cannot unilaterally support and sustain Iraq on its path to prosperity. The demands on personnel and resources are too great to be sustained credibly by one international actor. The extent of this commitment also suggests that if the international community does not have a role in brokering the peace, there will be less incentive to contribute seriously to the expensive and time-consuming process of building a viable state.

The next attempt at peace building in Iraq will be more difficult than the first failed U.S. efforts in 2003. Iraqis are disillusioned and lack trust. Life for Iraqis is worse in most ways than it was before the war: less security, less electricity, less water, less access to health care, more unemployment, and extreme risks from just sending children to school.[8] Even with a peace agreement, it will take time to build confidence that the agreement will hold.

The provisions of a political settlement must shape the details of a peace-building strategy. There are, however, lessons from Iraq and other international missions that should inform both the process and the substance of a peace-building strategy.

—*Common Strategy, Shared Expectations.* A reconstruction framework for Iraq must make expectations and commitments clear on the part of Iraqis and the international community. The International Compact for Iraq is a starting point, but it should be restructured in light of a peace agreement and the guidelines suggested below. Both donors and Iraqis should refrain from overpromising, yet at the same time, to build credibility, an agreement has to focus on short-term results on security and jobs. Most postconflict situations result in an initial euphoria and then lead to disappointment and resignation when expectations are not met.

—*Local Ownership, International Oversight.* Iraqis must believe in a unified Iraq, even if it takes a federal shape, for the state to be viable. A peace settlement will provide guidelines for compromise, but one has to expect that every aspect of any agreement will be tested. A key function for the UN will be to provide neutral oversight and perhaps a venue to work out disputes, so that Iraqis can begin to rebuild trust and to give practical meaning to "local ownership" from a national and not a sectarian perspective. The mechanism for UN oversight should be informed by the dynamics of the political negotiations, which will likely suggest a combination of actors who can retain local trust. At a minimum, a regular review mechanism should be created to drive implementation.

—*Security.* Most recent peace agreements in the wake of civil wars have required international peacekeepers to secure time and space for implementation. The goal should be to mobilize a UN-led force focused particularly on border security, with the United States continuing a significant but reduced military presence in Iraq. If one took troop ratios from Bosnia or Kosovo as a guide, the force presence would be as large as 250,000 in the non-Kurdish parts of Iraq.[9] A more realistic target for Iraq would be on the order of 150,000 total U.S. and UN troops in the first year, reducing this level to 100,000 if the agreement holds. Against the international requirement of 150,000 troops, the United States should propose to provide 100,000 in the first year and then scale down to 50,000 in the second year, while supporting the UN in recruiting the balance of forces. In principle, it would be attractive to have one force under UN leadership, but it is unrealistic to contemplate that the United States would place troops under UN command. The United States should seek a supplemental appropriation to fund a major share of these costs, while seeking contributions from the neighboring states. Burden sharing would be the most effective way to support the orderly reduction of U.S. forces in Iraq.

—*Rule of Law.* Restoring Iraqi confidence will require systematically administering the rule of law without regard to religion or ethnicity. This will require an overhaul of the police, the Ministry of the Interior, the courts, and the penitentiary system. In the short term, a combination of peacekeepers and international police will need to share basic law and order functions with Iraqis to stress that there is a new era in enforcing the rule of law. Ideally this would entail 20,000–30,000 international police as part of the international mission, but experience has shown that these numbers are not available. Out of necessity, designated units of the peacekeeping mission must take on this function. The cost of reconstituting the Ministry of the Interior and the police will be large, perhaps on the scale of $5 billion, and donors will resist getting involved. Yet if there has been a glaring lesson from Iraq and Afghanistan, it has been that failure to take a comprehensive approach to the full system of law and order has undermined progress in every other area of reconstruction.

—*Oil Revenues.* Disputes over revenue sharing were one factor driving the Sunni insurgency, and if the provisions of the political settlement in this area are not fully met and completely transparent, they will be the first factor to cause a political settlement to unravel. One should expect attempts to distort accounts and cut special deals. Given the trends in other resource-rich conflict states, corruption in the energy sector will be endemic. Even a perceived diversion of natural resource wealth to particular groups or individuals can reignite civil wars. This is a difficult area for the UN because of the legacy of the Oil-for-Food Programme during Saddam Hussein's period. That said, there is no alternative to an international oversight mechanism, monitored by an independent international firm, on oil revenues and the implementation of the natural resource provisions of the political agreement. The foundations for this mechanism exist, but it may be necessary to transition the current oversight framework for oil revenues to a new international mechanism with extensive publicity on measures taken to ensure transparency.

—*Militias and Jobs.* Few states have managed the disarmament, demobilization, and reintegration (DDR) of militias well. The first two components can be straightforward. The process generally unravels with reintegration. If former militia members are reintegrated into communities with 30 to 40 percent unemployment, the likelihood is that 30 to 40 percent of those reintegrated will be unemployed and disgruntled within a year. Hence, the strongest DDR program is one that is teamed with a massive, community-based job creation program throughout the country. Again, the most effective path to such job creation is local—through municipal works programs and, more important, through microcredit programs that can help jump-start local business development.[10]

—*Reconciliation, Governance, and Politics.* A common mistake after most peace agreements is to drive too quickly to elections. Elections in such an environment can reinforce sectarian competition. A track record of governance has to be established that allows the provisions of a political settlement to be implemented. The objective is not to discourage democratic progress but to make a democratic process credible with maximum participation from all groups in an environment that supports the process of reconciliation rather than reignites past tensions. Provincial elections are already scheduled for October 2008, and parliamentary elections follow in 2009. Should a political settlement modify or delay that schedule, the international community should be prepared to accept the change and not automatically dismiss it as undemocratic.

The failed attempts at reconstruction in Iraq and the serious struggles in Afghanistan in a mission that includes the UN, NATO, massive U.S. support, the EU, and other international donors should underscore the difficulty of helping a nation reestablish the functions of governance, the rule of law, security, and an environment to stimulate investment. A successful peace-building mission in Iraq will take a decade and massive resources. To be sure, Iraqi oil revenues should eventually finance most of the requirement, but an early international injection of funds will be needed to support job creation. The temptation on the part of most states will be to assume that a UN peace-building mission in Iraq can be done cheaply and quickly and thus to shortchange the process. The United States already made that mistake, and it should not be repeated.

CONCLUSION

Realities on the ground in Iraq and in U.S. and international politics will shift rapidly and affect the nature of what can be done in Iraq. U.S. policy has failed so far to deal with the complex nature of security and the political and economic challenges in Iraq, thereby creating new threats: risks of a wider sectarian conflict in the region between Sunni and Shi'a, an emboldened Iran, a network of al Qaeda franchises operating throughout the Middle East and North Africa, ungoverned spaces in Iraq that can become bases from which to export transnational terrorism, and instability and lack of resiliency in international oil markets.

These threats are regional and global. They call for multilateral engagement and a role for the UN to provide the political cover most nations need to reengage in Iraq. Yet there should be no illusions about simple success.

To maximize chances to advance a political settlement in Iraq, the next president will need to act quickly, when troop levels will be near their peak. While presidential candidates McCain and Obama differ on whether and how long to keep U.S. forces in Iraq, neither contemplates increasing U.S. forces. It should be made clear to Iraqis and the international community that if the Iraqis will not take advantage of a credible multilateral process to reach a political compromise, then U.S. troops will be withdrawn because they cannot make a sustainable difference in Iraq. What should not be forgotten is that diplomatic and military strategies must reinforce each other as part of a coherent policy.

The limits of unilateralism also apply to containing the spillover from war in Iraq if it is not possible to broker a political compact among the parties. The United States should encourage a UN role in diplomacy to get commitments from Iraq's neighbors to not fuel the Iraq civil war with money and weapons and by implication exacerbate the foundations for international terrorism. Perhaps other nations, not from the Middle East, could contribute troops or observers to control the spillover. An even broader lesson is that the disruption of diplomatic ties with perceived enemies only hampers our capacity when we have no choice but to find common ground. At present the very question of a dialogue with Iran has become an issue, when the real focus should be on the substance of such a dialogue.

America's image around the world has reached an all-time low. The Pew Global Attitudes Project survey report from June 2006 showed that the United States military presence in Iraq is seen by most nations as a greater threat to world peace and security than is Iran.[11] Pew's 2007 survey report showed that in nearly all countries surveyed more people view China's influence positively than they view U.S. influence.[12] A third worldwide survey, *World Public Opinion 2007,* shows that "In 10 out of 15 countries, the most common view is that the United States cannot be trusted to 'act responsibly in the world.'"[13]

The next president may well find that engaging the UN seriously in Iraq, working under a UN umbrella to restore international cooperation, respecting and abiding by international law, and resorting to unilateral action only under imminent threats could restore respect for U.S. leadership and serve our national security interests. In Iraq, U.S. advocacy for UN political and humanitarian leadership may not only help the United States, it may begin to give credence to a reawakening of American diplomacy and international engagement.

NOTES

1. General Petraeus and Ambassador Crocker have urged caution in withdrawing troops before security has been consolidated, and the Bush administration has used their advice to buy time on further withdrawals. For an example of this dynamic between field recommendations and Washington responses see Stephen Lee Meyers and Thom Shanker, "Bush Given Iraq War Plan with a Steady Troop Level," *New York Times,* March 25, 2008 (www.nytimes.com/2008/03/25/washington/25policy.html?_r=1&hp&oref=slogin).

2. David Petraeus, "Report to Congress on the Situation in Iraq," 110 Cong. 2 sess., April 8–9, 2008, pp. 2–4. Text from *Federal Document Clearing House Congressional Testimony* (www.defenselink.mil/pdf/General_Petraeus_Testimony_to_Congress.pdf).

3. Ryan Crocker, "Testimony of Ambassador Ryan C. Crocker before the Senate Foreign Relations Committee," 110 Cong. 2 sess., April 8, 2008, p. 8. Text from *Federal Document Clearing House Congressional Testimony* (www.defenselink.mil/pdf/Ambassador_Crocker_SFRC_Testimony.pdf).

4. General Petraeus cites their numbers at more than 91,000 in his April 2008 report to Congress, p. 3.

5. See Sudarsan Raghavan, "Basra's Wary Rebirth," *Washington Post*, June 1, 2008, p. A1 (www.washingtonpost.com/wp-dyn/content/article/2008/05/31/AR20080 53100971.html).

6. Carlos Pascual and Kenneth M. Pollack, "The Critical Battles: Political Reconciliation and Reconstruction in Iraq," *Washington Quarterly* 30, no. 3 (Summer 2007): 7–19.

7. Thomas E. Ricks, "Deals in Iraq Make Friends of Enemies," *Washington Post*, July 20, 2007, p. A1 (www.washingtonpost.com/wp-dyn/content/article/2007/07/19/ AR2007071902432.html?nav=emailpage).

8. For statistics on all these measures, see Michael E. O'Hanlon and Jason H. Campbell, *Iraq Index: Tracking Variables of Reconstruction & Security in Post-Saddam Iraq* (Brookings, October 1, 2007) (www3.brookings.edu/fp/saban/iraq/index.pdf).

9. Pascual and Pollack, "The Critical Battles," p. 9.

10. The experience of ProCredit Bank throughout the Balkans, a bank network funded through the European Bank for Reconstruction and Development (EBRD), has demonstrated that microcredit and small credit is viable and sustainable in places such as Bosnia and Kosovo. For more information on the ProCredit Bank, see (www.pro-creditbank.com.mk/).

11. *America's Image Slips, but Allies Share U.S. Concerns over Iran, Hamas* (Washington: Pew Global Attitudes Project, June 13, 2006), p. 3 (http://pewglobal.org/ reports/pdf/252.pdf).

12. *Global Unease with Major World Powers* (Washington: Pew Global Attitudes Project, June 27, 2007), p. 44 (http://pewglobal.org/reports/pdf/256.pdf).

13. *World Public Opinion 2007* (Chicago Council on Global Affairs and World PublicOpinion.org, June 25, 2007), p. 30 (www.worldpublicopinion.org/pipa/pdf/ jun07/CCGA+_FullReport_rpt.pdf).

9

Back to Balancing in the Middle East

A New Strategy for Constructive Engagement

MARTIN S. INDYK AND TAMARA COFMAN WITTES

SUMMARY ❱ A new Sunni-Shi'a fault line and a significant decline in U.S. influence frame the challenge to Middle East policy for the next president. That challenge requires a return to balance-of-power diplomacy and a better balancing of interests and values to contain the Iraq civil war, strengthen the forces of moderation, prevent Iran from becoming a nuclear power, and promote democratic reform.

An expanding arc of Iranian influence extends from Tehran over Baghdad, Damascus, and Beirut. Radicals under this arc have gained strength by exploiting the United States' own mistakes—our ineffectiveness in Iraq, disengagement from the Arab-Israeli peace process, enabling of anti-democratic forces to gain power through elections, and inability to halt Iran's quest for nuclear weapons. But the divide in the region is not a simple contest between extremists and moderates or even between Sunni and Shi'a.

Because the United States is no longer dominant in the region, the next president will have no choice but to return to balance-of-power diplomacy. Recognizing the complexity of Arab allegiances, the United States

A version of this chapter originally appeared as "Foreign Policy after Bush: Back to Balancing," in *The American Interest* 3, no. 6 (November–December 2007). The authors are grateful to *The American Interest* for permission to revise that article for this volume.

will need to cement and sustain a moderate coalition that can counter Iran's regional ambitions. Its strategy should include these elements:

—A renewed effort at Arab-Israeli reconciliation, which might also generate tension between Syria and Iran

—Containment of the spillover effects of civil war in Iraq

—Negotiations with Iran to attempt to head off its nuclear ambitions, including bilateral engagement to address broader concerns

—Regional security arrangements to contain the Iranian threat, prevent a Middle East nuclear arms race, and, if necessary, shelter our allies under a nuclear umbrella

—A political and economic reform agenda that helps create a new social contract between Arab governments and their citizens

—In less secure countries, much more of an emphasis on building democratic institutions rather than on holding democratic elections ❱

CONTEXT ❱ When President Bush explained his new "surge strategy" in Iraq to the American people in January 2007, he defined the challenge to the United States that is playing out across the broader Middle East as "the decisive ideological struggle of our time. On one side are those who believe in freedom and moderation. On the other side are extremists who kill the innocent and have declared their intention to destroy our way of life."

The problem with this good-versus-evil approach to the conflicts that wrack the Middle East is that it does not describe the decisive struggle as seen by the regional players. A more effective strategy for protecting and promoting U.S. interests must start with a more precise assessment of what is happening there and then determine what the United States can and should do about it.

Regional Trends

That assessment needs to take account of two broad trends in the region:

—*An emerging struggle for power between Shi'as and Sunnis.* For centuries, this sectarian rivalry has lurked just beneath the surface. Now it has broken out in full force because the sectarian killing in Iraq has fed, and been fed by, a regional contest between an Iranian-led Shi'a bloc and Sunni Arab states led by Saudi Arabia and Egypt. Each bloc encompasses moderates and extremists, severely complicating the effort to pursue a coherent U.S. strategy to bolster moderates at the expense of extremists.

—A declining ability of the United States to influence events in the region. U.S. influence was at its height after the successful application of force: first in 1991, when it kicked Saddam Hussein's army out of Kuwait, and then in 2003, when it toppled his regime. This influence was magnified by the 1991 collapse of the Soviet Union, which left America as the world's sole superpower. The United States' dominance in the Middle East is now on the wane, however, sapped by failure in Iraq, war-weariness at home, the administration's determined neglect (until recently) of the Arab-Israeli peace process, and Russia's and China's expanding influences in the region. This loss of dominance requires a return to realism: the United States will have to create a concert of powers to counter threats to its common interests. The next president will have to work cooperatively with others, in the region and outside it, to achieve U.S. purposes. In other words, the United States will have to return to a balance-of-power approach, with all the imperfections and moral dilemmas that such an approach implies. And it means that the United States will have to pursue, with flexibility and compromise, multilateral approaches to the region's many problems. ▋

STRATEGIC AIMS

The United States could confront a potentially dire situation in the Middle East. Civil strife in Iraq, Lebanon, or Gaza could spill over and destabilize neighboring states or trigger wider conflict. Iran's determined pursuit of nuclear weapons could provoke a nuclear arms race. Although, ideally, the United States should wean itself off imported oil, energy independence will take at least a decade to achieve. In the meantime, and because the global economy will still rely on oil and gas, the United States will retain a vital interest in the free flow of energy supplies from the Persian Gulf, which contains a majority of the world's oil and gas reserves. It will also retain an abiding commitment to the security and well-being of Israel and Arab allies. In these circumstances, even if U.S. military forces are pulled back from Iraq, wholesale disengagement from the region is both unwise and infeasible.

A strategy to protect U.S. interests at a time of greater conflict and declining influence should aim toward the following objectives:

—Containing civil conflict in Iraq, to prevent any implosion taking place there from exploding into a wider regional conflict;

—Strengthening the forces of moderation in the Arab world, so they can counter Iran's influence and blunt the impact of regional radicals;

—Relaunching an energetic Arab-Israeli peace process as the bond for a virtual alliance between Israel and Arab states against Iran and its proxies and as a way to keep radical forces from gaining a foothold in the Palestinian arena;

—Preventing Iran's development of nuclear weapons and, should that fail, developing a security framework that will deter their use and avoid a nuclear arms race in the Middle East;

—Pursuing an agenda of political and economic liberalization that will help meet the aspirations of the people of the region, thereby reducing the appeal of regional radicals and helping ensure the long-term stability of regimes that share U.S. strategic interests

THE SUNNI-SHI'A FAULT LINE

It took a war to expose the Sunni-Shi'a sectarian fault line running through the Middle East. For some time, Sunni Arab leaders in Egypt, Saudi Arabia, and Jordan had been warning that a "Shi'a arc" was spreading its influence across the region. Iraq's descent into civil war and Iran's defiant pursuit of nuclear weapons fed these Arab concerns. But it was only in 2006, when Hezbollah provoked a confrontation with Israel in Lebanon and when Damascus blocked Egypt from organizing a prisoner exchange to calm tensions in Gaza, that these leaders rang alarm bells. For them, it was simply unacceptable that a Shi'a-dominated, historically Persian Iran should blatantly interfere in Iraq, Lebanon, and Palestine and become the arbiter of Arab interests. They decried the Shi'a axis that appeared to stretch from its base in Iran to the Shi'a-led government in Iraq to the Shi'a-aligned Alawite regime in Syria and on to Hezbollah in Lebanon.

Differing U.S.-Arab Perceptions of the Sunni-Shi'a Split

From Washington's perspective, however, this new fault line was perceived as a division between the region's moderates and extremists. Indeed, the Lebanon War in the summer of 2006 looked like a proxy war between two sets of forces, each presenting competing visions of the Middle East's future. Hezbollah's dynamic leader, Hassan Nasrallah, and Iran's populist president, Mahmoud Ahmadinejad, put forward a vision of the region defined by unending "resistance" (meaning violence, terrorism, and perpetual confrontation) against Israel, the United States, and status quo leaders across the Arab world. Nasrallah and Ahmadinejad argue for the redemptive value of violence and offer the false promise of justice and dignity for Arabs humiliated by the long history of defeat at the hands of the West and Israel. It was violence, they assert, that forced Israel to withdraw unilaterally from Lebanon in May 2000 and from Gaza in August 2005. It is defiance, they claim, that has enabled Iran to proceed with its nuclear program in the face of United States–led international opposition. And, in their view, violence and defiance enabled Hezbollah to stand proudly in 2006 against the Israeli army and United States–inspired UN Security Council resolutions.

To moderate Sunni Arab leaders—including Egypt's president Hosni Mubarak, Jordan's king Abdullah II, and Saudi Arabia's king Abdullah, all friends of the United States—the Iranian-led challenge *is* deeply threatening on multiple levels. Even on the streets of these leaders' own cities, they are less popular than Nasrallah and Ahmadinejad.[1] The radicals' message of resistance is always combined with denunciations of Sunni Arab leaders for sheltering fecklessly under a U.S. security umbrella and making humiliating deals with Israel. In Lebanon, the Iranian-Syrian-Hezbollah axis openly attempts to topple the moderate Sunni-led government. In the Palestinian territories, the Shi'a axis provides critical backing for Hamas and Palestine Islamic Jihad (PIJ), which reject an Israeli-Palestinian peace to which the Sunni leaders are committed.[2] In June 2007 they helped Hamas launch a putsch in Gaza against the authority of President Mahmoud Abbas, which secured them a foothold on Israel's southern border to match the one on its northern border maintained by Hezbollah. In Iraq, Iran is aiding and encouraging Shi'a militias who oppose political reconciliation with Iraqi Sunnis, threatening to establish a virtual Shi'a state on the borders of Saudi Arabia and Kuwait—a menacing prospect.[3] Most alarmingly, Iran is attempting to achieve military dominance through a nuclear program that could put it in possession of nuclear weapons within five years.

Given these Arab concerns, the Shi'a rise presents the United States with a measure of opportunity. Sunni Arab leaders desiring to counter Iran's bid for regional hegemony seek U.S. support to strengthen the Lebanese government and the Palestinian presidency of Mahmoud

Abbas, promote an effective Israeli-Palestinian peace process, prevent an Iranian takeover in Iraq, head off Iran's nuclear program, and enhance their own security capabilities.[4]

However, these Arab leaders do not share Washington's antipathy for Sunni extremists, preferring to co-opt them rather than see them fall into the waiting arms of Iran and Hezbollah. Hamas, for example, became steadily more dependent on Iran for funding and training when Arab leaders acceded to the Bush administration's insistence that they cut off their support for the militant Islamist organization. But with the emergence of this new Sunni-Shi'a fault line, the Sunni leaders in Egypt and Saudi Arabia want to woo Hamas away from Iran and bring it back to the Sunni side. Egypt's denunciation of Hamas for its military takeover of Gaza was quickly smoothed over, and Egypt invested months in mediating an Israel-Hamas cease-fire. President Bush's speech in July 2007 on the peace process simplistically characterized Hamas as part of the broader global jihadist enemy (al Qaeda actually regularly denounces Hamas). He demanded that Arab states choose sides. The Saudi and Egyptian leaders, though, fear that U.S. isolation of Hamas will make Bush's words a self-fulfilling prophecy.

Similarly, Arab states will not support U.S. efforts to suppress the Sunni insurgency in Iraq if it leads only to unfettered Shi'a supremacy there. Arab governments remain deeply troubled by the prospect of a Shi'a-dominated Iraqi state—not just because it will strengthen Iran but because they fear it will mobilize demands from their own restive and disadvantaged Shi'a populations. If U.S. domestic politics forces a precipitate withdrawal and Sunni-Shi'a violence in Iraq escalates, Arab states will feel strong pressure to act on behalf of their Sunni brethren.

The challenge for U.S. policy in the coming period will be to forge and sustain a coalition of moderate forces in the Middle East to combat the newly emerging radical forces and the harsh vision of the region's future that they promote. But U.S. strategy will need to take into account that the United States' main Arab allies have divergent objectives from ours. Their cooperation in isolating Hamas in Gaza was a temporary, tactical convergence with our approach. They continue to reach out to Hamas in an effort to reconcile the group with Abu Mazen (President Mahmoud Abbas) and to wean them away from dependence on Iran and its allies. Rather than oppose a power-sharing arrangement, the United States needs to establish a consensus on what Hamas would have to do so that it can rejoin mainstream Palestinian politics.

In the meantime, the United States will need to work closely with the West Bank government of President Abbas and Prime Minister Salam Fayad to prove that moderation brings greater benefits to the Palestinian people than do the violence and defiance that Hamas currently preaches and practices. And it should insist on Arab state support for that effort. As a consequence of the violent ambitions of the Iranian-led coalition in Gaza, the Palestinians are in the ironic position of having, for the first time in their history, not one, but two governments vying for their support by competing to meet their needs. Who wins this competition will have profound consequences for the success of U.S. coalition building.

A similar divergence of objectives exists when it comes to dealing with Syria. While Sunni Arab leaders have little sympathy for the Asad regime, they recognize the benefits of offering it an alternative to its strategic alliance with Iran. If Syria could be split from Iran, it would create a crack in that axis that would physically separate Hezbollah from its Iranian lifeline. The Alawite regime is already conscious of its uneasy position atop a Sunni populace that could become restive if the regime plants itself firmly on the Shi'a side of the fault line. This may explain why the Syrian president is pursuing peace negotiations with Israel, while the Iranian president calls for Israel's destruction. As with Hamas, pressure and isolation have their uses in influencing the calculus of the Syrian leadership. But the door to Washington should also be left open to the Syrians should they want to change sides. This approach could bring Sunni Arab and U.S. strategies into greater alignment.

Similarly, the United States should seek neither Shi'a nor Sunni supremacy in Iraq but rather a pluralistic regime capable of protecting the interests of all of Iraq's communities. Although the intense sectarian violence may have made the goal of a pluralistic Iraq much more difficult to achieve, the United States cannot become involved in an effort to rescue the Sunni insurgents there, any more than it can condone Shi'a suppression of the Sunni community accompanied by the establishment of an Iranian sphere of influence. The United States must continue to co-opt Sunni political forces in Iraq to counterbalance Shi'a dominance while redeploying troops around Iraq's periphery to deter would-be sectarian provocateurs and meddlesome neighbors.

AMERICA'S DEARTH OF INFLUENCE

Another complication to the challenge of developing a coherent and effective U.S. strategy for the Middle East lies in the decline of Washington's ability to influence events there. During the era of U.S. dominance in the region, from 1991 to 2006, the United States was strong enough to preserve its regional interests without depending on the balance of power in the Gulf between Iran and Iraq. Earlier, Washington had sought to maintain a favorable balance, supporting first Iran under the shah and then Saddam Hussein's Iraq during his 1980s war with Iran's ayatollahs. The U.S. dominance, achieved by the eviction of Saddam's army from Kuwait and the collapse of the Soviet Union, enabled the Clinton administration to avoid a balance-of-power game in favor of a policy of containing both Iran and Iraq. Dual containment might have been sustainable had Clinton achieved the breakthrough he sought with respect to a comprehensive Arab-Israeli peace, which would have isolated both rogue states. But after Clinton's peace efforts collapsed in 2000, President Bush chose another path.

The failure of the Bush administration's efforts to transform the region through regime change in Iraq and assertive promotion of democracy has harmed the U.S. position in the region in three ways:

—First, Iraq's disintegration clearly has tipped the balance in favor of Iran, while dealing a blow to the U.S. image of invincibility and tarnishing its values.

—Second, President Bush's equation of democratization with early elections, even where political institutions, parties, and a democratic culture were weak, advantaged avowedly militant Islamist parties like Muqtada al-Sadr's supporters in Iraq, Hezbollah in Lebanon, and Hamas in the Palestinian territories. With superior organization; an anti-American, anti-regime message; and only a feeble central government to counter them, they were able to exploit elections and enter government with their militias and terrorist cadres intact. From there they have succeeded in further eroding the state institutions of Iraq, Lebanon, and the Palestinian Authority, advancing radical agendas and pushing those states to the brink of civil war.

—Third, the Bush administration's determined disengagement from the Israeli-Palestinian peace process contributed to Hamas's rise to power in the Palestinian Authority. Israel's decision to pursue a policy of unilateral withdrawal reinforced Hamas's and Hezbollah's claims that violence was the only way to make gains against Israel. All this further undermined President Abbas, who was committed to negotiating a two-state solution with Israel. Bush's isolation of Hamas did not weaken the movement as hoped. With their takeover of Gaza and authority over 1.3 million Palestinians, they can no longer simply be ignored. Moreover, President Bush's failure to engage in any serious effort to end the Palestinian intifada and promote a solution to the Palestinian problem convinced Arabs and Muslims regionwide that the United States cared little for their concerns.

While American influence waned, Russia and China were emerging as independent players in the Middle East in ways that vastly complicated U.S. diplomacy. President Vladimir Putin's Russia made lucrative deals to supply nuclear and missile technology to Iran. China's interest in secure lines of energy supply from Iran, its nearest Middle Eastern neighbor, made it as cool to sanctions as Russia has been. Both states seek to sell arms in the region and offer economic and political ties unencumbered by pressure over democracy or human rights.

Neither Russia nor China appears to be mounting a fundamental challenge to U.S. primacy in the Gulf, but both are happy to see the United States bogged down by security commitments while they secure preferential energy and trading relationships with regional states. Unconstrained by a weakened United States, Russia and China have so far undermined the one serious effort by the Bush administration to use diplomacy to achieve one of its goals in the Middle East: heading off Iran's nuclear program.

THE DIPLOMATIC AGENDA

The consequences of declining U.S. power are that the United States now finds itself in the position of *demandeur*. We no longer can insist, as President Bush once did, that "you're either with us or against us." Recognizing the limits of military power—demonstrated in Iraq and in Israel's experience in Lebanon in the summer of 2006—the United States is forced to turn to diplomacy. But it does so when its adversaries in the Middle East are less fearful of U.S. power and see less need for U.S. favor and when its allies are no longer sure that the United States is a reliable partner. That is why Iran in 2006 could spurn Secretary Rice's offer of negotiations over its nuclear program and scoff at the weak UN sanctions that resulted.[5]

Build a Moderate Middle Eastern Alliance

The United States now must build a counteralliance to the Iranian-Syrian-Iraqi Shi'a-Hezbollah alliance and correct the tilt in Iran's favor that was the unintended consequence of the misadventure in Iraq. As in previous eras when the United States did not dominate the region, this approach inevitably will put it in league with unfamiliar and unreliable allies, creating moral dilemmas and policy inconsistencies. The United States will not now enjoy the luxury of staying above the fray and demanding that local actors read from its script.

Use Diplomacy to Contain Iran

By necessity, the two major arenas for diplomatic activity will be the effort to head off Iran's nuclear weapons program and the attempt to resurrect a meaningful Arab-Israeli peace process. Although Secretary Rice's two-year effort to pressure Iran to suspend its uranium enrichment resulted in only a weak UN sanctions resolution and no suspension of Iran's nuclear program, diplomacy has by no means run its course. Iran still seems some years from being in a position to fabricate a nuclear device. The unanimous votes of the Security Council, combined with the threat of stronger sanctions, triggered unprecedented public criticism within Tehran of Ahmadinejad's confrontational approach. The stigma of international isolation that accompanies UN sanctions, however weak they may be, does not sit well with Persian pride. Nor is confrontation with the international community welcomed by Iran's more prudent leaders. Moreover, the isolation of Iran has advantaged U.S. efforts outside the Security Council to block financial transactions with Iran and to persuade other countries to divest from its economy. Consequently, those Iranians who argue for a more sophisticated stealth approach to acquiring nuclear weapons, using negotiations to divide the United States from its European, Russian, and Chinese partners, may well become ascendant again. If they do succeed in outflanking Ahmadinejad or reining him in, Iran's enrichment efforts may be temporarily suspended, and international negotiations on the nuclear program could resume.

Already, the United States and Iran are engaged in direct negotiations over Iraq. This presents an important test of Tehran's intentions. If it is willing to reduce its hegemonic ambitions in Iraq in favor of a common goal of stabilizing its neighbor, this could provide a foundation for higher-level talks about the many other troubling aspects of Iranian behavior that need to be addressed, such as sponsorship of terrorism, interference in Lebanon, and opposition to Israel and the peace process, to name a few.

Reengage in Arab-Israeli Diplomacy

In the Arab-Israeli diplomatic arena, the Iranian threat provides a new impetus to progress. Palestinian moderates are as concerned about Iranian interference in their internal affairs (through the backing of Hamas and Palestine Islamic Jihad) as Israel is concerned about Ahmadinejad's nuclear threats. Israeli and Sunni Arab leaders now share an interest in showing that negotiations can work better than resistance. The involvement of Arab states, via the Arab League Peace Initiative, provides a boost to President Abbas and an incentive to Israelis looking for a reliable Arab partner. The willingness of Israeli and Palestinian leaders to discuss the elements of a final agreement is also a positive development, since it will give both sides greater reassurance about the endgame as they take interim steps to build confidence in a partnership for peace.

The United States needs to nurture and sustain a viable peace process to cement this emerging commonality of interests among its Arab and Israeli partners. In this context, the Hamas coup in Gaza has served as a clarifying act. Beyond setting up a direct competition between the two visions of a Middle East advanced by the United States and Iran, it has simplified the diplomatic process. Since Israel withdrew unilaterally from Gaza, that territory is no longer in contention. That leaves the disposition of the West Bank and East Jerusalem as the only territorial issues still in dispute between Israel and the Palestine Liberation Organization (PLO, which has accepted Israel's right to exist within its 1967 borders). Abu Mazen is authorized by the Palestinian people, as the chairman of the PLO, to negotiate with Israel. And those negotiations are no longer complicated by the presence of Hamas, with its rejectionist attitude, in the Palestinian Authority government.

After six years of conflict, Israelis and Palestinians have also become more realistic about the terms of engagement for a final status agreement even though they have lost confidence in the willingness or ability of the other to live up to those requirements. That is why it is essential now to promote a two-track process that leads to final-status negotiations and a parallel rebuilding of confidence in the partnership through concrete reciprocal actions on the ground in the West Bank (for example, the curbing of Palestinian violence and Israeli settlement activity, the assumption of responsibility by reconstituted Palestinian security services and the removal of Israeli military roadblocks, and the ending of Palestinian incitement and the release of Palestinian prisoners). Since there is a Palestinian government in the West Bank willing to undertake this effort and an Israeli government willing to reciprocate, such an effort now has a greater chance of success than at any time since the breakdown of final status negotiations at Taba in January 2001. This is especially the case because for the first time in seven years there seems to be a common sense of urgency infusing these efforts caused by the threat from Iran and the Hamas takeover in Gaza.

Hamas, of course, will not stand by as Israel and Mahmoud Abbas undertake a new peace initiative. Despite its cease-fire commitments, it likely will continue to attempt to perpetrate terrorist attacks within Israel and challenge any reconstituted Palestinian security services in the West Bank. To be effective, a new United States–led peace process must also include concerted efforts to contain Hamas locally and regionally, using diplomatic, military, and financial means. The United States should use intermediaries to articulate clear criteria for any attempt to reintegrate Hamas into mainstream Palestinian politics. To be sure, forswearing violence and terror is an essential requirement. But rather than insist on empty rhetorical declarations, the United States should test Hamas's intentions through concrete actions. If the Israeli-Hamas cease-fire established in June 2008 holds, further steps by Hamas evidencing a rejection of violence and acceptance of a two-state solution could enable a reconciliation between Hamas and the PLO and a reintegration of Gaza into the Palestinian Authority.

A United States–led effort aimed at putting the peace train back on track and moving forward can succeed if it

—focuses on rebuilding Palestinian economic and security capabilities,

—defines the endgame and a time line for Palestinians and Israelis to get there,

—engages the Arab states, including U.S. support for Israeli-Syrian talks. Such a process will require active American diplomacy; but it will boost U.S. prestige, make it easier for Arab leaders to cooperate with the United States and Israel, and increase Iranian isolation.

But the U.S. government will need to be realistic about the obstacles to progress. On the Palestinian side, after six years of neglect of the peace process, Palestinians are left with a divided populace under two different authorities, crumbling social and political institutions, a desperately weakened moderate leadership, and an incipient failed terror statelet in Gaza. On the other side, Israeli prime minister Ehud Olmert has lower approval ratings than President Bush's. Olmert's best hope for survival lies in renewed peace talks with the Palestinians—yet Olmert's unpopularity, and Mahmoud Abbas's questionable ability to deliver, will make the Israeli leader hesitate to take the substantial risks inherent in negotiating a deal that would dismantle more than 100 settlements in the West Bank and tamper with the status quo in Jerusalem.

The structural flaw at the heart of such a reconstituted process is the lack of an effective Palestinian security capability. Without that, any easing of Israel's military presence will provide an opening that Hamas and its allies will do their best to exploit. One successful suicide bombing could shut down the whole fragile process. It is therefore essential to focus U.S. efforts on dismantling the corrupt security establishment that Yasir Arafat built and replacing it with untainted commanders who are willing to take on the complicated task of controlling the territory. This should be easier in the context of a reconstituted political process that provides Palestinians with a reason for supporting the suppression of violent gangs and terrorist cadres by their own security forces.

Contain the Impact of Iraq's Chaos

To be effective, U.S. diplomacy on Iran and the Arab-Israeli conflict needs to be backed by a security strategy that buttresses U.S. regional allies against the combined threats of growing instability and a potential nuclear arms race. The United States already has strong security relationships with Israel, Egypt, Saudi Arabia, and the Gulf Cooperation Council (GCC), our partners in the virtual alliance against Iranian ambitions. To maintain these partners' security, we now must successfully manage the challenges posed by Iraq's political stalemate and Iran's pursuit of nuclear weapons.

The United States needs to develop a containment strategy to prevent any implosion in Iraq from exploding into a regional conflagration and to deter external meddling in Iraq. An Iraqi civil war easily could draw in its neighbors: Turkey, Iran, and Saudi Arabia could decide to intervene; and massive refugee flows could overwhelm Jordan and Kuwait, among others. Containment of such possibilities will require maintaining a U.S. troop presence on the Iraqi periphery, probably at reduced numbers, for some time to come.

Build Long-Term Gulf Stability

Iran's determination to continue its nuclear program is already sparking preparations by Israel for a possible preemptive strike and by Iran's Arab neighbors for their own nuclear programs. If diplomacy fails to head off Iran's nuclear program, pressure will grow on the United States to resort to a preemptive strike of some type. At best, however, such a strike would only delay Iran's acquisition of nuclear weapons, and a strike alone will not be sufficient to prevent a regional nuclear arms race.

The next president should enter into urgent discussions with our regional allies—Israel, Egypt, Jordan, and the GCC states—to develop security agreements that would strengthen their own deterrent capabilities and at the same time extend a U.S. nuclear umbrella to them. In return they would need to commit to actions that bolster the region's nascent moderate alliance: nonproliferation, visible support for Arab-Israeli peacemaking, internal reform, border security cooperation, and regional counterterrorism efforts. Such arrangements would put U.S. ongoing regional security investments into a context that clarifies the mutual benefits of our deployments and that emphasizes reciprocal commitments by the regional beneficiaries of our presence. It could also help integrate post-Saddam Iraq into a stable regional security order. The fundamental objective would be to prevent a nuclear arms race and effectively deter aggression by a nuclear-armed Iran. Although such a NATO-like security framework for the Middle East will be controversial at home, it will be all but unavoidable if nuclear diplomacy fails. Conversely, if nuclear diplomacy succeeds in heading off Iran's aspirations for nuclear weapons, it too could be invited to participate in this regional security architecture.

THE ROLE OF ARAB REFORM

In forging a realistic new U.S. strategy for the Middle East, it would be easy to jettison the Bush administration's efforts to advance Arab democracy. After all, the Sunni leaders whose regimes the United States seeks to liberalize are the very ones whose support is most necessary to deflect Iran's bid for hegemony. How then can we insist that they undertake political and economic reforms that are inherently destabilizing?

Bitter experience teaches that repressing the region's radicals does not remove the threat they pose; instead, repression in one country often pushes radicals to safer havens in failing states (like Lebanon and Gaza) from which they can wreak more terrible damage. The appeal of Islamist radicalism lies in its ideology of revolutionary resistance to the stagnation and suffering in many Arab societies today. Countering that ideology requires a positive alternative vision of the future, one in which moderation, tolerance, and peace provide more benefits and opportunities than do resistance and violence.

To marginalize the radicals and rejectionists, this vision must encompass prospects for realizing Palestinian national aspirations. But this vision must also present the vast majority of Arabs outside Palestine with the opportunity to shape their own future. This promise can only be fulfilled through far-reaching political, economic, and social reforms that create a new social contract between Arab governments and their citizens.

Arab leaders feel keenly the threats from radical Islam within their own societies. The corruption, inefficiency, and nepotism pervasive in the Arab states have produced economic stagnation and an increasing inability to deliver basic government services to a burgeoning population. Islamists capitalize on this failing with charitable networks that provide efficient social welfare to the needy. Moreover, for decades, Islamist movements in Jordan, Egypt, and other states allied with the United States have steadily built up their grassroots popularity by attacking the passivity of these regimes in the face of U.S. and Israeli policies that are portrayed negatively. These movements benefit from the apparent successes of Nasrallah and Ahmadinejad. Likewise, the critique of regime performance at home and abroad that local Islamists provide echoes the rhetoric trumpeted by Iran and Hezbollah.

In this environment, U.S. efforts to persuade Arab leaders of the need to reform should resonate. The leaders are increasingly aware that the sheer size of the restless and underutilized youth cohort in today's Arab world combined with the relentless demands of a globalized economy produce mounting expectations. More than half of the Arab world's population is younger than the age of twenty-one. While current rulers can still manipulate political institutions, buy support with government resources, and call in their security forces when all else fails, their capacity to sustain this game is increasingly challenged. By increasing repression, they run high risks of alienating supporters. By relying primarily on U.S. military and economic support, they tarnish their image as defenders of Islam and Arab interests.

For now, Arab regimes believe that the best way to tamp down the threat from domestic Islamist opposition is to work at resolving regional conflicts such as in Iraq, Lebanon, and Palestine, relieving them of the burden of addressing domestic grievances. While the United States should work with them to resolve regional conflicts, the next president also needs to help them understand that the best insulation against the destabilizing effects of domestic Islamist movements is to repair the frayed social contract between citizens and the state.

Make Reform a Foundation of Partnership

Arab rulers face a dilemma: they know that regional stability demands their close cooperation with the United States, at a moment when their people view with fury the regional role of the United States. Enhancing Arab cooperation with U.S. regional diplomacy will thus result in increased repression at home. To extract Arab rulers from this dilemma, and to be sustainable and effective in countering the region's radical axis, U.S.-Arab cooperation must rest on a new foundation of partnership among the United States, moderate Arab governments, and their mostly moderate citizens—a partnership designed to produce a better future for the people of the Middle East.

Provide Material Support for Reform

Reform will come about only through the willingness of Arab regimes to undertake necessary changes. We have no alternative but to work with them. The U.S. role should be to reduce the risks and costs of undertaking essential, long-delayed reforms through material incentives, disincentives, and dialogue.

—With U.S. economic aid to Egypt declining to a minimum level in 2008, the United States should invite Egypt to begin a strategic dialogue that would encompass economic, security, and diplomatic cooperation and link new levels of aid to agreed-upon goals, including a vision for Egypt's political future.

—New aid through a "Democracy Challenge Account" could provide incentives to Arab states willing to take risks for reform.

—Democratic activists and politicians in the Arab world do not fear a U.S. "kiss of death"; instead, they fear U.S. abandonment. They already feel its effects in the form of crackdowns on journalists and activists in Egypt and elsewhere. As we did in South Korea and the Philippines, the U.S. government should provide visible support to democracy movements while maintaining strategic cooperation with governments.

Test Islamists' Willingness to Moderate

Under current conditions, the Islamist movements will be the first beneficiaries of any new political openings. But broader political freedoms, if enabled by Arab regimes, will allow non-Islamist alternative voices to emerge and will force Islamist movements to clarify their political agendas. If they advocate radical actions and views, or if they pursue violence or other antidemocratic means, they will become legitimate targets for state action. While countenancing such targeted crackdowns, we should not accede to any regime using the excuse of radical Islamist activity to repress *all* dissent. The United States can support harsh measures against domestic opposition movements, but only when they have demonstrated political irresponsibility—and when moderate alternatives exist.

In the Middle East, cultivating moderation is essential to building democracy, and cultivating democracy is essential to building moderation. If, over time, limited political openings are perceived as window dressing on autocracy, then moderates will be discredited as the radicals grow in popularity.

Focus on Our Strongest Allies First

Building democracy and moderation together requires focusing democracy-promotion efforts on those societies—like our allies Egypt, Morocco, and Jordan—with strong, capable governments and relatively tame domestic Islamist movements.[6] In such societies, immediate security concerns are lower for both government and citizens, radical arguments have the weakest hold, and Islamists have the greatest incentive to remain peaceful and moderate in exchange for the ability to play a public role in politics and society. There, regimes are strong enough to tolerate freedom of expression and association, and citizens are open to moderate alternatives to Islamic radicalism.

In weaker states, like Lebanon, Palestine, and Iraq, the priority should be on state building rather than on democracy promotion. In these settings, only when communal security is ensured with neutral and reliable state institutions will the militancy of local radicals lose its claim on public loyalty. Saudi Arabia is a special case, in which the line between the established brand of Islam that supports the state and the brand that justifies violent terrorism is blurred. Saudi domestic security forces face a real, if so far contained, challenge from domestic militants. Any effort to advance political reform in Saudi Arabia must therefore be undertaken cautiously, with these dynamics in mind.

The United States will need to be consistent and candid with Arab allies, voicing expectations about reform priorities and policies and integrating reform into the framework of bilateral relations as a precondition for long-term, reliable, and stable U.S.-Arab cooperation. The United States will be required to offer Arab states a great many security guarantees to offset the harmful consequences of Iraq's chaos and Iran's ambitions; Arab states should be expected to match this U.S. investment by making the changes necessary to build internal stability.

CONCLUDING OBSERVATIONS

The next president will face a Middle East in turmoil and an American public weary of engagement in the region. To disengage would have profound consequences for U.S. security interests at home and across the globe. To protect those interests, the United States will have to reinvent a diplomacy backed by security guarantees and the threat of force, in the service of a strategy designed to protect our allies, counter our adversaries, and promote a more peaceful and stable region with governments accountable to their people. This monumental challenge will require creativity, flexibility, and a willingness to work with players whose purposes may not always be consonant with our own. We will have to abandon the ill-fated combination of naïveté and muscularity that has characterized the Bush administration's approach in favor of a pragmatic realism that brings American values into balance with American interests.

ADDITIONAL RESOURCES

Byman, Daniel L., and Kenneth M. Pollack. 2007. *Things Fall Apart: Containing the Spillover from an Iraqi Civil War.* Analysis Paper 11. Brookings, Saban Center for Middle East Policy.
Wittes, Tamara Cofman. 2008. *Freedom's Unsteady March: America's Role in Building Arab Democracy.* Brookings.

NOTES

1. The latest Sadat Chair (for Peace and Development)–Zogby (International) poll shows Arabs in five key countries naming Hassan Nasrallah as their most admired leader worldwide, with Mahmoud Ahmadinejad in third place behind former French president Jacques Chirac. See (www.bsos.umd.edu/sadat).

2. In 2002, at an Arab League Summit in Beirut, leaders of all Arab states endorsed the Saudi peace initiative of then crown prince Abdullah, which offered Israel peace, recognition, normalization, and an end to the conflict if it withdrew from all the Arab territories occupied in 1967 and agreed to the establishment of a Palestinian state in the West Bank and Gaza.

3. These Sunni Arab states backed Saddam Hussein during the Iraq-Iran War of the 1980s for the express purpose of blocking the establishment of an Iranian foothold in southern Iraq. Saudi Arabia invested $60 billion in that successful effort, only to be repaid by Saddam's invasion of Kuwait after he had beaten back the Iranian onslaught.

4. The Bush administration's decision in July 2007 to sell Saudi Arabia $20 billion in sophisticated weaponry is a manifestation of this dynamic. See Robin Wright, "U.S. Plans New Arms Sales to Gulf Allies," *Washington Post,* July 28, 2007, p. A1.

5. Contrast this with Iran's quiescent behavior after the toppling of Saddam Hussein's regime in 2003, when they halted their mischief making momentarily and instead sought a "grand bargain" with the United States. Bush's spurning of that initiative mirrors Iran's response to Rice's initiative three years later.

6. Islamist movements in these countries have largely shifted tactics over the years away from violent opposition, and most now operate within red lines established by the regimes. But as radical regional voices gain strength and Arab regimes lose legitimacy, local Islamists feel greater temptation to push the boundaries of peaceful dissent. The longer politics remains tightly controlled and the worse the regional environment becomes, the greater the incentive of local Islamists to radicalize in both their ideology and their actions.

Bent but Not Broken

How the Next Commander in Chief Can Prevent the Breaking of the U.S. Military

P. W. SINGER

SUMMARY ❯ The good news for the next president is that he will become commander in chief of a military that is unmatched in its power and capability by any other nation's armed forces today or in history. The bad news is that this excellence is under siege. The U.S. military and its National Guard and Reserve components have been stretched thin and worn down by the combination of extensive deployments and a deferral of the hard questions of how a nation supports a military at war.

The U.S. military is far from broken. But warning symptoms are there. Trends in recruiting and retention show a force under great stress. This is more than a simple issue of raw numbers of troops but also the long-term effect on quality. Likewise, while the focus of defense budgeting remains on major program acquisitions years into the future, the reality is that a looming equipment gap harms our security in the here and now. Iraq has driven many of these challenges, but they will continue years after operations end there. The problems can no longer be passed on.

The author would like to thank for their comments and suggestions Colonel John Brush, USMC; Colonel Kenneth Dahl, U.S. Army; Terree Haidet; Colonel Gregory Lengyel, U.S. Air Force; Michael O'Hanlon, Brookings; Captain Brian Perkins, U.S. Coast Guard; Commander Christopher Robinson, U.S. Navy; and Ralph Wipfli, Brookings.

A critical test of the next commander in chief will not just be on when and where to use force, but whether to take the actions necessary to ensure that the military does not become broken on his watch. The next president will have to face looming trends and ensure that the U.S. military remains both ready and capable, avoiding any of its post-Vietnam hardships. Specifically, the president should commission a plan of action to shore up the personnel and equipment challenges in the early days of his new administration. Measures to take include the following actions:

—Formulate a national call to service to support recruiting for our military at war

—Ensure recruiting standards are not lowered to maintain a high-quality force

—Expand the force only in a manner that addresses severe gaps and needs rather than provides blanket numbers

—Create a Joint Stabilization Command to better plan and support operations

—Answer troops' quality of life concerns and establish a Military Families Advisory Board to better support retention

—End the "Don't Ask, Don't Tell" policy that puts social politics above national security

—Reevaluate weapons acquisitions in terms of actual needs and the realities of the 9/11 world

—End the abuse of supplemental budgets

—Eliminate and punish waste and corruption, which undermines security

—Reform the acquisition process to finally work the market rather than continue to be worked by it ❱

CONTEXT ❱ From a spent and broken force after Vietnam, the U.S. military has been built into the most professional, best-trained, and best-equipped military not just in the world today, but in human history. For all the challenges we face now in Afghanistan and Iraq, our military's combat capabilities are unmatched. Indeed, it is telling that the very threats we face come not from peer competitors but from foes that seek out weaknesses on other planes of battle.

But this excellence is under siege. Our military has been at war for the last seven years, but other than at our airports, our nation has not. There has been no call to service and no mobilization on a national scale. When asked what citizens could do to share in the risks and sacrifices of the soldiers in the field, the message sent from the commander in chief in the White House was, "Go shopping." As one article in the *American Conservative* magazine put it, "Rather than summoning Americans to rally to their country, he [President Bush] validated conspicuous consumption as the core function of 21st-century citizenship."[1]

Instead, our leaders have made compromises and deferred the tough challenges. As the following sections explore, these are beginning to create serious crunches on both military personnel and equipment that no serious candidate for president can ignore.

The U.S. military in general, and the Army in particular, is at a tipping point in terms of its ability to field sufficient forces of a high level of quality and equipment that ensure our security.[2] It is certainly far from broken, but warning symptoms are becoming clear. Small compromises such as accepting gaps in personnel and equipment are beginning to have huge consequences. For all the focus on the pressing issues of Iraq and orange alerts, the broader question of ensuring that the U.S. military does not break down under his watch will be a critical challenge that the next president cannot avoid. ▌

ALL THAT WE CAN BE? ENSURING THE QUALITY OF OUR ARMED FORCES

With its rigorous requirements, training programs, and extensive education system, the U.S. military is arguably the smartest, most educated military force in history. The days of outproducing and outnumbering the enemy are gone. Today, quality comes before quantity when trying to maintain American dominance on the battlefield. Indeed, with the United States having global responsibilities but just 4 percent of the world's population, there may be no other choice. The quality of our military's human capital cannot be underestimated; U.S. security rises and falls with it.

The current pressures on the military derive from an Iraq campaign that has turned out to be much longer and more arduous than planned. As Army lieutenant general John Vines notes, "the war has been going on nearly as long as the Second World War and we're asking a lot of the forces."[3]

In no service are the pressures more pronounced than in the Army. Even before President Bush's 2007 "surge" of forces back to Iraq, the stresses and strains resulting from the increasing pace and frequency of deployments were stretching forces thin and gradually wearing down units and individual soldiers. Former four-star general and secretary of state Colin Powell states, "The active Army is just about broken," while retired Army major general Barry McCaffrey notes, "The wheels are coming off."[4]

Within these challenges, the Army is beginning to fall short of its goals to bring in sufficient numbers of the best and brightest recruits to maintain a high-quality professional force. In 2005 the Army missed its recruiting target by 8 percent.[5] By itself, this largest drop in recruitment in more than twenty years is notable, but even more noteworthy is that it occurred despite the Army's throwing manpower and money at the problem. Between 2004 and 2007, the Army added more than 1,700 frontline recruiters, not including the approximately 700 additional civilian recruiters.[6] Since the start of the war, the Department of Defense Budget for Recruiting and Advertisement totaled $10.6 billion, and the Army's annual portion of it has increased by roughly 50 percent (from $452 million to $646 million) in the same time span.[7] Because of a greater use of bonus money, spending on selective reenlistment has increased to five times the levels in 2003.[8] These numbers do not even reflect the approximately 8,000 enlisted soldiers "involuntarily retained" under the Stop-Loss program that keeps soldiers with key specialties beyond the length of their enlistment, the 20,000 sailors and airmen put into ground roles, and the 15,000 pulled from Individual Ready Reserve.[9]

It is important to add that the problem is not limited to enlisted troops, but it also affects the military's ability to retain its leaders of tomorrow, reflected by falling officer retention rates. In 2003, at the start of the war in Iraq, the Army lost 8.5 percent of its captains. After a peak loss of 12 percent in 2005, the rate has declined to 11 percent in 2007.[10] At least part of the decline, though, may be due to a faster promotion cycle from lieutenant to captain. In addition, recent graduates of West Point are leaving the force at the highest rates in three decades (since 1977), "a sign to many military specialists that repeated tours in Iraq are prematurely driving out some of the Army's best officers."[11] In 1977, 90 percent of West Point graduates reenlisted after their five-year Active Duty Service Obligation. At the end of 2003, the rate was down by 10 percent and continued to decline until 2006, when it reached 66 percent. The 2007 retention of 68 percent is only slightly higher. West Point reenlistment after six years of commitment is down from 58 percent in 2003 to 51 percent in 2007.[12] In addition the effect of "stop-loss" and fears of being called back from the reserves immediately after departure weigh in on these numbers (that is, the departure rates would arguably be higher if not for these programs).

By 2006 it had become clear that the various stopgap measures were not enough. So, the Army began to alter the standards that had been at the heart of fielding the best force possible. The minimum required commitment was dropped from two years to fifteen months, meaning that just when recruits begin to master a skill, they could be on their way out. The maximum age allowed for recruits was raised from thirty-five years to forty years in January 2006. Notably, a mere six months later, it was raised again to forty-two years, not because of a policy conclusion, but because the recruit numbers were still tight. As numbers veered back and forth from being off by more than 1,000 in May and June 2007 to meeting them in March 2008, it appears that the raw numbers will largely now be met. But they are being met by moving the goalposts, such as recruiting greater numbers of individuals without high school degrees, issuing moral waivers, or accepting lower AFQT scores.[13]

Similarly, the Army is promoting mid-level officers at a rate well past previous standards, in an effort to fill growing numbers of vacancies. The Army had a goal of promoting 70 percent of eligible majors to lieutenant colonels. It was reported in 2007 that it ended up promoting 90 percent. Similarly, it promoted 20 percent more captains to majors than that stated in the guidelines. Likewise, the old practice was that if officers were passed over for promotion twice, they typically would be discharged within six months. Today under the "selective continuation" plan, officers are allowed to stay on, even though the Army has found them not qualified to make the cut. Even with these various measures in place, the Army is still 17 percent short of the number of major slots it needs to fill.[14]

The Marine Corps has met its goals but partly by pulling a higher number from the "start pool." The pool contains individuals who have enlisted but delayed their entry to training camp, such as high school students waiting to graduate.[15] For each person taken from this pool, though, a recruiter in the next cycle has to find an applicant willing both to enlist and ship to training camp in the same month, an onerous task. Taking recruits from the pool thus both lessens the time an applicant has to prepare for the rigors of recruit training and creates bigger recruiting problems down the line. As one U.S. Marine Corps recruiting officer put it, "We are shipping more to recruit training than replacing in our pool to ship—this will hurt the Marine Corps within the next few years."[16] The Marines are worried because their percentage of pooled recruits is down to 41 percent; it is even more telling then that the Army's start pool is down to 12 percent.[17]

Perhaps the most important adjustment was the lowering of quality standards for recruits. The U.S. military requires that all recruits take the Armed Forces Qualification Test (AFQT). The test consists of 100 multiple-choice questions designed to measure how well the person will perform once in uniform. The recruits' raw scores put them within four broad bands or categories, based on their percentile score relative to those of the other test takers, akin to the SAT rankings. Through the 1980s and 1990s, the military recruited only 2 percent of those who scored in the lowest 30 percent, known as category 4, usually picking out those few that had special aspects to consider. In 2005 the category 4 allowance was doubled to 4 percent. Still in 2005 and 2007, the rates for category 4 recruits were above the target at 4.4 percent and 4.1 percent respectively.[18] In addition, the military accepted double the number of recruits who did not graduate from high school. There was also a 50 percent increase in 2006 of waivers of enlistment standards for "moral turpitude, drug use, medical issues, and criminal records."[19] Overall, in 2006, the Army granted waivers for 15 percent of all recruits, and as of August 2007, 23 percent of recruits needed either a medical, moral, or drug waiver.[20]

It can be argued that such low scores do not affect the final military product in the field because of the training process involved. The military is renowned for helping to turn lives around in positive directions. This is where the testing rather than waivers may be more important, as studies have shown that AFQT scores are one of the best determinants of a soldier's aptitude to perform in the field.[21] To illustrate, category 3 soldiers, who are just one percentage bracket higher, on average hit their targets on shooting ranges 34 percent more times than do category 4 recruits.[22] The trends are even more apparent for highly technical skills that are more frequent in the modern military. In one test, a set of soldiers, who had all gone through advanced training, were assigned to troubleshoot a radio system. Nearly all (97 percent) of category 1 recruits, the highest-rated troops on the AFQT scale, fixed the problem.

Only 25 percent of category 4 soldiers could, and they are the set that the Army is increasingly enlisting.[23]

There are also indications that the training program itself is trending less difficult because of recruiting pressures. The proportion of recruits who washed out of training dropped from 18.1 percent in 2005 to only 7.6 percent in 2006, despite the higher numbers of candidates the Army had judged to be less qualified going into training.[24]

In addition, there are indications that the immense pressure to meet quotas has led some recruiters to cut corners. The Government Accountability Office (GAO) reported that the claims of recruiter misbehavior and violations of established policy are growing at a disturbing rate.[25] The report states that "some recruiters, reportedly, have resorted to overly aggressive tactics, which can adversely affect [the Defense Department's] ability to recruit and erode public confidence in the recruiting process."[26] As a result of investigations, 44 Army recruiters were relieved of duty and 369 were admonished. Perhaps the most noteworthy incident was an Army recruiter in Oregon who signed up an autistic boy to become an armor cavalry scout, despite his parents' objections.[27]

One should be clear that the force is not broken yet, nor anywhere near the troubles that occurred inside the force in the wake of Vietnam. However, the trend lines are quite clear and, indeed, perhaps more worrisome in the new types of conflicts in the twenty-first century.

Ensuring the best possible human capital for the force is essential in the era of the "strategic corporal."[28] In the conflicts of the twenty-first century, the pressures on individual soldiers are greater, and expectations and responsibilities are higher. Sergeants may coordinate air strikes, something once only decided by the highest-level officers. Talent is at a far greater premium than in the past.

At the same time, there is a darker side to the strategic corporal; mistakes made at the lowest unit level can have far greater consequences than they did in the past. Bad things happen in war, and bad apples exist in any human endeavor. However, the fear is that with greater numbers of less-qualified troops, there will be more bad apples let into the force and more resultant mistakes that undermine the reputation of the rest of the force. For example, Army private Stephen Green was arrested in 2006 for raping an Iraqi girl and then murdering her entire family. The impact was felt beyond the scene of the crime and greatly undermined the U.S. strategy to win hearts and minds in Iraq and the rest of the Muslim world. Notably, Green had been recruited to join the Army, despite his recruiter's knowing he was a tenth grade dropout with a history of psychological problems and a multiple arrest record. Again, such a recruit, and such an incident, was an immense exception to the rule, but any trend that allows more of such exceptions is worrisome.

The effect is starting to translate to less-prepared units deployed to the field. For example, the Fourth Brigade of the Army's Third Infantry division was deployed to Iraq in February as part of the surge of forces in 2007. More than half the brigade's soldiers at the rank of E-4 and below were straight out of basic training, and by one report, "the bulk of its midlevel non-commissioned officers in the ranks of E-5 and E-6 have no combat experience."[29] This is despite the unit's being reactivated a year ago.

The Marines and Army are also finding it difficult to give troops a break from the combat zone long enough to complete their full spectrum of training. The commandant of the Marine Corps, James Conway, testified to Congress that the Marines are not training for amphibious, mountain, or jungle warfare nor conducting large-scale live fire maneuvers. "We've got a little bit of a blindside there," he said. Similarly, Army vice chief of staff Richard Cody testified that "we're only able to train them . . . for counterinsurgency operations. They're not trained to full spectrum operations."[30]

The challenges of maintaining a high-quality force trickle down to specific sectors and specialties. At the tip of the spear in the war on terrorism are special operations forces, currently in their largest deployment ever. The Pentagon has planned to increase by one-third active-duty Army special forces battalions, psychological operations, and civil affairs; establish a Marine Corps Special Operations Command; and increase the number of SEAL teams.[31]

However, the force is already finding it tough to meet its numbers. The GAO found that the Navy is at just 86 percent manning levels for SEAL teams and has failed to meets its authorized enlisted levels for the last five years, much less meet higher goals.[32] Such plans will take years to implement and potentially water down quality. For example, in 2005 the Navy eliminated the winter session of training, traditionally the hardest to survive, "to lower attrition rates." Potentially related, the pass rate for physical screening for SEALs made a surprising jump from 34 percent to 77 percent last year.[33]

Even then, Special Operations Command believes that it will be stretched too thin to provide enough forces to meet the requests of the regional combatant commands.[34] Ninety percent of special operations forces' deployments are Middle East focused, leaving other volatile parts of the globe open.[35]

Indeed, many special operation forces units are already understrength or overdeployed, slowly wearing elite units out. For example, one elite soldier wrote that his unit in Iraq was at 55 percent strength.[36] Another, a Navy elite forces officer, discussed how since 9/11 his unit has been on deployment almost constantly, with ninety days back and forth between Afghanistan and Iraq, and with only a few months off each time in between. Several of his best soldiers have decided to retire early as a result, induced further by higher-paying contractor jobs.[37]

These gaps extend to an array of specialties that military officers refer to as "high demand–low density." The Army has a 40 percent shortfall in highly valued information operations soldiers and does not expect to fill the gap within seven years.[38] Other specialties such as civil affairs personnel, military advisers, or engineers are also understaffed. While not involved in direct combat, they are greatly valued by generals in the field, meaning these gaps have far greater weight. General John Abizaid said of a seventeen-member unit of Navy engineers in East Africa, "[They] achieve as much for us as a battalion of infantry on the ground looking for bad guys."[39]

Frequently, these resource problems and skill gaps force the military to outsource certain functions to private contractors. U.S. Central Command (CENTCOM) recently reported that it has outsourced some 160,000 jobs to private contractors in Iraq that would have once been done by soldiers. This trend, though, has proven problematic; examples range from the allegations of contractor abuse at Abu Ghraib by members of the CACI firm, the war profiteering accusations made against firm such as Halliburton and Custer Battles, and the 2007 Baghdad shooting episode involving members of the Blackwater firm.

The National Guard and Army Reserve are experiencing the same challenges.[40] Lieutenant General Clyde Vaughn, director of the Army National Guard, says that the Guard is experiencing "more turbulence now than any other time I've ever seen."[41] Secretary of the Army Francis Harvey said he was "very concerned" about the state of the National Guard and described the effects of multiple deployments as "stretching the Guard."[42] Michael Noonan of the conservative-leaning Foreign Policy Research Institute stated that "the National Guard and Army Reserve have also been used in numbers not seen since the Second World War. An increasing number of these units are rapidly reaching their limit on cumulative mobilization time (24 months) under current Presidential call-up authorization."[43] The number of service duty days for National Guard and Reserve soldiers has increased from 12.7 million in 2001 to more than 61 million days in 2006. At the peak of the campaign in Iraq in 2004, the reserve components made up more than a third of the U.S. military presence in that country.[44] All thirty-four National Guard Brigade Combat Teams (BCTs) have served at least one tour of service in either Iraq or Afghanistan.[45] As part of meeting the needs of the second wave of the surge, the Pentagon has announced plans to change the call-up authorization, allowing reservists to be called back, even if they have already reached the limit after which they were told they would not have to deploy again. This is viewed by many reservists and national guardsmen as a broken promise.

Overstretched forces, unit overuse, and frequent redeployments also pressure the home front. Soldiers often cite family strain as a key factor in deciding whether to reenlist. We have to face that with an older force, this has become what Bobby Mueller, president of Veterans for America, describes as "a family war."[46] Sixty percent of those deployed to Iraq and Afghanistan have family responsibilities, including 16,000 single mothers. Unfortunately, data confirm the negative impact on families: Marines and Army soldiers have seen a doubling of divorce rates since 2001; 47 percent of those killed left families behind.[47]

Finally, the demographics of the professional forces are gradually less representative of the United States. Recruiting disproportionately targets certain sectors and geographic regions. For example, recruitment numbers for economically disadvantaged and *legacy youths* (children of soldiers) are higher than numbers for the general populace, and ROTC programs in the South now predominate over other regions. This is not to challenge the qualities of youths from these areas but rather to note that recruitment focused on certain groups reinforces a distancing of the public from its military and a striking absence of the American upper class from the services.[48] For example, less than 1 percent of Ivy League school graduates enlist.[49] This becomes not just an issue of service now but leadership later. Because of the elites' increasing unfamiliarity with the military, they are more prone to make poorly informed decisions about the military and conflict.

Strikingly, unlike the tensions that characterized the Vietnam era, the current generation of youths is not in any antagonistic relationship with the military. Indeed, 70 percent of college students, the most liberal segment of the American public, trust the military above all other public institutions.[50] As one report noted of the new "9/11 Generation," "The traditional dove-hawk, liberal-conservative dichotomies describe little about today's youth. . . . They are simultaneously human rights crusaders and supporters of a strong military."[51] An opportunity is being missed.

An Agenda for Action on Personnel

Any serious candidate for president in 2008 will have to address recruiting and force quality and develop an action plan. What is needed is a series of short- and long-term policy responses designed to alleviate pressure on troop numbers while keeping troop quality high.

The next president should issue a national call to service. It is striking that a nation of 300 million cannot persuade the roughly 300,000 talented young individuals a year needed to serve their country. The next president should make it clear that it is not merely the U.S. military, but the United States of America that is at war, and the nation needs to share the burden.[52]

The next president should seek to energize today's youth the same way Presidents John Kennedy and Ronald Reagan did in the past. Their call to action would place the ethic of public service and sacrifice on the agenda again as goals to aspire to and would enlist the help of America's youth, as well as the parents, coaches, and teachers who influence them in meeting our national challenges.[53] The bully pulpit of the presidency can generate greater enthusiasm for volunteerism and draw in the best and brightest to serve their country. But the pulpit can be powerful only if it is utilized.

Demand that quality comes first. A force can quickly lose its edge; but as the experiences after Vietnam illustrate, restoring it can take decades. The next president should ensure that the first priority of his secretary of defense is to prevent the breakdown of the U.S. military. Anything less is unacceptable. Within 100 days, the new secretary of defense should issue to the president a plan of action addressing the personnel and recruiting issues, including benchmarks for progress that can be measured.[54]

Where necessary, this may require decisions that balance new acquisitions with troop quality and personnel requirements. For example, one could raise the entire recruiting budget by approximately 50 percent by purchasing one less F-22 fighter jet.[55] Between the security trade-off of 182 rather than 183 new jets and an increase of overall force quality, the next secretary should choose the latter.

High demand must equal high supply. Some have proposed expanding the forces with numbers ranging from 35,000 (in the president's 2007 State of the Union speech) to 100,000 or 200,000.[56] Any talk of expansion in generic numbers misses the point of where the need is most dire. Throwing numbers broadly at the problem is not an answer, nor is re-creating the Army of 1991. Rather, there are certain units and specialties that are incredibly overextended because of their constant demand, while other specialties are not called for by commanders in the field. If the Army simply uses its greater numbers to add a few more BCTs (which with rotation schedules would yield only one or more to operations), this historic opportunity to expand smartly will be squandered.

Within the first 100 days, the president must demand from the military services an evaluation of personnel demand relative to supply, using this as the baseline for further expansion. Any military personnel expansion should be made first in the areas in which the need is greatest. This means that the likely focus of any expansion will be in such areas as civil affairs, combat engineers, foreign area officers, training advisers, special forces, military police, information operations, and so on that will provide the greatest benefit to solving pressing needs.

The Pentagon should also be given the task of moving private contractors out of roles that are inappropriate for civilians. Over-outsourcing is not the answer for the military's future. Greater numbers of contract officers may also be needed to catch up to supervising the massive amounts of current contracting.

This expansion of high-demand–low-density areas also aligns well with the new interests and capabilities of the 9/11 generation and other elites who may not have been prone to volunteer for the military in traditional roles. A new recruiting effort would be made to tap into such sectors, including outreach to liberal arts and engineering programs.

Create a Joint Stabilization Command. Gaps within specialties particularly relevant to stabilization and advisory missions began to appear in the early 1990s and remain unfilled today. In addition, the planning side of the stabilization and advisory mission was grossly ignored in Iraq, leading to actions (and inactions) that fueled the insurgency and that continue to press our troops. The creation of a Joint Stabilization Command would ensure that such lessons are not forgotten and that specialized forces are available.[57] Much like the role that the Special Operations and Joint Forces Commands play, the command would also provide a joint military node for training, budgeting, and coordination with the interagency process that is presently missing.

Better Support Military Family Needs. As the saying among military recruiters goes, "You enlist an individual, you reenlist a family."[58] The next president should establish a board to support soldiers' families, of whom we are asking so much. Consisting of experts and family representatives from each service, it would be given the task of developing a series of actionable policy items that would ease the burden on spouses and families. The board would provide an institutionalized conduit to bring evolving concerns of military families to the attention of senior policymakers and the public that is currently missing. To hold feet to the fire, the board's yearly report to the president and secretary of defense would be made public and include status reports on the previous year's recommendations. Other areas to support include letting family members tap into their soldier's unused GI Bill education benefits; giving military spouses hiring preferences for federal jobs; improving military day care; and initiating a continuum of service plan, which allows military members to take leave of up to two years—for family or professional development reasons—but maintain health benefits and the ability to return to the force at the same rank.

Don't Ask, Don't Tell?—Don't Bother. Homosexuals in military service were a controversial issue at a time of relative peace in the early 1990s. The United States is now at war. The policy of discharging suspected gay soldiers has cost the U.S. military $320 million and more than 12,000 skilled soldiers in the last ten years, 800 of whom were in high-demand–low-density skill areas, such as Arabic linguists and combat engineers.[59]

More broadly, "Don't Ask, Don't Tell" has also undermined general recruitment efforts to get top-quality soldiers and leaders of the future. Recruiting officers cite access as a key challenge in tracking down likely recruits. But the policy has limited their access at any school requiring equal opportunity standards for on-site recruiting. While any company can get on campus to meet and mingle with students, military recruiters and ROTC programs are kept off many college campuses and out of job fairs as a result of "Don't Ask, Don't Tell." In any event, social and military attitudes have evolved. What was once controversial is increasingly acceptable both inside and outside the military. For example, 79 percent of Americans now support a policy that allows gays to openly serve in the military, while West Point's best thesis award in 2006 went to a heterosexual Army officer who argued that the policy should be scrapped for violating military values.[60] Given that no credible study has found that reversing the policy would harm America's combat capabilities (the integration of gay soldiers in the military of our ally Great Britain, for example, went by without incident), it is time to put national security above social politics.

WHEN THE WHEELS REALLY FALL OFF: FACING THE EQUIPMENT GAP

One of the less-discussed aspects of the Iraq War and other recent deployments is the more than 1,000 vehicles lost.[61] In many cases, the equipment is not destroyed in combat but is just wearing out, because of heavier-than-expected use in conditions tougher than planned. For example, the Association of the U.S. Army estimates that equipment is being used at rates five to six times more than in peacetime.[62] Some systems have even higher rates. The Congressional Budget Office (CBO) found that Army and Marine trucks are driven ten times more miles.[63] Likewise, the tough operating environment takes its toll. Humvees used in Iraq needed to be replaced after two years instead of the expected thirteen years and light armored vehicles after six instead of the expected thirty.[64]

Equipment age also adds to the challenge. The average age of the military's medium truck is twenty-one years, for the M-1 tank it is twenty years, and for the F-15 and F-16 fleet it is seventeen years. In sum, as a recent U.S. Army War College report argued, "The bills for the Iraqi counterinsurgency—or more specifically, for undertaking large-scale protracted counterinsurgency with a force not designed for it—were coming due."[65]

The impact is being felt far and wide. A GAO study looked at readiness rates for a basket of thirty different military equipment items. It found that across all military branches, readiness had declined, mainly because of heavy use in Iraq and Afghanistan and difficulties with complex and aging equipment.[66] For example, Marine Corps ground equipment readiness is at 81 percent. The result is not "enough weapons, communications gear, or properly outfitted vehicles."[67]

Equipment wear and tear not only affects readiness but also capacity.[68] As a stopgap measure, equipment has increasingly been taken from a variety of sources to meet needs in the field. Some is pulled from stateside units, which affects training down the line, and some pulled from prepositioned stocks. For instance, to meet needs in Iraq, the Marines have drawn down prepositioned stocks in the Pacific and Europe by up to 70 percent. These weapons and equipment are thereby unavailable for U.S. security commitments elsewhere.

The National Guard and Reserve are also being tapped to fill shortfalls and are experiencing the same equipment crunch. The Army National Guard has transferred more than 100,000 items to active units overseas, depleting key inventory items, including radios, generators, and armored Humvees.[69] The Army Reserve likewise has transferred more than 235,000 items.[70]

"Taking from Peter to pay Paul" has created great gaps. By mid-2005, nondeployed National Guard Units had only 34 percent of their essential equipment, while the Army Reserve only had 76 percent of its required gear.[71] To illustrate, the Army National Guard has 30,071 Humvees on hand, but the National Guard Bureau has an identified need for 50,473. Another 3,268 Humvees are scheduled to arrive in September 2008, which still leaves a shortfall of 17,134 vehicles.[72]

Our "fifth military service," the U.S. Coast Guard (USCG), is hammered by the equipment crunch as well. Following years of underfunding by Congress and the Transportation Department, the average age of the Coast Guard's Deepwater cutters has climbed to thirty-three years. Its fleet of High and Medium Endurance Cutters is older than thirty-seven of thirty-nine naval fleets worldwide. With delays in replacement caused by contractor problems (that is, the contractor was delivering ships that were at risk of sinking), USCG officers say it is a race to replace these aging assets before they cease to be operational.

These equipment shortfalls undermine our ability to fight and win the wars of today, reduce our ability to head off the potential wars of tomorrow, and limit the policy options of leaders as they wrestle with issues ranging from North Korea to Darfur. For example, the chief of staff of the Army noted that two-thirds of Army brigade combat teams are "not ready for combat."[73] The annual risk assessment by the Joint Chiefs of Staff has found that U.S. commanders around the world did not think that they could meet established standards.[74] We can be sure that America's adversaries look at this trend as a positive development.

Gaps in equipment also limit the ability of the National Guard, Army Reserve, and Coast Guard to perform emergency missions at home, including responses to terrorism or natural disasters. A worrisome indicator of this came when a tornado hit Kansas in May 2007. The National Guard, which was at just 51 percent readiness, took more time than usual to deploy, and even then, it depended upon the contributions from the federal government, neighboring states, and private businesses to carry out its mission. For example, it had 353 Humvees instead of its full complement of 660 and only 4 of its 19 helicopters at its disposal. According to officials, a second disaster of similar scale would not have been manageable, because of the shortfalls in equipment. Incredibly, other guard units have come back from Iraq without equipment, such as Mississippi's 890th Engineering Battalion, situated along a hurricane-prone coastline.

Equipment shortages will remain a challenge even if the Iraq War ended tomorrow. The GAO estimates that at the end of the Iraq deployment there will be a $13 billion to $16 billion backlog of equipment repair and replacement for the Army and Marine Corps that will take at least two years to complete.[75] According to the Commission on the National Guard and Reserves, equipment shortages for the Reserve Components total $48 billion and would take years to reset.[76]

Yet, this shortfall has been dodged by both the military services and policymakers. Rather than filling current backlogs, each of the services is focused on centerpiece programs for the future, specifically the Army's Future Combat Systems (FCS), the Air Force's F-22 and F-35, the Navy's DD-X and CGX, and the Marines' V-22 and EFV.

The budget supplementals would seem to be the appropriate funding source for equipment backlogs and emergency needs. However, the supplementals have ballooned, while their original purpose has been abused. For example, because of a lack of funding, Army repair depots have been operating only at half their capacity. One report stated that 530 tanks, 860 armored personnel carriers, and more than 1,000 Humvees shipped back from Iraq for repairs are "stacking up at all the Army depots."[77]

Instead, the services frequently have used the supplementals (estimated to total almost $700 billion for the wars in Afghanistan and Iraq since fiscal year 2001) to finance what they cannot get in the regular budget, such as long-term transformation projects like the Army's modularity program or the Joint Network Node.[78] Whenever Congress has balked at such add-ins, the Army has threatened to instead stop buying spare parts, "freeze" all new contracts, and "release service contract employees, [including] recruiters." Noah Shachtman of Defense Tech commented, "It's a form of blackmail, more or less: give us our money, Congress. Or risk being nailed as 'anti-soldier.'"[79]

Former Army officer and conservative columnist Ralph Peters is perhaps the most pointed commentator on the issue: "If you found your hilltop house on fire, would you A) put out the flames, or B) buy flood insurance? If your answer is B, you're suited for a job in the Office of the Secretary of Defense (OSD). At a time when our Army and Marines bear by far the heaviest load of our nation's security burdens, OSD proposes reducing the number of soldiers to free up funds for wasteful Cold War era weapons systems." He continued, "Faced with the urgent need to replenish Marine and Army equipment destroyed or worn out in Iraq, we're buying high-tech toys that have no missions. . . . Your tax dollars are being squandered while our troops are being betrayed."[80]

The equipment and budget shortfalls are also in part due to poor oversight and management of the Pentagon's acquisitions. Cost overruns happen in any business, but in defense contracting, it has become the norm. The GAO found that of the Pentagon's seventy-two major weapons acquisition programs, two-thirds are behind schedule an average of 21 months, and their acquisition growth costs have gone up from $42 billion in 2000 to $295 billion in 2007.[81] The F-22, for example, was originally projected to be $145 million and now is roughly $345 million per plane. Despite their failure to control the cost structure and time schedule of the program, contractors for the fighter jet have pocketed 91 percent of the performance bonus included in the contract, or about $850 million.[82]

Part of the cause is that the use of contractors in development and acquisition programs is as prevalent as it is in the military. The GAO reports that as much as 48 percent of the workforce employed in the fifty-two weapons programs investigated were civilian contractors that performed roles from engineering to program management.[83] That is due to "a critical shortage of certain acquisition professionals with technical skills as [the Department of Defense] has downsized its workforce over the last decade."[84]

There is also a worrisome trend toward old-fashioned corruption and profiteering. Deputy Attorney General Paul McNulty estimated that 5 percent of all federal spending in 2005 was lost to fraud, mostly in defense contracting and Iraq reconstruction efforts. He noted that many businesses saw federal spending, especially from the less-monitored supplemental funds, as "an increase in opportunity for fraud, misuse of funds, waste and corruption."[85] In addition to these losses, one must consider that the fiscal year 2007 Defense and Homeland Security Appropriations Act allocated $13.2 billion in pork money contained in 2,658 earmarks.[86] An apt example was the $3 million sneaked into the defense budget for "First Tee," a program that teaches "life-enhancing" golf skills to boys and girls. For any business, such results would be stunning. For a nation at war, they are shameful.

What is worse, the challenges will likely come to bear at the worst possible time, namely during a looming budget deficit crunch. The defense budget is already at its post–World War II high, equaling the Reagan era buildup. The Center for Strategic and Budgetary Assessments has stated that the Bush administration may be underestimating the accumulated costs of its planned budgets versus available funds by as much $900 billion or more.[87] The head of the nonpartisan CBO said he was "terrified" of the budget deficit and described it as a looming "fiscal hurricane."[88] The situation might be akin to getting a bill for overdue credit card payments just when the bank forecloses on your house.

An Agenda for Action on Equipment

Many of these issues are not easy to solve and will require difficult trade-offs. However, leaders are defined not by the easy choices they make but by how they handle the tough ones. The future president should be guided by a set of priorities that will resolve the looming equipment crunch, rather than continue to pass it down the line.

Place current needs first. As a nation at war, we must fulfill our troops' needs to ensure that they get the best possible support and equipment. However, as noted by Kori Schake, former director of Defense Strategy and Requirements at the National Security Council (2002–05), the Department of Defense has thus far avoided "making hard trade-offs between what it prefers to do (continue existing weapons systems) and what the nation most needs (an agile force that can quickly defend us against terrorists)."[89] The president should direct that each major defense program be reevaluated in light of current needs and gaps and likely future threat scenarios. More important, while many of the programs have merit in continuing, the number of platforms actually ordered must be weighed against other pressing needs.

The F-22 can illustrate the merits of such an evaluation, looking not merely at overall costs but the trade-offs that come with it. The cost of just one F-22 fighter jet would provide enough funds for twenty-five A-10s—a manned close air support aircraft—or, even more forward looking, forty-five Reapers, which is the next generation of the Predator unmanned plane. While the fighter jet is not even usable in Iraq due to electronic interference issues, such tactical drone planes have been in huge demand from commanders in Iraq and elsewhere (there are simply just not enough to go around, with General Robert Scales estimating that the force is meeting only about 5 percent of the requests for drones from ground commanders). The savings would also equal the annual costs of approximately 3,000 troops. Overall, the planned purchase of 183 F-22s will cost about $63 billion, or 40 percent of annual salaries for the entire U.S. military. This does not include sunk costs in research and development for the plane.

The point is not to beat up on the F-22. It is a fine aircraft that should be in the force (though perhaps not at the same numbers). Rather, it is to note that many of the most expensive centerpiece programs of the services are immense costs but are not the panacea for their current and arguably future needs. Their numbers and time frame for purchase need to be scaled to current priorities, with an eye kept open toward more advantageous trade-offs.

For example, the National Missile Defense program has absorbed a massive investment in a most difficult and still unproven technology, when more suitable and apt-to-succeed technologies, such as the Aegis and airborne laser, are available to confront the threat of ballistic missiles. This is not to mention that it seems unlikely to stop the most probable scenarios of terrorist weapons of mass destruction (WMD) use, nor deter major adversaries who could easily overwhelm its limited numbers. Likewise, the Navy's DD-X is projected to cost the equivalent of almost ten of the more agile and deployable Littoral Combat Ships (that is, if the cost overruns do not make their costs higher than expected). So, a future secretary of defense must seriously weigh whether gaining eight of these ships, plus spending the 20 percent overall savings elsewhere, might be better for U.S. capabilities than having just one of the DD-X. Equally, the Marine Corps V-22 Osprey has a troubled history and offers only marginal advantages for its steep price tag. It is illustrative that few Marines called for its expedited deployment to Iraq, and once on the scene, its engines rapidly needed to be replaced.

The Army's ambitious FCS plan entails buying an entire new suite of vehicles and computers for the force. The FCS is expected to represent up to 70 percent of the Army procurement budget from 2014 to 2022, even without future cost increases (which are likely, even with the FCS already 76 percent above the Army's original cost estimate).[90] As a result, if the Army proceeds with its plans, it will not have funds to either fill past backlogs or even buy needed items like matériel and ammunition, as well as vehicles outside of FCS. Even during the Reagan-era buildup, the Army only spent 20 percent on acquisitions of combat vehicles compared with the 70 percent planned for FCS.

Dating back a decade, it is another program that merits reevaluation of whether a commitment to a full buy still makes sense, based on the costs, the current shortages, and the fact that much of the FCS technology still remains under development. One alternative that the next president should give consideration to is the "network only" version of the FCS plan. Instead of the full buy of the entire FCS program, more than 30,000 newly designed vehicles and all accompanying equipment, this plan would focus on how to link many current systems into the FCS network of unmanned systems and sensors. This would not jettison the FCS program as a whole but instead would focus on the development of those technologies with the biggest payoff and least risk of failure, while leaving open the plan of vehicle replacement down the road. An added benefit is that the revised plan could be ready for the field as early as 2010, sooner than under current plans by several years, meaning it could make a difference for our troops earlier. Procurement could also take place at a faster pace, meaning more of the equipment would be available as well. Even after filling the equipment backlog, such a plan would save an estimated $22 billion through 2017. This could be spent to fund such areas as raised pay and benefits to help the recruit quality issue.[91]

End the supplemental gravy train. The supplemental appropriations were intended as emergency funding for operations that were not contemplated in the regular budget. As a first step to restoring fiscal sanity to military purchases, the new president must make it clear that the supplemental budgets are neither a catchall for funding nor a place to hide budget needs.

The next president should follow the bipartisan recommendation from Congress that future defense budgets do what was done during the Korean War and include funds for predictable wartime spending.[92] With a Congress afraid to make the request a requirement, the next president must ensure that budget requests meet the old standards. If there is a request for supplemental funding in Iraq or beyond, it should include only operational costs and the needed funds for the looming shortfall in equipment. It should not include programs that are long-term or transformative, which must be evaluated according to their own merits and included in the regularized budget process.

Cut the waste and corruption. The next president owes it to the troops and taxpayers to make it a priority to reduce corruption and routine cost overruns. To begin, the president should choose a secretary of defense who will act as a steward of the nation's bank account as well as its security. To improve the management of Pentagon funding, the next president should instruct the new secretary to formulate an action plan within the first 100 days of service, containing reasonable benchmarks to measure success or failure.[93]

Fundamentally, there is a lack of integration among the three decision support systems (budgeting, requirements generation, and acquisition management) that make up the larger defense acquisition enterprise. As a result, the Pentagon's acquisition process lacks the capability to accurately predict what systems need to be procured, what the costs are, what the delivery schedule is, and how the systems will perform.[94]

Acquisition reform will not come from a magic silver bullet, instantly creating a Pentagon process that looks like a Fortune 500 company. Instead, there are three priority areas in which defense leadership must enact steady change to rein in the current epidemic of cost, schedule, and performance failures.[95]

First, improve the process of developing requirements, better address the needs of joint capabilities, and align them with strategic goals. This may require shifting the primary responsibility for generating the requirements of their operational capabilities from the individual services to the combatant commanders (COCOMS). At the very least, a forum should be established in which industry leadership and the Department of Defense (DoD) can share and align strategic plans for achieving joint capabilities.

Second, DoD must restore the competency and value of the in-house defense acquisition workforce, which has been whittled away at a time it is needed more than ever. DoD needs to build a human capital strategy that attracts talent to the government acquisition workforce, rather than drives it away, and puts specific emphasis on recruiting program management and systems engineering competency. It must also reverse the trend in replacing government acquisition professionals with contractors (thus outsourcing decisionmaking power and responsibility) and establish a stable government acquisition workforce with "incentivized" leadership. It should also align the tours of government program managers and key engineering, financial management, and logistics personnel with planned system increments.

Finally, DoD must seek to break the hold of the "Beltway Bandits" (large federal contracting firms that maintain a stranglehold on contracting mainly because of their connections and understanding of the system) and find a way to reduce obstacles for traditionally nondefense small and large businesses to enter the mainstream of defense contracting. This step is necessary to improve the viability of the American defense industrial base and foster competition and innovation. The president should instruct the new secretary of defense to establish a blue ribbon panel made up of leaders from industry (beyond the usual suspects of traditional big contractors) and defense experts to focus on eliminating the barriers that prevent some of our most innovative and dynamic companies from doing business with the government.

Parallel to this program of reform, the government must take full advantage of the market, reversing a trend in which the market is taking advantage of the government. A regularized system of incentives must be offered to firms that come in *under* budget, including preferential status for future contract bids. For firms that fail to honor their contracts, punishments must be enacted, including greater use of financial sanctions and novel schemes such as the removal of a firm from pending or future contract bids, to ensure the cycle is broken.[96]

When it comes to corruption and war profiteering, no measure should be spared, as both hollow out the budget and undermine morale and values. Because supplementals have been prone to the most abuse, the next president should instruct the Department of Defense to create a special task force of inspectors for these funds. In addition, the president should request that the Department of Justice create a joint group of special prosecutors for wartime contracting.

A new punishment system must significantly raise the potential costs of such thievery to outweigh its perceived advantages for individuals and companies. The sanctions for any firm and executives guilty of profiteering should be immediate and heavy, including being eliminated from bidding on government contracts for a minimum of ten years. Second, the president should work with Congress to double the criminal sentences for individuals involved in government corruption and triple them during a time of conflict. The president should also ask the new attorney general to explore the possibilities of bringing treason charges against any individuals who line their pockets at the expense of our national security and troops' lives.

CONCLUDING OBSERVATIONS

The United States cannot afford to avoid the hard choices that come with having a military at war. Our military is not broken, but there are clear, unavoidable symptoms of distress. The challenges in ensuring force quality and filling equipment gaps must be faced now, before they hollow out the force.

For how significant these problems are, it is important to note that the solution is not simply to throw money at the problem. The looming crunches do not require massive increases in the budget to prevent them. But they also mean that we cannot take wide swipes at reducing the military budget.

In sum, building the best military in the world took decades. The next president must ensure it is not lost in a matter of years.

QUESTIONS FOR CANDIDATES:

—Is the United States at war or not? If so, what are your plans for engaging the broader public in supporting a military that is on a war footing?

—What assignments will be first on the list you give your new secretary of defense for action, and what benchmarks will you use to judge the secretary's success or failure on them?

—Do you have an action plan for meeting recruiting challenges, especially in ensuring quality levels, and, if so, what are its benchmarks for success?

—How will your proposed budget meet the looming military equipment crunch?

—Will you request a wartime supplemental, and what categories will and will not be included in it?

—Do you have an action plan for cutting military waste and corruption, and if so, what are its benchmarks for success?

NOTES

1. Andrew J. Bacevich, "The Right Choice? The Conservative Case for Barack Obama," *American Conservative,* March 24, 2008 (www.amconmag.com/2008/2008_03_24/article.html).

2. Malcolm Gladwell, *The Tipping Point: How Little Things Make a Big Difference* (Boston: Back Bay Books, 2002).

3. Frederick W. Kagan, "The U.S. Military's Manpower Crisis," *Foreign Affairs* 85, no. 4 (2006): 102.

4. Colin Powell, as quoted in Karen DeYoung, "Powell Says U.S. Losing in Iraq, Calls for Drawdown by Mid-2007," *Washington Post,* December 18, 2006, p. A20; General Barry McCaffrey (ret.) quoted in Frederick W. Kagan, "The U.S. Military's Manpower Crisis," p. 101.

5. The Army Reserve and the Navy Reserve also missed their targets.

6. See U.S. Department of Defense, *Office of the Secretary of Defense, Operation and Maintenance Overview, February 2007, Fiscal Year (FY) 2008 Budget Estimates* (www.defenselink.mil/comptroller/defbudget/fy2008/budget_justification/pdfs/01_Operation_and_Maintenance/FY_2008_OM_Overview_(All).pdf); Government Accountability Office (GAO), *Military Recruiting: DOD and Services Need Better Data to Enhance Visibility over Recruiter Irregularities,* GAO 06-846 (August 2006).

7. Department of the Army, *Fiscal Year (FY) 2004/2005 Biennial Budget Estimates,* vol. 1: *Operation and Maintenance, Army: Justification Book* (Washington: February 2003).

8. Department of the Army, "Retention Mission and SRB (Selective Reenlistment Bonus) Takers" (Washington: U.S. Army G-1, Directorate of Military Personnel Management).

9. Congressional Budget Office (CBO), *Recruiting, Retention, and Future Levels of Military Personnel* (October 2006), p. 15 (www.cbo.gov/ftpdocs/76xx/doc7626/10-05-Recruiting.pdf).

10. Data obtained from the Army.

11. Bryan Bender, "West Point Grads Exit Service at High Rate," *Boston Globe*, April 11, 2007.

12. Department of the Army, "West Point Graduate Retention after 5-Year Active Duty Service Obligation," Information Paper (Washington).

13. Prepared statement of David S. Chu, under secretary of defense for personnel and readiness, "Personnel Overview," before the Senate Armed Services Personnel Subcommittee, 110 Cong. 2 sess. (February 27, 2008).

14. Bryan Bender and Renee Dudley, "Army Rushes to Promote Its Officers," *Boston Globe*, March 13, 2007.

15. A youngster can enlist and then wait up to a year to start training, allowing a recruit to enlist while in school but join after graduation, for example. The start pool percentage, which has been normally at 50 percent, dropped to 41 percent.

16. Personal communication by e-mail from USMC officer, November 6, 2006.

17. CBO, *Recruiting, Retention, and Future Levels of Military Personnel*, p. 4.

18. National Priorities Project, "Military Recruiting 2007: Army Misses Benchmarks by Greater Margin" (Northampton, Mass.: January 22, 2008) (www.national priorities.org/militaryrecruiting2007).

19. Testimony of General Barry McCaffrey (ret.) to the Senate Armed Services Committee, 110 Cong. 1 sess. (April 17, 2007) (http://armed-services.senate.gov/ statemnt/2007/April/McCaffrey%2004-17-07.pdf).

20. Statement of Major General Thomas P. Bostick, Commander United States Recruiting Command, before the House Armed Services Subcommittee for Military Personnel, 110 Cong. 1 sess. (August 1, 2007).

21. The study was commissioned by the Office of the Secretary of Defense.

22. Fred Kaplan, "GI Schmo: How Low Can Army Recruiters Go?" *Slate*, January 9, 2006 (www.slate.com/id /2133908/ [September 1, 2006]).

23. Jennifer Kavanagh, "Determinants of Productivity for Military Personnel: A Review of Findings on the Contribution of Experience, Training, and Aptitude to Military Performance" (Santa Monica, Calif.: RAND National Defense Research Institute, 2005), p. 28; see also David Armor, "Manpower Quality in the All-Volunteer Force," in *The All-Volunteer Force: Thirty Years of Service*, edited by Barbara Bicksler and others (Dulles, Va.: Brassey's, 2004), pp. 90–108.

24. Tom Vanden Brook, "Army Reshapes Training to Spare Enlistees the Boot," *USA Today*, July 13, 2006, p. 1A.

25. Part of the increase, but certainly not all of it, may be explained by the increase in the number of recruiters.

26. GAO, *Military Recruiting: DoD and Services Need Better Data to Enhance Visibility over Recruiter Irregularities*. Criminal violations by recruiters are up 100 percent; claims of wrongdoing, proven and unproven, are up 50 percent; and substantiated claims are up 50 percent as well.

27. "Army Releases Autistic Teen: Parents Say Army Ignored Their Complaints until Newspaper Article," *CBSnews.com*, May 12, 2006 (www.cbsnews.com/stories/ 2006/05/12/national/main1613987.shtml [May 13, 2006]).

28. The term "strategic corporal" was coined by former Marine commandant Charles Krulak.

29. Lawrence Korb, "A Troop Readiness Crisis," *Boston Globe,* April 11, 2007.

30. Ann Scott Tyson, "Military Is Ill-Prepared for Other Conflicts," *Washington Post,* March 19, 2007, p. A1.

31. Ann Roosevelt, "SO/LIC Building Capability, Capacity for Irregular Warfare," *Defense Daily,* October 19, 2006; Ann Scott Tyson, "Plan Seeks More Elite Forces to Fortify Military," *Washington Post,* January 24, 2006, p. A1; U.S. Department of Defense, *Quadrennial Defense Review Report* (Washington, 2006), pp. 44–45. It is striking that "Q Course" for training special forces (SF) troops has been reduced from 63 to 48 weeks, while the number of troops going through it has tripled.

32. "SEALs Face Recruiting Woes," *Virginian Pilot,* May 7, 2007.

33. Ibid.

34. Ann Scott Tyson, "Crunch Time for Special Ops Forces," *Christian Science Monitor,* April 6, 2004; David Wood, "Special Forces Stretched Thin by Two Wars," *Baltimore Sun,* September 24, 2006, p. 1.

35. "SEALs Face Recruiting Woes," *Virginian Pilot.*

36. Sean Naylor, "The Spec Ops Stretch," *Armed Forces Journal,* November 2006, p. 32.

37. Personal communication from interview with special forces officer, September 7, 2006.

38. *Jane's Defense Weekly,* August 23, 2006, p. 29.

39. Greg Jaffe, "A General's New Plan to Battle Radical Islam—Learning from Hezbollah," *Wall Street Journal,* September 2, 2006, p. A1.

40. The National Guard currently has ten brigades deployed in Iraq, Afghanistan, and the Balkans, and another 50,000 troops were deployed after Hurricane Katrina.

41. As quoted in Michelle Tan, "Relief for U.S. National Guard," *Defense News,* October 9, 2006, p. 57.

42. Ibid.

43. Michael Noonan, "The Quadrennial Defense Review and U.S. Defense Policy, 2006–2025," E-Notes (Philadelphia: Foreign Policy Research Institute, March 9, 2006).

44. Commission on the National Guard and Reserves, *Transforming the National Guard and Reserves into a 21st-Century Operational Force* (Washington, January 31, 2008).

45. Ibid.

46. Bobby Mueller, statement at first meeting of the President's Commission on Care for America's Returning Wounded Warriors, Washington, April 14, 2007.

47. David Crary, "Iraq War Takes Toll on Army Marriages," Associated Press, June 20, 2005; Bobby Mueller, statement, the President's Commission on Care for America's Returning Wounded Warriors.

48. Kathy Roth Douquet and Frank Schaeffer, *AWOL: The Unexcused Absence of America's Upper Classes from Military Service and How It Hurts America* (New York: HarperCollins, 2006).

49. In addition, ROTC programs and military recruiters are increasingly absent from campuses as a result of the impact of the "Don't Ask, Don't Tell" policy.

50. Ganesh Sitaraman and Previn Warren, *Invisible Citizens: Youth Politics after September 11th* (Boston: Institute of Politics, 2003).

51. Rachel Kleinfeld and Matthew Spence, *The September 11th Generation: The National Security Beliefs of Voters under 30,* Truman National Security Paper (Washington: Truman National Security Project, May 2006).

52. As Colonel John Brush, U.S. Marine Corps, and Colonel Kenneth Dahl, U.S. Army, write, "While America's commitments have expanded steadily, America's leaders have stopped asking for service. It is a twenty-five-year-old sergeant on recruiting duty in Pittsburgh whom we've asked to tackle the weighty issue of who serves our country in uniform, instead of the people who should own the challenge—our political and leadership class, and in fact, all of us." See John Brush and Kenneth Dahl, "Don't Ask, Don't Serve" (Brookings, October 31, 2006).

53. It is a scary data point that only 35 percent of adults surveyed in a Defense Department research poll said that they would recommend to a youth that he or she consider service in the Army or Marines. See CBO, *Recruiting, Retention, and Future Levels of Military Personnel,* p. 26.

54. For example, returning to the old recruiting quota of 2 percent for category 4 applicants within two years.

55. The cost of an F-22 fighter is $345 million. Indeed, the Congressional Budget Office estimates that a mere increase in the number of Army recruiters by 800 to 1,100 would eliminate the shortfalls in raw numbers of Army recruits. This would cost between $98 million and $147 million annually. The cost to raise the sufficient number of recruiters for the National Guard and Army Reserve would be between $395 million and $569 million. See CBO, *Recruiting, Retention, and Future Levels of Military Personnel,* pp. xxii, 21.

56. See, for example, Frederick W. Kagan, "The U.S. Military's Manpower Crisis."

57. Hans Binnendijk and Stuart E. Johnson, *Transforming for Stabilization and Reconstruction Operations* (Washington: National Defense University, Center for Technology and National Security Policy, 2004), pp. 53–69; Thomas Barnett, *The Pentagon's New Road Map: War and Peace in the Twenty-First Century* (New York: Putnam, 2004); Thomas Barnett, *Blueprint for Action: A Future Worth Creating* (New York: Putnam, 2004).

58. Mark Thompson, "A War Machine for the Whole Family," *Time,* April 3, 2008 (www.time.com/time/nation/article/0,8599,1727490,00.html).

59. *Financial Analysis of "Don't Ask, Don't Tell"* (Santa Barbara: University of California, Michael D. Palm Center [Center for the Study of Sexual Minorities in the Military], February 2006) (www.gaymilitary.ucsb.edu/Publications/2006-FebBlueRibbonFinalRpt.pdf).

60. For further information on this, see also Lawrence Korb and others, *Restoring American Military Power: A Progressive Defense Review* (Washington: Center for American Progress, January 2006); "West Pointer Wins First-Ever Military Award for

Challenging Gay Ban" (University of California–Santa Barbara, Michael D. Palm Center [Center for the Study of Sexual Minorities in the Military], August 16, 2006) (www.gaymilitary.ucsb.edu/PressCenter/press_rel_2006_0808.htm); Aaron Belkin and Melissa S. Embser-Herbert, "A Modest Proposal: Privacy as a Flawed Rationale for the Exclusion of Gays and Lesbians from the U.S. Military," *International Security* 27, no. 2 (Fall 2002): 178–97.

61. These include 20 M1 Abrams tanks, 50 Bradley fighting vehicles, 20 Stryker wheeled combat vehicles, 20 M113 armored personnel carriers, 250 Humvees, and 500 heavy and medium transport trucks and trailers, reconnaissance vehicles, and mine-clearing vehicles. Add another 27 Apache attack helicopters, 21 Blackhawk utility helicopters, 23 Kiowa Warrior assault helicopters, and 14 Chinook cargo helicopters. See Greg Grant, "Army 'Reset' Bill Hits $9 Billion: Nearly 1,000 Vehicles Lost in Combat," *Army Times,* February 20, 2006, p. 16.

62. Association of the United States Army, "Resetting the Force: The Equipment Challenge," *Torchbearer National Security Report* (Arlington, Va., October 2005), p. 7 (www.ausa.org/pdfdocs/TB_Resetting.pdf).

63. Douglas Holtz-Eakin, "The Potential Costs Resulting from Increased Usage of Military Equipment in Ongoing Operations," testimony before the House Committee on Armed Services, Subcommittee on Readiness, 109 Cong. 1 sess. (Washington, April 6, 2005), p. 1 (www.cbo.gov/showdoc.cfm?index=6235&sequence=0).

64. General Michael Hagee, U.S. Marine Corps, testimony before the Senate Armed Services Committee, 109 Cong. 1 sess. (Washington, June 30, 2005), p. 9 (http://armed-services.senate.gov/statement/2005/June/Hagee%2006-30-05.pdf).

65. Stephen Metz, *Learning from Iraq: Counter-Insurgency in American Strategy* (Carlisle, Pa.: U.S. Army War College, October 2006).

66. Government Accountability Office, *Military Readiness: DoD Needs to Identify and Address Gaps and Potential Risks in Program Strategies and Funding Priorities for Selected Equipment,* GAO-06-141 (October 2005), pp. 6–7.

67. Bryan Bender, "Marine Units Found to Lack Equipment," *Boston Globe,* June 21, 2005 p. A1.

68. General Michael Hagee, testimony before the Senate Armed Services Committee, p. 8.

69. Government Accountability Office, *Plans Needed to Improve Army National Guard Equipment Readiness and Better Integrate Guard into Armed Force Transformation Initiatives,* GAO-06-111 (October 2005), p. 4.

70. Government Accountability Office, *Reserve Forces: An Integrated Plan Is Needed to Address Army Reserve Personnel and Equipment Shortages,* GAO-05-660 (July 2005), p. 14.

71. GAO, *Plans Needed to Improve Army National Guard Equipment Readiness,* p. 11; GAO, *Reserve Forces,* p. 15.

72. Other examples include night goggles: 276,734 are required and only 102,684 are on hand now. In 2008 there will be a shortfall of 143,613. See Michelle Tan, "Relief for U.S. National Guard."

73. William Matthews, "War Strategy," *Armed Forces Journal,* September 14, 2006, pp. 14–15.

74. Thom Shanker, "Pentagon Says Iraq Effort Limits Ability to Fight Other Conflicts," *New York Times,* May 3, 2005, p. 1; Josh White and Ann Scott Tyson, "Wars Strain U.S. Military Capability, Pentagon Reports," *Washington Post,* May 3, 2005, p. 6.

75. Government Accountability Office, *Military Readiness: Impact of Current Operations and Actions Needed to Rebuild Readiness of U.S. Ground Forces,* GAO-08-497T, statement of Sharon L. Pickup, director, defense capabilities and management, 110 Cong. 2 sess. (February 14, 2008).

76. Commission on the National Guard and Reserves, *Transforming the National Guard and Reserves into a 21-Century Operational Force.*

77. Ann Scott Tyson, "U.S. Army Battling to Save Equipment," *Washington Post,* December 5, 2006, p. A18.

78. The modularity program involves training and new equipment for long-term transformation and is budgeted to cost $6 billion a year from 2006 to 2011. As Cindy Williams, principal research scientist at MIT's Security Studies Program, put it, "Treating this transformative program as an emergency is illogical." See Cindy Williams, "Beyond Preemption and Preventive War," Policy Analysis Brief (Muscatine, Iowa: The Stanley Foundation, February 2006), p. 13. The Joint Network Node is a massive communications equipment program akin to a Wi-Fi network for the military.

79. Noah Shachtman, "Army's Contrived Cash Crunch," DefenseTech.org, May 31, 2006 (www.defensetech.org/archives/002457).

80. Ralph Peters, "Betraying Our Troops: Procuring More Useless Weapons Systems . . . ," *New York Post,* February 3, 2006.

81. Government Accountability Office, *Defense Acquisitions: Assessments of Selected Weapon Programs,* GAO-08-467SP (March 2008).

82. This is not an isolated incident. Contractors for the F-35 Joint Strike Fighter also received their full bonus of nearly $500 million from 1999 to 2003, despite the fact that it overran the budget by $10 billion and was almost a year behind schedule.

83. GAO, *Defense Acquisitions: Assessments of Selected Weapon Programs.*

84. Ibid., p. 30.

85. Dawn Kopecki, "On the Hunt for Fraud," Businessweek.com, October 11, 2006 (www.businessweek.com/bwdaily/dnflash/content/oct2006/db20061011_184367.htm? chan=top+news_top+news+index_businessweek+exclusives).

86. Citizens against Government Waste, "2007 Congressional Pig Book Summary," (Washington) (www.cagw.org/site/PageServer?pagename=reports_pigbook2007).

87. Steven Kosiak, *Cost Growth in Defense Plans, Wars in Iraq and Afghanistan Could Add Some $900 Billion to Projected Deficits,* Update (Washington: Center for Strategic and Budgetary Assessments, December 23, 2005) (www.csbaonline.org/4Publications/PubLibrary/U.20051223.CostGrowthInDefensePlans/U.20051223.Cost GrowthInDefensePlans.pdf).

88. Richard Wolf, "A 'Fiscal Hurricane' on the Horizon," *USA Today,* November 14, 2005.

89. Kori Schake, "Jurassic Pork," *New York Times,* February 9, 2006, Op-Ed, p. A27.

90. Senate Report 109-254, "National Defense Authorization Act for Fiscal Year 2007."

91. Note that this alternative includes the cost of modernizing the equipment in the rest of the Army. For more on this see Jeffrey Tebbs, "Smelting the Iron Triangle: Constraining Congress Defense Contractors, and the Military Brass to Restore a Fiscally Prudent Defense Budget," Brookings Economic Studies Paper, 2006; Congressional Budget Office, *The Long Term Implications of Current Defense Plans and Alternatives: Summary Update for Fiscal Year 2006* (Washington, October 2005).

92. William Matthews, "Bush Says He May Ignore New War-Funding Law," *Defense News,* October 23, 2006, p. 23.

93. Such as reducing by 50 percent the number of programs currently over budget.

94. Two comprehensive studies have been recently completed that address reforming the defense acquisition enterprise. Both studies support the conclusion that instability brought on by tremendous complexity of the enterprise and a lack of integration of the budgeting, requirements generation, and acquisition management processes are at the core of the systemic problems that lead to acquisition failures. See Assessment Panel of the Defense Acquisition Performance Assessment (DAPA) Project, *Defense Acquisition Performance Assessment Report* (Washington: January 2006); Center for Strategic and International Studies (CSIS), *Beyond Goldwater-Nichols: U.S. Government and Defense Reform for a New Strategic Era,* Phase 2 Report (Washington, July 2005), chapters 6–7.

95. The four priority areas are consolidated recommendations from recent studies (DoD, *Quadrennial Defense Review Report*; DAPA Project, *Defense Acquisition Performance Assessment Report*; CSIS, *Beyond Goldwater-Nichols*) and discussions with defense acquisition professionals. I am particularly indebted to Commander Christopher Robinson, U.S. Navy, in this section.

96. For example, for every failure to perform, a company is removed from one pending or future contract bid. To prevent companies from gaming the system and then bidding next on something they do not mind losing, the removal should be a randomized process, such that the firm will not know whether it will lose a future small or large contract.

Ensuring that Foreign Aid Is Effective

Raise the Level of Debate about Aid

KENNETH W. DAM

SUMMARY ❱ Presidential candidates can expect to encounter three competing concepts about foreign aid. They will hear that foreign aid does not work and is therefore wasted; that poverty, disease, and hunger are so pervasive in the developing world that foreign aid must be increased dramatically; and that U.S. foreign aid decisionmaking and management are so complex and convoluted that they need major reorganization.

To raise the level of discussion and ground the administration's decisions in better data, the next president should direct several *evaluative* initiatives:

—All foreign aid programs should be systematically evaluated, based on their unique goals, rather than the overarching, sometimes irrelevant criterion of economic development.

—Food aid policy, in particular, should be evaluated to determine its impact on hunger and on long-run agricultural development in recipient countries.

—A consistent method should be established for comparing foreign aid efforts across developed nations that takes into account the contributions of private philanthropy and foreign-born workers' remittances to their countries of origin, not just government outlays.

The new administration should build on—and presidential candidates should endorse—recent *programmatic* trends in foreign aid that reflect a bipartisan consensus. The administration should

—increase well-conceived health and education efforts, because they are valuable on their own terms and promote economic development;

—expand collaborations among federal agencies, with other countries, and with international institutions and nongovernmental organizations to reduce overlap and administrative burdens on recipient countries;

—place World Bank lending on a more rational footing, by demanding concrete moves away from corruption both within the bank and in recipient countries and by limiting the implicit loan subsidy to middle-income countries, especially China;

—continue the recent shift toward grants and away from loans.

The new administration should be skeptical of debt relief proposals, especially those that do not include meaningful reforms and should develop a comprehensive policy approach toward debt relief. Finally, even though the current organization of U.S. foreign aid operations is a morass, the new administration should refrain from reorganization until it determines clear objectives, forms a strong leadership team, and reviews the current system's strengths and weaknesses: "Think objectives and means first, reorganize later." ❭

CONTEXT ❭ Judging from experience, three sharply contrasting ideas about foreign assistance will surface during the 2008 presidential campaign—and subsequent congressional debates:

—Foreign aid does not work and is therefore wasted.

—Poverty, disease, and hunger are so pervasive in the developing world that foreign aid must be increased dramatically.

—U.S. foreign aid decisionmaking and management are so complex and convoluted that major reorganization is needed.

The first two views are often expressed in highly emotional terms. The second viewpoint, notably, is sometimes manifested through mass marches, targeted demonstrations, and celebrity tours and performances. ❭

COMPETING BELIEFS

Each of the three views is supported by substantial research. Most voters, though, are poorly informed about the size and scope of foreign assistance

Table 11-1. Portion of the President's FY 08 International Affairs Budget Devoted to Economic Development, by Selected Programs

Program	Amount (billions of dollars)	Percentage
Development Assistance	1.0	2.8
Millennium Challenge Corporation (MCC)[a]	1.1	3.0
Multilateral Economic Assistance (including International Development Association of the World Bank)	1.8	5.0
Subtotal	3.9	10.8
Total FY08 budget for international affairs	36.2	100.0

a. An additional $1.9 billion is requested for MCC funding in future years.

budgets and programs. In public opinion surveys, Americans grossly over-estimate the amount the United States spends on foreign aid, especially when compared with other countries' foreign assistance expenditures.

IS FOREIGN AID EFFECTIVE?

If foreign aid is ineffective, it truly is wasted. A large research literature is devoted to determining the effectiveness of aid. *The central question is: effective in achieving what?* Much of the literature measures its effectiveness only in promoting economic growth, reflecting the assumption that foreign aid is primarily intended to boost economic development. In truth, economic development consumes about one-sixth of the president's fiscal year 2008 budget for international affairs, which includes State Department operations (table 11-1). Some aid programs have economic aspects but are not designed solely to boost economic development (table 11-2).

Foreign aid is a diverse endeavor, encompassing a bewildering array of programs, both bilateral and international. Many of these programs are intended to achieve goals other than economic development, such as fighting disease, supporting a friendly government, or providing disaster relief, and the United States is by far the largest donor of humanitarian aid.

It should come as no surprise that the universe of U.S. foreign aid programs, intended to serve multiple purposes, achieves only mixed results in meeting the single purpose of enhancing economic development. This is especially true when one focuses on aid to a single country, such as the Democratic Republic of the Congo (formerly Zaïre), where for many

Table 11-2. Selected Foreign Aid Components Other than Economic Development
in the President's FY 08 Budget

Component	Amount (billions of dollars)	Percentage
Economic Support Fund (includes conflict recovery and counterterrorism projects)	3.3	9.1
Foreign and security policy support for former Soviet-bloc countries	0.7	1.9
Migration and Refugee Assistance	0.8	2.2
Subtotal	4.8	13.2

years bilateral aid was used essentially to bribe the corrupt and incompetent Mobutu regime.

An additional problem in measuring the effectiveness of foreign aid in terms of economic growth is that much of U.S. aid provides relief in the wake of war, famine, civil strife, or a natural disaster—when economic development already has experienced a serious blow and considerable time will be needed to regain previous economic levels. It is hardly fair to fault these relief efforts for failing to produce growth beyond previous levels, when countries are struggling to regain lost ground.

Efforts to Assess Effectiveness

Some aid programs nevertheless have been found to produce an economic development payoff, particularly "short-impact" aid programs—including budget and balance-of-payments support, investments in infrastructure, and aid for productive sectors, such as industry and agriculture.

Attitudes toward the necessary preconditions for successful economic aid are evolving. Earlier research seemed to show that economic assistance does work in countries with sound economic policies, including fiscal discipline, an independent central bank that enforces anti-inflation monetary policies, and openness to international trade (the components of the so-called Washington Consensus). But this conclusion has been largely discredited and replaced with a "neo-institutional" belief that the most important factor in economic development, whether or not foreign assistance is involved, is the quality of institutions. The Bush administration combined the "good policy" and "good institutions" approaches in creating the Millennium Challenge Corporation, a new component of U.S. foreign aid programming.

Methodology Problems

The neo-institutional approach does not readily lend itself to econometric measurement. Indeed, it remains doubtful whether foreign aid can improve either economic policies *or* institutions in the developing world. The traditional approach of conditioning aid on policy and institutional reforms is itself questionable:

—Does "conditionality" work?

—When countries do not meet aid agencies' conditions, are penalties adequate to make "conditionality" credible?

The best measure of effectiveness might be whether a program accomplishes what it purportedly sets out to do, but aid agencies rarely get around to serious evaluation of individual programs. Evaluation requires a clear, comprehensive definition of effectiveness. Take, for example, food aid. Yes, it is fairly simple to show that food aid feeds the hungry. However, a test for effectiveness also should include whether food provided gratis from outside the region undercuts local agriculture and whether it leads to better nutrition for the local population over time, taking into account its effects on local production. The analytical dilemma is exacerbated when the aid program becomes entangled with U.S. politics—in this instance, the desire to stimulate domestic U.S. agriculture. U.S. food aid programs normally require that food be shipped from the United States rather than purchased locally, thereby raising the cost and often undermining local agriculture and farm employment.

Despite these challenges, the next administration should emphasize serious evaluation in starting new assistance programs and in assessing inherited ones.

Are We Spending Enough?

Although the United States is the world's largest foreign aid donor in absolute terms, our contribution as a percentage of gross domestic product (GDP) is quite low. Under the definition of foreign aid set by the Development Assistance Committee of the Organization for Economic Cooperation and Development (OECD), which measures Official Development Assistance (ODA), the United States usually ranks either twenty-sixth or twenty-seventh among the twenty-eight industrialized OECD member countries in the percentage of GDP devoted to foreign aid. As a result, critics say the United States is stingy.

After declining in the early 1990s, U.S. foreign aid expenditures rebounded in the late 1990s and grew rapidly in the first half of the present decade. U.S. ODA has climbed from 0.12 percent of GDP in 1994–95 to 0.20 percent in 2004–05, while ODA for the European Union as a whole remained flat at 0.39 percent. U.S. aid to Africa has grown even more rapidly in this period, with a strong focus on HIV/AIDS (through the President's Emergency Plan for AIDS Relief) and a new focus on malaria. This rapid growth was helped by the fact that debt relief is now counted, rightly or wrongly, as ODA.

International comparisons are, however, weak. For one thing, the United States spends far more on *military* and other forms of non-ODA assistance than do other countries (a fact whose implications for development are controversial). Even more important, ODA comparisons take into account only expenditures by governments; yet *private philanthropy* plays a far larger role in international aid from our country than it does from nearly all other OECD nations. U.S. private philanthropy for developing countries is more than twice as large as ODA. According to a Hudson Institute study, U.S. philanthropic sources gave more than any other donor country in 2005—even without taking into account contributions by U.S. corporations, universities, and religious organizations. However, most countries do not collect comprehensive data on private and voluntary giving, which would enable more accurate international comparisons.

Remittances to home countries by foreign workers in the United States (some of whom are U.S. citizens) are also much larger than remittances from foreign workers in other countries, even on a per capita basis. Remittances from U.S. workers to developing countries are two and one-half times as great as the U.S. government's ODA. Although it is sometimes assumed that remittances go only from migrant workers to their families, the fact is that (in the case of Mexico, for example) groups of U.S. citizens and U.S. permanent residents of Mexican extraction have organized to send collective remittances to fund local infrastructure and community projects in Mexican villages.

Under these circumstances, it is hard to justify cross-country comparisons, and efforts to paint the United States as stingy are off the mark. To make international comparisons truly valid and reliable, global criteria and data collection for private philanthropy and remittances are needed to supplement data on ODA.

CHOOSING AMONG DIFFERENT TYPES OF AID

Foreign aid is not a key political issue in the United States.[1] In general, it is easiest to win congressional support for aid programs with broad appeal that are based partly on familiar U.S. models. To illustrate, the Bush administration was able to increase total foreign aid by emphasizing health interventions that have been credited with success in the United States, especially for HIV/AIDS and especially for Africa, where the disease burden is horrific. Even though it is easier to garner support for programs like this, it would be shortsighted either to abandon abstract goals like economic development or to assume that what works in the United States will work in the developing world.

Programs can serve multiple purposes. Health programs—ranging from medical care to nutrition—promote economic development, because hungry children do not learn, and sick adults do not work. Indeed, health and education programs often do more to boost growth in countries with poor economic policies and poor institutions than do most economic development projects. More important, health programs have eliminated smallpox, dramatically reduced polio, and expanded immunizations and oral rehydration therapy, saving millions of lives. This is not to say that all health programs are worthwhile—on their own terms or in economic terms. Health programs require a sound distribution network and sufficient trained personnel to ensure, for example, that medicine is properly administered and actually taken.

Similarly, education programs, by building human capital, can make a vital contribution to economic development. Yet some education programs fail to achieve positive results in economic *or* educational terms. In particular, programs that aim merely to increase the percentage of school-aged children in places called schools can lead to simple warehousing of children—as is the case in parts of India, where teacher attendance is strikingly low.[2]

Achieving economic development is elusive. Both donor and recipient countries struggle with a multiplicity of overlapping programs, some of which are too small to make a difference and which overwhelm developing countries' administrative capacities. To avoid cluttering the landscape in developing countries, diverse government aid agencies and nongovernmental organizations must combine or coordinate efforts. Meanwhile, even the best-intentioned programs and people may be unable to surmount deeply rooted systemic problems, whether in health, education, agriculture, commerce, or other sectors. Given the complexities involved, it is not at all clear that the current level of public discussion in the United States or in other developed countries is up to the challenge of devising a sound economic aid strategy.

DEALING WITH THE WORLD BANK

Issues surrounding the June 2007 resignation of World Bank Group president Paul Wolfowitz are likely to prompt the next administration to conduct a thorough review of U.S.-World Bank relations.[3] This reexamination could extend to regional aid institutions as well, but the World Bank is likely to be the main concern. Although the Wolfowitz controversy nominally involved conflict-of-interest issues, fundamental policy issues also were raised, and, since the resignation, even mainstream media coverage has turned from a focus on the man to an analysis of bank governance and policies.

One issue is corruption—both within the bank staff itself and in recipient countries. The new administration *must* address the staff dimension, because congressional appropriations help fund the World Bank's soft-loan component, the International Development Association (IDA). And, the new administration also *should* address the local dimension, because corruption within countries goes straight to the function of the bank—it compromises economic development. *At the end of the day, the bank must be seen as willing to cut lending to countries that fail to measurably reduce corruption.*

Loans to Middle-Income Countries

Another key issue facing the World Bank concerns global economic growth fueled by massive financial liquidity. Today, most of the bank's middle-income member countries are able, in normal situations, to borrow in private financial markets. (In crises, nations turn to the International Monetary Fund.) Loans to middle-income countries almost surely could be turned over to the private sector. However, these nations currently obtain conventional loans, repayable in hard currency, from the World Bank Group's International Bank for Reconstruction and Development (IBRD). The IBRD has a credit rating of AAA, based on the willingness of the

United States and other prosperous countries to stand behind the bank's obligations—in effect, to guarantee the loans. The IBRD funds these loans by borrowing in private markets and investing its available reserves. And it makes money on this $15 billion lending operation, using the proceeds to fund staff salaries and day-to-day operations.

The issue is whether the United States should continue its implicit subsidy of World Bank loans to middle-income countries. The argument *against* it is that private sector banks are able to serve this function. The argument *for* it is that the profits support World Bank staff salaries and services. These services assist not just middle-income borrowers but others as well, so that lending to middle-income countries subsidizes aid to poorer ones. Further, these services include research, reports, and initiatives in the health and social sectors, many of which have global reach and therefore should be considered "global public goods."

Loans to Poor Countries

Less controversial are loans to low-income countries, mostly in sub-Saharan Africa. These low-income borrowers, heavily burdened by debt and poor governance, simply do not have the financial standing to satisfy the requirements of private lenders. They are usually able to borrow from IDA at extremely favorable terms, and sometimes receive a grace period before payments begin and quite low interest rates. IDA activities on behalf of low-income countries are financed by triennial rounds of "replenishments" by the bank's more developed member countries.

Loans to Emerging Countries

China, India, and other large developing nations pose another issue for the World Bank. These countries could borrow in private markets, but they also have hundreds of millions of people living in poverty, often in subnational regions or enclaves (such as western China), where they constitute the vast majority of the population. As a device to reduce poverty, loans targeted to these groups would have considerable force. But U.S. contributions to IBRD loans to China, in particular, could be hard to explain to American voters, given current trade imbalances and China's ability to access private credit. (China no longer receives IDA loans.) The new administration should address at least the China aspect of World Bank lending instead of allowing the issue to drift into contentiousness.

PROVIDING DEBT RELIEF

The cause of debt reduction for developing countries gathered strength with the Jubilee 2000 movement and other initiatives in this century's first decade to help developing countries, especially in Africa, free up resources for development. "Drop the Debt," one of the slogans of the cause, captures the emotional level of the public discussion. Much of this emotion was contrived or misdirected. For example, debt did not cause children to die, for even the most indebted countries received more aid than was their debt service, and many of those countries were not servicing their debt. Further, debt relief involves new borrowing that creates new debt service obligations. Typically, debt relief is part of a package that includes relief of some portion of existing debt, payment of some remaining debt, and additional lending, which often exceeds payments on old debt.

In contrast to the public clamor, a quite different discussion was occurring between governments and inside the Washington Beltway among federal policymakers and World Bank officials. This discussion focused on the potentially negative effects of debt relief on future aid levels. If debt relief would reduce future aid, it could impede development. Another adverse effect would occur if debt relief would end some recipient countries' laudable practice of making debt payments, called "reflows." If reflows stopped, the IDA would have less money to lend (and to compensate staff) and would have to rely almost exclusively on its triennial replenishments, which are difficult to coax out of Congress and other political entities. Currently, reflows support one-fifth of the bank's new soft loans to poor countries.

U.S. Leadership on Debt Relief

The debt relief issue came to a head at the G-8 summit in Gleneagles, Scotland, in July 2005. There, the United States won G-8 support for comprehensive debt relief, including 100 percent relief for some countries, through an end run around the Europeans' advocacy of traditional debt relief packages, which included partial write-downs and new lending. The U.S. approach eliminated reflows from the countries receiving 100 percent relief, but only for IDA loans, not bilateral loans.

Why did the United States seek to exclude its own, bilateral loans from debt relief? As the Bush administration recognized, debt relief is more a political than a financial matter. U.S. politicians and diplomats have long been tempted to offer debt relief as a soft diplomatic option, to win hearts and minds in developing countries, even though its overall effect is mixed. To control this temptation, the government has for many years counted debt relief as an outlay in the federal budget "150 accounts," which fund international activities ranging from State Department salaries to bilateral economic assistance. Understandably, debt relief on bilateral loans was a sensitive issue within the U.S. foreign policy establishment.

Developing a New Policy

Debt relief can assist an overburdened developing country when it is accompanied by additional resources or induces domestic reforms. Moreover, across-the-board debt relief is unlikely to help developing countries significantly. The new administration should develop a coherent policy on debt relief that would guide new lending to poor countries, especially in Africa where—Republicans and Democrats agree—more aid is needed. Debt relief is likely to be a recurring problem, and a new policy also would guide U.S. attitudes toward debt relief by international lending organizations, which have their own institutional and strategic interests.

Shifting from Loans to Grants

Architects of foreign aid used to view loans as a better device than grants, precisely because repayments could fund new loans and finance development agency staff costs. During the Bush administration, though, following much international debate, a marked shift toward grants has taken place. Grants preempt the debt relief issue by avoiding a piling up of debt that, in many cases, is unlikely to be repaid. There is little reason for the new administration to reopen this issue.

REORGANIZING FOREIGN AID PROGRAMS

Every administration struggles with the question of how to organize U.S. foreign assistance efforts. Ever since the Kennedy administration, major studies and reports on the subject have blossomed periodically. Bush administration initiatives included

—Creating the Millennium Challenge Corporation, a quasi-independent agency, to reduce global poverty by promoting sustainable economic growth

—Launching a major initiative to combat HIV/AIDS

—Establishing a State Department office of Director of Foreign Assistance at the deputy secretary level to absorb many functions of the Agency for International Development, which remains in operation

Is reorganization indicated? As the Brookings Institution's Lael Brainard has depicted, the organization of the federal government's foreign aid operation is a nightmarish maze of boxes and lines. A key, if cynical, reason to choose the reorganization route is that reorganizing is easier for new political executives than the nitty-gritty work of improving existing entities.[4] Nevertheless, there are ample reasons to refrain from reorganizing, at least initially:

—Reorganization in government almost always makes things more, not less, complicated, especially when congressional action is required.

—Most reorganizations slow the pace of action, as new players are added, people move to new seats, new communications channels are put in place, and fresh bureaucratic rivalries take shape.

—Reorganization often substitutes for real action on concrete problems (following the maxim "When in doubt, reorganize").

One reorganization idea is to create a cabinet-level department of foreign assistance, along the lines of the Department for International Development in the United Kingdom. This idea is almost certainly politically unworkable, since the Departments of State and Defense—and their Capitol Hill oversight committees—are unlikely to allow such a department to operate independent of their control. The idea is also conceptually flawed, because foreign aid serves multiple purposes, not just economic development, and some aid programs relate directly to national security.

Even if reorganization is eventually undertaken—which could consolidate and regularize some of the Bush administration innovations—the new administration should defer this task, pending fundamental decisions about primary foreign aid objectives, the formation of an effective leadership team, and a systematic evaluation of the current system's strengths and weaknesses. The advice here is: "Think objectives and means first, reorganize later."

CONCLUSION

Foreign aid reform is a difficult matter. It has programmatic and organizational aspects. The programmatic issues are so complex, both substantively and politically, that commentators and review groups have recently tended to assume that all would be well if only the present maze of U.S. foreign aid organizations could simply be merged into a single U.S. foreign aid agency, preferably a separate cabinet-level department. The present organizational morass reflects, however, the multiple purposes of foreign aid, which include a variety of economic development, foreign policy, security policy, and social (health, education, poverty alleviation) objectives. Each individual program thus has its own constituency within the government, the Congress, and the American society. The present organizational and programmatic structure, together with untold mandates and restrictions, is written into statutes. Aside from the fact that a merger into, say, a new executive branch department would therefore be unlikely to pass Congress, such a new department could hardly resolve the issues of conflicting objectives without a struggle with State and Defense and perhaps other departments, with many resulting conflicts inevitably landing on the president's desk. It would, therefore, be far better for the new administration to decide on the balance of its foreign aid objectives and then propose to Congress an organization to carry out those objectives.

ADDITIONAL RESOURCES

Banerjee, Abhijit Vinayak. 2007. "Inside the Machine." In *Making Aid Work*, edited by Abhijit Vinayak Banerjee, pp. 123–65. MIT Press.
Birdsall, Nancy, and Devesh Kapur, with others. 2005. *The Hardest Job in the World: Five Crucial Tasks for the New President of the World Bank*. Washington: Center for Global Development (www.cgdev.org/content/publications/detail/2868).
Brainard, Lael, ed. 2007. *Security by Other Means*. Brookings.
Clemens, Michael, Steven Radelet, and Rikhil Bhavnani. 2004. *Counting Chickens when They Hatch: The Short-Term Effect of Aid on Growth*. Working Paper 44. Washington: Center for Global Development (www.cgdev.org/content/publications/detail/2744/).
Dam, Kenneth W. 2006. *The Law-Growth Nexus: The Rule of Law and Economic Development*. Brookings.
HELP Commission. 2007. *Beyond Assistance: The HELP Commission Report on Foreign Assistance Reform*. Washington (December). (www.helpcommission.gov/portals/0/Beyond%20Assistance_HELP_Commission_Report.pdf).
Hudson Institute. 2007. *The Index of Global Philanthropy*. Washington: Center for Global Prosperity (http://gpr.hudson.org/files/publications/IndexGlobalPhilanthropy2007.pdf).
Lancaster, Carol. 2006. *Foreign Aid: Diplomacy, Development, Domestic Policies*. University of Chicago Press.

———. 2008. *George Bush's Foreign Aid: Transformation or Chaos?* Washington: Center for Global Development (www.cgdev.org/content/publications/detail/16085/).

Lerrick, Adam. 2006. *Forgive the World Bank but Don't Forget: Debt Relief Should Fund a Turnaround in Development Aid. Development Policy Outlook* 1, Washington: American Enterprise Institute (www.aei.org/publications/filter.all,pub ID.23836/pub_detail.asp).

Mallaby, Sebastian. 2005. "Saving the World Bank." *Foreign Affairs* 84, no. 3 (May–June).

Radelet, Steven. 2006. "A Primer on Foreign Aid." Working Paper 92. Washington: Center for Global Development (July) (www.cgdev.org/content/publications/detail/8846).

Rajan, Raghuram. 2005. "Aid and Growth: The Policy Challenge." *Finance and Development* 42, no. 4 (December) (www.imf.org/external/pubs/ft/fandd/2005/12/straight.htm).

———. 2005. "Debt Relief and Growth." *Finance and Development* 42, no. 2 (June) (www.imf.org/external/pubs/ft/fandd/2005/06/straight.htm).

Rajan, Raghuram, and Arvind Subramanian. 2007 (forthcoming). "Aid and Growth: What Does the Cross-Country Evidence Really Show?" In *Review of Economics and Statistics* (also as IMF Working Paper 05/127, Washington, 2005).

U.S. Department of State. *Summary and Highlights, International Affairs Function 150, Fiscal Year 2008 Budget Request.* Washington (www.state.gov/documents/organization/80151.pdf).

World Bank. 2006. *Strengthening the World Bank's Engagement with IBRD Partner Countries.* Washington: World Bank, Development Committee (http://site resources.worldbank.org/DEVCOMMINT/Documentation/21046512/DC2006-0014(E)-MIC.pdf).

NOTES

1. This issue tends to be more important in northern European countries with proportional parliamentary representation; there, some minor parties hold strong positions on foreign aid, and coalitions are formed through compromises on party positions.

2. One UN Millennium Development Goal is to ensure that all children complete a full course of primary schooling.

3. Wolfowitz was replaced by Robert B. Zoellick, former deputy secretary of state, in July 2007.

4. For example, the Bush administration found it easier to create the Department of Homeland Security rather than to wrestle with the inability of multiple departments and agencies to communicate quickly and cooperate effectively. Meanwhile, Congress has simply avoided addressing the nearly crippling problem of overlapping committee jurisdictions affecting homeland security.

12

Managing Homeland Security
Developing a Threat-Based Strategy

JEREMY SHAPIRO

SUMMARY ❯ After 9/11 the United States acted swiftly to defend itself from terrorist attacks. The government implemented numerous far-reaching security measures, undertook a vast reorganization for the purpose of defending against terrorism, and more than tripled federal homeland security spending. Although substantial gaps remain, coordination of antiterrorist efforts has been significantly improved internationally and within the federal government.

There have been no terrorist attacks in the United States since 9/11, but it is far from clear whether the government's efforts have made the difference. Policy discussions of homeland security issues are driven not by rigorous analysis but by fear, perceptions of past mistakes, pork barrel politics, and insistence on an invulnerability that cannot possibly be achieved. It is time for a new, more analytic, *threat-based* approach, grounded in concepts of sufficiency, prioritization, and measured effectiveness.

The new president should put forward a threat-based homeland security strategy that would acknowledge that major terrorist attacks are unlikely in the United States and would reallocate resources accordingly. The strategy would focus specifically on enhancing four major efforts: coordination with foreign partners to degrade al Qaeda further; continued "overprotection" of civil aviation, including air cargo inspection and defense against surface-to-air missiles; public education to create more resilience in the event of an attack; and outreach to Muslim communities in the United States, whose unfriendliness to terrorist groups so far has made the United States less vulnerable than other countries to incidents of terror. ❱

CONTEXT ❱ "Homeland security"—both the term and the policy—were effectively born amid the crisis of September 11, 2001. The policy started with a simple purpose: to prevent further terrorist attacks on American soil. On these terms, the policy seems enormously successful: the country has seen no further Islamist terror attacks, despite numerous predictions to the contrary. Of course, neither were there any terrorist attacks in the United States in the five years before 2001, so whether our post-9/11 success is attributable to recent homeland security policies, offensive antiterrorism operations abroad, or just dumb luck is debatable.

Homeland security is such a new topic that explanations for success are difficult to assess. It also has become a politically charged question in a country traumatized by 9/11 and increasingly polarized along partisan lines. Perceived deficiencies in homeland security have become political cudgels for beating incumbents and establishing a politician's *bona fides* on national security issues. Neither these discussions nor homeland security policies themselves are squarely rooted in anything except the politics of fear and perceptions of pre-9/11 deficiencies.

In the early days after 9/11, it made sense to take measures that responded to the circumstances of that attack and reassured a nervous public. But seven years into the apparently endless war on terrorism, homeland security should evolve from a set of emergency policies into a permanent field of important government policy that, like any other, must justify its allocation of taxpayer funds through solid analysis.

Certainly, an extraordinary amount has been achieved in homeland security (see table 12-1). A multitude of specific initiatives to protect everything from ports to power plants has advanced from mere ideas to operational programs with, by governmental standards, lightning speed. Giant bureaucracies, including the Department of Homeland Security (DHS), the Office of the Director of National Intelligence (DNI), and the Transportation Security Administration (TSA), have emerged from nothing into large functioning organizations. Governments are rarely capable of reacting so rapidly and radically to new challenges.

Table 12-1. Major Post-9/11 U.S. Homeland Security Legislation

Legislation	Date	Purpose
Authorization to use military force	September 2001	Authorized the president to use force against those who committed or aided the 9/11 attacks
USA PATRIOT Act	October 2001	Expanded the authority of U.S. law enforcement, by breaking down barriers between law enforcement and intelligence and between domestic and foreign activities
Aviation and Transportation Security Act	November 2001	Established the Transportation Security Administration to improve security in all modes of transportation
Enhanced Border Security and Visa Entry Reform Act	May 2002	Increased resources for border security and for information sharing among intelligence, law enforcement, and border security agencies
Public Health Security and Bioterrorism Preparedness and Response Act	June 2002	Implemented measures to improve the ability to prevent and respond to bioterrorism and other public health emergencies
Homeland Security Act	November 2002	Established the Department of Homeland Security, whose primary mission is to help prevent, protect against, and respond to acts of terrorism
Terrorism Risk Insurance Act	November 2002	Created a financial backstop, enabling commercial insurers to provide affordable terrorism insurance
Maritime Transportation Security Act	November 2002	Implemented measures to protect the nation's ports and waterways from terrorist attack
National Intelligence Reform and Terrorism Prevention Act	December 2004	Created the Office of the Director of National Intelligence and the National Center for Counterterrorism to coordinate intelligence gathering and analysis
Security and Accountability for Every (SAFE) Port Act	October 2006	Increased safety measures for maritime and cargo security, including a new requirement that U.S. ports scan all imported containers for radiation
Implementing Recommendations of the 9/11 Commission Act	August 2007	Provided for the implementation of the remaining recommendations of the National Commission on Terrorist Attacks upon the United States relating to the Department of Homeland Security, the Visa Waiver Program, intelligence, and other issues
Protect America Act	August 2007	Amended the Foreign Intelligence Surveillance Act of 1978 to provide additional procedures for authorizing certain acquisitions of foreign intelligence information

And yet, as critics frequently point out, many gaps remain in homeland security. State and local governments, although critical to preventing attacks and managing their consequences, have not been well integrated into federal efforts. Similarly, the private sector has just begun to contribute to homeland security. As a result, targets that can be protected only at the local level—skyscrapers, subway systems, and chemical plants, for example—have inconsistent protection or none. Limited information sharing with other countries means that suspected terrorists continue to slip across borders. Within the federal government, DHS lacks the authority and intelligence assets to coordinate fully homeland security, while the department's dreadful response to Hurricane Katrina has raised questions about its competence. This list could go on and on.

But the difficulty in evaluation comes less from these well-known deficiencies than from the absence of any reasonable standard of judgment. That the U.S. homeland can never be made 100 percent secure has become a cliché. The country contains a half million bridges, 500 skyscrapers, 200,000 miles of natural gas pipelines, and 2,800 power plants; the list of critical infrastructure alone is far too long for all its components to be protected, and then there are subways, restaurants, movie theaters, schools, and shopping malls.

Yet, in the political arena, invulnerability *is* the standard by which homeland security policies are judged. Washington think tanks, federal agencies, and government commissions have produced a steady stream of reports since 9/11 detailing the myriad vulnerabilities of the homeland and the insufficiency of the government response before and after 9/11.[1] The attack scenarios they present demonstrate a degree of imaginative thinking that even the innovative strategists of al Qaeda could never match. Moreover, the scenarios are often connected only to vulnerabilities, not to threats. Each type of attack is said to be plausible, regardless of whether any particular actor in the world has both the desire and the capacity to carry it out. A vaguely defined enemy, usually labeled "al Qaeda," is assumed to be willing and capable of doing essentially anything.

In fact, in many cases, there simply is no such enemy. For example, no one has presented evidence of any group in the world currently willing and capable of carrying out a terrorist attack in the United States using nuclear weapons or any other weapon of mass destruction (WMD), reasonably defined. The federal government nevertheless spends $11 billion a year to research, develop, and deploy technologies to defend against "catastrophic threats." Similarly, no evidence of a realistic plot against a U.S. port has surfaced; nor is one included among the ten terrorist plots that President Bush says the U.S. has disrupted since 9/11. Nevertheless, the government's 2009 homeland security funding request provides $3 billion for port security, because a terrorist attack against a U.S. port could be "economically devastating"—regardless of how likely it is.[2]

Vulnerability analyses do little to promote wise policy, but they are very meaningful politically. They usually make the case that an investment of just a few billion dollars would fix the problem. If another terrorist attack occurs—and one certainly could—a report will doubtless already exist that demonstrates that the attack could have been prevented for a few billion dollars, and yet the government did nothing. Having watched the "blame game" surrounding the 9/11 commission hearings, any U.S. official may assume that this situation represents a serious *political* vulnerability.

Partly for this reason, the last several years have witnessed a massive increase in homeland security expenditure. For fiscal year 2009, the president requested $66 billion for homeland security—a sum greater than the British or French defense budgets and more than three times the estimated level of pre-9/11 homeland security spending.[3] This spending generally lacks any firm connection to a specific terrorist threat; at worst, it serves as a source of government pork, promoting the growth of a nascent "homeland security–industrial complex." Nevertheless, the only real criticism to date, from both sides of the aisle, has been that America remains vulnerable in key areas. This type of criticism arises not because anyone believes or asserts invulnerability is possible, but because no other standard is used to evaluate homeland security policies.

There is, as yet, no measure of sufficiency in U.S. public debate on homeland security: How much are we willing to spend to be how safe? What civil liberties are we willing to give up, and what inconveniences should we tolerate? Which vulnerabilities should we address, and which should we live with? These questions remain unanswered—actually they have barely even been posed in U.S. politics.

After seven years of willy-nilly and often wasteful expansion, we now should have both the breathing room and the wisdom to find a better approach. The key challenge is not to persist in the quixotic effort to eliminate vulnerabilities through new bureaucracies or greater expenditures. Rather, it is to establish some concept of *sufficiency,* to create *priorities* within the expanding array of homeland security initiatives, and to determine *measures of effectiveness* to assess policies already implemented.

Planning for homeland security appears to be based on the notion, expressed on page one of the U.S. government's *National Strategy for Homeland Security*, that "today's terrorists can strike at any place, at any time, and with virtually any weapon." In fact, the primary lesson of the past few years is that they cannot. The enemy is neither omniscient nor omnipotent—and, at this point in the war on terrorism, we know an extraordinary amount about al Qaeda and about Islamist terrorists in general. We know about terrorist groups' goals and motivations, their multiple strengths, and their even more myriad weaknesses. We can discern very consistent operational styles and patterns.

Certainly, these groups include many intelligent, adaptive enemies that constantly innovate, and we need to be able to meet new challenges. But any terrorist group's operational flexibility is limited by the nature of its political goals, its organizational responses to counterterrorism, and the constituencies it seeks to please. An understanding of those limits will yield a much smaller field of possible terrorist targets and methods that deserve our greatest attention. In general, we can use our knowledge of the enemy to inform our homeland security policy, to efficiently and effectively allocate resources, and to resist the pressure to pursue an invulnerability that we know we can never achieve. ❯

WHERE WE ARE TODAY

After 9/11, the United States undertook by far the broadest government reorganization response to terrorism in modern history. The sheer size and symbolic power of an attack on what had previously been considered an inviolable continental sanctuary forced an entire rethinking of U.S. national security policy. Indeed, the perceived causes, both proximate and long-term, of the 9/11 attack have been used to justify all subsequent major changes in U.S. homeland security policies.

The government put the population on alert, providing a first, crucial line of defense. Air travel was quickly made much safer. The federal government created an entirely new agency, the TSA, which nationalized airport security, adding at one stroke tens of thousands of employees to the federal workforce—a stark contrast to the general trend of privatizing

U.S. government functions. The TSA quickly improved passenger screening procedures, began inspection of all luggage, installed hardened cockpit doors on large commercial aircraft, employed thousands of air marshals, and armed some pilots. The years since 9/11 have been among the safest in aviation history. There have been no further successful terrorist attacks and indeed only one crash of a large U.S. passenger jet for any reason.

Intelligence sharing, particularly about individuals with terrorist ties, was another early focus, reflecting a widely held belief that information sufficient to prevent the 9/11 attacks had existed within disparate parts of the government and private data sources in the United States. Rather than an overall lack of information, the problem was thought to be that no single agency or decisionmaker had enough aggregate information and power to recognize the full pattern and to act on what it knew.

To solve this "connect-the-dots" problem, Congress speedily passed the USA PATRIOT Act, giving the government broad new powers and breaking down long-held distinctions in American law and practice between domestic and foreign intelligence and between intelligence and law enforcement. The Terrorist Threat Integration Center (now the National Counterterrorism Center) was created to integrate and analyze all terrorist-related intelligence and information. The government also embarked on an immense effort, still very controversial and far from complete, to link various federal, state, local, and private sector databases to enhance "information awareness." These initial efforts were reinforced in 2004 by the creation of the Office of the Director of National Intelligence to oversee and coordinate all sixteen agencies within the U.S. intelligence community.

It made sense to move quickly after 9/11 to reassure a nervous public. From a longer-term perspective, however, the success of the 9/11 plot did not mean that the U.S. government was wholly unprepared for terrorism or even that U.S. intelligence was strategically surprised by these attacks. The government had done an enormous amount of work before then on homeland security. It was spending by some measures $16 billion a year to prevent attacks, protect critical targets, and prepare to deal with the consequences of WMD attacks.[4] The intelligence community had even focused specifically on al Qaeda as the principal terrorist threat. Of course, more could have been done. But the real change after 9/11 was in the prioritization of the fight against terrorism and in the wider public's perception of its importance, not in the awareness of the threat within the state security apparatus. For a nation at peace, the United States was enormously aware of terrorist and al Qaeda threats.

Still, after 9/11, many in the U.S. government saw a huge and probably fleeting opportunity to reorganize the government in a manner they had understood to be necessary but politically impossible. They believed that the government security apparatus, a legacy of World War II and the cold war, made little sense for dealing with new problems, including transnational terrorism. For example, border security was divided among numerous agencies in six departments (State, Treasury, Justice, Transportation, Agriculture, and Defense).

The most drastic change was the creation of DHS in 2003, the biggest reorganization of the federal government since 1947. DHS brought together twenty-two previously separate agencies, with more than 200,000 employees and a fiscal year 2009 budget of $50.5 billion. It now includes the Coast Guard, Customs and Border Protection, Immigration and Customs Enforcement, the Secret Service, and the new TSA. The White House also created a Homeland Security Council, analogous to the National Security Council, to coordinate homeland security policy across the federal government. The existence of this council acknowledges that DHS, despite its size and scope, still does not contain all of the governmental assets necessary for homeland security, not the least of them being the FBI, which remains in the Justice Department. Similarly, a National Joint Terrorism Task Force now coordinates efforts between the federal government and state and local officials.

Complementing these reorganizations is an enormous increase in resources. Beyond the tripling of overall homeland security expenditures, the share of FBI resources devoted to counterterrorism has doubled, and the combined total of CIA and FBI personnel working on terrorist financing alone increased from under a dozen to more than 300 in the two years following 9/11.[5] International cooperation in sharing information on suspected terrorists has improved, extending beyond countries that have been helpful over many years, such as France and Britain, to include many other states, particularly Pakistan and Saudi Arabia, who now take the threat more seriously.

Suspicious ships entering U.S. waters are now more likely to be screened. The country's exposure to biological attack has been lessened by stockpiling tens of millions of doses of antibiotics and enough smallpox vaccine for every U.S. resident.[6] Oversight has been tightened on labs working with biological materials. Terrorism insurance is now back-stopped by a new federal program. Certain types of major infrastructure, such as well-known bridges and tunnels, are protected by police and National Guard forces during terrorism alerts. Nuclear reactors have better protection. Federal agencies are required to have security programs for their information technology networks, and many private firms have backed up their headquarters and their data banks so that operations could continue after the catastrophic loss of a main site.[7]

THE WAGES OF HOMELAND SECURITY

Many of these measures were eminently sensible and, along with operations abroad, have helped prevent another major terrorist attack: in essence, we are safer. But, they have not been cost free.

First, there are direct costs, not only $66 billion in fiscal year 2009 federal dollars but also some unknown multiple of that figure in nonfederal spending. Los Angeles International Airport, for example, has to spend $100,000 per day for additional security when the alert goes from yellow to orange. Multiply that sum for alerts at other major airports and for more orange days, and the numbers rise quite quickly.[8] This level of spending also means that other priorities go unfunded. For example, the FBI investigated only about half as many criminal cases in 2004 as in 2000 and conducted 70 percent fewer drug-related investigations.[9]

Because much of this spending is not driven by any threat analysis, nearly any expenditure can be justified, and one has little basis for saying whether these trade-offs are worthwhile or whether the money was wasted. The allocations of homeland security funds to rural areas far from the terrorist radar screen and for the protection of miniature golf courses are ample indications that much of the spending is simply pork.[10] Terrorism is used to justify increases in expenditure on everything from antipoverty programs to gun control to HIV/AIDS. One enterprising senator applied it to prescription drug benefits, citing the "terror" caused by lack of access to medications.[11]

Second, the shift of so many organizations to DHS, whose overriding goal and ethos is counterterrorism and homeland security, has slighted other missions. So, for example, transferring the Federal Emergency Management Agency (FEMA) to DHS meant that FEMA paid less attention to natural disasters, with the result that an organization that in the 1990s excelled at hurricane response was unready for Hurricane Katrina in 2005.

Third, homeland security measures impose less tangible costs. Stepped-up security imposes great inconvenience on the public and increases the general level of anxiety. Increased surveillance necessarily compromises civil liberties and privacy. Controversies over warrantless wiretapping, for example, stir up divisive political debates and divert attention from other important issues. Insidiously, these measures often fall hardest on specific ethnic minorities and foreign nationals, especially those from Islamic countries, whose goodwill is most necessary for any long-term victory in the war on terror.[12] The increased difficulties that foreign students, workers, and tourists have in entering and living in the United States may have helped protect the homeland, but also they have reduced our competitiveness, restricted our access to foreign talent, and hurt our standing abroad. We have no way of assessing whether this trade-off was worthwhile.

THE ENEMY WITHOUT

The key to understanding how to make such trade-offs lies in understanding the nature of the terrorist threat. There can be little doubt that al Qaeda and like-minded terrorist groups retain the desire to carry out attacks within the United States. According to an October 2005 speech by President Bush, the United States has disrupted three attempted al Qaeda strikes inside the United States and intercepted at least five more terrorist efforts to case targets or infiltrate the country. Terrorism continues to flourish abroad, with attacks in Spain, Morocco, Tunisia, Saudi Arabia, Pakistan, Indonesia, and the United Kingdom. And of course, the war in Iraq seems to be incubating an entire new generation of jihadis.

Intent, though, is not capability. Given the loose international environment and well-documented holes in U.S. homeland security, the failure of jihadis to carry out even one small-scale attack in the United States in more than six years implies that they have some serious weaknesses, weaknesses that can inform an analytical approach to homeland security.

Terrorism analysts typically divide the jihadist threat into three categories.[13] First is the al Qaeda core, an organization based in the border region of Pakistan and Afghanistan with tentacles in many other countries. This is the organization that carried out the 9/11 attacks. The second category contains local, organized groups such as the Moroccan Islamic Combatant Group (GICM) and Jemaah Islamiyah in Indonesia. Sharing the general ideological disposition of the al Qaeda core and maintaining some links with it, these groups have carried out recent attacks in numerous countries—and they plague Iraq. Finally, there are specific lone individuals or isolated cells, inspired by al Qaeda or Islamist ideology, such as the perpetrators of the London attacks in 2005.

The al Qaeda Core

Since 9/11, the U.S. counterterrorism campaign has greatly weakened the al Qaeda core. Its sanctuary and training camps in Afghanistan have been eliminated, large numbers of its leaders have been killed, captured, or at least identified, and the remaining leaders spend much of their time and effort avoiding capture. Stepped-up cooperation between U.S. and allied intelligence services and increased monitoring of communications have made it far more difficult to carry out, undetected, a global conspiracy of the size and complexity favored by the core. Improved border security and greater identification of al Qaeda members have forced them to rely on local groups, of which there are none in the United States, and have disrupted key members' communications and travel, particularly to this country.

The core has proved very innovative in its techniques, but it has demonstrated a penchant for spectacular attacks against certain types of targets, especially symbolic targets of American power, military targets, and civil aviation. This pattern is not merely a result of habit; it reflects the core's strategy of demonstrating that it is engaged in a legitimate and effective war against the United States, while not alienating its recruiting base of ordinary Muslims through wanton, indiscriminate violence. As Bruce Hoffman has observed, "Radical in politics, terrorists are frequently just as conservative in their operations, adhering to an established modus operandi."[14]

The rather grandiose summer 2006 plot against airliners leaving the United Kingdom—apparently the first serious plot by the al Qaeda core in years—demonstrated that it remains wedded to large, complex schemes against civil aviation and also how hard it has become to carry such schemes to fruition. The plot was apparently discovered through intelligence several months before it was to have been carried out, and it was not even attempted in the United States. None of this means that the al Qaeda core is vanquished. Indeed, there is evidence of a revival in the tribal regions of Pakistan. But its ability to conduct complex, spectacular attacks, particularly in the United States, has been dramatically diminished.

Domestic Organized Groups

The most serious weakness of terrorists in attacking the U.S. homeland is that organized groups that share Islamist ideology and resort to terrorism do not exist in the U.S. homeland. Such local groups would apparently garner no real support in the American Arab or Muslim community, a precondition for their emergence. In the immediate aftermath of 9/11, American officials estimated that al Qaeda might have up to 5,000 affiliates in the United States. After extensive searching, however, an FBI report in 2005 concluded that there apparently were no al Qaeda cells or affiliated organizations in the United States.[15] The 9/11 plot originated abroad and apparently did not receive any help from coconspirators resident in the United States. The absence of such indigenous groups is what most sets the United States apart from countries, including many in Europe, that have experienced Islamist terror attacks since 9/11.

Isolated Terrorists

Perhaps the most worrisome category from the perspective of U.S. homeland security consists of lone individuals or isolated cells that are inspired by Islamist ideology but operate mostly on their own, with few links to the international jihad. As was demonstrated in London and Oklahoma City (by domestic terrorists), these disgruntled elements could construct homemade bombs and conceivably kill dozens or even hundreds of people. There have been many examples of people contemplating various types of small-scale attacks within the United States since 9/11.

Fortunately, terrorists in this category are the least skilled. The attacks that they have considered have been generally very small scale, and indeed most have failed or been foiled long before coming even close to fruition. Many did not progress beyond the discussion stage, and a few aspiring terrorists had to be instructed in terrorism targets and techniques by FBI informants. Others involved plots that were hopelessly absurd, including a scheme to attack the Brooklyn Bridge with a blowtorch. It would certainly be rash to dismiss the possibility that an attack from this quarter might occur at any time and that it might kill many people. But it would certainly be much smaller than the 9/11 attack and essentially without consequence for the functioning of American society. Because of the isolated nature of these groups, it would not be a harbinger of a sustained terrorist campaign within the United States.

CREATING A THREAT-BASED HOMELAND SECURITY STRATEGY

This analysis of the terrorist threat implies several priorities for U.S. homeland security—and, conversely, several areas that do *not* need greater attention or spending. *Catastrophic WMD scenarios dominate U.S. homeland security planning, but the weakness of the al Qaeda core and its inability to operate in the United States, the lack of organized indigenous groups, and the low skills of the isolated cells make such an attack unlikely.* The main priority should be to keep al Qaeda on its heels through cooperation and intelligence sharing with foreign partners; to track members of the al Qaeda core; and to inhibit their ability to rest, plan, communicate, or travel. This implies that alienating foreign partners for the purposes of fighting terrorism abroad may be counterproductive for homeland security

Even assuming a revival of the al Qaeda core, previous patterns suggest that it will continue to attempt to strike at already well-guarded targets, particularly civil aviation, military targets, and symbols of American power. It has indicated an interest also in attacking nuclear plants but has not attempted such an attack so far. Efforts to protect nuclear power plants and continued "overprotection" of civil aviation are reasonable investments. In particular, we should prioritize efforts to better inspect air cargo and checked luggage and to protect civil airliners against surface-to-air missiles.

At the same time, some potential targets merit *less* attention. Enormous expenditures on protecting less glamorous economic targets—so-called critical infrastructure such as ports, food distribution systems, and information systems—are largely misplaced. These systems are certainly vulnerable and important to the U.S. economy, but concern for them reflects a certain mirror imaging: we reason that if we wanted to cripple the U.S. economy, we would attack these targets. Yet the al Qaeda core has been wholly uninterested in these targets for reasons of ideology and audience. According to terrorism analyst Dan Byman, "When selecting their targets,

[Islamist terrorists] prefer to impress Islamists, and particularly *jihadists,* over Americans. An attack that devastates a dam along a river in the Midwest may be costly for Americans, but it has far less appeal than an attack on a national icon."[16]

By contrast, protecting the broad array of targets that might be attacked by isolated cells or individuals is both impossible and inordinately expensive, given the limited damage they could conceivably inflict. Some argue that these attacks must be stopped at all costs, not because of the damage they inflict but rather because of the damage that would be caused by the public reaction. Thus, just as 9/11 is said to have crippled the aviation industry because people were afraid to fly, an attack on a subway or bus in the United States would suppress economic activity across the country. To the extent that this is the case, it makes more sense to confront this reaction directly rather than to attempt to avoid every attack. Priority should be given to building a degree of *resilience* into U.S. society. Rather than asserting that such attacks represent a concerted effort to, in the words of former DHS inspector general Clark Kent Ervin, "terrorize the entire nation," the government should help educate the public that such attackers have limited capabilities and that extraordinary protective measures are unnecessary.[17]

Finally, and most important, we need to recognize that the relative safety of the U.S. homeland compared with that of other countries comes less from our broad oceans or our antiterrorist measures than from the absence of any indigenous terrorist groups. A top priority for homeland security should be to *avoid creating grievances within the American Arab and Muslim communities.* The outlook for this is fairly good at the moment—there is little indication that American Muslims are leaning toward such action in any sort of numbers.[18] Nonetheless, the federal government, in coordination with local governments, needs a sustained effort to reach out to these communities, to consult them on counterterrorism measures, and to create a process that will ensure that their concerns are taken into account in formulating policy. Homeland security actions that, in the name of closing vulnerabilities, alienate this community are probably counterproductive in the long run and should at the very least be complemented by positive efforts to engage the community. For example, most of the Islamic charities in the United States have been shut down since 9/11 on suspicion that they fund terrorism. But Islamic charities are an important outlet for American Muslim communities, and the federal government has essentially ignored their requests for assistance in forming charities that can pass governmental scrutiny.

CONCLUDING OBSERVATIONS

Implementing a threat-based homeland security strategy will be politically difficult. Although U.S. policymakers often say that homeland invulnerability is impossible, they are rarely able to accept the political consequences of that fact. Vulnerability means accepting that we cannot always be protected and that terrorist attacks can occur. It means that we have to make hard choices about how much to spend and what to leave vulnerable. It means that we may need to accept greater risk to preserve the friends we need and to avoid alienating those who might do even greater harm in the future. None of these are messages that the public may want to hear, but they are the realities of the age in which we live. The president should make it clear that the alternatives are wasteful spending, costly diversion from other essential tasks, wholesale suppression of civil liberties, and, ironically, heightened danger of terrorist attacks.

NOTES

1. For some government planning scenarios along these lines, including such novel plots as terrorist cyber attacks and attacks on the U.S. food supply, see GlobalSecurity.org's webpage (www.globalsecurity.org/security/ops/ter-scen.htm).

2. Office of Management and Budget (OMB), *Analytical Perspectives, Budget of the United States Government, Fiscal Year 2009* (Government Printing Office, 2009), table 3-7.

3. Veronique de Rugy, "Facts and Figures about Homeland Security Spending" (Washington: American Enterprise Institute, December 14, 2006); see also OMB, *Analytical Perspectives,* table 3-1.

4. Before 9/11, there was no "homeland security" spending category, so pre-9/11 homeland security spending can only be estimated. One estimate of pre-9/11 homeland security spending appears in James Jay Carafano and Steven M. Kosiak, "Homeland Security: Administration's Plan Appears to Project Little Growth in Funding" (Washington: Center for Strategic and Budgetary Assessments, March 12, 2003).

5. Speech of President George W. Bush at the FBI Academy at Quantico, Virginia, September 10, 2003.

6. Tom Ridge, "Since That Day," *Washington Post,* September 11, 2003.

7. On labs, see Martin Enserink, "Facing a Security Deadline, Labs Get a 'Provisional' Pass." *Science* 302, no. 5647 (November 7, 2003), p. 962; on nuclear reactors,

see Jim Wells, *Nuclear Regulatory Commission: Preliminary Observations on Efforts to Improve Security at Nuclear Power Plants*, testimony before the Subcommittee on National Security, Emerging Threats, and International Relations, Committee on Government Reform, House of Representatives, 108 Cong. 2 sess., GAO-04-1064T (Government Accountability Office, September 14, 2004); on information technology, see John Moteff, "Computer Security: A Summary of Selected Federal Laws, Executive Orders, and Presidential Directives," Congressional Research Service Report for Congress RL32357 (Library of Congress, April 16, 2004), p. 2.

8. John Mueller, *Overblown* (New York: Free Press, 2006), p. 161.

9. U.S. Department of Justice, Office of the Inspector General, "Top Management and Performance Challenges in the Department of Justice—2006" (www.usdoj.gov/oig/challenges/2006.htm).

10. James Fallows, "Success without Victory," *Atlantic Monthly* (January–February 2005).

11. Mueller, *Overblown*, p. 43.

12. On the treatment of foreign nationals, see David Cole, *Enemy Aliens: Double Standards and Constitutional Freedoms in the War on Terrorism* (New York: New Press, 2003).

13. This division of the threat follows Dan Byman and others. See, for example, Daniel Byman, *The Five Front War: The Better Way to Fight Global Jihad* (Hoboken, N.J.: Wiley, 2007). Appendix I of this book includes a list of people charged with contemplating terrorist attacks in the United States since 9/11.

14. Bruce Hoffman, "The Modern Terrorist Mindset: Tactics, Targets, and Technologies," Columbia International Affairs Online Working Paper ((St. Andrew's University, Scotland: Centre for the Study of Terrorism and Political Violence, October 1997), p. 10.

15. On the 5,000 figure, see Mueller, *Overblown*, p. 38; on the FBI report, see Eric Lichtblau, "Security Report on U.S. Aviation Warns of Holes," *New York Times*, March 14, 2005, p. A6.

16. Byman, *The Five Front War*, chapter 5.

17. Clark Kent Ervin, *Open Target: Where America Is Vulnerable to Attack* (New York: Palgrave Macmillan, 2006), p. 34.

18. For an examination of how homeland security measures are affecting the American Muslim population, see Paul Barrett, *American Islam: The Struggle for the Soul of a Religion* (New York: Farrar, Straus and Giroux, 2006).

PART

OUR SOCIETY

13

Empowering Moderate Voters

Implement an Instant Runoff Strategy

JOHN EDWARD PORTER

SUMMARY ❱ U.S. elections and the conduct of elected representatives in recent years have been characterized by excessive partisanship that impedes their performance and, more important, thwarts the fundamental purposes of representative government. The next president should promote the concept of "instant runoffs" in U.S. elections in order to give candidates who appeal to a broader range of the electorate a better chance to win their races and serve our citizenry. Specifically, the next administration should work to achieve either

—more competitive districts in which the parties must nominate candidates who appeal to moderate and independent voters, or

—instant runoff voting elections that permit voters to participate in deciding the final victors without narrowing the field in a party primary or two separate elections. ❱

CONTEXT ❱ The problem of gerrymandered districts for seats in the U.S. House of Representatives is not new, but it reached new heights during the 1990s. In recent years, redistricting patterns have created an extraordinarily high number of "safe districts," in which the incumbent or the incumbent party is highly likely to gain reelection. The 2006 election, in which a relatively large number of seats changed party, was an exceptional case, and it should not blind us to the general problem—even in 2006, more than seven in ten U.S. House elections (73 percent) were won by landslide margins of more than 20 percent. Nor should it reassure us that future elections will be competitive.

The U.S. Supreme Court has adopted three basic principles for congressional redistricting: one person, one vote; protection for minorities; and observance of traditional political boundaries when it does not interfere with observance of the first two principles. (Only a minority opinion has intimated the need for *competitive* districts.) Legislative redistricting proposals are subject to federal court review to determine whether they comport with these three principles.

Redistricting plans generally are drawn up by the state's legislature and governor. In only two states is redistricting conducted by a nonpartisan commission and in only a few by a bipartisan commission. Thus, in almost every case, the map of one party or another becomes the redistricting template, creating relatively safe districts for the majority and minority party alike. Only rarely does the party whose map is adopted put its own incumbents at risk.

In "safe districts," the primary often is the real election, and it does not represent moderate Americans' views well. In a predominantly one-party district, the candidate who wins the primary is very likely to win the general election. Considering that the more liberal Democrats and the more conservative Republicans—usually a small fraction of a district's eligible voters—are the people most likely to vote in primaries, the more extreme candidates are the ones most likely to prevail.

Unfortunately, the "moderate middle"—some 70 percent of the electorate—is left out of this process. Many moderate voters do not feel comfortable declaring a party affiliation, and many independent voters simply refuse to vote in primaries. And, in some states, people who are not registered with a party—that is, independent voters—are barred from voting in primary elections, even if they want to. Finally, many voters do not understand the importance of primaries and choose to vote only in the "real election." ❱

REFORMING THE ELECTION PROCESS

The purpose of primary elections is, in theory, to give voters the best candidates. In practice, primaries are a dismal failure.

Reassessing the Primary System

In the days of the party bosses, when candidates were picked in the legendary smoke-filled back rooms, the bosses at least had to consider which individuals would have broad enough voter appeal to win the elections. But today, with redistricting done according to Court principles and with the primary system used to select candidates, a small number of voters can ensure that the nation consistently elects the farthest left and the farthest right candidates.

Do our elected representatives then go to Washington intending to work with one another to try to solve the nation's problems in a cooperative and collegial atmosphere? Clearly, and sadly, no. Members of Congress come to Washington believing that they have a voter mandate to uphold their party's principles and that those principles—and only those principles—directly reflect the national interest. Such individuals have no intent or interest in compromising or collaborating with the "enemy" on much of anything. For example, for a long while the California congressional delegation—the nation's largest, containing many of the House of Representatives' most liberal Democratic and most conservative Republican members—never met to work together for the benefit of their state; in fact, many never even spoke to one another.

Campaign finance reform that would result in public funding of elections and eliminate as much party, political action committee (PAC), and individual support as possible is, without question, the most important change needed in our broken election system. However, achieving reform is difficult and its prospects doubtful. Meanwhile, the next president could make a substantial contribution to achieving a more representative democracy by working to fix another problem—that is, often the primary election serves, for all practical purposes, as the general election. That can be accomplished by ensuring that, wherever possible, we have either competitive districts in which the parties must nominate candidates who appeal to moderate and independent voters or elections that permit voters to participate in deciding the final victors without voting in a party primary or two separate elections.

Models for Change

Competitive districts are more likely to occur in states like Iowa, where an independent commission is charged with initially drawing the redistricting maps and the political culture generally respects the commission's judgment. But other states have been unable to move toward such commissions. In California, Governor Arnold Schwarzenegger is now making his third attempt to design a fairer redistricting process, working with reformers from across the political spectrum.

Even Louisiana, which has had more than its share of political scandals, has devised a better election system, one that eliminates party primaries in state races. When Louisianans go to the polls to select a governor, for example, they find all the candidates for each office on one ballot, identified by party or not, as the candidates choose. If no candidate receives more than 50 percent of the votes cast for a particular office, the top two vote-getters appear in a runoff election several weeks later.

The preceding two reform models are not necessarily appropriate for national implementation. Iowa's redistricting system probably will not work in states with a more contentious political culture, and Louisiana's approach involves frequent runoff elections that require voters to make a second trip to the polls.

A third—and extremely promising—way to move to a more representative democracy is through what is called "instant runoff voting" (IRV) or sometimes "ranked choice voting." IRV was invented by Professor W. R. Ware at the Massachusetts Institute of Technology in 1870. It was first used in governmental elections in the 1890s and is used today to elect Australia's house of representatives, Ireland's president, and the mayors of Wellington, New Zealand, and London, England. Recommended by Robert's Rules of Order as a means to elect majority winners, IRV is used for student elections in more than three dozen American universities and for the leadership of the American Political Science Association.

With IRV, winners must demonstrate both strong first choice support and acceptability to the majority. Voters indicate their choices as first, second, third, fourth, and so on, up to the number of candidates on the ballot for a particular office. If one candidate receives a majority of first-choice votes, he or she wins. If no candidate receives a majority of first-choice votess, the candidate with the *fewest* first-choice votes is eliminated. His or her votes are then added to those of the remaining candidates those voters chose second. The process repeats until one candidate wins with a majority of the votes. In one trip to the polls, the election is over, no party affiliation needs to be expressed, no later runoff is held.

Table 13-1. Frank's Voters' Second Choices

Candidate	Round 1: All voters' first choices	Round 2: Frank's voters' second choices	Final tally
Mark	38 votes	17 votes	55 votes
Ellen	42 votes	3 votes	45 votes
Frank	20 votes	Eliminated	

HOW INSTANT RUNOFF VOTING WORKS

Several methods of instant runoff voting are used in the United States and numerous foreign countries. The following examples show how the process might work in two-way and three-way (or more) races. For simplicity's sake, in this example, assume that there were 100 voters, so that the number of votes a candidate receives and the percentage of the vote received are the same. Our candidates are Mark and Ellen. Let's say that, in a traditional two-way race, the results are as follows:

Mark: 55

Ellen: 45.

Mark is the obvious winner.

Now Frank enters the race. The same voters voting for the same office might generate this result:

Mark: 38

Ellen: 42

Frank: 20.

Ellen receives even fewer votes than she did in the two-way race, but in a conventional election, she would win despite having less than a majority of the votes.

But with instant runoff voting, the election would not be decided until one candidate has a majority. If that cannot be achieved based on voters' first choices, then the second choices of some of them come into play. In this example, candidate Frank is eliminated, because he finished in last place. Frank's votes are then reassigned to his voters' second-choice candidate. Frank's voters' second choices are depicted in table 13-1.

In this example, Mark wins, just as he did when there were only two candidates. The effect of a "spoiler" candidate—that is, one who cannot win but draws enough votes from others so that no one has a majority—is thus avoided.

In elections with more than three candidates, the runoff process can be repeated, each time dropping the lowest vote-getter and reallocating his or her votes until one candidate has a majority of the votes—the "50 percent plus one" system. This system produces a result that better reflects the preferences of the majority of voters.

THE POLITICS OF INSTANT RUNOFF VOTING

IRV has drawn the support of the League of Women Voters in several states and of leading elected officials such as 2008 presidential candidates Senators John McCain and Barack Obama. Since 2002 IRV has been adopted by at least a dozen U.S. cities for their nonpartisan elections, including San Francisco and Minneapolis, and has proved both fair and efficient. Certainly the outcomes better reflect the preferences of the electorate and, in all types of elections, can mitigate the impact of a "spoiler" candidate who splits the majority vote.

In partisan elections, IRV can be used in three basic ways. First, states could use IRV only in their primary elections to ensure nominees have majority support within their party; several states already hold two-round runoff elections to accomplish this objective, although voter turnout typically plunges in the second round. Second, states could hold IRV in general elections without changing their primary system; in 2008 Vermont's legislature passed a bill to establish IRV for general elections to the U.S. House of Representatives and U.S. Senate.

The most promising approach for promoting both increased voter choice and moderation, however, is to make use of IRV's ranked-choice feature to fold its primary into the general election. Pierce County, Washington, will use this system for its county executive election in 2008. There will be no primaries. Candidates will go straight to the November ballot, and voters will use IRV to elect a majority winner among a full array of choices. Even in a "one-party district," all general election voters will have more choices among candidates of the majority party, along with candidates who are independent or aligned with other parties. Winners will need to work harder and be more inclusive to earn a majority of the general election vote—certainly more so than if they only needed to win in a low-turnout primary followed by a separate general election.

IRV remains a new idea, but my own experience with a different election method in my home state of Illinois suggests the value of experimentation. Implemented for state house of representatives elections after the Civil War as a means to help heal the wounds of that conflict in a divided state, cumulative voting meant that three representatives represented every district. Almost every district elected representatives of both major parties because voters could choose to award all their three votes to one candidate or split them among two or all three, and rarely could one party sweep all three seats. I won my first election in this system in 1972 and enjoyed a politics in Springfield founded on more cooperation across party lines and more independent voices within parties. Its repeal in 1980 when the state decreased the size of the legislature remains much lamented by elders in both parties.

With the new administration's support, IRV can turn U.S. elections from an embarrassment into a much closer representation of the democratic ideal.[1]

CONCLUDING OBSERVATIONS

Our next president should work aggressively toward bringing moderate and independent voters back into the election process. The election of less partisan, more mainstream candidates to offices of all kinds will reduce the rancor and extremism that currently characterize U.S. politics, drive more and more Americans away from the polls, and even discourage them from seeking political careers. Assuredly, it is in our president's best interest to have a Congress (and other elected officials) willing to compromise and collaborate on solving the many serious issues that confront the United States today.

NOTE

1. More information about IRV can be found at www.fairvote.org.

14

Rethinking U.S. Rental Housing Policy

Build on State and Local Innovations

BRUCE KATZ AND MARGERY AUSTIN TURNER

SUMMARY ❯ The subprime mortgage crisis has suddenly brought housing back on the national policy agenda. But while federal policymakers naturally focus their attention on crisis abatement, the country's broader housing challenges, particularly in the rental sector, also deserve attention and demand structural reform. If we are serious about our commitment to grow the national economy, make work pay, leave no child behind, and grow in environmentally sustainable ways, we must more effectively tackle today's rental housing problems. The next president should reinvigorate national rental housing policy, building on the innovations being tested in various states and locales. Specifically, the president should promote a housing policy under which

—the federal government assumes responsibility for boosting the purchasing power of low-income renters to cover the cost of decent quality housing through a combination of an increased minimum wage, an expanded Earned Income Tax Credit, and targeted housing vouchers;

—state and local governments take the lead in expanding the supply of moderately priced rental units, using a combination of regulatory tools and capital subsidies;

—the federal government employs a carrot-and-stick strategy to ensure that state and local governments reduce regulatory barriers that artificially constrain housing production and drive up costs; expand the stock of affordable rental housing in locations where it is needed; and ensure full and fair access to regionwide housing opportunities for low-income and minority households.

This new blueprint for federal rental housing policy responds to the root causes of current challenges, respects the creativity and capacity of state and local governments, catalyzes private market forces, links housing reform more closely to transportation and energy policies, and creates new housing opportunities for many more low- and moderate-income Americans. ❚

CONTEXT ❚ One-third of all Americans—more than 37 million households—rent, and a growing share of renters cannot find homes or apartments that they can reasonably afford. Moreover, as metropolitan areas sprawl outward and jobs become increasingly dispersed, fewer low-wage renters can find housing near their workplace. While employment growth is fastest in the low-density counties on the fringes of U.S. metropolitan areas, affordable housing—and affordable rental housing in particular—remains disproportionately located in inner-city and older suburban neighborhoods. In fact, in many metropolitan areas, a substantial share of the affordable rental stock is concentrated in distressed, high-poverty neighborhoods.

These challenges warrant more serious and sustained policy attention than they currently receive, both because they create hardship for low- and moderate-income families across the country and because they undermine other high-priority policy agendas. Specifically, the lack of affordable housing hinders economic productivity and undermines the premise that full-time workers should be able to achieve a decent standard of living. The concentration of affordable housing in distressed inner-city neighborhoods traps low-income children in dangerous places where public schools are failing. And the mismatch between employment and affordable housing locations contributes to environmentally and fiscally wasteful patterns of sprawl.

Today's rental housing market challenges reflect a confluence of demographic, economic, and social forces that the current array of federal housing programs can no longer effectively address.

Nationwide, rents are rising faster than incomes for a growing segment of the workforce. Specifically, gross rents (which include utility costs) have been growing faster than inflation, while the median renter's monthly income has declined 7.3 percent since 2000. As a result, average gross rents as a share of renter income have grown from 26.5 percent in 2000 to 30.3 percent today. This trend is primarily the result of widening income inequality—with incomes rising much more slowly for low- and moderate-wage workers than for those in high-skill, high-wage jobs.

The increase in rents is matched by increases in the costs of other, related necessities—transportation and energy. The burden of transportation and housing costs approaches 60 percent of income in the top 100 metropolitan areas and is increasing as gasoline prices rise. Very low-income households face especially painful trade-offs as they struggle to pay for rising home energy costs, particularly in older homes and in apartments that are not energy efficient.

Moreover, *in prosperous metropolitan areas,* the supply of housing is not keeping pace with employment and population growth. Local zoning laws, land use controls, and other regulatory barriers limit total housing production, raise the cost of new units, and often prevent the production of low-cost units. As population expands in a market with constrained supply, the increased competition for units causes prices to rise, even for households that do not typically rely on new construction for their housing. In effect, the traditional "filtering" process—in which older housing units become more affordable over time while the most affluent households trade up to new units—cannot function properly when supply falls too far short of growing demand.

According to Harvard's Joint Center on Housing, the ongoing subprime crisis has placed even more pressure on the rental market. The homeownership boom of the early part of this decade caused the production of new rental properties to decline for five straight years between 2002 and 2007. Foreclosures have further diminished rental housing availability; in New York City, for example, 60 percent of foreclosures in 2008 were two- to four-unit or multifamily buildings. And at the same time that supply has fallen, demand for rental housing has grown, because of the foreclosure crisis and larger demographic forces.

Within metropolitan areas, affordable rental housing is especially scarce in communities where job opportunities are expanding. Historically, both jobs and affordable rental housing were concentrated in central city locations. But over the last few decades, employment growth has become increasingly dispersed, while exclusionary zoning laws have limited the development of rental housing in many suburban communities. Central cities, then, remain the primary source of affordable rental housing within most metropolitan regions. Nationally, 45 percent of all renters and two-thirds of poor renters live in central cities.

The clustering of affordable rental housing in *central city neighborhoods* concentrates minority poverty and exacerbates distress. Although most poor Americans live in non-poor neighborhoods, 7.9 million poor people still lived in "extreme poverty" census tracts in 2000, and more than half of all high-poverty neighborhoods are predominantly Black or Hispanic.[1] Residents of these distressed neighborhoods often fall victim to a host of undesirable outcomes: higher rates of crime, teenage pregnancy, and educational failure; poor health and mental health; reduced private sector investment and higher prices for basic consumer goods; and greater dependence on overburdened local governments.

The existing panoply of federal rental housing policies can claim credit for some important accomplishments, but it now suffers from serious failures of scale, design, and implementation. Most significant is that the gap between housing needs and subsidy resources is steadily widening, with no resolution in sight. Since federal housing assistance is not an entitlement, only about one-third of eligible households receive assistance.[2] In essence, low-income renters participate in a national "housing lottery" in which the distribution of housing has ceased to be fair or rational.

In addition, programs to produce more rental housing units continue to focus on inner-city neighborhoods—further concentrating poverty rather than expanding access to opportunity. A recent analysis revealed that central cities received 58 percent of all metropolitan Low-Income Housing Tax Credit units built during the 1990s, even though they are home to only 38 percent of metropolitan residents. And one of every seven tax-credit projects sited in a central city is located in a neighborhood of extreme poverty.

Finally, federal programs provide few incentives to states and localities to remove the regulatory barriers that raise production costs and distort the location of rental housing. Thus, scarce federal production resources do not go as far as they could, with per-unit costs of production increased by burdensome local regulations and administrative procedures. And the federal government "looks the other way" when local jurisdictions implement policies that effectively disallow the construction and operation of affordable rental housing.

In the absence of federal leadership on rental housing policy, many local and state governments have stepped into the void because *they increasingly recognize the connection between the availability of affordable housing and future economic vitality.* As a consequence, they have begun to build effective coalitions in support of policies that

—boost incomes so that more working families can afford the cost of housing,

—reorient the regulatory environment to encourage the production of new rental housing where it is needed most,

—expand support for the production and preservation of moderately priced housing.

On the income side, twenty-nine states plus the District of Columbia have enacted minimum wages higher than the federal standard and twenty-two states plus the District now have their own earned income tax credit programs, which—like the federal program—supplement the incomes of workers who earn up to twice the poverty-level income. On the regulatory side, more than 130 localities nationwide are boosting the production of affordable housing through inclusionary zoning ordinances, and a handful of states, like Illinois and California, have enacted anti-NIMBY ("Not In My Back Yard") statutes to expand supply, particularly in restricted communities. And on the production side, thirty-eight states and more than 500 counties and cities have created housing trust funds and are collectively spending nearly $1.6 billion annually on the production and preservation of affordable housing. ❱

BLUEPRINT FOR RENTAL HOUSING POLICY

The federal housing policy debate can and should be reinvigorated during the next presidential election and beyond, building on the imaginative new solutions arising from state and local governments and the vibrant state and local political coalitions that are successfully promoting meaningful housing reforms and initiatives. These coalitions are using fresh language, deploying new arguments, and involving powerful partners from the business community in their push for change—presenting a potential model for building broader support for a reinvigorated housing policy at the federal level as well.

A New Division of Responsibility

The reawakening of policy innovation at the state and local level is inspiring, but without a renewed commitment from the federal government, it will never be sufficient to address the breadth and depth of the affordable housing challenges that we face today. If the new president is committed to tackling the challenges outlined here, we will need a new division of responsibility. No single level of government can or should try to address today's complex rental housing challenges on its own. Federal, state, and local government all have an essential role to play. Therefore, we propose a new division of responsibility—and accountability—between the federal government and states and localities.

Only the federal government has the fiscal capacity to address the consequences of stagnant wage growth and income inequality nationwide. As long as incomes for a substantial segment of the population fall short of what it takes to cover the costs of producing and operating adequate housing, state and local governments simply cannot afford to close the affordability gap for enough households. Therefore, federal policies should target the demand side of the housing affordability equation, ensuring that all households have sufficient income (or a housing voucher) to make adequate housing affordable.

If the federal government addresses the demand side of today's housing affordability crisis, state and local jurisdictions can and should assume lead responsibility for the remaining, supply-side challenges. Using both regulatory policies and supply-side subsidies, states and localities should create incentives that induce private market actors (both for-profit and nonprofit) to produce and maintain rental housing that is affordable for people with moderate incomes.

Under this basic framework, the federal government would retain a strong interest in the impact of state and local supply-side policies, because federal efforts to boost incomes will come to naught in markets where the housing supply is artificially constrained. Therefore, the federal role with respect to supply-side policy must be to create strong incentives for states and local jurisdictions to reduce regulatory barriers that unnecessarily constrain supply and inflate costs. The goal is to produce affordable rental housing where it is needed most, as well as to ensure that families are not excluded from opportunity-rich communities because of their race or ethnicity.

This proposed strategy goes beyond narrow housing goals to advance a broader set of national priorities that currently are being undermined by the failures of federal housing policy. Specifically, by expanding the availability of affordable housing in regions where jobs are plentiful and the population is expanding, this strategy enhances the economic productivity and competitiveness of the nation as a whole. By raising after-tax wages to a level sufficient to cover the cost of decent housing, it lives up to the fundamental premise that people who work full-time should be able to provide their families with a decent standard of living. By tackling the regulatory barriers that have concentrated affordable rental housing in distressed central-city neighborhoods, it expands opportunities for low-income families to raise their children in safe and healthy communities with well-performing public schools. And by ensuring that quality, affordable housing is built in locationally efficient places, it makes housing part of the sustainability solution.

Boosting Families' Purchasing Power

Ensuring that people who work full-time earn enough to afford decent housing is the critical first step in a twenty-first-century housing policy. The federal minimum wage standard and the Earned Income Tax Credit (EITC) program both represent powerful tools for accomplishing this goal. According to estimates from the National Low Income Housing Coalition, a full-time worker would need to earn close to $16.31 per hour (more than double the federal minimum wage that is scheduled to go into effect in 2009) to afford the average rent for a modest, two-bedroom house or apartment (that is, one costing 30 percent of gross income). Clearly, a substantial increase in the federal minimum wage must be part of a strategy for ensuring that full-time workers earn enough to afford minimally adequate housing.[3]

The minimum wage cannot fill the income gap alone. Currently, the federal Earned Income Tax Credit provides a substantial wage supplement for many working families. In fact, estimates indicate that the EITC already reduces the number of households with a severe housing cost burden by 18 percent. Increasing the EITC, extending it to childless workers, and expanding participation would substantially reduce the number of working families paying an unaffordable amount for housing, even at the current minimum wage. Combining a modest increase in the federal minimum wage with a substantial expansion of the EITC (or the refundable tax credit for renters proposed by John Quigley) offers an administratively efficient strategy for making housing more affordable for many working families.

One of the limitations of a national, income-based strategy is that it fails to reflect variations across markets in the cost of decent housing. In other words, the strategies above may be sufficient in some low-cost markets but still leave working families in high-cost markets with unaffordable rents. One option would be to adjust EITC payments to reflect local housing costs. However, the federal government's primary responsibility should be to bring working people's incomes up to a single, national standard, while creating incentives for state and local governments to reduce the costs of housing locally and to expand the availability of units that are affordable by the national standard.

For households headed by elderly or disabled people who cannot work and for families with children in which adults are not working (or are not working full-time), pools of housing vouchers could be linked to appropriate incentives and services. For example, one pool might be designed to provide a dignified safety net for those who cannot work and who lack the resources to obtain decent housing. Elderly and disabled families could use these vouchers to live in conventional rental housing or to move into supportive housing. Another pool of vouchers might target families leaving welfare, combined with a rent formula that encourages work and a requirement that families enter into a self-sufficiency contract, in order to make the best possible use of housing assistance. A third pool of vouchers might target families with young children living in severely distressed neighborhoods, providing support and help to relocate to communities with well-performing schools.

A potential strategy for encouraging states and localities to expand rental housing production and reduce market rent levels would be to set a single national payment standard for the new vouchers in conjunction with a supplemental fund that local authorities would be required to use to "top up" vouchers to a level sufficient to cover the costs of adequate housing in the local market area. As other state and local policies brought local housing costs down and expanded the stock of moderately priced units, money from this fund that was not needed to supplement federal voucher payments could be redirected to other, locally determined housing purposes.

The federally funded voucher program should be administered regionally, not by individual, local jurisdictions (as is the current Housing Choice Voucher Program). Administration by local public housing agencies fragments the metropolitan rental market, making it difficult for low-income families, particularly minority families living in central cities, to know about and act on the full range of housing options that a voucher makes affordable. Moreover, by automatically assigning responsibility to local public housing agencies, the current system prevents other capable public and private sector entities from administering the program, stifling the innovation that competition can bring. In nonmetropolitan areas, the vouchers should be administered by a state-level entity.

Expanding the Supply of Affordable Housing

If the federal government tackled the income side of the rental housing affordability challenge as outlined above, its supply-side intervention could focus on leveraging the full panoply of state and local powers and policies. More specifically, federal production resources should be designed to encourage state and local governments to be "affordable housing friendly" in the design and application of their regulatory regimes. In that way, federal programs can catalyze the production of substantially more affordable housing than is possible with current or even substantially higher funding levels. Federal production resources also should be allocated in a way that ensures that affordable housing is built in the right places—in communities of choice and opportunity that have good schools and quality jobs.

The federal government should employ a combination of carrots and sticks to effectively guide state and local action. First, existing metropolitan planning organizations (MPOs) should receive federal funding (and technical assistance) to prepare regional housing strategies that complement the regional transportation plans already mandated by federal law. These housing strategies should ensure that all communities in a metropolitan area, including the prosperous ones, participate in the production of housing for families with a broad range of incomes. MPOs are a logical choice for the development of regional housing strategies, given that they are generally governed by elected representatives of city and county governments, have been responsible for metropolitan transportation decisionmaking since the early 1990s, and increasingly are staffed with professionals with planning expertise.

To complement the metropolitan focus of the MPOs, new federal resources should be made available to support and nurture the creation of nonprofit regional housing corporations. The principal task of these corporations would be to develop and preserve affordable rental housing in growing suburban areas. Some would, by necessity, be new nonprofit entities; others would likely evolve from existing community development corporations.

Within this new regional planning framework, cities and urban counties would continue to receive funds from the Home Investment Partnerships (HOME) and Community Development Block Grant (CDBG) programs, but they would be required to implement housing programs in ways that further and are consistent with regional housing strategies. MPOs would have the authority to certify compliance, and cities and counties that did not comply would be given a designated period in which to correct deficiencies or lose federal funding for either housing production or transportation.

To induce more regional collaboration on housing strategies and more affordable rental production in suburban communities—many of which do not currently qualify for HOME or CDBG funding—we propose two new federal incentive funds. A regional sustainability challenge, perhaps enacted as part of federal climate legislation, could entice metropolitan areas to link housing, transportation, land use, and energy policies as a means to reduce greenhouse gas emissions. And a local, affordable housing incentive fund would reward jurisdictions that reduce regulatory barriers and expand the supply of moderately priced rental housing within their borders.

States would continue to administer the Low-Income Housing Tax Credit Program (LIHTC), but the formula for allocating credits would be recalibrated to increase the availability of credits in areas where new rental production is demonstrably needed. And LIHTC income limits and incentives should be adjusted to discourage the concentration of more affordable housing in distressed neighborhoods and to support both housing developments serving a broad range of incomes within revitalizing communities and developments that expand the availability of rental housing for low- and moderate-income households in opportunity-rich communities.

FIRST STEPS

Even if the basic thrust of this new housing policy framework gained wide acceptance, it would take time to transform federal programs and incentives and to build local, state, and regional capacity to perform more effectively. Moreover, the transition to a new system of federal responsibilities would have to include a responsible strategy for dealing with the existing stock of federally subsidized housing—public housing and privately owned rental housing alike. The following are four short-term, high-priority next steps that the new president should take with respect to federal rental housing policy.

—*Require existing metropolitan planning organizations to produce regional housing plans in conjunction with their already mandated transportation plans.* This requirement would begin the process of linking regional housing and transportation and could encourage some metropolitan regions to begin addressing regulatory barriers and other rental housing supply constraints. To support MPOs in this expanded mandate, the federal government should provide funding to enable hiring of qualified housing staff, as well as technical assistance.

—*Create new pools of federal housing vouchers,* to be awarded competitively to local and regional entities that can implement innovative programs linking vouchers with effective support services. The new voucher pools would be explicitly intended to encourage and support work among welfare-leavers and to enable low-income families with children to relocate to communities with high-performing public schools.

—*Expand and retarget the Low-Income Housing Tax Credit program.* First, LIHTC resources should be reallocated to provide more credits to states where rental housing is in short supply and fewer credits to states with sufficient (or excess) supply. In addition, LIHTC income limits should be adjusted so that credits support two distinct types of housing developments: mixed-income housing in revitalizing communities (where the broadest possible mix of incomes is needed) and affordable housing in opportunity-rich communities (where more of the LIHTC units should target low- and moderate-income levels within mixed-income neighborhoods).

—*Preserve and transform the current inventory of public and federally assisted housing through new initiatives.* These new initiatives include a reinvigorated HOPE VI program to demolish and replace severely distressed public housing; reliable federal funding for the renewal of Section 8 contracts; a new block grant program for acquisition and recapitalization of affordable housing by nonprofits, guaranteeing long-term affordability; and the elimination (or reduction) of tax liabilities for owners of federally assisted housing who sell to a nonprofit entity that commits to ensuring the long-term affordability of the housing.

These four steps, all of which could be implemented immediately and at varying scales, offer the new president the opportunity to begin moving federal rental housing policy in a new direction—toward a framework that addresses the fundamental challenges facing the country today. How much would these steps cost? Although the scale of each of the proposals is flexible, a desirable five-year package would include

—1 million new incremental vouchers (phased in over ten years),

—a 20 percent expansion of the LIHTC program,

—restoration of the HOPE VI program to its original scale,

—a comparable annual investment in preservation matching grants,

—exit tax relief for the owners of older subsidized properties.

The cost of this package would total about $2.6 billion in the first year, rising to $6.3 billion in year five. The increased expenditures could be directly accommodated in a broad budget reconciliation package, which undoubtedly will be the subject of congressional action in the next few fiscal years. Increases in appropriations for vouchers, HOPE VI, and preservation will also depend on a new federal budget compact (and specifically the room to expand nondefense discretionary spending) but will be subject to annual decisions by Congress.

CONCLUDING OBSERVATIONS

Ever since its inception in the 1930s, federal rental housing policy has been evolving—responding to market trends, changes in political circumstances, and the shifting philosophies of the day. The pressing housing challenges facing the nation at the start of the twenty-first century require a renewal of the federal rental housing policy, because—left unchecked—current trends threaten to undermine national economic, social, welfare, environmental, and even educational priorities.

These recommendations build on the energy and innovation emerging from state and local leaders across the country. Accordingly, they are meant to be federalist rather than federal and to fully acknowledge the preeminent role of state and local governments in setting the rules of housing production. The recommendations focus primarily on closing the growing gap between wages and rents in the United States They also recognize that the federal role in producing affordable housing must catalyze markets, stimulate the overhaul of regulatory restrictions, promote mixed-income housing, decommission federal enclaves of poverty, support city and suburban collaboration, and diminish the ill effects of balkanized, duplicative, and fiscally wasteful administration.

There are, no doubt, risks to pursuing this strategy, and many constituencies will find greater comfort in protecting their piece of a shrinking pie than in striking out for new, uncharted territory. Yet political risk taking and political leadership are essential if the current stalemate over housing policy is to be broken. The next president should forge a new national compact on housing and launch a period of meaningful policy debate, reform, and action.

ADDITIONAL RESOURCES

Berube, Alan, and Bruce Katz. 2005. "Katrina's Window: Confronting Concentrated Poverty across America." Brookings.

Freeman, Lance. 2004. "Siting Affordable Housing: Location and Neighborhood Trends of Low-Income Housing Tax Credit Developments in the 1990s." Brookings (April) (www.brookings.edu/metro/publications/20040405_freeman.htm).

Glaeser, Edward L., and Joseph Gyourko. 2002. "The Impact of Zoning on Housing Affordability." Discussion Paper 1948. Harvard Institute of Economic Research (March).

Glaeser, Edward L., Joseph Gyourko, and Raven E. Saks. 2005. "Why Have Housing Prices Gone Up?" Discussion Paper 2061. Harvard Institute of Economic Research (February).

Harvard Joint Center for Housing Studies. 2005. "The State of the Nation's Housing 2005" (www.jchs.harvard.edu/publications/markets/son2005/son2005.pdf).

———. 2006. "America's Rental Housing: Homes for a Diverse Nation" (March).

———. 2008. "America's Rental Housing: The Key to a Balanced National Policy." (www.jchs.harvard.edu/publications/rental/rh08_americas_rental_housing/rh08_americas_rental_housing.pdf).

Jargowsky, Paul. 2003. "Stunning Progress, Hidden Problems: The Dramatic Decline of Concentrated Poverty in the 1990s." Presentation at the meeting Stunning Progress, Hidden Problems: The Dramatic Decline of Concentrated Poverty in the 1990s. Brookings (May 19) (www.brookings.edu/metro/speeches/20030519_jargowsky.htm).

Katz, Bruce J., and Margery Austin Turner. 2001. "Who Should Run the Housing Voucher Program? A Reform Proposal." Housing Policy Debate 12, no. 2: 239–62.

Khadduri, Jill, and Charles Wilkins. 2006. "Designing Subsidized Rental Housing Programs: What Have We Learned?" Paper prepared for Revisiting Rental

Housing: A National Policy Summit. Harvard Joint Center for Housing Studies (November 14–15) (www.jchs.harvard.edu/publications/rental/revisiting_rental_symposium/index.htm).

Nagle, Ami, and Nicholas Johnson. 2006. "A Hand Up: How State Earned-Income Tax Credits Help Working Families Escape Poverty in 2006." Washington: Center on Budget and Policy Priorities (March) (www.cbpp.org/3-8-06sfp.htm).

National Low Income Housing Coalition. 2005. "Out of Reach 2005." Washington.

Pendall, Rolf, Robert Puentes, and Jonathan Martin. 2006. *From Traditional to Reformed: A Review of the Land Use Regulations in the Nation's Fifty Largest Metropolitan Areas.* Brookings.

Pettit, Kathryn L. S., and G. Thomas Kingsley. 2003. "Concentrated Poverty: A Change in Course." Washington: Urban Institute.

Quigley, John M. 2006. "Just Suppose: Housing Subsidies for Low-Income Renters." Program on Housing and Urban Policy Working Paper W06-005. University of California–Berkeley, Institute of Business and Economic Research (September) (http://urbanpolicy.berkeley.edu/pdf/QJustSuppose092006.pdf).

Stegman, Michael, Walter Davis, and Roberto Quercia. 2003. "Tax Policy as Housing Policy: The EITC's Potential to Make Housing More Affordable for Working Families." Brookings (October) (www.brookings.edu/metro/publications/200310_stegman.htm).

NOTES

1. This report defines "high-poverty neighborhoods" as those with poverty rates of more than 30 percent and "extreme-poverty neighborhoods" as those with poverty rates of more than 40 percent.

2. This estimate is derived by dividing the total number of directly assisted rental units (4.9 million) by 13.7 million, which is the total number of extremely low-income (less than 30 percent of U.S. average monthly income) and very low-income (less than 50 percent) households, given that most direct federal assistance programs target these income levels.

3. On May 25, 2007, President Bush signed the Fair Minimum Wage Act of 2007 to increase the minimum wage to $7.25 per hour over two years.

15

Attacking Poverty and Inequality

Reinvigorate the Fight
for Greater Opportunity

RON HASKINS AND ISABEL V. SAWHILL

SUMMARY ❱ Although the nation's poverty rate is higher now than it was in the 1970s, no president since Lyndon Johnson has made fighting poverty a major plank of his campaign or a goal of his administration. With large and growing gaps between the rich and the poor, it is now time for presidential candidates and the next president to focus on poverty and inequality in the United States. Evidence suggests that the American people are ready to support a reinvigorated fight.

Three effective ways to reduce poverty are to increase work levels, reverse the growth of single-parent families, and improve educational outcomes. Past initiatives that produced strong results, including welfare reform in the 1990s, can be models for the aggressive pursuit of all three strategies.

Specifically, the next president should undertake a comprehensive assault on poverty and inequality focusing on work, family, and education, which could launch a new generation of effective policies that might include the following:

—Strengthening work requirements in government assistance programs
—Ensuring that the minimum wage does not lose its value to inflation
—Expanding the Earned Income Tax Credit
—Subsidizing child care for low-wage workers
—Promoting marriage as the best environment for rearing children

—Funding effective teen pregnancy prevention efforts, premarital education, and family planning

—Investing in high-quality early childhood education

An effective strategy to expand opportunities will target the bottom third and help people onto and up the ladder that leads to the middle class. It also will draw them into the labor market, reduce dependence on government assistance, create more taxpayers, and improve people's lives.

A comprehensive new strategy would cost about $38 billion a year in new federal funding; the strategy should be enacted only if it is fully paid for by reducing other expenditures. ❚

CONTEXT ❚ Poverty engulfs 13 percent of the total population and 18 percent of the children in the United States. Following an impressive drop in the late 1990s, especially among female-headed families, the poverty rate is higher now than it was in the 1970s. (The federal poverty level was defined as income below $15,700 for a family of three in 2005.) Although the nation has made some progress against poverty in some subgroups of the poor, such as the elderly and female-headed families, a great deal remains to be done.

A major factor in both generating and fighting poverty is the state of the economy. The years since 1979 have seen big increases in income for those at the top of the income distribution, modest increases for those in the middle, and almost no change at all for those at the bottom. What is needed is to pull up the bottom third and help lower-income individuals get their foot on the ladder that leads to the middle class.

Even though the nation has made only modest progress against poverty since the early 1970s, fighting poverty has not been a major part of any president's campaign or a goal of his administration since Lyndon Johnson, and few presidential candidates have put poverty or inequality on the front burner of their campaigns. Ronald Reagan talked about the importance of protecting the "truly needy," but that was a minor theme, at best, during his administration. Bill Clinton quietly expanded assistance for the working poor but avoided talking about poverty, preferring to focus on a middle-class tax cut and "ending welfare as we know it." John Edwards talked about the "two Americas" in his 2004 campaign, but the defeat of the Kerry-Edwards ticket left the issue unaddressed. In 1999–2000, candidate George W. Bush promised to be a compassionate conservative and to "leave no one behind," but poverty has increased under the Bush administration.

The American people may be ready for a fresh look at the question. First, many people across the political spectrum always have believed that helping the poor is a worthy public policy goal, and the Hurricane Katrina experience may have swelled their ranks. Second, welfare reform, because it has successfully moved poor adults into jobs, has refocused attention on the working poor—a group that elicits far more sympathy than those who depend on government assistance. Third, inequality is growing, and the public appears increasingly concerned about the gap between the richest Americans and the poorest. In polls conducted in the fall of 2006, inequality ranked second only to gasoline prices as the economic issue of greatest concern.[1] ❭

FOCUS ON WORK, FAMILY, AND EDUCATION

Why has the nation not made more progress against poverty? After all, in 2004, after adjusting for inflation, the amount that federal and state governments spent on means-tested programs designed to assist the poor— more than $580 billion—had more than quadrupled since 1968.[2] Two factors have undermined both public and private efforts. The first is a set of poverty-increasing trends: the breakdown of the family, stagnation in real wages among low-skilled workers, and the failure of the education system to equip students with the skills needed in the new economy. The second factor is that many antipoverty programs, which merely provide people with cash and other benefits, have failed to address the main causes of poverty—and in some cases have made them worse. We need a new generation of antipoverty policies that focus on requiring and rewarding work, reversing the breakdown of the family, and improving educational outcomes.

Simulation research performed at Brookings demonstrates that increasing workforce participation, increasing marriage rates, and improving education are the three best ways to reduce poverty. Securing full-time jobs for all would reduce poverty 40 percent, restoring marriage rates to 1970s levels would reduce it 30 percent, and achieving universal high school graduation would reduce it 15 percent. By contrast, even doubling cash welfare payments would reduce poverty less than 10 percent.

These projections are consistent with experience. In the 1990s, a robust economy, welfare reform that required mothers to work, and increases in federal benefits for low-income working families combined to increase the work rate of never-married mothers heading families—women with the lowest education and the least job experience—by nearly 40 percent in five years. This is a feat without parallel for any other demographic group in Census Bureau records. Partly as a result of this increased maternal employment, the poverty rate for children in female-headed families fell 30 percent between 1993 and 2000, while poverty among Black children reached its lowest level ever.

One reason for welfare reform's success is that it combined sticks with carrots. Mothers who failed to search for a job could lose their benefits, and there was a five-year time limit on cash welfare payments. The carrots consisted of generous work-support benefits in the form of wage supplements, child care, health insurance, and food stamps for mothers who joined the workforce. Under the old welfare system, when parents left welfare for work, health coverage and other benefits virtually ceased as soon as the paychecks started coming in. In short, policy changes made welfare less desirable and work more desirable. Government action that emphasizes personal responsibility yet supports those who play by the rules can have a major impact on poverty—including concentrated poverty of the kind exposed by Katrina.

ADOPT ALL THREE STRATEGIES TO REDUCE POVERTY

A full package of work-family-education proposals is, in our view, the best bet for ensuring that more children have the skills needed for adult success and that more unskilled adults are able to support their families through work. However, any one of the proposals described below would be a good start on achieving these objectives.

Require and Reward Work

One way to require and reward work is to strengthen work requirements in housing programs. Another way is to adjust the minimum wage to keep it in line with market developments and provide low-income working families with wage supplements and child care assistance.

Strengthen Work Requirements in Housing Programs

As the welfare reform experience shows, increasing work levels reduces poverty, when combined with government benefits that help low-income working families. Yet work requirements in other federal and state programs, including the Food Stamp program, are either weak or nonexistent.[3] One fertile area for strengthening work requirements is housing programs.

Each year, 4.8 million housing units involve some type of federal subsidy, at a total cost of $30 billion. Only units that are in public housing projects impose a work requirement; even there the requirement is just eight hours a month, and it is observed in the breach. Worse, most housing programs actually contain substantial work disincentives: the general rule that beneficiaries must pay 30 percent of their income toward the cost of their unit means that, if they accept a job, their rent goes up by as much as 30 cents for each dollar of earnings. When this obligation is added to FICA and state taxes, many workers in low-wage jobs pay 50 percent or more of their earnings in taxes and extra housing payments. It would be challenging to envision a system that would discourage work more effectively.

A major congressional objection to work mandates is the fear that sanctions will make some residents homeless.[4] However, the large-scale Jobs-Plus demonstration program conducted in public housing units in six cities found that a voluntary program featuring incentives and social supports for work produced very high rates of participation and substantial increases in both work and earnings.[5]

One approach to increasing work would be to give local housing authorities, for a time, the power to impose work mandates and sanctions and allow them to decide whether and how to use them. Under this approach, the Department of Housing and Urban Development (HUD) would have authority to negotiate with local authorities over such particulars as the percentage of housing beneficiaries who would be required to participate, the hours of participation, and the definition of work. The emphasis would be on private sector jobs, with the work program providing jobs of last resort. Participating local authorities would be allowed to forgive the 30 percent rent charge on earnings, with resulting lost local revenues compensated by the federal government. If, after several years, a high percentage of housing beneficiaries still were not working, the approach could be revisited.

Make Work Pay

Some people choose not to join the labor force or to work only sporadically simply because wages for low-skill jobs, which have stagnated in recent decades, are very low and often are not competitive with other sources of income, including crime, government programs, and friends and relatives. To make work pay, the federal government should ensure that the minimum wage does not lose value to inflation, expand the Earned Income Tax Credit (EITC) for those working full-time at low wages, and subsidize child care enough to cover expenses fully (along a sliding scale linked to income).

In combination, these three measures would reduce poverty by about 14 percent, lift 6 million Americans out of poverty, and provide more than 20 million working families with an average benefit of almost $1,500 a year. They also would attract 800,000 more people into the labor market, thereby cutting welfare expenditures and increasing tax revenues.

For low-skilled men, especially minority men, special policies are needed. This group is experiencing falling employment, declining rates of marriage, and distressing rates of crime and incarceration.[6] Along with higher wages, targeted initiatives might dilute this witches' brew of negative outcomes. Increasing the EITC to provide payments up to $2,700 to all low-wage workers over the age of twenty-one who work at least thirty hours a week is one way to reach male low-wage earners who do not have custody of children.[7] In addition, state officials could be given authority to suspend past-due child support obligations for men who obtain jobs and meet future child support obligations. Similarly, a program of early release from prison could target nonviolent offenders who participate in work preparation programs and then hold jobs for prescribed periods of time. All these approaches are promising and merit limited federal funding of state demonstrations.[8]

Restore the Two-Parent Married Family

Restoring the share of children being reared by married couples to 1970s levels would reduce the poverty rate by 20 to 30 percent. Two ways to reduce the prevalence of single-parent families are to reduce teen and out-of-wedlock childbearing and to reduce the incidence of divorce.

Reduce Teen Pregnancies and Out-of-Wedlock Births

Happily, since the early 1990s, teen pregnancy and birth rates have declined about one-third, slowing growth in the proportion of children born outside marriage. If that decrease had not occurred, the number of children from birth to age six living in poverty would be 8.5 percent higher than it is today. Explanations for the decline include more conservative attitudes among the young, heightened concern about sexually transmitted diseases, and greater efforts to prevent teen pregnancy, including messages about abstinence and more effective use of contraception.[9] A future drop in teen childbearing will save taxpayers money since it now costs the federal government at least $9 billion per year in direct costs for health care, foster care, criminal justice, and public assistance programs and in lost tax revenues.[10] Because unwed mothers are less likely to marry than other similar women, a decline in births outside marriage will increase marriage rates as well.[11]

New public messages are vital to reducing teen pregnancy further. Many young people, especially teens, have not fully absorbed the message about the normative ordering of events that is critical to achieving life's goals: finish high school (and, if possible, obtain a two-year or four-year degree), do not marry before your twenties, and wait to have children until after you marry and at least one parent is stably employed.[12] The broadcast media and other communications venues, including the bully pulpit of the presidency, can disseminate knowledge about this success sequence to a broad cross section of society and can send a message about responsibility into the cultural ether.[13] Our nation's leaders should actively discourage unwed childbearing, especially among teens; building on the examples set by Presidents Bill Clinton and George W. Bush, they should promote marriage as the best environment for rearing children.

In addition, the federal government should fund programs that teach values and relationship skills to younger Americans, while providing information about preventing unwanted pregnancies (Such information would include sex education that encourages abstinence among teens but provides accurate information about contraception for those who are sexually active.) Programs that teach responsibility and engage young people in constructive activities through community service are effective in reducing teen pregnancy.[14]

Another way to reduce unplanned pregnancies outside marriage is to provide more family planning services to low-income women. Through Medicaid family planning waivers, states have reduced unintended pregnancies and births and saved money in the process. Providing low-income women with greater access to family planning services through Medicaid is a cost-effective way to reduce the number of children living in poverty.

Reduce Divorce

Divorce rates have leveled off since the 1980s, but divorce nonetheless contributes substantially to the number of children living in single-parent families. One effective way to reduce the risk of divorce (and, thereby, single parenting) is to teach relationship skills to couples who are married or are contemplating marriage.[15] Doubling the number of couples who receive premarital education could reduce divorce rates by 7 percent and, over a decade's time, reduce the number of children living in poverty by at least 160,000. However, not all such programs have been successful. The marriage demonstration programs launched by the Bush administration can serve as a useful foundation. The next president should build on that foundation, supporting investment in learning what works to reduce births to teens and unmarried women while promoting healthier marriages and better relationships.

Improve Educational Outcomes

Americans have long believed that education is the key to economic success. Recent research has added three important insights about the role that education plays in reducing poverty and improving opportunity. First, gaps in skills related to school achievement are present as early as the age of three and persist throughout the school years.[16] Second, from preschool through college, education usually reinforces rather than mitigates preexisting differences between groups defined by race and socioeconomic status. Third, although improvement is needed at every level of schooling, improving preschool programs is more effective than virtually any other intervention in boosting test scores, helping children perform at grade level and avoid special education, increasing high school graduation rates, and producing better economic and social outcomes in the adult years.[17]

To reduce education gaps and promote opportunity, intensive, high-quality preschool programs are needed for disadvantaged three- and four-year-olds. Such programs produce more positive effects than do typical Head Start programs or state-run preschool programs, although Head Start does modestly enhance learning and behavior.[18] Characteristics of high-quality programs include extensive teacher training, evidence-based curricula, small classes, and low staffing ratios. These high-quality programs, although small in scale, have dramatically improved high school graduation rates, college enrollment, adult earnings, crime rates, teen childbearing rates, and other outcomes. One challenge, however, is to retain the effectiveness of model programs as they go to scale and successive generations of adopters try to implement them "on the cheap."

According to the evidence, the benefits of such a program will be greater than the costs.[19] Consequently, it makes sense to provide new federal funds to states that design programs that meet certain broad quality requirements. State proposals should include plans for integrating funds from Head Start, federal child care programs, Title I, and state preschool programs. States also should be required to match new federal funding, dollar for dollar. States would be required to agree to rigorous, independent evaluations so that administrators and policymakers could find out what is and is not working and use that information to improve the program.

PAYING THE BILL

Rough estimates of the costs of the proposals described above are summarized in table 15-1. Most are not very expensive and are designed to achieve their objectives as cost effectively as possible. The most expensive component is the proposal to expand the EITC and child care assistance to low-income working families. This proposal is designed to provide the largest benefits to those who work full-time; these are the individuals who play by the rules but who do not have the skills to earn a wage that would allow them and their children to join the middle class. As shown by polling data and public support for a higher minimum wage, most Americans want to help this group.

Nonetheless, new initiatives should not be undertaken, in our view, unless the costs can be fully covered by eliminating spending or tax preferences in other areas. For several years, Brookings scholars have been

Table 15-1. Proposed New Annual Federal Antipoverty Expenditures

Item	Amount (millions of dollars)
Housing work program[a]	1,000
Wage and child care assistance	25,000
Teen pregnancy prevention programs[b]	1,400
Expanded Medicaid family planning	1,000
Expanded premarital education	200
High-quality early childhood education[c]	10,000
Total	$38,600

Source: Authors' calculations.

a. Under HUD estimates, about 100,000 to 150,000 adults living in public housing are required to meet the very modest work requirement. Assuming that a similar number of nonexempt households are in Section 8 housing and using the midpoint of the HUD estimate, some 250,000 adults would be subject to the new work requirement. If the average cost of the work program could be held to around $4,000 per adult, the cost of a fully implemented program would be around $1 billion. The cost of the incentive could add another billion dollars to the cost. If implemented gradually, the program would cost a few hundred million dollars per year for the first five years.

b. Saul D. Hoffman, *By the Numbers: The Public Costs of Teen Childbearing* (Washington: National Campaign to Prevent Teen Pregnancy, October 2006) (www.teenpregnancy.org/costs/); Julia B. Isaacs, *Cost-Effective Investments in Children,* Budgeting for National Priorities Paper (Brookings, January 2007).

c. Costs for a program that serves three- and four-year-olds for a half-day, offers wraparound child care to working parents, and is funded partly by a sliding fee scale tied to income would approximate $20 billion per year, about half of which would be new money. Overall, the program might eventually cost $10 billion at the federal level, but because it would be phased in gradually as states readied their plans, initially it would cost less, perhaps $7 billion per year.

calling attention to the impending federal fiscal crisis, and a number of our publications have suggested areas where such offsets might be found.[20] We refer readers to these publications for suggested savings in other areas of the budget.

CONCLUDING OBSERVATIONS

Americans have never liked welfare and tend to believe that anyone who gets an education and works hard can succeed. Policies intended to reduce poverty and inequality must be consistent with those beliefs. The proposals described above, by emphasizing work, marriage, and education, meet that test. The next president need not adopt this particular menu of policies but should improve opportunities for those left behind by adopting programs that balance personal and public responsibility in a way that a majority of Americans can support.

ADDITIONAL RESOURCES

Bloom, Howard S., James A. Riccio, and Nandita Verma. 2005. *Promoting Work in Public Housing: The Effectiveness of Jobs-Plus: Final Report*. New York: MDRC.

Campbell, Frances A., and Craig T. Ramey. 1999. *Early Learning, Later Success: The Abecedarian Study*. Chapel Hill, N.C.: Frank Porter Graham Child Development Institute.

Frenzel, William, and others. "Taming the Deficit." 2007. Budgeting for National Priorities Paper, Brookings (January).

Hoffman, Saul D. *By the Numbers: The Public Costs of Teen Childbearing*. 2006. Washington: National Campaign to Prevent Teen Pregnancy (October).

Isaacs, Julia B. "Cost-Effective Investments in Children." 2007. Budgeting for National Priorities Paper, Brookings (January).

Mincy, Ronald B., ed. *Black Males: Left Behind*. 2006. Washington: Urban Institute.

Rivlin, Alice M., and Isabel Sawhill, eds. 2004. *Restoring Fiscal Sanity: How to Balance the Budget*. Brookings.

Schweinhart, Lawrence J., and others. 2005. *Lifetime Effects: The High/Scope Perry Preschool Study through Age 40*. Ypsilanti, Mich.: High/Scope Press.

Whitehead, Barbara Dafoe, and Marline Pearson. 2006. "Making a Love Connection." Washington: National Campaign to Prevent Teen Pregnancy.

NOTES

1. Deborah Solomon, "Democrats' Risky Strategy: Trumpeting the Wealth Gap," *Wall Street Journal*, October 2, 2006, p. A1. Twenty-four percent of those polled said that the "gap between rich and poor" is the most pressing economic issue. This places it second to "gas prices and energy costs," which was selected by 26 percent.

2. Congressional Research Service, *Cash and Noncash Benefits for Persons with Limited Income: Eligibility Rules, Recipient and Expenditure Data, FY2002–FY2004*, RL33340 (Washington: Penny Hill Press, March 27, 2006), p. 5.

3. The Food Stamp program now has two types of work requirements, both weak. Although these two work requirements look strong on paper, they are mostly observed in the breach. The biggest flaw is that states are not required to have all or even a federally specified percentage of their adults in a work program. By contrast, the 1996 welfare reform legislation that contributed to the decline in the welfare rolls and the major increases in work specified that states must have at least half their caseload in a work program or suffer the imposition of stiff financial penalties. We think it would be good policy to provide states with more funding to impose much stronger work requirements and then enforce them vigorously. Opponents of this approach argue that the sanction of losing food stamp benefits for failing to meet work requirements is too harsh, especially because some families already lose their cash welfare benefit for failing to meet work requirements.

4. Maggie McCarty, *Community Service Requirements for Residents of Public Housing,* RS21591 (Washington: Congressional Research Service, January 5, 2007).

5. The Jobs-Plus demonstration study, launched in 1998 in six cities, involved nearly 5,000 residents of public housing. The program consisted of three major components: a services component in which housing staff members met with residents, explained the program to them, encouraged them to find employment, and offered employment and training; a neighbor-to-neighbor component that aimed to provide social support for work; and a financial incentive that reduced or eliminated the 30 percent housing "tax." Across all sites combined, nearly half the residents offered the incentive took advantage of it; in one site almost three-quarters of the residents enrolled. Similarly, averaged across all sites, the typical resident, as compared with similar residents not participating in the program, increased his or her earnings by around 6 percent per year. In three sites in which the program was well implemented, the earnings gain averaged 14 percent a year over four years and was 20 percent in the final year. Even compared with other welfare-to-work programs, many of which have been successful in moving people into jobs, these are large impacts and are highly encouraging. See Howard S. Bloom, James A. Riccio, and Nandita Verma, *Promoting Work in Public Housing: The Effectiveness of Jobs-Plus: Final Report* (New York: Manpower Demonstration Research Corporation [MRDC], March 2005).

6. Ronald B. Mincy, ed., *Black Males: Left Behind* (Washington: Urban Institute, 2006); Peter Edelman, Harry J. Holzer, and Paul Offner, *Reconnecting Disadvantaged Young Men* (Washington: Urban Institute, 2006).

7. Gordon Berlin, "Rewarding the Work of Individuals: A Counterintuitive Approach to Reducing Poverty and Strengthening Families," *Future of Children* 17, no. 2 (Fall 2007): 17–40. States would volunteer for the federally financed demonstrations and would, in turn, agree to allow the data collection that would be necessary to determine whether the program is boosting wages, increasing marriage, or having other detectable effects. Given the number of states that already have EITCs (earned income tax credits), it would be possible to require states to make a financial contribution to the benefit so that they could participate in the experiments and thereby capture the federal dollars.

8. Lawrence Mead, "Toward a Mandatory Work Policy for Men," *Future of Children* 17, no. 2 (Fall 2007): 43–72; Hugh B. Price, "Transitioning Ex-Offenders into Jobs and Society," *Washington Post,* special to washingtonpost.com, April 10, 2006.

9. John S. Santelli and others, "Can Changes in Sexual Behavior among High School Students Explain the Decline in Teen Pregnancy Rates in the 1990s?" *Journal of Adolescent Health* 35, no. 2 (2005): 80–90.

10. Saul D. Hoffman, *By the Numbers: The Public Costs of Teen Childbearing* (Washington: National Campaign to Prevent Teen Pregnancy, October 2006) (www.teenpregnancy.org/costs/pdf/report/BTN_Executive_Summary.pdf).

11. Daniel T. Lichter and Deborah Roempke Graefe, "Finding a Mate? The Marital and Cohabitation Histories of Unwed Mothers," in *Out of Wedlock: Causes and*

Consequences of Nonmarital Fertility, edited by Lawrence L. Wu and Barbara Wolfe (New York: Russell Sage, 2001), pp. 317–43.

12. More description of this "success sequence" can be found in Barbara Dafoe Whitehead and Marline Pearson, *Making a Love Connection: Teen Relationships, Pregnancy, and Marriage* (Washington: National Campaign to Prevent Teen Pregnancy, 2006).

13. Sara McLanahan, Elisabeth Donahue, and Ron Haskins, "Introducing the Issue," *Future of Children* 15, no. 2 (Fall 2005): 3–12.

14. Two of the more effective programs, as identified by Douglas Kirby for the National Campaign to Prevent Teen Pregnancy, are the Teen Outreach Program (TOP) and the Children's Aid Society–Carrera Program. These programs focus on youth development, not just on family planning or abstinence. See Douglas Kirby, *Emerging Answers: Research Findings on Programs to Reduce Teen Pregnancy* (Washington: National Campaign to Prevent Teen Pregnancy, 2004).

15. Paul R. Amato and Rebecca A. Maynard, "Reducing Nonmarital Births and Increasing Marriage to Reduce Poverty," *Future of Children* 17, no. 2 (Fall 2007): 117–41. The best-known and most successful premarital education program is the Prevention and Relationship Enhancement Program (PREP).

16. Christopher Jencks and Meredith Phillips, eds., *The Black-White Test Score Gap* (Brookings, 1998); Ron Haskins, "Putting Education into Preschools," in *Generational Change: Closing the Test Score Gap,* edited by Paul Peterson (New York: Rowman & Littlefield, 2006), pp. 47–87; Cecilia Rouse, Jeanne Brooks-Gunn, and Sara McLanahan, "Introducing the Issue," *Future of Children* 15, no. 1 (Spring 2005): 3–12.

17. See, for example, W. Steven Barnett, "Long-Term Effects of Early Childhood Programs on Cognitive and School Outcomes," *Future of Children* 5, no. 3 (1995): 25–50; Janet Currie, "Early Childhood Education Programs: What Do We Know?" *Journal of Economic Perspectives* 15, no. 2 (2001): 213–38; James J. Heckman and Dmitry V. Masterov, "The Productivity Argument for Investing in Young Children," Working Paper 5 (Washington: Invest in Kids Working Group, October 4, 2004); Craig T. Ramey and others, *Early Learning, Later Success: The Abecedarian Study* (Chapel Hill, N.C.: Frank Porter Graham Child Development Institute, 1999); Lawrence J. Schweinhart and others, *Lifetime Effects: The High/Scope Perry Preschool Study through Age 40* (Ypsilanti, Mich.: High/Scope Press, 2005).

18. W. Steven Barnett, Cynthia Lamy, and Kwanghee Jung, *The Effects of State Prekindergarten Programs on Young Children's School Readiness in Five States* (Rutgers, N.J.: National Institute for Early Education Research, December 2005); Haskins, "Putting Education into Preschools"; Jens Ludwig and Deborah A. Phillips, "The Benefits and Costs of Head Start," Georgetown University, Working Paper 12973 (Cambridge, Mass.: National Bureau of Economic Research, March 2007); Jens Ludwig and Isabel Sawhill, "Success by Ten: Intervening Early, Often, and Effectively in the Education of Young Children," Hamilton Project Discussion Paper (Brookings, February 2007).

19. Total gross cost of the program is estimated to be around $30 billion, $20 billion of which is new spending. The authors argue that the benefit-cost ratio of such a program would be from more than 2 to 1 by the most conservative estimates to 7 to 1 or higher, making it extremely cost effective. Greg Duncan, Jens Ludwig, and Katherine Magnuson, "Reducing Poverty through Preschool Interventions," *Future of Children* 17, no. 2 (Fall 2007): 143–60; Julia B. Isaacs, "Cost-Effective Investments in Children," Budgeting for National Priorities Paper (Brookings, January 2007).

20. Alice M. Rivlin and Isabel Sawhill, eds., *Restoring Fiscal Sanity: How to Balance the Budget* (Brookings, 2004); William Frenzel, Charles Stenholm, William Hoagland, and Isabel Sawhill, "Taming the Deficit," Budgeting for National Priorities Paper (Brookings, January 2007).

16

Pathways to the Middle Class

Ensuring Greater Upward Mobility for All Americans

HUGH B. PRICE, AMY LIU, AND REBECCA SOHMER

SUMMARY ❱ Middle-class prosperity is the cornerstone of the American Dream. Americans believe that through hard work and education families can enter the middle class and keep on climbing. However, recent evidence shows that, even with a rebounding U.S. economy, working-class and middle-class families are struggling more than in decades past, and upward economic mobility is slowing, even for those who work hard and play by society's rules. Moreover, the road to middle-class prosperity is even rockier for minorities. Several time-honored pathways that lead to the middle class are postsecondary education, good jobs, living in viable neighborhoods, personal financial responsibility, and entrepreneurship. This paper focuses on all but the last of these pathways to opportunity.

The next president of the United States should strengthen opportunities for hard-working Americans to reach the middle class and ensure that middle-class families can continue to enjoy improved economic prosperity and upward mobility. Specifically, the next president should concentrate on increasing the number of lower-income people enrolled in and completing postsecondary education programs; improving access to good jobs that pay middle-class wages, offer benefits, and provide opportunities

The authors wish to thank Oliver Sloman, Brookings research assistant, for his substantive contributions to this paper.

for advancement; fostering economically viable and diverse communities and neighborhoods that facilitate wealth building; and promoting personal financial security through financial literacy and access to fairly priced financial services and products. ❯

CONTEXT ❯ A core American value holds that individuals and families who take advantage of opportunities for education, employment, homeownership, or entrepreneurship ought to be able to enter the ranks of our nation's middle class. Once there, through additional hard work and commitment, middle-class families ought to enjoy greater economic security and further upward mobility. Pursuit of the American Dream has created a sizable middle class that is the bedrock of U.S. society and the envy of the world.

But is the dream fading? Several recent and long-term trends suggest that may be so; among them are the nation's growing income inequality, stagnant economic mobility, and for many families, meager wealth accumulation. People of color face even more daunting obstacles to attaining and maintaining middle-class status, and given the growing proportion of minorities in the U.S. labor force, this trend has especially troubling implications for the future economic and civic health of our country.

The next president should mount a concerted effort to enable more Americans to climb the ladder to middle-class status and help ensure that they prosper once there. This can be accomplished by fortifying and expanding four major pathways to the middle class, namely: education, quality jobs, viable neighborhoods, and financial well-being. These measures will encourage and equip aspirants to embark on the journey to middle-class status and preserve the ethos of opportunity that is the hallmark of the United States. ❯

CHALLENGES TO THE ASPIRING MIDDLE CLASS

Today, working-class and middle-class Americans face greater economic stress and have less upward mobility than do wealthier Americans. They are also relatively worse off than previous generations were. While the U.S. economy will always go through periods of expansion and contraction, with concomitant swings in public opinion about personal economic security, mounting evidence indicates that the first decade of the twenty-first century is marked by some discouraging economic trends.

Who Are the Middle Class?

The middle class can be defined by income, education, occupation, values, lifestyle, or a combination of these attributes. For ease of measurement, in this paper, the term *middle class* is synonymous with middle income, and *middle-class households* are ones whose members earned annual incomes between $35,000 and $80,000 in 2000. This income range spans the third and fourth quintiles of the nation's income distribution.

Even before the recent home mortgage crisis and the subsequent economic downturn, few of the economic gains from this decade have benefited the nation's working poor and large segments of the middle class. Much of the wealth has increasingly been concentrated in the nation's richest 1 percent, which has seen its after-tax income grow by 176 percent since 1979. This increase is nearly ten times faster than that of the bottom fifth of income earners. Thus the income gap between those who are wealthy and those who are not has been widening, and in fact, according to economist Isabel Sawhill, the gap has reached its widest point "at any time over the past half century." Average hourly earnings have been stagnant or slipped every month since October 2007. At the same time, Americans face rising costs in housing, gas prices, health care, and college tuition, plus the most mountainous levels of consumer debt in the last thirty years.

A new study by the Pew Charitable Trust's Economic Mobility Project, conducted by scholars at the Brookings Institution, found that the wide income inequality in the United States may not be offset by gains in upward mobility across generations, which is much less than the upward mobility experienced in other developed nations, such as Canada and Germany. The result is that while two-thirds of today's adults earn higher incomes than their parents did, a full one-third of American adults do not earn as much or have experienced net *downward* mobility. According to another recent study, since the early 1990s, middle-class families are experiencing more frequent downward income shocks and more income volatility, placing them at heightened risk of defaulting on loans or incurring greater debt.

Upward mobility is highly dependent upon the economic fortunes of one's parents. Unfortunately, children born to parents who are lower income or African American face acute challenges.

To start, less than one-third of all African-American households earned middle-class incomes in 2000, the smallest middle class among racial and ethnic groups, compared with 36 percent of Latino and 40 percent of White households who earned middle-class incomes. Furthermore, middle-class minorities are less likely than middle-class Whites to own their own homes and to invest in stocks, reducing the chances of upward mobility and wealth accumulation for future generations.

Overall, upward income mobility is less likely for African American children than for White children. First, Black children of middle class parents earn lower median incomes today than did their parents, which stands in stark contrast to the higher incomes earned by most children of White parents. Downward mobility among African Americans is exhibited in another way: almost half of Black children whose parents were solidly middle class in the late 1960s fell to the bottom of the income distribution by the time they were adults compared with 16 percent of solidly middle class White children.

CLEARING THE PATHWAYS TO THE MIDDLE CLASS

While households can follow a number of pathways to economic advancement, this paper focuses on four of the primary ones: postsecondary education, good jobs, economically viable and diverse neighborhoods, and sound financial practices and services. For far too many strivers, these pathways are strewn with formidable obstacles.

Postsecondary Education

The correlation between income and education is strong. According to the U.S. Census Bureau, the estimated lifetime earnings of an individual with a high school diploma are almost $1 million less than earnings for an individual with a college degree. Even possessing an associate degree increases lifetime earnings by about $400,000 over those of a high school graduate. In short, having a good education, especially a college degree, remains a driving force behind economic progress.

Unfortunately, Latinos and African Americans, along with Native Americans, are not well served across the entire educational continuum, including in higher education. Their educational advancement matters enormously, because by 2020, some 30 percent of our working-aged population will be Latino or African American—nearly double the percentage in 1980.

Yet, as Charles Kolb of the Committee for Economic Development warns, only 20 percent of Black students and 16 percent of Latinos who graduate from high school are adequately prepared for college.

The share of the U.S. workforce with high school and college degrees may not only fail to keep rising over the next fifteen years, it could actually decline slightly. As highly educated baby boomers retire, the face of the workforce will change. Not only will it have a greater proportion of minorities, but it also could have a greater proportion of people without college degrees. Since workers with fewer years of education on average earn so much less, U.S. living standards could plunge unless the college pathway is cleared, especially for African American, Latino, and low-income youngsters.

Good Jobs

Achieving middle-class prosperity obviously necessitates a job or business income that can provide a middle-class lifestyle and offer opportunities for advancement. But more than wages per se, access to the middle class also depends on quality jobs that either offer health insurance and retirement plans or pay enough so that workers can purchase these protections on their own. Unfortunately, obtaining—and holding onto—quality jobs is becoming increasingly problematic. Overall, wages have eroded since the 1980s, as employment growth shifted away from well-paying industries that produce goods toward lower-paying enterprises that mostly provide services. Fewer jobs offer health coverage and guaranteed pensions—a phenomenon that affects the solidly middle class as well. In 1979, 69 percent of workers had employer-provided health insurance coverage. By 2004, only 56 percent did.

Once again, people of color face more hurdles than do Whites. To begin with, minorities are overrepresented in low-paying jobs. In 2000 the occupations that paid the lowest median hourly wages were found in food preparation, farming, personal services, health support services, and sales. Together, people in these occupations made up 25 percent of the workforce. However, only 23 percent of White workers were employed in these low-paying occupations, compared with 28 percent of African Americans and 32 percent of Latinos. Similarly, Black and Latino employees are less likely than Whites to be in jobs offering health insurance benefits. While 60 percent of White employees have health care coverage, only 54 percent of African American and 40 percent of Latino employees are insured.

Moreover, fewer minorities tend to have any kind of job—one of quality or not. Only 61 percent of Black men are in the workforce—the lowest participation rate of any group of men in the country. Not surprisingly, this problem dovetails with their lack of educational preparation. In 2000 among Black men aged twenty to twenty-four, the unemployment rate was a staggering 36 percent if they were high school dropouts but only 6 percent if they held bachelor's degrees. Improvements in educational outcomes for Blacks and Latinos undoubtedly will help boost their prospects in the labor market. But additional reforms are needed to improve the supply of and access to quality jobs, especially within the expanding sectors of the economy.

Economically Viable and Diverse Neighborhoods

A range of studies over the past two decades has documented the adverse impact of extremely poor neighborhoods on the overall well-being of families and children. Recently, studies also have shown the benefits to households from living in mixed-income neighborhoods: less crime, better employment prospects, improved school performance, higher property values for homeowners, and stronger retail markets. There also is evidence that owning a home in stable neighborhoods with little poverty improves the benefits of homeownership for the household's children. Enabling aspiring middle-class families to own homes in economically viable and diverse neighborhoods with good schools can help put families on the course to economic prosperity.

Clearly, the opportunity to live in good neighborhoods, especially middle-class neighborhoods, is a key pathway to achieving the American Dream. And as families improve their economic fortunes, they typically aspire to move up to a better home and neighborhood. Unfortunately, the nation's middle-income neighborhoods are steadily disappearing—and at a faster clip than the decline in the size of the middle class itself. The total share of U.S. neighborhoods in metropolitan areas (which encompass 85 percent of the U.S. population) that are middle income decreased from 58 percent in 1970 to 41 percent in 2000, while the share of middle-income households declined by 6 percentage points. And as these neighborhoods disappear, the opportunity to move up may also be slipping. In 1970, 55 percent of low-income families lived in middle-income and economically integrated neighborhoods. But by 2000, only 37 percent did.

The decline in middle-income neighborhoods not only means that fewer low-income working families can take advantage of a key stepping-stone into the middle class but also that middle-class, or marginally middle-class, families also may soon be priced out of economically sound neighborhoods, undercutting their ability to accumulate wealth.

Finally, research shows that middle-class minorities, especially African Americans, may be living in racially or economically segregated neighborhoods that constrain their wealth-building potential. In 2000 Black middle-class households earning $60,000 or more lived in neighborhoods in which the median income was $44,668. Whites in the same income bracket lived in neighborhoods with a median income of $60,363. As a result, when minority residents do own their own homes, their property tends to be worth less than that of White homeowners. Developing more viable neighborhoods protects and promotes wealth building and the other benefits of homeownership, particularly for persons of color.

Financial Acumen and Fairness

Financial acumen helps individuals along the path to the middle class. It helps them avoid unduly burdensome debt; use appropriate and fairly priced financial services; and build financial security through homeownership, investment, and retirement savings. Overall, a larger proportion of Americans have inadequate savings and are deeper in debt than ever. The latest figures from the Bureau of Economic Analysis put the U.S. personal savings rate at negative 1 percent, demonstrating that personal spending and payments are outstripping disposable personal income. No wonder then that 70 percent of U.S. households live paycheck to paycheck. These numbers suggest the difficulty that many Americans would have in entering or maintaining middle-class prosperity and security.

On the other side of the household budget are expenses. Ironically, lower-income families often pay higher prices for everyday goods and services, such as auto and home loans, groceries, furniture, and appliances, than do other consumers. For example, lower-income homeowners generally pay 1 percentage point more in mortgage interest than their higher-income neighbors do, which adds tens of thousands of dollars in additional charges over the life of the loan. Low-income people who do not have health insurance are charged full price for medical services, while those with insurance pay (in combination with their insurer) a discounted price. While some of these differential prices are rationally set and take into account legitimately higher risks, they also can result from unscrupulous market practices, as well as a lack of financial savvy among low-income consumers.

AN AGENDA FOR ADVANCING OPPORTUNITY FOR ALL AMERICANS

To preserve and expand the American middle class, the next president should concentrate on improving four important pathways to upward mobility: postsecondary education, quality jobs, economically viable and diverse neighborhoods, and financial well-being. While numerous possible reforms would strengthen these pathways, the following low-cost, proven programs and easy-to-implement steps, if universally and conscientiously applied, promise to close the racial and ethnic gaps in economic well-being and help all middle-class aspirants climb the ladder of opportunity.

Help Students Afford and Complete Postsecondary Education

The top priority for expanding the middle class is to significantly increase the number of students who complete postsecondary education in our nation's community colleges, four-year colleges and universities, or specialized training programs geared to specific occupations. To increase access and completion rates at four-year colleges and other postsecondary institutions, the next president should promote a four-point policy agenda.

Increase the Value of Pell Grants to Make College More Affordable

Affordability of higher education has been a growing problem for years now. Even at public two-year and four-year colleges, financial aid has not kept pace with tuition. In 1976–77 Pell Grants, the primary source of aid for low-income students, covered 94 percent of average two-year college costs and 76 percent of average four-year college costs. As of 2004 they covered only 68 percent and 34 percent, respectively.

Addressing this problem will require political will but not necessarily radical policy departures. In Pell Grants, the federal government already has an effective vehicle for aiding the aspiring middle class. Policymakers in both political parties acknowledge the need to increase the value of Pell Grants. In 2007, they joined together to pass the College Cost Reduction Act, which raises the maximum Pell Grant award from $4,310 in the 2007–08 award year to $5,400 by the 2012–13 award year. While this increase is sorely needed, a $1,100 increase does not go far enough to help the nearly half of all Pell Grant recipients who face a total price tag of more than $15,000 to attend higher education institutions. The next president should support further increases in the value of Pell Grants and other forms of direct, need-based aid.[1] Unlike tax credits or loans, tuition grants positively influence students' decisions about *whether* to apply to college, and from the government's perspective, the increased tax revenues and host of other benefits that result from generating more college graduates could be considerable.

Invest in Counseling that Helps Students Apply to College

The quality and amount of guidance that students receive in high school influences the likelihood that they will pursue higher education. Students whose parents attended college and can better assist their children with the application process are twice as likely to apply. Unfortunately, counseling receives scant attention amid schools' current emphasis on high-stakes testing. Effective counseling steers students toward courses that will place them on track for postsecondary education and helps them successfully navigate the process of applying for college or career training programs.

College-oriented counseling programs can be quite effective. For example, College Summit, established in 1993 by a former inner-city high school student, runs four-day summer workshops on college campuses around the country to help low-income students with every component of their college applications. Through these efforts, which include assistance with financial aid forms, essay writing, and college selection, College Summit connects low-income students who are qualified for college with the help they need but probably will not otherwise receive. According to College Summit, 79 percent of its participants enroll in college, nearly twice the national rate for low-income high school graduates. Of these, *80 percent* have graduated or are still enrolled six years later. The average participant has a GPA of 2.8, and half are African American.

Policymakers have long realized the importance and effectiveness of college preparation programs. Unfortunately, federally funded programs like TRIO, which assist low-income, first-generation students to apply to and complete postsecondary programs, reach perhaps just 10 percent of the eligible population. College Summit estimates that 200,000 high school seniors who are college material do not enroll annually.

The next president should increase federal investment in the nation's human capital by significantly expanding the well-designed and demonstrably effective counseling programs offered by schools and community-based organizations for able, low-income students who otherwise might not pursue postsecondary education.

Expand Programs that Boost Graduation Rates

Within five years of entering a four-year college, 40 percent of students from the top quartile, but only 6 percent from the bottom quartile, will earn their degree. To help narrow this gap, the next president should push to increase the quantity and quality of academic and social support services available to low-income students who are struggling in college or postsecondary training programs. As a first step, the government could tie funding for support services to Pell Grant funding. This way, low-income students will always receive help completing their degrees as well as paying for them.

Because failure to complete one's degree is so costly for students, colleges, and society, the federal government should evaluate new approaches to improve retention and graduation rates and, if they are found to be effective, provide significant funding for them. For example, federal studies have consistently demonstrated that students who work more than fifteen hours per week are more likely to not complete college in a timely fashion. In an attempt to deal with this issue, a program called Opening Doors gave low-income parents attending community colleges $1,000 scholarships for completing a semester with a C average or above. A rigorous evaluation has found that students helped by Opening Doors were more likely than nonparticipants to attend college full-time and pass more courses, and their retention rate from one semester to the next was substantially higher.

Extend Financial Aid to Part-Time and Nontraditional Students

Nontraditional students are fast becoming the new "normal" in post-secondary education. In 1991 a third of all college students were aged twenty-five and older, and a mere decade later, nearly half (47 percent) were. At present, most financial aid formulas offer little or no support to students enrolled less than half-time, even though many of these students are working adults of modest means who are trying to become qualified for jobs that pay middle-class wages.

This paucity of support can discourage part-time students concerned about their ability to pay tuition by themselves. They may not enroll, or they may take too few classes, delaying degree completion and increasing the chances that unforeseen circumstances will cause them to abandon the effort altogether.

To help nontraditional students, the 2007 College Cost Reduction Act, which recently passed the House, includes a provision to make Pell Grants available year-round, not just during the spring or fall, to make them more practical and valuable to nontraditional students. The next president should ensure that these and other kinds of flexible financial aid are available to assist strivers whose lives cannot accommodate traditional course loads.

Create Ladders to Quality Jobs

The next president should promote programs and tax incentives that help low-income workers access quality jobs—those that provide a good living and opportunities for advancement—through job training, matching, and placement.

Expand Job Training that Works

Solid research shows that welfare recipients who receive job training, especially when provided by organizations that collaborate with prospective employers, reap many benefits. Compared with recipients who do not participate, the trainees typically end up earning significantly higher wages and are more likely to receive crucial fringe benefits, such as health coverage, paid sick leave, and vacation. As a result, their labor force participation and retention rates are better as well. Employers in turn benefit from reduced turnover, improved operations, a reliable source of qualified workers, and reduced hiring costs.

Having legislated stringent time limits on the receipt of welfare benefits, the federal government should ratchet up its investment in programs that successfully channel former recipients into jobs that start them on the path toward economic self-sufficiency and the American mainstream.

Provide Funding and Incentives to Channel Low-Wage Workers into Better Jobs

Many workers in low-wage jobs could climb higher if employers recognized their potential and invested in their advancement. However, it may take an external catalyst to spur this needed investment in human capital.

In Boston, the nonprofit SkillWorks brings together businesses, government, foundations, and unions to create the collaborative climate and operating conditions to help these workers advance. Through so-called Workforce Partnerships, SkillWorks encourages employers, such as hospitals and office-cleaning companies, to create career ladders for their low-wage employees. In return, SkillWorks makes certain these employees receive the training and education they need to succeed in their new positions. By arranging nontraditional internal promotion paths from low-wage jobs to better ones, SkillWorks creates a win-win situation for workers and employers alike.

The federal government should invest in more such experiments and, if they work, widely implement them. Federal aid can take the form of operating grants for community colleges and local nonprofit organizations, with tax incentives for employers willing to upgrade low-wage workers who rise to the challenge of qualifying for better jobs. The more that government agencies at all levels, community-based organizations, employers, and unions collaborate to help low-wage workers access better opportunities, the more the middle class will grow, to society's overall benefit.

Foster Economically Viable and Diverse Communities

For years, racial integration, affordable housing, and community development have ranked low among federal priorities. The next president should rekindle the federal commitment to fostering viable communities that are economically diverse and that enable striving families to take their place in the mainstream by purchasing a home in a good neighborhood. These communities offer other opportunities customarily associated with the middle class, such as solid schools, a sound local labor market, essential retail and other services, and stable housing values.

Reform Affordable Housing Programs to Promote Quality, Economically Integrated Communities

As noted earlier, middle-class neighborhoods are dramatically shrinking. One possible reason for this phenomenon is that federal policies continue to limit the development of affordable housing almost exclusively to low-income neighborhoods in the urban core, even though the majority of low-income and working families live in the suburbs today. Removing this constraint on the construction of federally financed affordable housing would enable low-income families to enjoy the considerable economic and social advantages of living in more viable neighborhoods, which have better schools and job opportunities.

The federal government can take several steps to promote the creation of healthy, mixed-income neighborhoods that are ripe with opportunities for upward mobility. First, the federal government should require existing metropolitan planning organizations to produce regional housing plans in conjunction with their already mandated transportation plans to ensure that all urban and suburban jurisdictions accommodate the need for affordable housing, particularly near job growth centers. Second, the federal government should expand and reform the federal housing voucher program so that it can better serve renters throughout a metro area and allow low-income families with children to live in neighborhoods with high-performing public schools. Third, the federal government should expand and retarget the Low-Income Housing Tax Credit (LIHTC) program, our nation's largest producer of affordable housing today. These credits should reward private developers who build two types of developments: mixed-income housing in emerging or revitalized neighborhoods and affordable housing in hot-market or opportunity-rich communities, such as those near transit stations, downtowns, or good schools. These reforms would help create economically integrated neighborhoods that can help lift lower-income and middle-class families toward greater wealth accumulation and upward mobility.

Promote Financial Literacy and Encourage the Wider Availability of Mainstream Financial Services

Reaching and remaining in the middle class require at least some financial literacy, including an understanding of how to manage personal finances and the necessity of building assets instead of debts. Families also need to guard against and be protected from unsavory financial practices that rob them of income and wealth. There is much the next president can do to help households strengthen their financial status.

Promote Financial Literacy Courses in High School

Many low-income and minority children receive little if any formal or informal instruction in basic financial management, building wealth and assets, saving for college, or preparing for retirement. As Alan Greenspan has noted, financial literacy is no longer simply knowing how to balance a checkbook. Consumers must be able to navigate a wide range of financial products and services.

To better prepare young people for the financial realities and responsibilities that await them, the federal government should accelerate the momentum that is already building in many states. Currently, a dozen or so states mandate financial education as part of the secondary school curriculum. Some experts suggest that financial literacy should be incorporated into existing curricula for math, social studies, and English in elementary schools and that it should be offered as a stand-alone class in high school. Research suggests that high school students who take such a course have higher savings rates and net worth as adults. The federal government also should provide states with financial literacy matching grants for school districts that serve low-income students, who have the greatest need for such knowledge.

Create "Banking Innovation Zones" to Encourage Mainstream Financial Services to Locate in Low-Income Neighborhoods

The federal government could use its considerable depository power to encourage mainstream financial institutions to locate in low-income neighborhoods. The New York State Banking Department has done just that. Its Banking Development District program identifies neighborhoods that do not have any banks and may not have enough depository power to attract mainstream banks. The state then encourages banks to enter these neighborhoods by depositing money at market and below-market interest rates. The bank gains access to inexpensive state money, and the neighborhood has access to a mainstream financial institution. This low-cost, win-win strategy could be replicated on the federal level to promote banking access to low-income neighborhoods nationwide.

CONCLUDING OBSERVATIONS

One of the utmost priorities of the next president should be to uphold the core American value that people who work hard and play by the rules should be able to enjoy the fruits of a middle-class lifestyle and to share such rewards with their families and children. As we contemplate America's future as the most diverse nation on earth, it will be essential that all Americans—regardless of economic circumstances or race and ethnicity—

have a realistic chance to enjoy upward mobility and join the middle class. Strengthening the four pathways to middle-class prosperity—post-secondary education, quality jobs, economically viable and diverse neighborhoods, and sound personal financial practices—should define and then drive the domestic agenda of the next president of the United States.

ADDITIONAL RESOURCES

Booza, Jason C., Jackie Cutsinger, and George Galster. 2006. *Where Did They Go? The Decline of Middle-Income Neighborhoods in Metropolitan America.* Living Cities Census Series. Brookings, Metropolitan Policy Program (www.brookings.edu/metro/pubs/20060622_middleclass.htm).

Fellowes, Matt. 2006. *From Poverty, Opportunity: Putting the Market to Work for Lower Income Families.* Brookings, Metropolitan Policy Program (www.brookings.edu/metro/pubs/20060718_povop.htm).

Harkness, Joseph M., and Sandra J. Newman. 2003. "Effects of Homeownership on Children: The Role of Neighborhood Characteristics and Family Income." Federal Reserve Bank of New York, *Economic Policy Review* 9, no. 2 (June): 87–107.

Hertz, Tom. 2006. *Understanding Mobility in America.* Washington: Center for American Progress (www.americanprogress.org/issues/2006/04/b1579981.html).

Isaacs, Julia B., Isabel V. Sawhill, and Ron Haskins. 2007. *Getting Ahead or Losing Ground: Economic Mobility in America.* Economic Mobility Project. Washington: Pew Charitable Trusts and Brookings.

Katz, Bruce. 2004. *Neighborhoods of Choice and Connection: The Evolution of American Neighborhood Policy and What It Means for the United Kingdom.* Brookings, Metropolitan Policy Program (www.brookings.edu/metro/pubs/20040713_katz.htm).

Katz, Bruce, and Margery Austin Turner. 2008. "Rethinking U.S. Rental Housing Policy: Build on State & Local Innovations." Opportunity 08 Project. Brookings.

Kolb, Charles. 2006. "The Cracks in Our Education Pipeline." *Education Week* (July 12).

Logan, John R. 2002. *Separate and Unequal: The Neighborhood Gap for Blacks and Hispanics in Metropolitan America.* Albany, N.Y.: Lewis Mumford Center for Comparative Urban and Regional Research (October).

Mishel, Lawrence, Jared Bernstein, and Sylvia Allegretto. 2006. *The State of Working America 2006/2007.* Cornell University Press.

McMurrer, Daniel R., and Isabel V. Sawhill. 1998. *Getting Ahead: Economic and Social Mobility in America.* Washington: Urban Institute (www.urban.org/pubs/getting/).

Sawhill, Isabel, and John E. Morton. 2007. *Economic Mobility: Is the American Dream Alive and Well?* Washington: Pew Charitable Trusts.

Turbov, Mindy, and Valerie Piper. 2005. "HOPE VI and Mixed-Finance Redevelopments: A Catalyst for Urban Renewal." Discussion Paper. Brookings, Metropolitan Policy Program (www.brookings.edu/metro/pubs/20050913_hopevi.htm).

NOTE

1. Courtney McSwain, "Window of Opportunity: Targeting Federal Grant Aid to Students with the Lowest Incomes." (Washington: Institute for Higher Education Policy, 2008).

PART

OUR PROSPERITY

17

Taming the Deficit

Forge a Grand Compromise for a Sustainable Future

WILLIAM FRENZEL, CHARLES W. STENHOLM,
G. WILLIAM HOAGLAND, AND ISABEL V. SAWHILL

SUMMARY ❱ Currently projected deficits are unsustainable and pose serious risks to the economy, make us dangerously dependent on other countries, impose a "debt tax" on every taxpayer, send the bill for current spending to future generations, and weaken the government's ability to invest in the future or respond to emergencies. The next president will have to act to meet the deficit challenge.

Specifically, presidential candidates should commit to restoring fiscal balance over the next five years and to constructing a sustainable fiscal course over the long term by reforming entitlements and taxes as soon as possible. They should emphasize to the public that the deficit matters and pledge to work in a bipartisan way to tame it; they should agree to putting all options on the table, provide an outline of the reforms needed on both the tax and spending sides of the ledger, and be candid with the American people about the magnitude of the problem. Candidates also may want to propose reforms to the budget process, but these alone will not restore fiscal balance. ❱

This paper presents detailed proposals to illustrate what a defensible deficit reduction package might contain. None of the authors entirely support every component, but the package as a whole shows that it is possible for people of good will to come together and produce a deficit reduction plan that gets the job done.

CONTEXT ❯ *The federal government is spending beyond its means.* Surpluses of the late 1990s have been transformed into deficits that hovered around $300 billion to $400 billion a year in the first half of the current decade and stood at $162 billion in fiscal year 2007. Although this may have been an improvement over the previous several years, any good news is likely to be short-lived, for two major reasons. First, and most important, the retirement of the baby boom generation and rapidly rising per capita health care costs will soon produce substantially larger deficits, unless action is taken to reform Social Security, Medicare, and Medicaid. Second, although official projections show the deficit withering away, this rosy outlook is due to the statutory requirement that the Congressional Budget Office (CBO) adopt several unlikely assumptions, including the complete expiration of recently enacted tax cuts. Under a more realistic scenario, deficits could swell to $700 billion by 2018 and continue increasing in subsequent decades as the population grows older and health care spending keeps climbing.

By the early 2040s, assuming health care costs continue to grow faster than the economy, the three major entitlement programs will absorb *all* of the federal government's projected revenues (figure 17-1).[1] To prevent the elimination of the rest of government, either taxes would have to be raised by half, or benefits for seniors would have to be drastically curtailed. In short, projected deficits are enormous and unsustainable, and almost everyone agrees that there is no plausible rate of economic growth that will enable us to "grow our way out" of the problem.[2] ❯

WHY DEFICITS MATTER

Why is it vital for any candidate for president to address this issue? Continuing deficits pose a serious threat to the economy. At present, the effects of deficits are masked by the willingness of other countries to lend us money, thereby allowing us to live beyond our means. Three-fourths of recent-year deficits have been financed by foreigners, including the central banks of China, other Asian nations, and oil-exporting countries in the Middle East.[3] Without this influx of money from abroad, our economic strength would erode. It would be more expensive for both businesses and households to borrow; interest rates could rise by several percentage points, increasing the cost of a typical mortgage by more than $2,500 per year; the value of the dollar would fall; a recession would likely follow;

Figure 17-1. Projected Spending Growth for Major Entitlement Programs

Percentage of GDP

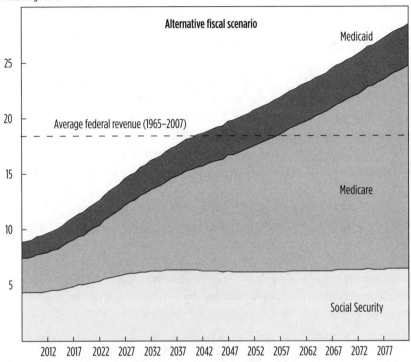

Source: Congressional Budget Office, *The Long-Term Budget Outlook* (December 2007), alternative fiscal scenario.

and growth in the American standard of living would slow.[4] The exact scenario is unpredictable: it could be a gradual adjustment (soft landing) or a full-scale economic crisis. Either way, our mounting indebtedness to foreign countries means that we are losing control of our economic destiny.

Besides threatening the economy, continuing deficits enlarge the national debt and require that more tax dollars be devoted to servicing it. These interest payments absorb nearly one-fifth of all income tax revenue and in 2006 cost the average household nearly $2,000.[5] When Americans pay their taxes each year, they increasingly are paying for the privilege of borrowing more and forgoing the opportunity to reduce tax burdens or devote these dollars to defense, education, or other programs.

Deficits shift the costs of government from current to future generations. Sometimes, borrowing is justified: to cover the costs of a national emergency or to bolster the economy during a recession. However, currently projected deficits are *structural* and not the result of special needs—such as a recession, the wars in Iraq and Afghanistan, and Hurricanes Katrina and Rita.

Finally, deficits limit the nation's ability to respond effectively to future emergencies or to make public investments in areas such as national security or education. In an avian flu epidemic or deep recession, the federal government's ability to act would be encumbered by red ink.

In short, the nation's current fiscal stance threatens the economy, makes us dangerously dependent on the rest of the world, imposes a "debt tax" on every American, sends the bills for current spending to future generations, and weakens the ability of the federal government to invest in the future or respond to crises.

Solutions to this problem will require that elected officials take what initially may be unpopular steps to raise taxes and cut spending. Congressional leaders are well aware of the problem but are hampered by the breakdown of the budget process in recent years and a lack of trust between the two political parties. *Presidential leadership is needed to break the impasse and move the country toward fiscal balance.*

ADDRESS THE ISSUE SQUARELY

Presidential candidates should not be expected to provide detailed blueprints for reducing the deficit. Before entering office, candidates do not possess the detailed knowledge and staff resources necessary to navigate complex budget issues. However, all candidates can and should do the following:

—State unequivocally that deficits *do* matter

—Commit to restoring fiscal balance over a reasonable time period, such as five years, and to putting the nation on a sustainable fiscal course by reforming entitlements as soon as possible

—Pledge to work in a bipartisan way to achieve this objective

—Put all issues and options on the table: entitlements, revenues, defense, and all other spending categories

—Outline the spending cuts and revenue increases needed to achieve short-term fiscal objectives and the changes needed in Social Security and Medicare to maintain long-term fiscal discipline

—Be candid with the American people about the nature and magnitude of the challenge, acknowledging that the problem cannot be solved simply by cutting fraud, waste, and abuse; curbing earmarks; raising taxes on the very wealthy; or streamlining government

—Propose reforms to the budget process without assuming that these alone will be sufficient to restore fiscal balance

These are the minimal requirements for any candidate asserting a claim to fiscal responsibility. In their absence, the next president will have no mandate to lead the way to a solution.

AIM TOWARD A GRAND COMPROMISE

Serious deficit reduction will require bipartisan support, regardless of which political party holds the White House. Enacting a durable solution will depend on respecting certain principles and values that each party holds dear:

—*A balance of spending cuts and revenue increases* and an agreement that the bulk of the savings will be devoted to deficit reduction and not to tax cuts or increased spending; however, to sweeten the package and in recognition that some high-priority tax reductions (for example, reform of the Alternative Minimum Tax, or AMT) and additional funding for selected cost-effective investments can strengthen the nation as much as reducing the deficit can, some of the savings could be devoted to these purposes

—*Sensitivity to conservative concerns* that higher tax rates might reduce incentives to work, save, and invest, thereby weakening economic growth, and that in the absence of constraints on spending the government will absorb too large a proportion of national income

—*Sensitivity to liberal concerns* that tax burdens and spending cuts should be fairly distributed and that government has a positive role to play in improving the economy, providing a safety net for the vulnerable, and making strategic investments undervalued by the private sector

—*Improving the efficacy of government* through the elimination of poorly performing programs and the reallocation of some funding to more cost-effective uses to meet the objective of not bigger government or smaller government, but smarter, more efficient government

—*Recognition that entitlement programs, especially Medicare, drive spending growth* and that the small, nondefense discretionary portion of the budget (18 percent) cannot carry the deficit reduction load

The illustrative plan that follows applies these principles. It would eliminate the deficit within five years and set the budget on a sustainable

Table 17-1. One Path to a Balanced Budget[a]

Measure	Fiscal year 2013 (billions of dollars)
Revenue increases	206
Outlay reductions	219
Discretionary spending (hard freeze)	124
Social Security, Medicare, and Medicaid reforms	38
Reduced debt service	57
Subtotal	425
Additional investments	(37)
Net impact of proposals	388
Projected deficit	(388)
Resulting surplus (deficit)	0

Sources: Authors' calculations from various sources: Capretta (2007); Isaacs (2007); Tebbs (2007); Rogers (2007); Rivlin and Sawhill (2005) .

a. The cost estimates for new investments include the associated debt service.

and fiscally responsible trajectory (table 17-1). The package is about evenly divided between expenditure reductions and revenue increases. Over time, spending reductions will come primarily from curbing the growth in entitlements. For the first five years, though, to protect current beneficiaries and allow time for political compromises to emerge, most cuts come from discretionary programs. The plan would raise revenue through broadening the base of the tax system, instituting a tax on energy, and promoting tax compliance. Once the steps needed to achieve balance are in place, a portion of the projected savings in interest—a "fiscal responsibility dividend"—is earmarked toward initiatives to strengthen the nation. The remainder is reserved for deficit reduction.

RESTRAIN SPENDING

The federal government spent $2.7 trillion in fiscal year 2007. While much of the public believes that the federal budget is bloated, interest groups lobby vigorously to maintain favored programs, with support from relevant agencies and congressional champions. As a result, spending has grown through Democratic and Republican administrations alike, although rarely more rapidly than during the last five years.[6] Scores of programs have accumulated that, at best, have had modest impacts, have cost far more than they were worth, and have increased burdens on the average taxpayer while benefiting relatively small but politically powerful groups. Specific examples of programs that could be cut will be found in a series of Brookings papers and books (see Additional Resources).

We propose a very simple, if draconian, solution: *set a freeze on all discretionary programs.* This cap would permit trade-offs between programs but require that any increase above current levels be paid for by cuts in other programs. A freeze would save $268 billion over five years, starting in 2009.[7] This approach spreads the pain widely and puts the onus on the president and Congress to make the case for any exception. Presidential candidates should commit to a freeze and promise to veto any breach. Combined with short-run adjustments in the major entitlement programs and revenue increases, discussed later, this approach would balance the budget in 2013, when constraints could be eased.

Not just domestic spending needs to be reined in. Department of Defense spending totaled $530 billion in fiscal year 2007, exceeding real expenditures at the height of the Korean War and approaching a level not witnessed since the Second World War. A significant component of the increase is attributable, broadly, to the global war on terrorism. However, the Defense Department continues to fund numerous weapons systems with little regard for their relevance to current threats or to their performance on measures of cost-effectiveness, ability to meet production timelines, or likelihood of delivering promised capabilities. The defense acquisitions budget reasonably could be trimmed by $35 billion per year.

REFORM ENTITLEMENTS

Social Security, Medicare, and Medicaid are popular because they help a large portion of the population meet essential retirement and health care expenses. However, these three programs, especially Medicare, are the major reason that we are on an unsustainable course *after* 2013. No amount of reasonable cuts in other programs or revenue increases can meet the long-term fiscal challenge they pose, and the next president and Congress must address this challenge.

Social Security

President Bush's attempt in 2005 to reform Social Security was unsuccessful, and the entire system still must be placed on a more solid financial footing.[8] According to the program's trustees, benefit payments will exceed payroll tax revenues within the decade. The only ways to restore solvency to the system are to reduce benefits or to raise taxes, but almost no one supports changes that would harm current beneficiaries. Instead, many experts believe the solution will entail adjusting the age of retirement to reflect greater longevity, encouraging people to remain in the workforce longer, reducing the future growth of benefits for the more affluent, and encouraging workers to save more for their own retirement in personal accounts outside Social Security.

Further, Social Security revenues could be increased by raising payroll taxes. Removing the cap ($102,000 in 2008) on payroll taxes would increase funding especially if it were combined with a change in the benefit formula for those at the top of the earnings scale. Some of the resulting additional revenue could be used to reduce the payroll tax rate.

Significant progress also can be made within the next five to ten years, by changing the way in which benefits are indexed for inflation and by accelerating implementation of the scheduled increase in the normal retirement age from 66 to 67. These changes would yield close to $20 billion in annual savings within a decade. Presidential candidates should consider these or other options, publicly outline their thinking on the issue, and pledge to work with members of the opposite party to craft a solution.

Medicare, Medicaid, and the Health Care System

Health care expenditures in the United States have been growing 2.5 percentage points faster than the economy since 1960. Further, the U.S. health care system is inefficient, costing far more while delivering no greater benefits than do more heavily government-financed systems in other developed countries.[9] Reforming the *entire* health care system, not just the public programs, should be a very high priority. The next president must address the challenge of reducing the growth of health expenditures, while ensuring that patients have access to the benefits of cost-effective medical advances. Although the task is exceedingly difficult, the stakes could not be higher. Indeed, the entire U.S. fiscal problem can be viewed, in essence, as a health care problem. Slowing the growth of health care spending would enhance the nation's competitiveness while reducing most of the nation's long-term deficit.

Experts have suggested diverse strategies: collecting more evidence on effective treatments and creating incentives for patients and providers to use that evidence, instituting electronic health records, emphasizing more preventive care, and more effectively managing chronic diseases, such as diabetes and asthma. Health care financing ideas for encouraging consumers to make thriftier choices include greater reliance on prepaid managed care and high-deductible health plans linked to health savings accounts. Some experts believe that the states are the best place to introduce these or other reforms; however, the most notable example of state-based reform to date—the one being implemented in Massachusetts—contains little in the way of real cost containment and thus may not be an ideal national model. In any case, the federal government should take the lead. As large payers, Medicare and Medicaid have tremendous influence over practice patterns and prices overall and can access huge data sets on the costs and outcomes of clinical care.

The above-mentioned strategies are designed to work within the current employer-based system, supplemented by public programs that provide subsidies to the elderly, the disabled, and the poor. More fundamental reforms that replace the existing system may be needed. An example would be guaranteeing everyone access to a basic health insurance plan, with income-related subsidies for the less affluent and constraints on total public spending that would automatically trigger a tax increase if exceeded. Americans should have whatever level of publicly sponsored health care they want, but only if they are willing to pay for it. (See Additional Resources for more details.)

Are such comprehensive financing reforms feasible? We cannot know, unless more effort is expended on fully articulating their designs and putting them on the agenda for debate and discussion. The essence of the social contract implicit in such plans should be universal access to care in the short run, coupled with limits on spending in the longer run.

Presidential candidates should educate the public on both the nature of the health care financing problem and the solution they favor. Leadership is critical. Past failures to achieve consensus do not justify inaction; indeed, the difficulty of achieving consensus is the reason to start now.

ENHANCE REVENUE

Adopting the changes proposed so far would reduce discretionary spending 11 percent relative to adjusted baseline projections for 2013. In addition, Social Security, Medicare, and Medicaid would each undergo extensive restructuring, yielding modest savings in the near term ($38 billion in 2013) and substantial savings over the long term, as each of the major entitlement programs assumed a sustainable trajectory. The shorter-term savings come from more accurate indexing of Social Security benefits, charging higher premiums to more affluent Medicare beneficiaries, and other similar changes (see Additional Resources for more detail).

Unfortunately, the proposed expenditure reductions can stanch only half the budgetary red ink within the five-year horizon. Limiting spending further would require draconian cuts in domestic discretionary spending, imprudent reductions in resources for national security, or reneging on promises to current Medicare and Social Security beneficiaries. Spending cuts of this sort almost certainly would derail any political compromise between moderates in both parties. Accordingly, a nonnegligible component of any effort to balance the budget must involve revenue enhancements. This phrase is not merely a coy term for tax hikes, but a strategy to increase tax receipts in a way that will facilitate economic growth, improve economic efficiency, simplify the tax code, and promote fairness.

The following revenue package respects these principles and has four components: collecting more of the taxes already owed, broadening the tax base by curbing various deductions and exclusions, imposing a new tax on energy consumption to combat global warming and improve energy security, and reforming the AMT (table 17-2).

Promote Compliance with Existing Tax Law

Collecting taxes that are lawfully owed should be a high governmental priority. In its most recent review, the IRS estimated a 14 percent noncompliance rate for 2001, resulting in $290 billion in missing revenue. Tax gaps of this magnitude necessitate higher tax rates for those who do pay and could induce a downward spiral in compliance, as honest taxpayers abandon what they perceive as an unfair system.

The IRS should be given statutory authority to require more third-party information reporting and withholding (such as reporting cost bases of securities transactions and subjecting corporate taxpayers to similar 1099 requirements as unincorporated businesses). In addition, new resources should be devoted to enforcement. The IRS enforcement workforce declined 36 percent between 1999 and 2005. IRS commissioner Charles Rossotti estimated that $2.2 billion in additional enforcement

Table 17-2. Revenue Proposals[a]

(billions of dollars)

Revenue-raising measures	2009	2010	2011	2012	2013
Narrow the tax gap	25	26	27	29	30
Broaden the base[b]	98	128	133	136	139
Limit itemized deductions to 15 percent	50	68	70	71	71
Limit exclusion on employer-paid health insurance	49	60	63	66	69
Impose a carbon tax	10	21	33	34	36
Net effect[b]	133	176	193	199	206
Revenue-neutral reform of the Alternative Minimum Tax (AMT)					
Index AMT exemption levels	-1	-2	-4	-5	-7
Freeze estate tax at 2009 level	0	16	18	19	21
Net effect[b]	-1	14	14	14	13

Sources: Urban Institute and Brookings Tax Policy Center, Microsimulation Model (version 1006-1): tables T07-0032, T07-0034, T07-0035, T07-0036; (version 0305-3A): T06-0124, T06-0214; Rogers (2007).

a. The AMT reform produces revenue over the next five years but is revenue-neutral over a longer time frame. For a more detailed discussion of these components and several variants, see Frenzel, Stenholm, Hoagland, and Sawhill (2007).

b. Components may not sum to totals due to rounding.

funding would recover $30 billion from identified, noncompliant taxpayers in 2002. Although most experts are skeptical about the ability of such enforcement efforts to increase revenues in the absence of reform and simplification of the tax system, we assume some $25 billion in additional first-year net revenue could be obtained by narrowing the tax gap through better enforcement.

Broaden the Tax Base

Since the 1986 Tax Reform Act, the tax code has been riddled with 14,000 new exclusions, exemptions, deductions, credits, and preferential tax rates. From 1974 to 2004, the Treasury Department reported that the number of such losses, known as tax expenditures, more than doubled. Tax expenditures introduce complexity, needlessly raise the costs of compliance, provide little benefit to the two-thirds of households who do not itemize, are regressive, conceal subsidies, and often provide tax breaks for behavior that would have occurred even without the tax benefit. Consider this: the revenue loss from savings incentives in the tax code is greater than total personal savings.

There are a number of ways to broaden the tax base. One is to eliminate most itemized deductions in favor of a standard deduction for everyone, with a few exceptions for unusually high expenditures (like medical
care), which might reduce one's tax-paying ability. A more politically feasible alternative, endorsed here, is to turn almost all itemized deductions
into a 15 percent credit against taxes. Further, the tax code should limit
exclusions from income of employer-paid health insurance premiums and
certain other health-related tax expenditures. The limit could be set at the
average premium paid in the year of enactment; assuming the limit was
not indexed over time, it would gradually increase the incentive for
employers and employees to make better health care choices. Finally, if
the taxable income threshold for the Social Security payroll tax were
increased, the additional revenues could be used either to shore up the
financing of Social Security benefits in a progressive fashion or to finance
a small reduction in the payroll tax rate (for example, from 6.2 to 5.35
percent for both employers and employees). In total, these changes would
raise $139 billion in 2013.

Enact an Energy Tax

A new energy (carbon) tax would promote energy efficiency, reduce
dependence on oil imports from unstable parts of the world, and combat
global warming. The current level of energy taxation in the United States is
anemic by international standards, measuring only two-thirds of the Organization for Economic Cooperation and Development (OECD) average.

Experts from Resources for the Future, the Brookings Institution, and
the World Resources Institute support a carbon tax, administered
upstream, where carbon-laden fuels are imported or produced. Recommended here is a modest carbon tax of $15 per metric ton, phased in
over three years, to produce revenue of $35 billion per year once com-
pleted. Under a cap-and-trade system with a "safety valve" pricing mechanism, the government would cap permissible emissions but allow firms
to buy and sell allowances among themselves. When the price reached the
"safety valve" level, the government would auction off additional
allowances to bring in more revenue.[10]

Reform the Alternative Minimum Tax

As currently structured, the AMT, originally designed to prevent high-
income households from evading federal taxes, will impose higher tax

rates on an increasing proportion of households—nearly 30 million tax-payers by 2010. Revenue-neutral reform of the AMT would neither lower nor raise tax rates overall but would simply create a fairer, more sustainable tax structure. This can be accomplished by holding constant the percentage of taxpayers subject to the AMT and recouping the revenue this would lose by freezing the estate tax at its 2009 exemption levels ($3.5 million per individual, $7 million per couple) with a 45 percent rate of taxation. With these parameters, less than one-half of 1 percent of estates would be subject to estate taxes, and the AMT would no longer threaten middle- or upper-middle-income families.

REINVEST A PORTION OF THE FISCAL RESPONSIBILITY DIVIDEND

The plan outlined here would slow the accumulation of debt and reduce interest costs, producing a "fiscal responsibility dividend" that would total about $57 billion by 2013—more than enough to close the remaining fiscal hole.[11] We propose devoting $20 billion of this dividend to deficit reduction and the remaining $37 billion to investments in the nation's future, although none of the dividend should be spent until the CBO certifies that the deficit has been lowered enough to truly produce the dividend. Following this verification, areas for spending might include

—sliding-scale subsidies for early childhood education, at an estimated cost of $18 billion in 2009 and $97 billion over five years (even under conservative assumptions, these programs return more than $2 in benefits for every $1 in costs);

—international assistance, a long-run strategy that would help defuse terrorism;

—biomedical research, electronic medical records, and covering the uninsured, as a prelude to fundamental health care reform.

BREAK THE LEGISLATIVE STALEMATE

The politics of deficit reduction are extraordinarily difficult. Some process reforms could provide political cover for the tough choices that need to be made and thus could help break the stalemate.

In 2006, President Bush called for a bipartisan entitlement commission. Democrats balked at participating, mainly because taxes were not part of the deal. A future commission would need highly respected cochairs (similar to the 9/11 Commission), an equal number of Democrats and Republicans, a mandate to tackle not only entitlements but also tax reforms to enhance revenue, and a requirement that a supermajority of commissioners support its recommendations. In addition, the president and Congress should agree to consider commission recommendations on a fast-track basis.

For discretionary programs, the recent revision of House rules to reinstate pay-as-you-go financing is promising—although a firmer, statutory version of PAYGO that cannot be waived by the House Rules Committee would be preferable. Other process reforms worth considering include stating the long-term costs of present commitments in budget documents, giving the president enhanced rescission authority (a modified line-item veto), and creating a rainy-day fund in lieu of using supplemental appropriations to fund emergencies. Reforms could also include biennial budgeting and appropriations, automatic continuing resolutions when Congress fails to pass appropriations bills, and simplified committee operations.

CONCLUDING OBSERVATIONS

The nation will face a fiscal tsunami once baby boomers begin to retire. Any candidate for president who downplays the problem or avoids talking about specifics will ill serve the public and forfeit any mandate to lead. This issue is too important to ignore until after the votes are counted.

ADDITIONAL RESOURCES

Aaron, Henry J., and Stuart M. Butler. 2004. "How Federalism Could Spur Bipartisan Action on the Uninsured." *Health Affairs,* web exclusive (March 31).

Antos, Joseph, and others. 2008. "Taking Back Our Fiscal Future." Brookings–Heritage Fiscal Seminar (Washington, April).

Auerbach, Alan J., William G. Gale, and Peter R. Orszag. 2006. "New Estimates of the Budget Outlook: Plus ça Change, Plus C'est la Même Chose." *Tax Notes.* Washington: Brookings–Urban Institute Tax Policy Center (April 17).

Capretta, James C. 2007. "Restraining Federal Domestic Spending." Budgeting for National Priorities Paper. Brookings (January).

Frenzel, William, Charles Stenholm, William Hoagland, and Isabel Sawhill. 2007. "Taming the Deficit." Budgeting for National Priorities Paper. Brookings (February).

Gluck, Frederick W. 2007. "Plain Talk about Health Care." Budgeting for National
    Priorities Discussion Paper. Brookings (February).
Isaacs, Julia B. 2007. "Cost-Effective Investments in Children." Budgeting for
    National Priorities Paper. Brookings (January).
Rivlin, Alice M., and Isabel V. Sawhill, eds. 2004. *Restoring Fiscal Sanity: How to
    Balance the Budget.* Brookings.
———, eds. 2005. *Restoring Fiscal Sanity 2005: Meeting the Long-Run Challenge.*
    Brookings.
Rogers, Diane Lim. 2007. "Reducing the Deficit through Better Tax Policy."
    Budgeting for National Priorities Paper. Brookings (January).
Sawhill, Isabel, and Emily Monea. 2008. "Old News." *Democracy,* no. 9 (Summer):
    20–31.
Tebbs, Jeffrey M. 2007. "Pruning the Defense Budget." Budgeting for National
    Priorities Paper. Brookings (January).
White, Chapin. 2007. "Trends: Health Care Spending Growth—How Different Is the
    United States from the Rest of the OECD?" *Health Affairs* 26, no. 1 (January–
    February):154–61.

NOTES

1. In November of 2007, the Congressional Budget Office (CBO) released a new metric for projecting health care consumption and costs. Rather than assuming that excess cost growth rates continue indefinitely at some specified level, the new metric assumes that these rates will eventually moderate to some degree, as Americans will ultimately demand changes to the health care system to prevent their consumption of other goods and services from declining in real (inflation-adjusted) terms. See Congressional Budget Office (CBO), *The Long-Term Outlook for Health Care Spending* (Washington, November 2007), pp. 9–12. Figure 17-1 also assumes that the spending by the federal government will follow the alternative fiscal scenario defined by the CBO. This scenario assumes that physician payment rates grow with the Medicare economic index and that other spending excluding interest remains at the 2007 share of GDP. For further details, see CBO, *The Long-Term Budget Outlook* (Washington, December 2007), table 1-1.

2. According to the CBO, an increase in the growth rate of real GDP of one-half of 1 percent per year for each of the next five years would reduce the deficit by only $75 billion. See CBO, *The Budget and Economic Outlook: Fiscal Years 2007 to 2016* (Washington, January 2006), appendix C, p. 123.

3. Authors' calculations, based on data from U.S. Treasury Department, table: "Major Foreign Holders of Treasury Securities" (Washington, through August 15, 2006) (www.treas.gov/tic/mfh.txt); Bureau of the Public Debt, *Monthly Statement of the Public Debt of the United States* (Washington: Treasury Department, through July 31, 2006) (www.treasurydirect.gov/govt/reports/pd/mspd/mspd.htm).

4. Authors' calculations for the increased cost of a mortgage, assuming a 20 percent down payment on a $225,000 house, with a thirty-year fixed rate mortgage. (In 2005, $225,000 was the median sale price for an existing single-family home, as reported by the Joint Center for Housing Studies at Harvard University, *The State of the Nation's Housing: 2006* [October 2006].)

5. Authors' calculations based on data from CBO, *An Analysis of the President's Budgetary Proposals for Fiscal Year 2009* (Washington, March 2008), data from Baseline Budget Projections; U.S. Census Bureau, *Statistical Abstract of the United States: 2008*, Table 58: "Households, Families, Subfamilies, and Married Couples: 1960 to 2006."

6. From fiscal year 2002 to fiscal year 2006 (estimated), total federal spending grew at a faster inflation-adjusted rate than during any administration since Lyndon Johnson's. Authors' calculations based on data from Office of Management and Budget, *Budget of the United States Government: FY 2007* (2006), tables 1.3, 4.1, and 8.2.

7. Authors' calculations from CBO, *The Budget and Economic Outlook: Fiscal Years 2007 to 2016*, tables 1-3 and 1-8; Tax Policy Center, "Outlook Tables" (Washington, August 2006); CBO, *Long-Term Implications of Current Defense Plans and Alternatives: Summary Update for Fiscal Year 2006* (Washington, October 2005). Baseline assumptions regarding discretionary spending are explained in "Taming the Deficit" (Frenzel, Stenholm, Hoagland, and Sawhill 2007).

8. Whatever one thinks about the merits of carve-out private accounts, they do not address the fiscal challenges facing the current system and instead would only make matters worse for a number of decades, because the diversion of payroll taxes into private accounts would leave the current system of benefits underfunded, requiring more borrowing to make up the difference.

9. As an illustration of this point, U.S. per capita health expenditures were more than twice those of most other Organization for Economic Cooperation and Development (OECD) countries in 2005.

10. In conjunction with the carbon tax, the president and Congress also could eliminate harmful, inefficient, and redundant tax subsidies related to energy. These include, but are not limited to, expensing of exploration and development costs for extractive industries, corn-based ethanol subsidies, and the "percentage depletion" rules for extractive industries. These additional measures should recover $15 billion to $20 billion in revenue each year.

11. In part, the interest savings occur because of the reduction in the accumulation of debt and in part because interest rates are likely to be lower in response to less borrowing. We conservatively include only the first of these effects.

18

Realistic Approaches to Head Off a U.S. Economic Crisis

WARREN B. RUDMAN, J. ROBERT KERREY,
PETER G. PETERSON, AND ROBERT BIXBY

SUMMARY ❱ An honest assessment of the nation's long-term fiscal outlook almost makes one wonder why, in 2008, anyone would want to be elected president. And why so little attention is being paid to a problem that budget analysts of diverse perspectives routinely describe as "unsustainable."

One thing is clear: the status quo is not acceptable. The next president will inherit a fiscally lethal combination of changing demographics, rising heath care costs, and falling national savings. The public should take care to not buy the proposals of presidential candidates that either ignore the magnitude of the long-term fiscal challenge or lock candidates into positions that make these problems insoluble. Improving the nation's long-term fiscal outlook will require hard choices on spending and tax policy. Presidential candidates and their consultants might shy away from endorsing such choices on the campaign trail, but they should not rule them out.

The next administration must enter office with a mandate to act on this problem. Doing so will likely require a mix of options arrived at through bipartisan negotiations. The more options taken off the table through ironclad campaign promises, the more difficult it will be to find meaningful solutions once the campaigns are over and the time for governing begins. Candidates must acknowledge the magnitude of the problem, the need for trade-offs, and the necessity for prompt action. Vague promises of "fiscal responsibility" give the public insufficient insight into how well candidates understand the task at hand.

Comprehensive solutions may take considerable time to develop, and once implemented, they should be subject to periodic review. However, as a framework for action the next president should

—commit to a balanced budget;

—take every reasonable step to constrain the rising costs of heath care and the retirement programs Social Security and, most especially, Medicare;

—make clear to Americans that taxes cannot be cut over the long term unless programs are cut commensurately;

—prevent total spending, taxes, or debt from reaching levels that could reduce economic growth and future standards of living. ❯

CONTEXT ❯ The basic facts are not in dispute. What they portend is not just a short-term budget crunch but the long-term budgetary impact of an unprecedented demographic shift to an older society—one that will exert great pressure on the economy from programs such as Social Security, Medicare, and Medicaid. Key features driving the impending fiscal crisis are as follows:

—Social Security, Medicare, and Medicaid already constitute 42 percent of the federal budget—before the baby boomers have begun to retire in any numbers.

—Over the next thirty years, the number of Americans aged sixty-five and over is expected to grow from 13 to 20 percent of the population. The ratio of workers paying into Social Security and Medicare relative to the number of beneficiaries will fall by roughly one-third.

—For the past forty years, health care spending has consistently grown faster than the economy. If the same growth rate continues over the next forty years, Medicare and Medicaid alone will absorb nearly as much of our nation's economy as the entire federal budget does today.

—Higher saving levels today would contribute to a larger economy tomorrow, and that would make the looming fiscal burden more affordable. Unfortunately, Americans' personal savings rate as a percentage of disposable income has steadily declined—from more than 7 percent in the early 1990s to essentially zero today. Net national saving, public and private combined, has plummeted from 8.5 percent of gross national income twenty-five years ago to less than 2 percent today.

—In the absence of domestic saving, foreign sources have taken up the slack. The portion of the government's privately held debt owned by foreign investors has risen from 36 to 46 percent since 2001. Reliance on foreign borrowing increases the budget's exposure to international capital markets and decisions made by foreign interests. Moreover, interest payments on the national debt go to bondholders from abroad—a growing mortgage on our future national income.

—Raising tax revenues to cover projected government spending would require today's tax levels to increase by a third to a half by 2030, depending on the growth of health care costs. If we try to keep government revenues at today's level and pay for the increase in Social Security, Medicare, and Medicaid by reducing spending on other programs, it would require a cut of between one-half to four-fifths by 2030—again depending on the path of health care spending.

Another way to look at the size of the problem is to total up the government's explicit liabilities, such as the national debt, and its implicit obligations, such as future Social Security and Medicare benefits. According to the Government Accountability Office (GAO), all such "fiscal exposures" have a present value of $53 trillion—almost as much as today's net worth of all household assets and far more than the commonly cited national debt, which is now over $9 trillion.[1]

No one can say when all this might end up in a crisis nor what a crisis would look like. Indeed, there might be no crisis at all—just a long, slow erosion in our nation's standard of living. In either case, it is a dismal future, and doing nothing now to avoid it would be an act of fiscal and generational irresponsibility.

Despite the clear warning signals, presidential candidates will face enormous pressure to look the other way. The problem is not that the public cannot handle the truth—we believe they can—the problem is the poisonous political environment in Washington and an election process that rewards the most obstinate forms of partisanship. The very idea of bipartisan cooperation seems highly offensive to ideological purists of both Left and Right. Politicians who truly wish to seek consensus solutions are confronted with the double burden of working out their differences, which can be substantial, while fending off their ideological guardians, who insist that any compromise is both unnecessary and unwise.

Campaign platforms will therefore burst with "base"-pleasing pledges. If history is a guide, Democrats will tout plans to expand entitlement benefits, not just for those in need but for middle-income and upper-middle-income people as well. They will be much less forthcoming about where the money will be found. For their part, Republicans will likely insist that all of the Bush tax cuts must be made permanent and that more tax cuts would be even better.[2] They, in turn, will have little to say about the specific spending cuts that would be needed to accommodate the revenue loss. These are politically convenient evasions. The real choices require scaling back federal expenditures for health care and Social Security, raising revenues, or some combination.

Some people might believe that the federal government should both tax and spend at about 18 percent of GDP, while others might believe it should tax and spend at about 30 percent. No reasonable person, however, would argue that the government should tax at 18 percent and spend at 30 percent. The resulting annual deficits and accumulated debt would shatter the economy. Yet this is the future we will get if we try to fund the spending *required by current law* with today's level of taxation.

While candidates will not necessarily agree on specific solutions, even within their respective political parties, they can prepare the ground for action in the next administration by acknowledging that each of the realistic options discussed in the next section comes with economic and political consequences. There must be trade-offs.

—Those who want to raise taxes must consider what level of taxation they are willing to support and how the new revenue should be raised.

—Those who believe that spending must come down must consider which programs they would target for reduction and how the savings would be achieved.

—Those who are unwilling to do either must consider how much debt they are willing to impose on future generations. ▐

TOWARD A BRIGHTER FUTURE

There is no quick fix. There are, however, actions we can begin taking now that will improve the economic prospects for future generations.

Commitment to a balanced budget is a good first step. Restoring a balanced budget would increase national savings, lower future interest costs, signal to world financial markets that we are serious about getting our fiscal house in order, and reduce our dependence on foreign lenders. Yet, even with a near-term balanced budget plan, current fiscal policy would remain unsustainable over the long term.

The most effective long-range solution would be to *constrain the rising cost of heath care and retirement programs—primarily Medicare and Social Security.* This will require difficult choices regarding who should receive benefits, what level of benefits can be provided, and how those benefits should be delivered.

Raising future taxes to meet rising costs of government programs is another option, but conceptually this would be similar to borrowing in that it would place a claim on the expected earnings of today's children—in effect confiscating their economic futures. There is, however, a necessary corollary: if spending does not come down, taxes will have to go up. Trying to borrow our way through the problem does not reduce the tax burden; it will simply impose even *higher* taxes on future generations who would be saddled with the rising costs of entitlement programs in addition to exploding interest costs.

Treating taxes and spending as "separate deals" is an economic fantasy. To be sure, low taxes theoretically encourage economic growth by providing incentives for work, saving, and investment. However, if taxes fall too far below government spending for too long, the resulting deficits will eventually cancel out any positive economic gains. In the final analysis, government revenues must be sufficient to pay its costs. Tax cuts make attractive campaign rhetoric, but unless they are accompanied by reduced spending over the long term, we are merely shifting the tax burden from ourselves to our children. Debt is not a painless alternative to taxation.

The best fiscal policy is one that aims to *prevent total spending, taxes, or debt from reaching levels that could reduce economic growth and future standards of living.* For that reason, we do not favor a blanket extension of the expiring 2001 and 2003 tax cuts. Instead, the decision on whether to extend them should be made within the context of sustainable, long-term fiscal policy. Adhering to the pay-as-you-go (PAYGO) budget rules now in effect in the House and Senate would facilitate the necessary balancing of tax and spending priorities.

SOCIAL SECURITY REFORM

Basic Principles

We believe that Social Security reform plans should meet three fundamental objectives—ensuring Social Security's long-term fiscal sustainability, raising national saving rates, and improving the system's generational equity:

—*Long-term fiscal sustainability.* The first goal of reform should be to close Social Security's financing gap over the lifetimes of our children and beyond. The only way to do so without burdening tomorrow's workers and taxpayers is to reduce Social Security's long-term cost.

—*Increased national savings.* As the United States ages, the economy will inevitably have to transfer a rising share of real resources from workers to retirees. This burden can be made more bearable by increasing the size of tomorrow's economy. The surest way to do this is by raising national saving rates and hence, ultimately, productivity growth. Without new saving, reform is a zero-sum game.

—*Generational equity.* As currently structured, Social Security benefits offer each new generation of workers declining value on their contributions. Reform must not exacerbate—and ideally should improve—the generational inequity underlying the current system.

Paths to Avoid

Candidates tempted to take the path of least resistance may rely on criteria that minimize the size of the problem or on options that merely shift and conceal the cost. Here are a few examples of such shortsighted approaches:

Trust Fund Accounting

The traditional method of measuring Social Security's future is the seventy-five-year actuarial balance of its trust funds. By this measure, Social Security is said to be solvent until 2041. That may sound reassuring, but all it really means is that the government owes itself a great deal of money. Trust fund accounting obscures the magnitude and timing of Social Security's financing gap by assuming that trust fund surpluses accumulated in prior years can be drawn down to defray deficits incurred in future years. However, the trust funds are bookkeeping devices, not a mechanism for savings. The special-issue U.S. Treasury bonds that the trust funds contain represent a promise from one arm of government (Treasury) to satisfy claims held by another arm of government (Social Security). They do not indicate how these claims will be satisfied or whether real resources are being set aside to match future obligations. Thus, alone, their existence does not ease the burden of paying future benefits. The real test of fiscal sustainability is whether reform closes Social Security's long-term gap between outlays and dedicated tax revenues.

Reliance on New Debt

Paying for promised benefits or financing private account options by issuing new debt defeats the objective of increasing savings. To the extent that reform relies on debt financing, it will not boost net savings and may result in a decline. Without new savings, any gain for the Social Security system must come at the expense of the rest of the budget, the economy, and future generations. When we resort to borrowing, we are ultimately increasing taxes for our kids.

Reliance on Outside Financing

Ideally, reform should achieve all necessary fiscal savings within the Social Security system itself. Unrelated tax increases and spending cuts may never be enacted, or if enacted, may at any point be neutralized by other measures.

Realistic Reform Strategies

There is no one right answer to Social Security reform. However, adjusting the program for Americans' increasing longevity and constraining the growing value of its scheduled monthly benefits are the two most logical steps for constraining growth in the program's cost. Personal accounts would help improve generational equity and improve savings—if the accounts are fully funded and mandatory.

Longevity Adjustments

Raising the age at which retirees are eligible for full benefits (now sixty-six and scheduled to go up to sixty-seven by 2027) makes good sense for several reasons:

—Longevity is increasing steadily, and longer life spans mean longer, and more costly, lifetime benefits.

—Older Americans are generally healthier than in the past and can work more years, especially as jobs have become less physically demanding.

—In coming decades, the pool of working-age Americans will virtually stop growing, depriving our nation of this engine of economic growth. Raising the eligibility age for full benefits could help augment the labor force by encouraging older people to remain at work for a few more years.

Some proposals would raise the full-benefit age in the future. Others would set up an automatic provision, referred to as "longevity indexing," that would have the full-benefit age or initial age rise periodically if longevity continues to rise. As a practical matter, these options should be combined. Raising the eligibility age to a higher fixed target may balance the system for awhile. But without longevity indexing, the system will again drift out of balance.

Price Indexing

Another good option would be to index initial benefits to the growth in prices for commonly used goods and services, as measured by the consumer price index.[3] This reform has two advantages: it is simple, and it creates large savings. According to the most recent estimate by the Social Security program's actuaries, moving to price indexing would more than close the program's projected gap. Assuming this change took effect in 2012, the actuaries estimate that the system's annual shortfall would peak in 2032 at 2.33 percent of taxable payroll. By 2055 the system would show a positive balance, and by 2080 it would be running a surplus equal to 2.23 of taxable payroll.

Under the rules by which Social Security operates today, it is virtually impossible to close its deficit by increasing national productivity. True, higher productivity would result in higher wages and thereby boost payroll tax revenue. But higher wages also would result in higher benefits that would largely cancel out the gain. With price indexing, however, benefits would shrink indefinitely relative to taxable payroll and GDP—and the faster that wages grow, the more that benefits would shrink as a share of the economy.

This dynamic, of course, means that retirees would receive smaller benefits, relative to the wages of the working population. To the extent that Social Security is viewed as a type of safety net program, this does not pose a public policy problem. To the extent that Social Security is viewed as an income replacement program, it does.

For this reason, price indexing makes the most sense as part of an overall reform that also incorporates funded benefits like personal accounts. On one hand, the price-indexed, pay-as-you-go benefit would ensure that the purchasing power of benefits would remain the same for each new generation of retirees. On the other, the funded benefits would help ensure that the relative living standard of retirees is not eroded.

Another approach, called progressive price indexing, would mitigate the effects of reform on low-income and moderately low-income workers by wage-indexing benefits for the lowest third of benefits (as under current law), phasing in an element of price indexing for the middle third, and fully price-indexing benefits for the top third. This would generate program savings from moderate- and high-income workers but protect lower-income workers. According to the Social Security actuaries, this reform would close roughly 80 percent of the cash deficit by 2080.

Although this change alone would not be enough to close the system's financing gap, Congress should give it serious consideration as part of an overall reform plan. It would substantially improve the system's fiscal sustainability while preserving all promised benefits for those who rely on them most.

Tax Options

Raising the payroll tax rate to meet benefit obligations would be neither economically sound nor generationally equitable. The burden would fall most heavily on lower- and middle-income workers and on future generations. A popular alternative to an across-the-board increase is to make more of the earnings of higher-income workers taxable by raising the cap on taxable wages. Currently, the Social Security payroll tax (12.4 percent) is levied on wages up to $102,000. Raising this cap would bring in more money, but as a means of ensuring the program's sustainability, it would be considerably less effective than its proponents allege. It would provide only a few more years of positive cash flow to the system, and unless the link between taxable earnings and benefits were to be eliminated, it would add to the system's long-term cost by providing higher benefits to those who need them least.

Certainly, raising taxes in some form would be more fiscally responsible than would unlimited borrowing. It may also be a necessary component in any plan that is capable of winning broad bipartisan support. But before resorting to this option, policymakers must carefully weigh the magnitude of the looming demands that Social Security and health care entitlements will place on the income of future workers and the economy overall. Levying higher taxes to meet rising costs could hinder an economy that will also have to cope with near-stagnant workforce growth. Moreover, a Social Security tax increase now would simply be used to support other government operations and perhaps would even encourage higher government spending while pretending that we are shoring up the trust fund.

In short, increasing Social Security revenues today will not reduce the program's future burden unless a mechanism is in place to ensure that the extra money generates increased personal saving and a larger future economy.

Personal Accounts

One way that higher Social Security contributions could generate new saving would be if they were used to create personally owned accounts within the Social Security system. This reform could increase saving by providing a more reliable method of pre-funding promised benefits than government trust funds can ensure. The funds would be beyond the reach of government, and Congress could not double-count personal account assets in the federal budget. In other words, they would provide a "lockbox" no politician could pick.

However, the money to establish personal accounts must come from somewhere. To the extent that the source of funding is additional government borrowing, no new savings for the economy will result, because the increase in government borrowing would cancel it out. Moreover, personal accounts alone do nothing to close the existing gap between dedicated revenues and promised benefits. In any true transition to a funded system, workers will have to pay more, retirees will have to receive less, or both. Reform plans that do not face up to this transition cost will not result in new net saving or a larger economy.

It thus makes sense to use the *add-on approach* to personal accounts, meaning that they should be funded from additional worker contributions. These contributions would be personally owned savings, and so they would not function as a tax increase. They would increase national and personal savings rather than increase the size of government. Such accounts should be a mandatory part of the system. The government has a legitimate interest in seeing that people do not undersave during their working lives and become reliant on the safety net in retirement.

MEDICARE REFORM

Medicare is a much bigger problem than Social Security, not just fiscally but also politically and ethically. Its costs are projected to grow faster than the economy and faster than can be reasonably supported by the federal budget. Health care prices have outpaced overall economic growth since 1960. This phenomenon greatly compounds the growing fiscal problems associated with the rising number of aged Americans. Unless health costs slow, by 2050 the share of GDP consumed by Medicare and Medicaid will be four times what it is today. Most of that increase would come from the rising cost of health care rather than from the larger number of elderly Americans.

Before we begin to think about specific ways to address the Medicare problem, here are criteria for evaluating presidential candidates' Medicare reform proposals:

—*Scope of benefits.* Medicare should cover a level of care commensurate with the care available to working-age people. This does not mean that taxpayers must be expected to finance a high-option insurance plan for all seniors.

—*Fiscally responsible.* A fiscally responsible program is one that can reasonably be expected to operate within the resources available to finance it. A program that assumes a perpetually open spigot from the Treasury is not fiscally responsible.

—*Income-related cost sharing.* As a group, seniors enjoy a better income and less poverty than do other age groups, particularly children. Therefore, Medicare's premiums, which help fund Parts B (physician care) and D (prescription drugs), should be geared to income levels. Currently, premiums cover only 25 percent of program costs. General tax revenues cover the rest. Given this large subsidy and the need for long-term program savings, beneficiaries who can afford to pay more of their fair share should do so.

—*Efficient provision of medical care.* Whatever new system of medical insurance for the elderly is devised, it should contain incentives for both providers and patients to use resources cost-effectively. Treatments that have little or no promise of achieving any appreciable improvement in a patient's well-being should not be financed with taxpayer dollars.

Political leaders like to pretend that there are simple fixes to Medicare that will not require anyone to give up anything. Just clamp down on "fraud and abuse," or cut back on excessive paperwork, and the problem will be solved. Health policy experts see it differently. Pure waste is no easier to pinpoint in the health system than it is in the federal budget. And, even if we could identify and eliminate all of it, the underlying cost drivers—from technology to expectations of good health to aging—would soon cause spending to grow again as fast or faster than before.

The hard truth is that there are only two direct ways to reduce the growth in Medicare costs: pay health care providers less, or reduce the amount of health care that patients consume. Although both political parties agree that the goal is to deliver better quality of care while controlling costs, that goal is much easier enunciated than achieved.

The United States has the only open-ended, cost-plus health care financing system in the world. As a result, we spend more than twice as much per capita as do other developed countries. Yet there is very little evidence that our overall health outcomes are any better—and on some key measures, they are worse. Following are described some of the more significant contributing factors to this situation.

Resource Intensity

The resource-intensive style of medicine is the single most important reason why so much more is spent on health care in the United States than in other nations. Some of the resource-intensity comes from new technology and some from simply doing more—more tests, more visits, more procedures, more administrative costs, and so on. Society's definition of health itself has also expanded. In recent decades, we have steadily broadened the definition of insurable health care to include whole new realms of social life.

Lack of Cost Containment Incentives

"Good health" is a subjective standard and one that naturally rises as society becomes more affluent. As these trends interact with technological progress, they are transforming the practice of health care. While once health care meant an occasional visit to the doctor or hospital, it is fast becoming a lifelong process of diagnostics and fine-tuning in which any extra dollar spent is expected to confer some perceived benefit. And with consumers' out-of-pocket share of their personal health care costs having fallen from more than 30 percent in 1975 to 15 percent in 2005, they have little incentive to demand the most cost-effective treatments. Moreover, fee-for-service reimbursement and fear of malpractice claims give providers every incentive to prescribe any additional treatment regardless of its relative cost-effectiveness.

Aging Society

Then again, there is the aging of the U.S. population. Nearly every measure of illness, disability, and health care utilization rises with age. On average, each older American consumes about four times as much in medical services as a younger adult and about seven times as much as a child. Although the elderly now are just 12 percent of the U.S. population, they account for nearly 40 percent of U.S. medical bills.

No Cost-Effectiveness Standards

Businesses run on best practices. Medicare does not. Many studies have shown that comparable patients receive very different care—at very different costs—depending on where they get care, because of different styles of practice from one region to another or even from one hospital to another. For example, comparable patients are six times as likely to have back surgery if they live in some areas of Oregon than if they live in Indiana. One reason for this is that insufficient data exist to guide caregivers and patients on which treatments work best. Any package of reforms should include greater attention to research on the comparative effectiveness of treatments, as well as incentives for patients and providers to use the results of such research in making decisions on the best care.

Better targeting of resources could lead to substantial savings. It is well documented, for example, that cost variations are dramatic for care near the end of life. A recent study of large California hospitals found that Medicare spending per patient in the last two years of life ranged from $24,722 to $106,254—*with no demonstrable difference in health status, quality of health care, or longevity.* Over the five-year study period, Medicare could have saved $1.7 billion in the Los Angeles area alone, if the resource-intense hospital care in Los Angeles had matched the pattern of care in lower-cost areas of the state.[4] With more than a quarter of annual Medicare spending going for beneficiaries in the last year of life, policymakers must begin asking some tough questions about the causes and potential cures for such anomalies in cost patterns.

The most striking finding from these comparisons of costs among regions is that higher spending and more resource-intensive care do not produce better patient outcomes. For policymakers, the key point is that there are choices in the way care is delivered and that the most expensive choice is not necessarily the best—not for patients and not for society.

Americans have yet to confront these choices, but other countries have been dealing with them for years. Go through the intensive care unit of NewYork-Presbyterian Hospital and count the number of octogenarians who are there with heroic intervention techniques and a dismal quality of life. Then go to a hospital in London and observe the difference in the age composition. What is done in Great Britain? Medical costs have been capped. A neurologist caring for stroke patients with a dismal prognosis turns them over to their general practitioner, who sends them home to die quietly of pneumonia, the "old man's friend." Would Americans accept the level of health care rationing that this implies? Maybe not. But we will soon need to face the question.

Spending on health care for the elderly will continue to grow far faster than the economy so long as we pretend that costs can be controlled without any sacrifice. Costs are not rising because of the proliferation of completely useless medical services. They are rising because medical science can do more for more people—and because what it can do is often very expensive, even if the benefit is incremental. Ultimately our nation must decide what level of health care we wish to provide as an entitlement and how much we are willing to pay for it. Setting limits in Medicare will mean moving toward a whole new paradigm—one in which prospective budgets at the program level and capitation at the beneficiary level finally compel us to make trade-offs between health care and other national priorities.

In short, Medicare should be put on a budget. If program costs exceed targeted levels, Congress and the president should be required to take corrective action. If they decide that program costs should be permitted to increase (for example, by filling the prescription drug "doughnut hole" or by adding long-term care coverage), then the demands of fiscal responsibility require that they identify a commensurate stream of revenue to pay for the expanded coverage.

No matter what vision of health care reform we adopt, it would make sense to end the current open-ended tax exclusion for employer-paid health benefits. According to GAO, this exclusion cost the federal government an estimated $188 billion in forgone revenues in fiscal year 2006 alone.[5] Subsidized health insurance is also one of the main reasons that Americans spend so much on health care. It encourages employees to choose more generous coverage than they otherwise would, channeling resources toward health care consumption and away from other priorities. It also gives the same preferential tax treatment to the last dollar spent on health care as to the first and thus subsidizes not just basic coverage, but "gold-plated" health benefit plans.

The tax exclusion thus adds to the deficit and drives up health care costs. It would be counterproductive in a single-payer national health system. It even would be counterproductive in a system that mandated employer-based coverage. If desired, to maximize coverage, it would be possible to reform this tax exclusion so that much, or even all, of the benefits went to lower earners. This could be done by using a flat refundable tax credit or a sliding-scale credit.

Ultimately, the growth in Medicare costs must be addressed through fundamental health care reform. That is no reason, however, to avoid incremental steps that make sense on their own and that can achieve substantial savings. Medicare is quite influential, accounting for 20 percent of the nation's total spending on health care. If the next president can agree with Congress on meaningful Medicare reforms, it may well lead the way for necessary reforms of the broader health care system.

CONCLUDING OBSERVATIONS

Daunting as the long-term projections for the U.S. economy are, there is nothing inevitable about a fiscal crisis. The problem we face—essentially a structural imbalance between what government promises and how much it collects in taxes to pay for those promises—is one that can be cured if we begin to address it now.

Fundamentally, this is not about numbers. There are basic philosophical questions:

—Is it morally acceptable to pursue a fiscal policy that threatens to place ever-tighter constraints on future generations' ability to determine their own priorities or to meet new challenges?

—Have we become so insistent on our own claims to government benefits, regardless of need, that we have forgotten about the well-being of the very people we expect to pay for those benefits—our children and grandchildren?

—Can any modern media–dominated society, fixated on the short term and the next election, deal on a timely basis with silent, slow-motion, long-term challenges, or is a costly crisis needed to spur action?

These are not easy questions, but they are ones that all of the 2008 presidential candidates should confront, publicly and explicitly.

NOTES

1. Government Accountability Office, "Government Accountability Office Statement," in *Fiscal Year 2007 Financial Report of the United States Government* (December 17, 2007).

2. The tax cuts enacted in 2001 and 2003 were written with *sunset dates* that cause them to expire by 2011. The estimated revenue loss of extending them is $3.6 trillion through 2018, including extension of relief from the Alternative Minimum Tax. If this revenue loss is not offset, the additional borrowing would add another $740 billion in debt service costs.

3. Under current law, initial benefit awards are indexed not to prices but to wages—that is, the wage history on which benefits are based is updated at the time of retirement to reflect the rise in the economy's overall wage level over the course of the beneficiary's working career.

4. See Dartmouth Atlas Project, "Supply-Sensitive Care," Topic Brief (Lebanon, N.H.: Center for the Evaluative Clinical Sciences at Dartmouth, January 2007) (www.dartmouthatlas.org/topics/supply_sensitive.pdf).

5. David M. Walker, *Long-Term Fiscal Outlook: Action Is Needed to Avoid the Possibility of a Serious Economic Disruption in the Future*, testimony of the U.S. comptroller general before the Senate Committee on the Budget, 110 Cong. 2 sess., GAO-08-411T (Government Accountability Office, January 29, 2008), p. 13.

Extending Deregulation

Make the U.S. Economy More Efficient

ROBERT W. CRANDALL

SUMMARY ❱ Since the 1970s, deregulation has succeeded in increasing overall economic welfare and sharply reducing prices, generally by about 30 percent, for transportation—including air travel, rail transportation, and trucking—and for natural gas and telecommunications. Few industries remain subject to classic economic regulation in the United States. To help remove some of the last vestiges of such controls, the next president should do the following:

—Promote full deregulation of all voice telephone services

—Oppose "network neutrality" initiatives for broadband telecommunications that would interfere with pricing innovations designed to relieve network congestion

—Within the electricity sector, support market reforms (such as real-time pricing) and incentives for expanding or preventing overloads in transmission grids and distribution networks and allow states to proceed at a measured pace in deregulating electrical generation

—Promote competition among airports and privatization of air traffic control in order to improve the pricing of airport landing rights and to reduce air traffic congestion

—Back "open skies" or "cabotage" approaches to international air travel and allow more foreign investment in domestic airlines

Even more important, the next president should act to restrain government interference in markets that does not quite amount to classic economic regulation. Examples of beneficial strategies for such regulatory reform include auctioning more of the electromagnetic spectrum, encouraging efficient pricing of water to take into account the highest-value uses of water and to facilitate conservation, and proposing the use of some federal interstate highway funds for demonstration projects for congestion-pricing on major urban highways. ❱

CONTEXT ❱ Analysts distinguish between economic and social regulation. The former is the control of prices, service quality, and entry conditions in specific sectors, such as transportation, communications, and energy. The latter is the regulation of risks to health, safety, and the environment. In this chapter, I focus primarily on economic regulation.

Deregulation of major industries in the United States began in the 1970s and spread to the United Kingdom and, to a lesser extent, to the European continent. Despite enormous success, the deregulatory movement may be stalled and even subject to reversal in the wake of spectacular failure in the perceived "deregulation" of the electricity industry in California, doubts about the wisdom of British electricity and rail privatization, the recent surge in oil prices, and debates over access of content providers to new broadband telecommunications services.

The next president should act to eliminate many remaining pockets of economic regulation. But a wider assault against myriad forms of inefficient government intervention in markets—beyond classic "regulation"—is more urgently needed. There simply is not much traditional economic regulation left in the United States, outside the telecommunications and electricity sectors. However, a great deal of federal interference with the market still occurs, including government control of the electromagnetic spectrum, non-price allocation of water and highways, regulation of airport landing rights, and air traffic control. Moreover, new forms of energy regulation are surely going to be proposed if the price of oil remains above $100 per barrel. Reducing these interventions may benefit the economy more than hunting down the last vestiges of traditional economic regulation.

The Benefits of Deregulation: Why Markets?

Deregulation has greatly improved economic welfare, and the improvement builds over time. For example, the U.S. airline industry is still

Table 19-1. Effects of Deregulation in the United States

Sector	Nature of deregulation	Consumer benefits
Airlines	Total	33 percent reduction in real fares
Trucking	Total	35–75 percent reduction in real rates
Railroads	Partial; rate ceilings and floors on "monopoly" routes	More than 50 percent decline in real rates
Natural gas	Partial; distribution still regulated	30 percent decline in consumer prices
Telecommunications	Partial; local rates and interstate access still regulated	More than 50 percent decline in long-distance rates
Banking	Consumer rates deregulated; entry liberalized	Increased interest on consumer deposits; improved productivity

Sources: Winston (1993, 1998); Crandall and Ellig (1997).

adjusting to unregulated competition twenty-three years after passage of the Airline Deregulation Act. In virtually every deregulated industry, there have been substantial gains in efficiency (table 19-1). The firms supplying the service—new entrants and incumbents alike—produce it at a cost that is about 30 percent lower than the cost would have been under the old regulatory regime. In addition, service quality tends to improve. Deregulation reduced airline fares, trucking costs, and railroad transportation costs by about $35 billion per year (in 1995 dollars), largely through improvements in efficiency. Similarly, reductions in long-distance telephone rates came about because of improved efficiency and the Federal Communications Commission's (FCC's) more efficient pricing of interstate carrier access, not from reduced telephone company profits.

By contrast, the U.S. government's inadvertent foray into controlling the field price of natural gas in the 1960s resulted in huge losses in economic welfare. Between 1968 and 1977, regulators kept natural gas prices artificially low and thereby transferred $39 billion from producers to consumers. However, doing so created shortages in natural gas that subsequently cost consumers and producers $59 billion (in 1982 dollars). Subsequently, natural gas deregulation was phased in between 1978 and 1984, and prices were kept artificially high during most of that period. This spurred a "sell-off" of gas at artificially low prices that cost producers $45 billion more than the gains to consumers. In all, seventeen years of regulating the previously competitive natural gas extraction industry cost the United States more than $160 billion (in 1995 dollars), according to Paul MacAvoy.

Table 19-2. Estimated Scope of Economic Regulation in the United States

Sector or industry	Regulated in 1975	Regulated in 2001	Percentage of 1999 GDP regulated in 1975	Percentage of 1999 GDP regulated in 2006	Percent decline in regulation
Oil and gas extraction	Yes	No	0.89	0	100
Railroads	Yes	No[a]	0.25	0	100
Trucking	Yes	No	1.25	0	100
Air transport	Yes	No	1.02	0	100
Pipelines	Yes	Yes	0.07	0.07	0
Electricity	Yes	Yes	1.19	1.19	0
Telecommunications	Yes	Partially	2.10	0.70[b]	75
Radio and television	Yes	Partially	0.70	0.23[b]	67
Financial depository institutions	Yes	No[c]	3.28	0	100
Insurance	Yes	Yes	0.77	0.77	0
Total			11.52	2.96	74

Sources: Winston (1993, 1998); Crandall and Ellig (1997).
a. Still some minor rate regulation.
b. Author's estimate.
c. Interest rates and entry are no longer regulated; solvency regulation remains.

Decline of Traditional Regulation

The twenty-five-year deregulation movement that began in the 1970s had a remarkable impact on the United States and many other countries. In the United States, the entire national transportation sector was substantially deregulated; the energy, financial, and video distribution sectors were heavily deregulated; and even telecommunications witnessed considerable deregulation and regulatory reform. About two-thirds of the communications sector (including long-distance services, broadband services, telephone terminal equipment, and cable television) has been deregulated, while local telephone service and broadcasting are still regulated. Overall, the amount of regulation has fallen by roughly 74 percent (table 19-2).

Unfortunately, this does not mean that government intervention in the operation of markets has withered away in the United States. Many other forms of government intervention survive. The sectors of the economy that are subject to some government control of prices and output are, in fact, quite numerous. Although not full economic regulation, these interventions generally involve direct or indirect control of prices or output. The following are the major examples of intervention in the United States:

—*Housing:* rent control

—*Housing finance:* government guarantees (subsidies) to home mortgage financing (Fannie Mae, Freddie Mac, Federal Housing Administration)

—*Agriculture:* price supports; marketing agreements

—*Trade protection:* regulation of minimum import prices under 1974 Trade Act (applying mainly to metals and chemicals)

—*Water supply:* government prohibition of the use of market prices to ration water among competing uses

—*Roads and highways:* government provision of roads and highways (overwhelmingly offered at zero prices even in the most congested hours and locations)

—*Airport access:* regulation and pricing of landing rights

—*Health care:* regulation of hospital and physician fees through Medicare and Medicaid, with resulting influence on fees paid by private insurers

—*Electromagnetic spectrum:* government control of a large share of this valuable resource and non-price allocation of much of the rest of it

Much remains to be done to free water, spectrum, roads, and land from inefficient government controls. ❯

DEREGULATE KEY INDUSTRIES MORE FULLY

The most important sectors still under formal government economic regulation are telecommunications and electricity. In addition, international air transportation and the air transportation network, including air traffic control and airport access, are still subject to government control.

Telecommunications

Although the incredible rate of technological change precludes anyone from safely predicting how the telecommunications sector will evolve under continued regulation or deregulation, it is difficult to see how further deregulation could hurt. Any remaining monopoly power lies in the provision of local access to residential and small business subscribers, but even this market is now buffeted by competition from cellular carriers, cable television companies, and independent Voice over Internet Protocol (VoIP) providers.

There are 175 million switched access lines in the United States, including (roughly) 45 million large business lines, 110 million residential lines, and 20 million small business lines. Most of the large business lines are located in dense business districts where competition now thrives. Thus, further deregulation of local access/exchange service would affect principally the 130 million residential and small business lines. Any attempt by the carriers to raise local rates significantly would induce substantial substitution of cellular, VoIP, and cable telephone service or even the remaining competitive local exchange carrier services.

At a monthly rate as low as $30, cellular subscribers may now purchase plans that provide free calling to all fifty states. Moreover, if local rates were to rise from their current $25 monthly average for residential subscribers, cable television systems would attract large numbers of subscribers to the VoIP and traditional telephone services that they now deliver over their broadband connections. For this reason, local telephone companies are not likely to raise rates even if they were fully deregulated. Indeed, these companies are now being forced to offer low bundled rates for local and long-distance telephone service, broadband Internet service, and even video and wireless services just to stem mounting defections by their traditional fixed-wire customers.

Full formal deregulation of all voice telephone services would convey enormous benefits for two reasons. First, the inefficient pricing of local and long-distance services, defended as a "universal service" policy, would end. Deregulated firms would not mark up their prices by exorbitant amounts for long-distance services with high elasticity of demand in order to provide low-cost local service. The gains to the economy from just this change would be as much as $7 billion a year. Second, regulatory barriers to both entry and investment in new services would be lowered. Regulatory delays in licensing cellular systems and approving Bell company offerings of voice messaging cost U.S. consumers $51 billion for each year of regulatory delay, according to an estimate by economist Jerry Hausman; even if that estimate is high by a factor of ten, the potential benefit of deregulation surely swamps any gains from continued regulation. For these reasons, the vestiges of telecommunications regulation should be abandoned as soon as possible—though not by creating new forms of control, such as prohibiting tiered pricing arrangements in order to ensure "network neutrality."

Network Neutrality

Over time, Internet subscribers have been able to obtain access at greater speeds. In turn, higher-speed access and the ubiquity of personal computers have induced network operators and content providers to offer new services, such as real-time video and VoIP. But many of these new services require improvements in network architecture and large capital expenditures by network providers. These network owners are now seeking new approaches to prioritizing traffic, potentially including the imposition of higher charges to applications providers or to network subscribers for priority services.

As network providers continue to build out infrastructure to facilitate the distribution of new services, some observers and market participants worry that the networks will begin to engage in "discriminatory" pricing or "exclusionary" conduct—particularly if they begin to invest in creating their own content or network applications. These critics' solution to this potential problem is to establish a policy of "network neutrality," either through new legislation or FCC regulation. While some details of the proposed policy remain obscure, most advocates of network neutrality appear to focus on nondiscrimination requirements for Internet content and on limitations—or an outright ban—on allowing content providers or subscribers to pay higher prices to receive priority on the network. Such a policy would be premature at the very least and could prove counterproductive.

Broadband communications technologies are evolving rapidly. There is no reason to believe that any of the current providers of high-speed subscriber connections, such as cable television operators and local telephone companies, will have enough market power to exploit consumers through discriminatory actions. Moreover, new wireless and satellite technologies are being deployed that may challenge current providers of high-speed Internet access. Finally, there is no evidence that the existing major network providers have engaged in exclusionary conduct.

Nor is it clear that all content should be treated equally and priced equally, given different degrees of priority in delivering and receiving the content. A consumer may be willing to wait a few seconds to download a complete PDF file but unwilling to wait a few seconds between words of a telephone conversation transmitted over the Internet. Network congestion problems are much more likely to be solved efficiently by using variable pricing than simply by requiring everyone to wait in line at a constant (and even zero) price. The fact that Internet traffic has traditionally been handled on a first-come, first-served basis should not lead to the conclusion that such a pricing policy will be optimal as network traffic soars and applications become much more varied. Network operators should be permitted and even encouraged to experiment with alternative pricing strategies in an open, competitive marketplace.

Electricity

Potentially, the electricity sector offers the greatest gains from further deregulation, although there is no consensus about the optimal mix of markets and regulation within this sector. Electricity generation has been substantially deregulated in many states and has become quite competitive, but transmission and distribution remain network bottleneck monopolies. There is little empirical evidence about the potential for competitive transmission grids or competitive local distribution networks. However, telecommunications provides an illustration of the range of possibilities. In most jurisdictions, at least two and sometimes three communications lines are available to residential and business subscribers— one or two fiber-coaxial cable lines and one copper telephone wire. Additional terrestrial networks connect the cell sites of the four national and several smaller, regional cellular phone carriers. Moreover, the United States is blanketed by a highly competitive long-haul telecommunications sector that provides voice/data services and is the backbone of the Internet. It is thus reasonable to suggest that competition could eventually emerge in electricity transmission and distribution as well.

The U.S. electricity sector is currently a mix of vertical integration and vertical fragmentation. In some states, generation is divorced from transmission; in others, the traditional utilities still provide generation, transmission, and distribution. Retail competition can coexist with vertically integrated incumbent electric utilities, but it probably will be most successful where generation is separated or transmission is "unbundled."

Although evidence exists that wholesale competition in generation on the state level reduces prices, the disastrous effects of California's flawed electricity reform in 2000–01 have substantially slowed deregulatory advances. California forbade utilities to enter into long-term contracts, which allowed generators to exploit the short-term scarcity of power created by natural forces, such as a shortfall in precipitation and a rise in fossil fuel prices. The result was an approximately $12 billion extra annual increase in the state's electric bill. (The total increase appears to have been about $20 billion, $8 billion of which would have occurred regardless, due to drought and higher oil prices.) Given this enormous failure, states should be cautious in opening generation markets to competition and should experiment with various market designs involving access of competitive generators to transmission networks. Such decisions can be left to state authorities without much federal guidance.

Predictions of how a deregulated market will evolve are notoriously unreliable. In the case of electricity, however, deregulation would likely lead to a much more decentralized system of supply and distribution. One response to deregulation might be that several generators enter the transmission business. In addition, small distribution networks could conceivably develop and use wires strung in parallel with those of current distributors, if these new entities could gain access to the poles. The bargaining power of large numbers of such sub-networks could even induce large grid operators to grant relatively competitive rates for transmitting power from large, distant generators.

The most important role for the federal government in furthering electricity deregulation would appear to be developing incentives for additional investment in transmission networks—whether that means expanding current networks or beginning to develop new ones. The shortage of transmission capacity is quite apparent, given the systematic differences in average wholesale electricity prices across narrow geographical areas, particularly in the Northeast. New investments in transmission would improve the performance of deregulated wholesale markets as they spread across the states. In addition, the federal government should encourage experiments in real-time retail pricing, so prices would rise during peak hours or periods of transmission-generation failures. Real-time pricing would have mitigated the worst effects of the California debacle.

Air Transportation

Although the domestic airline industry is now fully deregulated, air service between the United States and its international trading partners is not. U.S. carriers are not free to offer service to any foreign destination, and foreign carriers cannot freely offer service in the United States, even if they have succeeded in obtaining the right to serve an international route that terminates here. Moreover, the federal government continues to manage the air traffic control system, while state and local airport authorities regulate the prices and availability of landing rights. Large gains loom from liberalizing all these policies.

Airport Landing Rights and Air Traffic Control

Air space is an abundant resource whose scarcity is largely contrived by those who regulate it. In many countries, the air traffic control system has been privatized. In the United States, however, the Federal Aviation Administration (FAA) controls air traffic, and government-owned airports impose weight-based landing fees. The combination of FAA and airport regulation has created much more congestion than is necessary or optimal. Almost twenty years ago, Steven Morrison and Clifford Winston projected an $11 billion gain in economic welfare from a shift to congestion fees for air traffic, better pricing of aircraft landings, and improved investment decisions in building runways. In today's dollars, even with traffic held to 1988 levels, that estimate rises to more than $16 billion per year.

Cabotage

Gains from "open skies" agreements governing entry into international routes to and from the United States could be very large. The United States and the European Union have recently negotiated such an agreement for trans-Atlantic routes. A simple step in liberalizing other international routes would allow cabotage, or the extension of an international flight to continuing service in each other's domestic markets. Such liberalization would increase competition both here and abroad.

A further step toward increasing competition in domestic markets would be to eliminate all restrictions on foreign ownership of domestic airlines. This would allow foreign entrants, such as Virgin Airways, to compete with domestic carriers and permit foreign entities to hold major equity positions in domestic carriers.

Other Sectors

While few traditionally regulated industries remain to be deregulated, federal and state government policies affect the prices of a number of resources and could be relaxed or at least reformed. Chief among these resources are the electromagnetic spectrum, water, and the highway system.

The Electromagnetic Spectrum

Only recently have governments begun to privatize the electromagnetic spectrum by auctioning rights to it for various commercial purposes.

Unfortunately, only a very small share of commercially usable spectrum has been auctioned; the remainder is still allocated without regard to its economic value in alternative uses. The potential gains from freeing the remaining spectrum from government management—particularly that set aside for defense, public safety, and broadcasting—are extremely large. Were this spectrum allocated through market mechanisms, substantial economic value could be created.

For example, if the television broadcasting spectrum were freed for competing uses, much of it might be bought by telecommunications companies seeking to provide higher-valued traditional cellular services or new broadband services. If public safety and defense authorities were required to use a similar market mechanism, they might find it prudent to sell off some of their spectrum at high prices and use more spectrum-efficient technologies.

Given the results of recent spectrum auctions, the 400 megahertz of very desirable bands of the U.S. commercial television spectrum could be worth as much as $120 billion in alternative uses. This shift could require the abandonment of free off-air television broadcasting, leaving some households with dark television sets. However, given that fewer than 15 percent of U.S. households now watch television off the air, it would not cost much to shift them to cable television or broadcast satellites. Assuming a $20 monthly marginal cost of shifting these households to a basic tier of service, the annual cost would be $240 per household, and the present value of these costs in perpetuity, evaluated at a 5 percent discount rate, would be $4,800. With fewer than 15 million households to move, the total cost would be less than $72 billion. Therefore, the net gain from moving a small part of the spectrum to a higher-valued use would be about $48 billion. A total shift to a market allocation of spectrum would obviously unleash enormous value.

Water

Water may fairly be considered even more important than the electromagnetic spectrum, given its ubiquitous contribution to daily life. Unfortunately, despite the volumes that have been written on the costs and benefits of dams and other water resource projects and the many individual studies of the inefficiency of government allocation of water, there are very few comprehensive estimates of the social cost of failing to use the price mechanism efficiently in allocating this scarce resource.

The inefficiencies in allocating scarce water supplies derive from two causes. First, water is generally taken from rivers, lakes, and streams for use by farmers, businesses, and municipal water authorities without use of a price mechanism. Second, municipal authorities typically set the prices for water distributed to households at levels that fail to reflect the opportunity cost of the water. Without well-functioning markets and efficient municipal pricing, there is simply no assurance that water is being directed to its highest-value uses, and there is very little incentive for conservation.

According to a recent econometric study by Christopher Timmins, the annual net cost to the economy of inefficient pricing by municipal water authorities in California is $111 for each household in the state, because prices are set too low. If that result were extrapolated to the entire country—clearly an arbitrary exercise—it would suggest that inefficient pricing of water by municipalities could cost the economy in excess of $10 billion per year.

Highways

One of the most serious urban problems is rush-hour highway congestion. Long commuting times have huge impacts; the average commuting time to work in Washington, Los Angeles, Chicago, Philadelphia, and New York is more than 35 minutes per day, or roughly 150 hours per year. Obviously, this time is affected by the peak-hour congestion on major routes. If space were rationed more efficiently through some form of peak-load pricing of highways, commuters might save valuable time. For instance, if commuters value their time at half of their earned income, on average, and commuting times of, say, one-third of the population could be reduced by just 10 percent, the improvement would be worth $8.7 billion a year nationwide.

Very few private highways exist in the United States. Most public highways are free, and even public "toll" roads are rarely priced efficiently. Does any country use prices to ration highways? Norway, Sweden, Singapore, and the United Kingdom are four prominent examples. Stockholm residents voted last year to continue the city's congestion-pricing program, demonstrating that the use of the price mechanism in rationing this public good can gain public support.

The United States is now just beginning to use the price mechanism to ration capacity on urban highways with "high occupancy toll" lanes on major arterials in Minneapolis, Houston, and San Diego. Political opposition to charging for use of the "people's roads" has blocked this rational approach in many areas, including Washington, D.C. The next president should support use of federal interstate highway funds to stimulate congestion pricing on arterial highways serving major urban areas.

ADDITIONAL RESOURCES

Crandall, Robert W., and Jerry Ellig. 1997. *Economic Deregulation and Customer Choice: Lessons for the Electricity Industry.* George Mason University, Mercatus Center (January 1).

Crandall, Robert W., and Leonard Waverman. 2000. *Who Pays for Universal Service? When Telephone Subsidies Become Transparent.* Brookings.

Hausman, Jerry A. 1997. "Valuing the Effect of Regulation on New Services in Telecommunications." *Brookings Papers on Economic Activity (BPEA), Microeconomics:* 1–38.

Joskow, Paul L. 2006. "Markets for Power in the United States: An Interim Assessment." *Energy Journal* 27, no. 1: 1–36.

MacAvoy, Paul W. 2000. *The Natural Gas Market: Sixty Years of Regulation and Deregulation.* Yale University Press.

Morrison, Steven A., and Clifford Winston. 1989. "Enhancing the Performance of the Deregulated Air Transportation System." *BPEA, Microeconomics:* 61–112.

Newberry, David M. 2005. "Introduction." *Energy Journal* (Summer, special issue, *European Electricity Liberalisation*): 1–10.

Nivola, Pietro S., and Robert W. Crandall. 1995. *The Extra Mile: Rethinking Energy Policy for Automotive Transportation.* Brookings and Twentieth Century Fund.

Timmins, Christopher. 2002. "Measuring the Dynamic Efficiency Costs of Regulators' Preferences: Water Utilities in the Arid West." *Econometrica* 70, no. 2 (March): 603–29.

Winston, Clifford. 1993. "Economic Deregulation: Days of Reckoning for Microeconomists." *Journal of Economic Literature* 31, no. 3 (September): 1263–289.

———. 1998. "U.S. Industry Adjustment to Economic Deregulation." *Journal of Economic Perspectives* 12 (Summer): 89–110.

———. 2006. *Government Failure versus Market Failure: Microeconomics Policy Research and Government Performance.* AEI-Brookings Joint Center for Regulatory Studies.

20

Strengthening Higher Education

Simplify Student Aid and Emphasize Vital Science, Math, and Language Skills

PETER BERKOWITZ

SUMMARY ❯ The importance of higher education to the future of the nation can hardly be exaggerated. Economic growth and responsible political participation increasingly depend on a well-read and scientifically literate citizenry. Social mobility and higher incomes are closely tied to the acquisition of a college diploma and the communications skills and critical thinking that higher education fosters. And for many, a liberal education introduces students to the many dimensions of their own civilization and to the diversity of human civilizations and enlarges sensibility and understanding.

American universities are strong in many ways. No nation on earth can boast universities of greater overall quality or diversity. Millions of American students compete for admission. In fact, undergraduate and graduate students from around the world eagerly seek enrollment.

Yet, today, higher education in the United States faces formidable problems: unaffordable tuition, lack of accountability, students ill-prepared for college, declining enrollment in math and science, and too few graduates fluent in critical foreign languages. The next president can take several specific steps to strengthen U.S. higher education:

—Make college education more attainable for low-income students by simplifying the grants process and reducing inefficiency in the distribution of financial aid

—Encourage universities that receive federal dollars to fashion responsible ways to measure student progress and track college costs

—Create federally funded fellowships in biology, chemistry, and physics that require recipients, after graduation, to teach high school for one to four years

—Create a signature program of federally funded fellowships not only to support students who study critical foreign languages but also to build much-needed capacity within the Departments of State, Education, and Defense ▌

CONTEXT ▌ In September 2006 the Department of Education issued *A Test of Leadership: Charting the Future of U.S. Higher Education*, written by the Commission on the Future of Higher Education, which included leaders in the worlds of U.S. business and education.[1] The bipartisan reach of the report was reflected in the assertion of Senator Edward Kennedy (D-Mass., and chair of the Senate Education Committee) that it "laid out a promising agenda to keep our colleges and universities strong in this demanding age."[2] The commission's work provides a useful point of departure for examining higher education policy in the United States.

The report affirmed the common observation that U.S. higher education is in many ways the envy of the world and stressed that, in the twenty-first century, higher education would serve more than ever as an engine of social mobility, of innovation, and for creating a knowledgeable democratic citizenry. At the same time, it noted that the United States has fallen to twelfth place among major industrialized countries in overall higher educational attainment and sixteenth in high school graduation rates.

The report highlighted several specific causes for concern. Many students, particularly poor and minority students according to the report, do not obtain a college education because they lack information about college, it is too expensive, and the financial aid system is confusing. High schools fail to provide many students—again, especially poor and minority students—with the skills in reading, writing, and math that they need to do college-level work. Little reliable information is available about the actual cost of higher education or its quality or about the intellectual skills students develop in college and the knowledge they acquire.

Nor are these the only challenges American universities face. Since the tightening of immigration procedures in the aftermath of 9/11, many foreign students who would benefit from exposure to America and who would benefit Americans by exposing us to their culture have been denied visas. While science and technology play a larger role in all areas of our lives, scientific and mathematical literacy is on the wane. At a time when the United States' involvement in the world is rapidly growing, American colleges and universities produce a meager number of readers and speakers of critical foreign languages, such as Arabic, Persian, Turkish, Hindi, and Chinese. And America's elite universities, which set the tone for universities around the nation and train many of the next generation's leaders, have retained the rhetoric but abandoned the content and aims of liberal education.

To meet these challenges, the report recommended that the federal government

—increase financial aid for low-income students, make financial aid programs simpler and more straightforward, and engage in outreach to make information about financial aid more readily available to high school students and guidance counselors;

—renew efforts to improve the quality of high school education because of the dependence of college performance on basic skills in reading, writing, and math;

—improve transparency and accountability for parents and students, by creating a consumer-friendly information database dealing with the cost and quality of individual institutions; for policymakers, researchers, and the general public, by collecting and publishing better information on the quality and cost of higher education; and generally, by encouraging effective measurement of student performance;

—undertake new initiatives to improve the quality of instruction, especially in math and science;

—expand opportunities for adult education to enable citizens to participate in higher education throughout life;

—enlarge federal investment in fields critical to global competitiveness and security, including science, engineering, medicine, and foreign languages.

The report was greeted with three major criticisms. First, it was faulted for not adequately dealing with the challenge of providing greater financial assistance to needy students. Second, the creation of a national database that tracks student performance from kindergarten through college was deemed an intolerable threat to privacy. Third, the attempt to develop national testing, it was said, would impose a "one-size-fits-all" framework on higher education, encourage teachers to "teach to the test" rather than to students' needs and subject matter requirements, and shift power over education from college administrators and faculty to distant government bureaucrats.

The emerging politics of higher education reform reflect an altered policy landscape. In contrast to the Reagan administration, which considered abolishing the Department of Education, the Bush administration has sought to expand the role of the federal government in education, first in relation to K–12 schooling with its signature No Child Left Behind program and now in relation to higher education with the commission's report.[3]

Some of the criticism may reflect partisan posturing, but the objections raise serious issues and must be addressed. Reform will not be easy. Although low-income students need financial help, proposals for increased funding are made against the backdrop of increasingly severe budget constraints created by growing expenditures for the military and homeland security, rising costs of Social Security and health care, an already sizable deficit—plus concern that increases in financial aid only encourage colleges to raise tuition. National databases, though a potentially valuable tool for tracking student performance as well as university costs and effectiveness, do create the potential for serious abuse by reducing educational attainment to easily quantifiable units. And while the federal government certainly can provide incentives to encourage colleges and universities to pursue particular lines of study and research, a majority of Americans probably believes that it is not the government's place to legislate what it means to be an educated person or to establish a single goal for U.S. higher education.

This last point must be stressed. The great strengths of higher education in the United States—its vastness and its variety—also make it challenging to develop effective federal policy. As Peyton R. Helm, president of Muhlenberg College, observes,

American higher education has more than 4,200 institutions, including public, private, for profit, technical, secular, and faith-based schools with enrollments ranging from fewer than 10 students to more than 115,000. Four-year graduation rates range from less than 1 percent to more than 97 percent. Costs range from a few hundred to more than $45,000 per year. Teaching styles range from the intimate student-faculty interaction of residential liberal arts colleges like Muhlenberg to the on-demand (if less personal) on-line programs of the University of Phoenix. Colleges and universities prepare future engineers, scientists, rabbis, farmers, journalists, bankers, accountants, doctors, nurses, artists, technicians, dancers, lawyers, and teachers.[4]

Federal policymakers must respect this diversity of forms and goals in higher education, while establishing priorities among the nation's needs and constantly keeping in mind the limits of the federal government's role. ❯

CLEARLY ARTICULATE POLICY GOALS

Currently, U.S. lawmakers in both parties agree on two goals. First, priority should be placed on policies aimed at improving the educational attainments of poor and minority students. And second, support for science and math education is crucial for developing the skills that Americans need to compete in the global marketplace. Public opinion converges in significant measure with these goals: a majority of the public favors strengthening requirements in math, science, and foreign languages and making college more affordable. However, the majority also believes "it is more important to raise education standards and accountability than to increase funding."[5] Our new president, therefore, will have an opportunity to take advantage of a developing consensus on improving higher education through the careful crafting of initiatives that will achieve shared goals effectively.

The most urgent issues that stand the greatest chance of winning majority support are improving financial aid to low-income students, enhancing university accountability, strengthening math and science education, and promoting the study of critical foreign languages. Additional support for community colleges and technical schools is another worthy goal, but much of the support that the federal government is in a position to provide comes through loans and grants to the neediest students.

And while the number of foreign students studying in the United States declined sharply in the immediate aftermath of 9/11, the government has made significant strides in overcoming security-related delays in processing student visas and restoring the former numbers.[6]

IMPROVE FINANCIAL AID

College education is expensive, and costs continue to rise. According to a College Board study released October 2006, average 2006–07 tuition costs are $5,836 to attend a state school and $22,218 to attend a private college.[7] At elite private universities, the yearly price tag can approach $50,000. While the rate of increase has slowed recently, in the last five years state school costs have risen 35 percent and private college costs have increased 11 percent.

Currently, the federal government administers some twenty aid programs for postsecondary education. Pell Grants, the single largest source of support, are based on need and do not have to be repaid. Congress made available $12.75 billion dollars for the program in fiscal year 2006, with an average new award of $2,445 (minimum, $400; maximum, $4,050). Extremely needy students are eligible to receive grants also from the Federal Supplemental Educational Opportunity Grant Program, for which Congress made $975 million available in 2006. In addition, through aid totaling $1.172 billion in 2006, the Federal Work-Study Program offers jobs to students, and the Federal Perkins Loan Program provides $1.135 billion in low-interest loans.

In July 2006, the Bush administration made available $790 million for new National SMART (Science and Mathematics Access to Retain Talent) Grants and Academic Competitiveness Grants, two programs that are expected to total $4.5 billion over the next five years. National SMART Grants supplement the Pell Grants with up to $4,000 for college juniors and seniors. Academic Competitiveness Grants provide $750 for freshmen and up to $1,300 for sophomores who are Pell Grant recipients and who have completed rigorous high school coursework. Overall, in its budget for fiscal year 2006, the administration called for an increase of $28 billion for student aid programs through 2015, and these programs overall will help more than 10 million needy students cover the costs of college.

Despite this substantial federal support, the average student borrower graduates from college with $17,500 in student loan debt. To reduce this burden, many Democrats want to increase the federal funds available for outright grants and decrease the interest that students pay on their loans from 6.8 to 3.4 percent. Notwithstanding the commission's recommendation to increase federal funding, many Republicans will resist a further increase, and even the Bush administration is likely to resist one of the magnitude that Democrats will support.

In part these reservations stem from concern that more government support might be counterproductive:

> A large share of the cost of higher education is subsidized by public funds (local, state and federal) and by private contributions. These third-party payments tend to insulate what economists would call producers—colleges and universities—from the consequences of their own spending decisions, while consumers—students—also lack incentives to make decisions based on their own limited resources. [This] provides perverse spending incentives at times.[8]

In other words, there is reason to believe, rooted in economic analysis, that increasing federal financial aid will not ultimately help students because it encourages colleges and universities to raise tuition, enriching universities at the expense of taxpayers, while leaving students no better off financially.[9]

However, one policy initiative that should attract support from the new president and a majority in both houses of Congress would be to simplify and streamline the process by which students apply for financial aid, to improve the quality of the information that reaches low-income high school students, and to clarify the terms under which universities receive federal dollars in support of low-income students. Specifically, the Department of Education should undertake a major review and reduction of the hundreds of pages of regulations that currently govern the distribution of financial aid, eliminate unnecessary paperwork, and reach out to high school principals, guidance counselors, teachers, and students themselves through programs designed to keep them informed on new and existing grants. This would ensure that a larger proportion of current funds finds its way to the students most in need.

ESTABLISH ACCOUNTABILITY

The national commission proposed that college and university accountability could be improved through the establishment of a national database and the development of standardized tests to track student and university performance. Both proposals respond to serious problems, while raising serious concerns. However, carefully crafted reforms—advancing core educational goals while avoiding trampling on other important national goals and goods—should have the backing of the new president and could win majority support.

On its face, testing is an appealing way to hold universities accountable and determine what students are learning. Test scores provide a tangible and relatively objective measure of at least some of the intellectual skills and some of the knowledge that universities purport to teach. Furthermore, grades have become an increasingly unreliable measure because of an epidemic of grade inflation sweeping the nation, particularly at elite schools.[10]

Yet new national tests are not the answer. Numerous tests designed and administered by private companies are already in use. Achievement tests are available in many disciplines for those students who continue on to graduate school. Tests to measure analytical abilities are available for graduate school in the arts and sciences (GRE) and for professional education in business (GMAT), law (LSAT), and medicine (MCAT). Moreover, a single national test, or even a set of national tests, fails to reckon with the variety of disciplines and the interdisciplinary and special majors that have for decades been springing up around the nation. In addition, one can expect a bitter and protracted debate concerning who should devise the exams and what they should contain. Indeed, as long as the nation lacks a common higher education curriculum—and there is none to speak of, nor is there any likelihood of one emerging any time soon—debates about the authorship and content of national exams are doomed to be angry and inconclusive.

In general, tests used to evaluate student performance can be implemented in a "high-stakes" version or in a "low-stakes" version. The stakes in question are the students'. The high-stakes version provides information about individual students. The low-stakes version is anonymous and provides information about aggregate outcomes. As a result, the low-stakes version does not impose another nerve-wracking hoop for students to jump through, and it does not threaten student privacy. But it would still provide information to students, parents, companies, donors, and the public about the progress that students in general are making at particular colleges and universities. Similarly, the proposal to establish a national database—containing narrowly tailored information about financial aid, student progress, and graduation rates—could be valuable.[11]

STRENGTHEN SCIENCE AND MATH EDUCATION

In the United States, science and math education is on the decline, with American students ranking twenty-fourth in math out of twenty-nine developed nations. The number of students studying math and science is falling, and less than half of high school students are prepared for college math and science. Science courses for nonmajors are often light and unchallenging, which signals to students that learning about science is both difficult and unnecessary. These developments are disadvantageous for the nation. Science and mathematics provide rigorous intellectual training. And knowledge of biology, chemistry, physics, and advanced mathematics is increasingly valuable in many fields.

In fiscal year 2006, the federal government allocated $790 million for Academic Competitiveness Grants and National SMART Grants. For fiscal year 2007, the Bush administration proposed an increase of $60 million, which would enable grants to be distributed to an estimated 541,000 students. These programs, however, are not enough. To begin to reverse the decline, Congress should allocate an additional $60 million to create a new fellowship program administered by the Department of Education that is designed to encourage students to study science and math in college, as well as to improve high school science education. Students who maintain a B+ or better average in their science and math courses would remain eligible for fellowship support. Strings should be attached: in particular, in exchange for each year of support to study biology, chemistry, physics, or mathematics, students would be obliged to give back one year in teaching this discipline to high school students. In this way, the fellowship program both increases the number of science and mathematics graduates and improves the number and quality of high school teachers.

ENCOURAGE STUDY OF CRITICAL FOREIGN LANGUAGES

Initiatives to promote the study of critical foreign languages make sense whether one is a hawk or a dove, Democrat or Republican, and so they have the chance to command wide and deep bipartisan support. *Indeed, such an initiative could become a signature program of our next president.*

More than five years after 9/11, even highly educated Americans know little about the Arab Middle East, and universities have made few changes to educate the nation and train experts on the subject. According to the 9/11 Commission report, in 2002 U.S. colleges and universities granted a sum total of six undergraduate degrees in Arabic; similarly, the State Department reports that less than 1 percent of U.S. high school students are studying any of these critical languages: Arabic, Chinese, Farsi, Japanese, Korean, Russian, or Urdu. No surprise, then, that the 9/11 Commission found that the government has too few translators and those it does employ lack, in many cases, the requisite proficiency in Arabic and the languages of the regions they serve. Finally, according to the recently released Iraq Study Group report, the U.S. Embassy in Iraq employs only six fluent Arabic speakers.

The nation's security depends on acquiring knowledge of critical foreign languages. This was once well understood. As Stanford political scientist Mike McFaul observed,

> To fight a sustained battle against communism, the United States also invested billions in education and intelligence about the enemy. The U.S. government sponsored centers for Soviet studies, provided foreign-language scholarships, offered dual competency grants to compel graduate students to gain expertise in both security issues and Russian culture. Such programs aimed to combat the new "ism" exist today but are underdeveloped. We lack "human intelligence"—covert agents, spies, and informants—in the Middle East. But we also suffer from shortages of NSA [National Security Agency] linguists, academic scholars, and senior policymakers trained in the languages, cultures, politics, and economics of the Middle East. In the departments of political science at Harvard and Stanford—the two highest ranked programs in the country—there is not one tenured faculty member who is a specialist on the Islamic world.[12]

Those who prefer to emphasize the United States' commercial and diplomatic engagement with the world also should see foreign language study as a high priority for our colleges and universities. The study of a foreign language opens doors to culture, history, and politics. It disciplines the mind. And it allows people to reach out to foreigners by showing them the respect that inheres in addressing them in their mother tongue. Knowledge of foreign languages is an invaluable asset in an era of globalization in which the United States must cooperate and compete in myriad ways and at many levels with nations around the world.

On January 5, 2006, the Bush administration announced a National Security Language Initiative intended to improve America's "ability to engage foreign governments and peoples, especially in critical regions, to encourage reform, promote understanding, convey respect for other cultures and provide an opportunity to learn more about our country and its citizens."[13] The initiative, for which the president requested $114 million in fiscal year 2007, involves cooperation among the Departments of State, Education, and Defense and the director of national intelligence.

The initiative has three broad goals: to expand the number of Americans mastering critical-need languages and encourage students to begin language instruction at a younger age; to increase the number of advanced-level speakers of foreign languages, especially critical-need languages; and to increase the number of foreign language teachers and the resources available to them. In pursuit of these goals, the administration will

—allocate $51 million to revamp old programs and create new ones for language training from kindergarten through university levels;

—provide State Department scholarships to enable high school students to study critical-need languages abroad;

—establish new programs to increase the number and quality of language teachers;

—provide $13.2 million through the National Flagship Language Initiative to produce 2,000 advanced speakers of Arabic, Chinese, Russian, Persian, Hindi, and Central Asian languages by 2009;

—create new summer immersion programs;

—increase support for foreign language study abroad;

—establish a National Language Service Corps whose members, adept in critical foreign languages, will work as schoolteachers or in the federal government;

—create web-based distance-learning resources for critical foreign languages;

—expand teacher training programs.

These programs represent a good start in responding to urgent commercial, diplomatic, and national security needs. Yet they should be seen as only the beginning. The National Security Language Initiative draws upon the combined resources of the Departments of Education, State, and Defense. For fiscal year 2006, the president's budget for these three departments was $489 billion. Thus the $114 million earmarked for supporting the study of critical foreign languages represents a meager 0.02 percent of the departments' combined budgets.

By 2009 the country should triple the resources allocated to higher education in support of the study of critical foreign languages, from today's $114 million to $342 million. Though a drop in the bucket of the combined budgets of Education, State, and Defense, these investments in critical foreign language study would, by the administration's own analysis (and as the U.S. experience in funding critical foreign languages during the cold war suggests), bring huge rewards.

The most efficient and effective way to invest this money is to support college students directly. A substantial portion of the funds should be channeled into fellowships awarded and supervised separately by the Departments of Education, State, and Defense. Recipients of such support for the study of critical foreign languages should be required to maintain a B+ average in their language courses to maintain eligibility. They would be encouraged to spend a summer or semester in intensive foreign language study, preferably abroad. And they would be obliged to take at least one course in the history, politics, or religion of the people who speak the language they are studying. Students who receive more than two years' support would be required to work for one to three years in the department that is granting and supervising their fellowship. So, for example, students receiving Department of Education support might be required to work as high school language teachers, students receiving Department of State support might be required to work in the Foreign Service, and students receiving Department of Defense support might be required to work for the Pentagon.

Such a fellowship program has several advantages. It is more immune to politicization than are most others. The acquisition of vocabulary, the conjugation of verbs, and the mastery of cases and tenses provide relatively few opportunities to push partisan agendas. It prepares students not only for careers in government but also for careers in business, law, medicine, and the nonprofit sector—crucial sectors as U.S. interests become increasingly bound up with a peaceful, prosperous, and democratic world. It is entirely consistent with the highest ideals of liberal education in America. Indeed, the decline of the serious study of foreign languages at American universities and the concomitant ignorance of other peoples and the diversity of nations are an academic scandal. Such a program will make the job of U.S. diplomats easier. When the secretary of state and the thousands of State Department officials and U.S. ambassadors around the world undertake to explain American aims and principles to citizens of other countries through traditional and public diplomacy, they will be able to point to this country's funding of foreign language study as an illustration of our democratic commitment to understand better the peoples and nations with which we share the planet. Finally, such a program transcends partisan differences, and with suitable adjustments here and there, it should appeal to voters across the political spectrum.

CONCLUDING OBSERVATIONS

The next president will inevitably face challenges with respect to improving Americans' social mobility and economic prosperity, enhancing the nation's competitiveness in the global marketplace, cultivating informed and engaged democratic participation, and bolstering national security. *Strengthening higher education is essential to all of these,* and it should be a top priority for the people, their representatives in Congress, and our next president. Broad consensus exists on many of the most pressing problem areas in U.S. higher education, which should enable a committed president to make substantial progress.

NOTES

1. Secretary of Education's Commission on the Future of Higher Education, *A Test of Leadership: Charting the Future of U.S. Higher Education* (Washington: U.S. Department of Education, September 2006) (www.ed.gov/about/bdscomm/list/hiedfuture/index.html).

2. Edward M. Kennedy, "What Spellings Got Right and Wrong," *Inside Higher Ed,* October 3, 2006 (www.insidehighered.com/layout/set/print/views/2006/10/03/kennedy).

3. This has prompted hard-hitting conservative criticism of the Bush administration's higher education policy. See, for example, Larry P. Arnn, "Why the GOP Is Flunking Higher Education," *Claremont Review of Books* VI, no. 4 (Fall 2006).

4. Peyton Helm, "Spellings Report Would Weaken Higher Education," *Philadelphia Inquirer,* September 27, 2006.

5. Bryan Friel, "No Funding Left Behind," *National Journal,* September 9, 2006.

6. "Open Campuses," *Washington Post,* November 16, 2006, p. A26 (www.washingtonpost.com/wp-dyn/content/article/2006/11/15/AR2006111501343_pf.html).

7. Jay Matthews, "Spikes in College Price Tags Not So Sharp," *Washington Post,* October 24, 2006, p. A4.

8. Commission on the Future of Higher Education, *A Test of Leadership,* p. 10.

9. Richard K.Vedder, *Going Broke by Degrees: Why College Costs Too Much* (Washington: American Enterprise Institute Press, 2004).

10. John Merrow, "Grade Inflation: It's Not Just an Issue for the Ivy League," Carnegie Foundation for the Advancement of Teaching (Stanford, Calif., 2006) (www.carnegiefoundation.org/perspectives/sub.asp?key=245&subkey=576).

11. Such a database is not unprecedented. The Clery Act, signed in 1990, requires all universities participating in federal financial aid programs to report on crime statistics on and near their campuses. For more information about disclosure of campus security, see the website "Security on Campus, Complying with the Jeanne Clery Act" (www.securityoncampus.org/schools/cleryact).

12. Michael McFaul, "The Liberty Doctrine," *Policy Review* no. 112 (April and May 2002) (www.policyreview.org/apr02/mcfaul.html).

13. U.S. Department of State, Office of the Spokesman, "National Security Language Initiative," *Fact Sheet* (Washington, January 5, 2006) (www.state.gov/r/pa/prs/ps/2006/58733.htm).

21

Meeting the Dilemma of Health Care Access

Extending Insurance Coverage while Controlling Costs

HENRY J. AARON AND JOSEPH P. NEWHOUSE

SUMMARY ❙ Health care is the nation's largest—and, in many respects, most important—industry. It accounts for a large share of the nation's economy and is a major source of employment, to be sure, but by improving people's health and reducing disability, it promotes productivity across the economy and improves quality of life. The dollar value of Americans' improved health over the last three decades approximates the value of all other economic growth combined, and much, though not all, of that gain is traceable to improved health care.

The U.S. health care sector is growing rapidly and, on the private side (hospitals, doctors' offices, clinics), provides jobs for more than 15 million people. Government programs pick up about half of all health care spending.

—In 2008, total health care spending is projected to reach $2.4 trillion, or 16.6 percent of gross domestic product (GDP), accounting for a larger share of GDP than any other single industry.

—The federal government spends more on health care than on Social Security or national defense, the next most costly items.

—Federal spending on Medicare and Medicaid is projected to double between 2008 and 2032 and to triple by 2054.

In addition to rising costs that are straining public and private budgets, the financing and delivery of health care is marked by pervasive problems:

—Although *total* benefits from health care–related reductions in mortality and morbidity vastly exceed the increase in *total* health care spending, additional dollars spent at a given time appear to buy little or nothing of value.

—Geographic variation in spending is large, with residents of high-spending regions gaining no apparent benefit in health status or longevity.

—Nearly 47 million Americans had no health insurance coverage in 2006, and millions more had minimal coverage. If current cost trends continue, the number of uninsured will keep rising, potentially reaching 56 million by 2013. Quality of care is seriously flawed. The Institute of Medicine has estimated that each year between 44,000 and 98,000 Americans die because of medical errors. Millions more receive the wrong care or fail to receive appropriate care.

—Fewer than 10 percent of those who suffer injury or death from medical negligence receive compensation. Though few are compensated, much is spent on the cumbersome administration of the malpractice system. And inept providers face only weak incentives to improve their skills or cease practicing.

The next president and Congress will confront major health policy decisions with far-reaching effects on the life of virtually every American. What candidates say about health care policy will therefore be central in voters' judgments about whom they will support. This brief guide to health care reform describes basic characteristics of the U.S. health care system and four broad strategies for change. Most likely, the next president will have to choose some variant of the following specific options:

—Increasing consumers' share of health costs through high-deductible insurance, as an alternative to expanding employment-based coverage

—Incremental change to strengthen and extend employment-based health coverage, through reinsurance or making federal insurance programs (Medicare, Medicaid, or the Federal Employees Health Benefits Program) more widely available

—Universal health insurance by means of "Medicare-for-all"

—Support for state-level reforms, which may be the most politically feasible of these alternatives ❭

CONTEXT ❭ Compared with the ten other wealthiest nations, the United States spends nearly twice as much per capita on health care, yet life expectancy at birth is shorter—77.8 years versus 79.8 years—and

Box 21-1. Technological Change: Is Health Care Different from Other Industries?

How technological change affects health care spending is much misunderstood. Technical advances usually result in lower prices but increased total spending as the technology is widely adopted. This pattern has been evident in transportation (rail, air), entertainment (movies, television, recorded music), telecommunications, and data processing. That technological advances have increased health care spending seems obvious. The impact on price is less clear. Official health price indexes are seriously flawed. The fundamental problem is that it is very hard to measure quality and to value capabilities that did not exist previously. Careful studies of the price of treating victims of heart attacks and mental illness, however, indicate that improved technology has lowered prices after adjustment for improvements in quality.

People generally celebrate technological advances, as demonstrated by their spending patterns. They buy a DVD player to replace their VCR; they upgrade their home computer. In other words, they think the goods are worth what they cost or more. By contrast, many analysts believe that, because health insurance pays for most or all of care, the link between payment made and value received is broken, and much health care spending goes for services that provide few benefits relative to cost. The challenge is to squeeze out low- and no-benefit uses and bring down prices without unduly sacrificing beneficial care.

infant mortality rates are higher—6.8 versus 4.2 deaths per 1,000 live births. Our health care system spends so much more than most other nations' systems because it treats more patients intensively, because the care it provides uses more advanced technologies, and because the unit price of health care services is higher (see box 21-1). In addition, our financing system is uniquely cumbersome and costly.

In truth, the United States does not have a health care financing "system" but rather a bedlam of uncoordinated payment arrangements. In most other developed nations, one or a few organizations pay hospitals and physicians, often through annual budgets or simple formulas (such as set fees per patient day). But here, money flows to providers based on complex price lists for services rendered, detailed diagnoses of patients at admission, and myriad contractual arrangements. Payments come from various federal agencies (primarily the Centers for Medicare and Medicaid Services, the Defense Department, the Indian Health Service, and the Veterans Health Administration), from every state, from hundreds of counties and municipalities that run public hospitals, from thousands of insurers (each regulated by one of fifty independent state insurance regulatory agencies), from tens of thousands of self-insured employment-based plans (subject to federal regulation), and from the millions of patients who directly pay for at least part of the cost of care that they receive.

In all developed nations, health care spending has outpaced income growth for decades. According to data from the Organization for Economic Cooperation and Development, between 1970 and 2004 or 2005, annual health care spending grew 2.3 percentage points a year faster than income in the United States, 2.1 percentage points faster in France, 1.8 faster in the United Kingdom, 1.7 in Germany and Japan, and 1.0 in Canada. The size of this differential depends on public policy, changes in the average population age, the pace of technological change, and GDP growth in the specific country. During the 1990s, the gap between growth of health care spending and income temporarily vanished in the United States, as managed care encouraged modest restrictions on the use of health services and billing scandals triggered aggressive federal government efforts to root out fraud and overbilling by hospitals and physicians. However, the gap reemerged in 2000, and, if it persists, health care's share of total spending will inevitably rise. ▶

HEALTH CARE SPENDING: PUBLIC

Federal and state governments pay for a large and growing fraction of health care spending, principally through Medicare and Medicaid (figure 21-1), with other programs covering Native Americans, veterans, and members of the military forces and their dependents. Government health care spending is expected to continue increasing rapidly, less because of the much ballyhooed aging of the baby boom generation than because per capita health care spending is expected to continue to grow much faster than income.

Current projections indicate that total federal spending will grow far faster than revenues between 2007 and 2050, producing large and unsustainable deficits. The projected growth of Medicare and Medicaid spending is responsible for all of the gap (figure 21-2). To say that future budget problems are traceable to excessive government spending on "entitlements" in general therefore is misleading. If Medicare and Medicaid

Figure 21-1. Government Health Care Spending as Percentage of Total, 1960–2017[a]

Percent

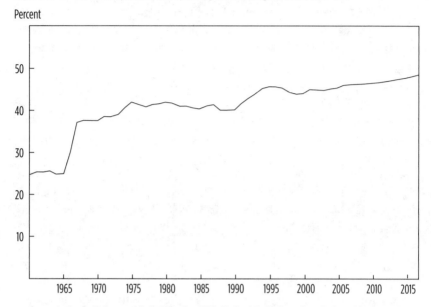

Source: Centers for Medicare and Medicaid Services (CMS), "National Health Expenditures by Type of Service and Source of Funds, CY 1960–2006" (www.cms.hhs.gov/NationalHealthExpendData/02_NationalHealthAccountsHistorical.asp) and "National Health Expenditures: Historical and Projections, 1965–2017" (www.cms.hhs.gov/NationalHealthExpendData).
    a. First projected year is 2007.

expenditures and all revenues earmarked or currently committed to them are removed from the equation, projected government revenues will be adequate to pay for all other government spending, including growing outlays on such entitlements as Social Security, food stamps, and the Earned Income Tax Credit.

Of greater importance is that the economic challenge that arises from increases in health care spending is the result of increases not only in government spending but also in private spending. Unless the U.S. citizenry is prepared to allow health care standards to fall when people become old, disabled, or poor, private health care spending increases must be controlled in order to significantly slow the growth in Medicare and Medicaid spending.

The stakes in achieving such control are enormous. If health care spending outpaces income growth by the current rate of 2.5 percentage points a year—a bit more than the historical average of the past three decades and a half—and if economic growth proceeds at the rate projected by the

Figure 21-2. Projected "Primary" Budget Deficit (−) or Surplus (+): Including and Excluding Medicare and Medicaid, Selected Years, 2007–50[a]

Percentage of GDP

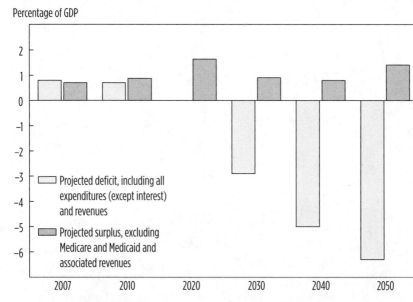

Source: Henry Aaron's calculations based on unpublished data underlying the Congressional Budget Office (CBO), *The Long-Term Budget Outlook* (December 2007); CBO, "Update of CBO's Economic Forecast," letter to Senator Kent Conrad, chairman of the Senate Committee on the Budget, 110 Cong. 2 sess. (Washington, February 15, 2008); FHI Board of Trustees, *2008 Annual Report.* The data combine CBO's extended baseline scenario for expenditures (adheres most closely to current law and assumes physician payment cuts as scheduled under the SGR [sustainable growth rate]) and its alternative fiscal scenario for revenues (assumes that none of the changes to tax law scheduled after 2007 will take effect and that the AMT [Alternative Minimum Tax] will be indexed to inflation).

a. The "primary" deficit or surplus is defined as all government spending, excluding interest on the debt, less all government revenue. Projected deficit excluding Medicare, Medicaid, and associated revenues is computed as follows: (1) projected Medicare and Medicaid spending are subtracted from CBO's projection of total long-term spending, excluding interest payments (following CBO's convention, beneficiary premiums are included in outlays as offsetting receipts); (2) from projected total revenues the following items are subtracted: projected Medicare payroll taxes, revenues from taxation of certain Social Security benefits that are transferred to Medicare, Part D "clawback" payments by states, and general revenues used to finance Medicare and Medicaid in 2007. The "projected deficit, excluding Medicare and Medicaid and associated revenues" is the difference between (1) and (2). It excludes from the projected deficit the anticipated increase in general revenues that will be needed to support Medicare and Medicaid if health care spending per beneficiary continues to outpace income growth by amounts as projected by the CBO in *The Long-Term Outlook for Health Care Spending* (November 2007).

Congressional Budget Office, per capita income available for purposes other than health care will still grow strongly for the next decade, but then stagnate (figure 21-3). Simply put, *the United States faces a health care financing challenge*—public and private—*that it cannot ignore.* It does not face a general government entitlement problem.

Figure 21-3. Projected Real per Capita Income, Various Series, 2007–50

Real per capita income index (2007 = 100)

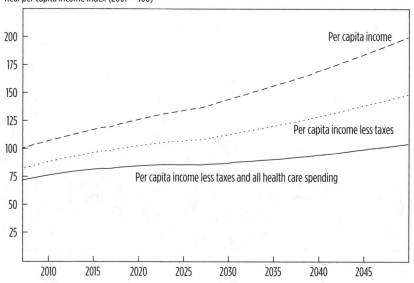

Source: Henry Aaron's calculations based on unpublished data underlying the Congressional Budget Office (CBO), *The Long-Term Budget Outlook* (December 2007); CBO, "Update of CBO's Economic Forecast," letter to Senator Kent Conrad, chairman of the Senate Committee on the Budget, 110 Cong. 2 sess. (Washington, February 15, 2008); Office of Management and Budget, *FY 2009 Historical Tables.* The calculations use CBO's extended baseline scenario for expenditures (adheres most closely to current law and assumes physician payment cuts as scheduled under the SGR [sustainable growth rate]).

HEALTH INSURANCE COVERAGE

Trends in health insurance coverage are not encouraging. Overall, coverage has fallen gradually and unevenly for two decades. The availability and generosity of employment-based insurance oscillates with the business cycle, and recently the proportion of Americans with this type of coverage has fallen sharply. Government-sponsored health insurance, particularly Medicaid and the State Children's Health Insurance Program (SCHIP), has taken up some of the slack. As a result, a larger fraction of U.S. children had health insurance in 2006—more than a quarter of them covered by Medicaid—than in any other year since 1987, when comprehensive statistics were first published.

Continued rapid growth of health care spending threatens our system of employment-based health insurance. The average annual health insurance premium for a family—$12,106 in 2007—about equaled the earnings of a full-time, minimum-wage worker. Economists argue about whether small changes in the minimum wage have much effect on employment, but few doubt that doubling the minimum wage would cause many workers to become unemployed.

Perceptions that employer-based insurance is providing less generous benefits and requiring higher deductibles and other cost sharing are widespread. Unquestionably, out-of-pocket spending has risen since 2000, but so has per capita health care spending. The net result is that the *share* of total health care spending paid directly by individuals actually has not increased, nor has the share paid by insurance fallen.

REFORM CHOICES ADDRESSING SYSTEMWIDE COST CONTROL AND INCREASED INSURANCE ACCESS

Rising costs and narrowing coverage mean that the next president must decide whether to push reform of the U.S. health care system, and, if so, how. The electorate has every right to expect each candidate to say whether he will make systemwide reform a top priority and, if so, which of the following four broad strategies the candidate proposes.

High-Deductible Insurance

The Bush administration sought to make high-deductible health insurance the norm, and the next president could sustain that effort. Under this approach, patients must pay directly for health care spending up to a dollar limit higher than most current insurance plans require. Beyond that limit, insurance would cover all or nearly all costs of care. Tax incentives would encourage most people to set aside monies in special health savings accounts (HSAs) to pay for most outlays below the deductible. The government would subsidize HSA deposits for low-income households. Unused balances would eventually be available for general consumption or for bequests, which advocates claim would encourage account holders to spend these dollars more carefully than they do when insurance lets them spend "other people's dollars." They predict that the growth of health care spending would slow, making health insurance more affordable and thereby slowing or reversing the loss of insurance coverage.

The effect of such plans is more complex than this simple argument suggests. Large deductibles do greatly reduce spending, compared to first-dollar coverage—perhaps by as much as 30 percent. But few people have first-dollar coverage now. Furthermore, spending by some people would likely increase, notably by the currently uninsured who, because of tax incentives or reduced premiums for high-deductible insurance, could finally afford coverage. The bottom line is that net savings are hard to gauge.

Incremental Change

The second strategy seeks to strengthen and extend employment-based coverage, rather than replace it. One means to this end would be for the federal government to provide reinsurance for all health spending above some threshold. The most immediate effect of such reinsurance would be to reduce insurance premiums, in effect shifting costs that are now paid through a premium to tax financing. Like any subsidy to insurance, this would make insurance more affordable and so decrease the number of uninsured. Nonetheless, there is some consensus across the political spectrum that unless the subsidy were large (that is, unless the reinsurance threshold were low), the reduction in the number of uninsured would be modest. One advantage of this approach is to decrease the cost to insurers of covering people deemed to be bad risks, making insurance somewhat more available to them. In general, the effects of this strategy on consumers may be weak. Approximately half of large and medium-sized establishments self-insure and commonly buy reinsurance already. In the individual and small group markets it would reduce the insurers' incentive to select against bad risks, but it would not eliminate it, since even with reinsurance such individuals would be unprofitable.

A second incremental strategy would be to authorize currently ineligible individuals or groups to "buy in" to Medicare or to the Federal Employees Health Benefits Program (FEHBP). The right to buy in could be extended to employer groups or other organizations. Premiums could be actuarially fair or subsidized. A third strategy would be to expand Medicaid eligibility—for example, to parents of currently eligible children.

The major advantage of the incremental strategy is also its principal weakness. It disrupts current arrangements least and requires few large shifts in financing that might necessitate large tax increases, generate windfall reductions in costs for businesses, or impose large payments on individuals. For the same reasons it would do little or nothing to simplify the current crazy quilt of financing arrangements. Nor is it clear how it could significantly reduce the alarming growth in health care spending.

Medicare-for-All

A sizable minority of Americans has long embraced the principle that a single, nationally uniform insurance plan should cover all Americans. One current embodiment of that strategy would enroll everyone in Medicare with a single menu of benefits financed jointly by earmarked taxes and premiums. As now, Medicaid could cover some or all premiums, cost sharing, and additional charges for low-income enrollees. Medicare beneficiaries would continue to be able to join health maintenance organizations, where available, and Medicare would pay their premiums in place of covering standard benefits.

No advocate of Medicare-for-all has fully explained how it would work. Would employers be required to pay taxes equal to some or all of what they now spend on health insurance for employees? If so, how would the taxes be designed? What charges, if any, would be imposed on employers who currently do not offer health insurance benefits? In general, how would revenues be raised to cover insurance costs? What premiums and cost sharing would people face? What relief from those charges would low-income households receive? Would supplemental insurance, which most Medicare beneficiaries now have, be folded in? Would people now eligible for Medicaid shift to Medicare? Any candidate who embraces this approach should be prepared to answer such questions.

State-Sponsored Reform

The final option is one of procedure. It arises from frustration with the fact that for seven decades national decisionmakers have been unable to agree on how to reform health care financing and from recognition that the same system may not be optimal for a nation as large and diverse as the United States. Under this approach, the federal government would authorize individual states or groups of states to develop their own plans to extend health insurance coverage. If the plans met certain standards, the federal government would defray part of the cost of extending coverage, adjusting its payments as state coverage expands. Congress would have to waive some restrictions in current federal health care programs so that states could combine funds in new ways. As states gather experience on what works, consensus on a national reform strategy might emerge. Alternatively, we might come to accept differing state or regional systems that reflect economic and political differences. Meanwhile, some of those now without health insurance would be covered.

This approach offers greater promise for extending health insurance coverage than it does for immediately controlling the growth of health care spending. It could build on experiments taking place across the country, as states try desperately to fill the vacuum in federal policymaking. It skirts the need for an elusive national consensus. It also might avoid a congressional showdown, since it already has garnered bipartisan support. In short, encouraging state-sponsored reforms may offer the only politically achievable way to extend health insurance coverage in the near future.

WHAT NO ONE WILL MENTION

No reform strategy that extends health insurance coverage to most of the nearly 47 million uninsured will immediately slow the growth of health care spending. On the contrary, added expenditures by the newly insured will boost health care spending, at least in the short term. But achieving long-term control of government health care spending will require near-universal coverage, unless the nation is willing to offer to the elderly, disabled, and poor health services that are grossly inferior to those available to other Americans. First, to slow the growth of spending on a sustained basis, the federal government would have to adopt regulations to control outlays (which are generally accepted in other nations that spend far less than we do), including limits on total and institution-specific spending. Without near-universal coverage, hospitals and other health care providers that were subject to spending controls would of necessity curtail care for the uninsured. The result could be widespread rationing of effective therapies for those now insured through public programs, with potentially serious health care consequences. However, eliminating waste and inefficiency in the current system could reduce the severity of any required rationing or delay it. Second, the currently fragmented organization of U.S. health care financing precludes effective limits. Our costly "non-system" of health care financing needs to be streamlined and simplified before effective cost control is even possible. Thus, *achieving universal coverage is a necessary precondition to effective cost control.*

Whether universal coverage would be sufficient to solve the problem of rising health care costs is unclear. To rein in health care spending will require rationing—that is, eliminating health care services that are not worth what they cost. Rational resource reallocation presupposes that we know a great deal more than we do currently about which services cost more than they are worth, that we can develop fair and politically acceptable limits, and that we will be willing to enforce them.

CONCLUDING OBSERVATIONS

As population aging proceeds and the menu of beneficial medical technologies continues to lengthen, per capita health care spending will increase. Consequently, the disposition of employers to drop coverage and of employees to refuse it even when it is offered will grow. These insecurities intensify during economic recessions. Presidential candidates will feel strong pressure to speak to the issue of expanding health insurance in the face of rising health care costs. Each of the four strategies outlined above promises to extend insurance coverage, some more than others, and provide a starting point for that conversation.

ADDITIONAL RESOURCES

Aaron, Henry J. 2007. "Budget Crisis, Entitlement Crisis, Health Care Financing Problem—Which Is It?" *Health Affairs* 26, no. 6 (November/December): 1622–633.

Aaron, Henry J., and Stuart M. Butler. 2008. "A Federalist Approach to Health Reform: The Worst Way, except for All the Others." *Health Affairs* 27, no. 3 (May–June): 725–35.

Blumenthal, David. 2006. "Employer-Sponsored Health Insurance in the United States—Origins and Implications." *New England Journal of Medicine* 355, no. 1 (July 6): 82–88.

Fisher, Elliott S., and others. 2003. "The Implications of Regional Variations in Medical Spending, Part 1: The Content, Quality, and Accessibility of Care." *Annals of Internal Medicine* 138, no. 4 (February 18): 273–87.

Gilmer, Todd, and Richard Kronick. 2005. "It's the Premiums, Stupid: Projections of the Uninsured through 2013." *Health Affairs,* web exclusive (April 5): W5-143–W5-151 (http://content.healthaffairs.org/cgi/reprint/hlthaff.w5.143v1).

Gruber, Jonathan. 2005. "Tax Policy for Health Insurance." In *Tax Policy and the Economy,* vol. 19, edited by James M. Poterba, pp. 39–63. MIT Press.

Institute of Medicine. 2001. *Crossing the Quality Chasm: A New Health System for the 21st Century.* Washington: National Academy Press.

McGlynn, Elizabeth A., and others. 2003. "The Quality of Health Care Delivered to Adults in the United States." *New England Journal of Medicine* 348, no. 26 (June 26): 2635–645.

Newhouse, Joseph P. 1992. "Medical Care Costs: How Much Welfare Loss?" *Journal of Economic Perspectives* 6, no. 3 (Summer): 3–21.

Nordhaus, William D. 2006. "The Health of Nations: The Contribution of Improved Health to Living Standards." In *Measuring the Gains from Medical Research: An Economic Approach,* edited by Kevin M. Murphy and Robert H. Topel, pp. 9–40. University of Chicago Press.

Swartz, Katherine. 2006. *Measuring Health: Why More Middle-Class People Are Uninsured and What Government Can Do.* New York: Russell Sage Foundation.

22▶

Meeting the Challenge of Health Care Quality

Achieve Reforms in Medicare, Quality, and Malpractice

HENRY J. AARON AND JOSEPH P. NEWHOUSE

SUMMARY ❚ The cost of the U.S. health care system is high and rising at unsustainable rates, and a growing number of Americans have inadequate health insurance or none at all. The American public has a right to expect both presidential candidates to address the overall problem of rising costs and decreasing access to care due to consumers' increasing inability to pay for services. But it also should expect candidates to address certain specific health system shortcomings, including the need to reform Medicare, improve quality of care, and tackle medical malpractice reform.

Each of these issues has figured prominently in recent political debates. Medicare threatens large and growing federal budget deficits as baby boomers retire or become disabled, especially if per capita health care spending continues to outpace per capita income growth. Scientific advances can reduce the number of needless deaths and injuries that result from shortcomings in the quality of health care, but these advances will not come cheaply, and many will require revolutionary change in the way that health care is delivered. And the compensation system for victims of medical malpractice is widely recognized as flawed, but the most commonly suggested solution—a cap on awards for non-economic damages—could actually worsen problems with the current system.

This chapter provides background for interpreting the positions that various presidential candidates may take on these issues. While the outcome of many policy initiatives is uncertain, some specific recommendations are warranted in each area:

—*Medicare reform:* With respect to Part D—the drug benefit—allow Medicare to select, through a competitive bidding process, a single pharmacy benefits management company for each region of the country and standardize plan offerings so that consumers do not have such a bewildering array of options; increase the deductible for Part D and use the savings to close the "doughnut hole."

—*Quality improvement:* Encourage development of cost-effective approaches to personalized medicine, tailored to individual patients' specific makeup, and the use of health information technology; continue to test quality improvement strategies in Medicare and Medicaid.

—*Malpractice reform:* Support a streamlined dispute resolution system that would more fairly compensate a larger proportion of patients injured by negligent health care providers.

With its enormous investments in health care programs, the federal government is uniquely able to mount the research necessary to stimulate widespread system improvements in quality and efficiency. The next president can use specific issues such as these in his first forays into what needs to be a complete overhaul of the system. ❚

CONTEXT ❚ Medicare finances health care for the elderly and for workers who become disabled. A distinct insurance program for these groups is logical, because, for most adults, health insurance is linked to employment. When people can no longer work because of age or disability, they generally lose access to employer-based insurance and may not have sufficient income to purchase it on their own.

Enacted in 1965, Medicare from the beginning was a political compromise. Part A, sponsored originally by Democrats, covers hospital and skilled nursing care, and Part B, sponsored originally by Republicans, covers physician care and certain other services. Not coincidentally, private health insurance then typically consisted of parallel plans covering hospital and physician services. Congress later allowed Medicare beneficiaries to enroll in managed care plans such as health maintenance organizations (Part C) and enacted limited outpatient prescription drug coverage (Part D), effective in 2006. ❚

REFORMING THE MEDICARE SYSTEM

Budgetary and health policy analysts see several problems with Medicare that need to be fixed. First, Medicare and Medicaid account for the entire projected long-term gap between federal revenues and federal spending, plus a little more. Second, Medicare can expose beneficiaries to financially ruinous cost sharing, particularly from lengthy hospital stays. Third, coverage of long-term care—nursing homes, home care, and other services typically needed by people with multiple chronic conditions—is spotty. Finally, the payment system is enormously detailed and hard to administer, with somewhat arbitrary fees based on patients' diagnoses or services rendered.

Because of gaps in Medicare coverage, most beneficiaries also have some kind of individual supplemental insurance—from former employers, Medicaid, or private purchase. About one-third receive retiree health coverage. Unfortunately, this benefit is eroding fast, because high costs are driving employers to cut retiree benefits or drop them entirely. About 14 percent of beneficiaries also qualify for Medicaid, which pays some or all of their cost-sharing obligations and in many states covers more services than does Medicare. According to the Medicare Payment Advisory Commission, the lack of coordination between Medicare and Medicaid degrades quality of care. Nearly 30 percent of beneficiaries purchase supplemental insurance—called "Medigap" coverage—and another 20 percent are enrolled in managed care plans (Part C), almost all of which provide some supplementary benefits. The resulting coverage is complex and uneven and boosts Medicare spending by insulating enrollees from cost sharing that would otherwise dampen demand.

Medicare's third major problem is quality. Patients with the same diagnoses are treated in widely different ways—at markedly different costs—depending on where they reside. Many patients, especially those treated simultaneously by several physicians, receive conflicting or counterproductive interventions. Nor do beneficiaries reliably receive the specific services recommended for their conditions. (None of these problems are confined to Medicare.)

Reforming Medicare's Benefit Structure

Three broad categories of reforms have been suggested for Medicare. Each has the potential to correct certain flaws in the current system, but each is difficult to design and implement well.

One approach would convert Medicare into high-deductible insurance linked to health savings accounts to which the government would make an annual contribution. Beneficiaries would pick an insurance plan, while the federal government would do little more than pay premiums. This approach reflects market-based ideas, popular with conservatives, that create disincentives for consumers to purchase excessive health services.

A second approach, premium support, would give Medicare enrollees a sum each year that they could use to buy private insurance. The payment would be adjusted periodically to keep up with rising insurance costs. Beneficiaries who selected plans costing more than the government payment would have to pay the difference, but if they bought less costly insurance, they could keep all or most of the savings.

The third approach would add an optional "super-Medicare" benefit to the current program by combining benefits from Parts A, B, and D and include special coverage, such as a limit on patient liability. Enrollees would pay a single premium, set to cover the cost of any added benefits (assuming universal enrollment). This option would add little to the growth of net federal health care spending.[1] Those who did not join when first eligible would have to pay higher premiums to join later. Assistance for the poor, now provided by Medicaid, would be folded into Medicare.

THE TROUBLED BEGINNINGS OF THE MEDICARE DRUG BENEFIT

The Medicare drug benefit rolled out to negative reviews, especially regarding the bewildering array of plans and lack of good information for choosing among them. Most of the confusion around initial implementation has passed, but several larger issues remain, relating to the administration of the benefit, the government's role in negotiating drug prices, and the structure of cost-sharing arrangements.

PBMs: To Choose or Not to Choose

Unlike Medicare, private insurers typically contract with a single pharmacy benefits manager (PBM) to administer their drug benefits. The PBM's profits depend on negotiating discounts with drug manufacturers. Periodic rebidding among PBMs ensures a competitive price. Thus, people with private drug insurance rarely, if ever, have to choose among

PBMs. By contrast, Medicare beneficiaries confront many drug plans offering widely different formularies (drug menus) and cost-sharing arrangements.[2]

Each approach has advantages and weaknesses. Competing plans enable some people to match their particular needs with plan formularies. In fact, Medicare's drug costs have turned out to require lower-than-anticipated premiums. But if the Part D legislation had permitted Medicare to choose a single PBM for each geographic region with periodic rebidding, it could have avoided the rampant confusion that has deterred some who are eligible from enrolling and led others to choose plans that are not in their best interest. (Medicare has such arrangements with the fiscal intermediaries and insurance carriers that administer Parts A and B.)

Drug Prices to Drug Manufacturers

Simply including drug benefits in Part B also would have simplified beneficiary choices but would have raised the explosive issue of how to determine drug prices. Under traditional Medicare, the government sets nonnegotiable prices that approximate the cost of service provision for most hospital and physician services. However, Medicare has a hard enough time matching prices to the costs of providing hospital services and sometimes makes mistakes. Drugs are even harder to price than hospital services. The biggest costs—for research and testing—occur before the first dose is administered. Once approved for sale, most drugs cost little to produce. As long as drugs are under patent, manufacturers can charge prices far above production costs and earn large profits, part of which finances research to develop future drugs. Although some complaints about high drug prices are quite justified, simply setting prices at production costs would hobble pharmaceutical research and discourage venture capital investment in drug development. Today's taxpayers and beneficiaries would gain; future patients would lose.

If the federal government changed from a "hands-off" buyer into an aggressive price negotiator, investors might fear that negotiation would become price setting. For example, Medicare and Medicaid administrators would likely point out that they must stay within a congressionally set budget and make what amounts to a take-it-or-leave-it offer. Or Congress could simply step in to set prices.

The "Doughnut Hole"

The current benefit formula, set up by the Medicare Modernization Act of 2003, defies all principles of insurance. The standard plan includes the so-called doughnut hole. In 2008, this means that, for beneficiaries with the standard plan, benefits are interrupted after out-of-pocket expenditures reach $834 and resume when outlays reach $4,050, at which point the program covers 95 percent of the cost of nearly all drugs on the plan's formulary without limit.[3] The no-benefits region—found in almost no commercial policy—emerged as a way to meet conflicting goals. The fiscal year 2004 budget resolution capped the bill's total cost, but Congress wanted to give some benefits to virtually everyone—even those who spend little on drugs—yet protect those who spend a lot on drugs from ruinous bills.

The result was a design that makes little sense as insurance. Having Medicare pay for small outlays may improve some patients' compliance with a medication regimen, but it "wastes" money paying for drugs that people can easily afford. It also led to a needlessly complex payment scheme. On balance, the situation would be improved if Medicare could choose a single PBM from competing bidders to serve a given region, increase the deductible, and use the money saved to eliminate the doughnut hole. The complexity and irrationality of the benefit formula for the newly added drug benefit is yet another reason to redesign the entire Medicare program.

IMPROVING HEALTH CARE QUALITY

The quality of health care improves when science finds new, beneficial interventions and when health care practitioners use them appropriately, which in turn requires that appropriate information is fully available to guide patient care. In this section, we focus on issues that will confront the next president—the promise and cost of "personalized" medicine, the need for more coordination of care across providers, how to use the vast quantity of information that has been or could be gathered by the federal government in its capacity as the largest single payer for medical care, and the unique problems and opportunities for medicine created by health information technology.

Personalized Medicine

A new approach to medical care—personalized medicine—promises both remarkable improvements in treatment and staggering increases in expenditures. Most diseases arise because one or more genes malfunction. The defective genes cause too much or too little of some protein to be produced or change the protein in a harmful way. Furthermore, not only are people genetically unique, they also accumulate added biological variation in the course of their lives through interactions with differing environments. What are regarded as single diseases are generally a large set of slightly different cellular, molecular, or genetic malfunctions that manifest themselves in similar, even indistinguishable, ways. Thus, drugs employed to treat what is considered a single disease may really be treating many slightly different illnesses. For these reasons, when two people with the same diagnosis take a medication, either they or their disease may not react the same way. Drugs typically help some patients, harm others, and produce no effect in still others; many produce different side effects in some or all who take them. At present, few of these reactions are predictable. As physicians become able to read the makeup of each person's genes and proteins, they will come to understand much more clearly whether particular drugs will work on particular patients and what the side effects will be.

Reading each person's biological characteristics also will make it possible to identify who is likely to be afflicted with certain diseases, so that treatment may begin before the conditions even manifest themselves. Already today, in the best-known example, women with particular genes that predispose them to develop breast cancer may undergo prophylactic mastectomies. As personalized medicine advances, offering treatment before illness occurs could become commonplace.

One might think that the benefits from personalized medicine would be an unalloyed blessing. But the full flowering of personalized medicine will also bring profound problems. Screening tests will become a fundamental element of primary care. Even if they are automated, the cost will be high. These tests will indicate much earlier than is now possible the need for therapies in vast numbers of people. Far more important is that personal medicine will mean personal drugs—special products developed because they will work reliably for a particular individual without undue side effects. The potential cost of this advance is almost unlimited, as companies would be asked to develop, in essence, an "orphan drug" for a single individual, rather than a blockbuster, "one size fits all" medication. So too are the ethical and political challenges that will arise if reversing or forestalling illness becomes feasible but unaffordable or if people predisposed to certain diseases are stigmatized.

These challenges will not appear full blown at some specific date. They will emerge gradually as scientific advances proceed and will intensify pressure to determine how much the nation is prepared to spend on health care. Careful, ongoing research on both the science and the economics of such advances is needed so that they can be developed in ways that benefit the health of the population without breaking the bank.

Increasing Coordination of Care

The explosion of medical knowledge has created the possibility of vast improvements in the quality of health care. To fully realize this potential requires fundamental change in how physicians practice medicine and, possibly, in how the delivery of care is organized.

Several decades ago, physicians were expected to know the recommended therapies for most diseases. Solo practice was the norm. Doctors did not usually need to consult with medical colleagues or other health professionals. Now, the menu of beneficial interventions is so vast that no one can master—or keep up with—more than a tiny bit of it. Countless medications are available. Patients with multiple conditions, who account for most of the medical spending, typically have several physicians. They receive both inpatient and outpatient care. When the activities of multiple providers are well coordinated, when medications are monitored to avoid harmful interactions, and when health professionals act carefully to avoid error, the results can be impressive.

Too often this standard is not met. The Institute of Medicine has concluded that tens of thousands of patients die or suffer injury from avoidable medical errors. According to a study by Elizabeth McGlynn and colleagues, about half the time patients simply do not receive the treatments recommended for their condition. Some problems arise because paper records are lost, others because one physician does not know what another physician has already discovered, and still others because the wrong medication or the wrong dose is dispensed. In general, the norm of the physician as solo operator obstructs the kind of cooperation and communication that has become essential to the delivery of optimal care for a growing fraction of patients. Optimal care increasingly requires physicians, hospitals, and other providers to be linked in a single system.

Information technology holds the promise to link together various providers and organize information about patients with multiple conditions to improve the quality of clinical decisionmaking. At the institution or community level, information technology can scan for indications of an outbreak of hospital-acquired infections or inefficient patterns of care. Information technology also will change the locus of care. Many patients do not need to be in a physician's office or hospital for their heart disease, diabetes, or blood pressure to be monitored; increasingly, that can be done at home, with the results transmitted to the provider and tracked. Even kidney dialysis can be performed at home. This enables physicians' time to be used more efficiently, saves patients the trouble of repeat physician visits, and offers the possibility of earlier intervention if a patient's condition changes. Certain high-cost specialists do not need to be at a patient's bedside—intensive care doctors now monitor multiple intensive care units remotely. These and other trends have the potential for improving the safety, effectiveness, patient centeredness, and timeliness—that is, the quality—of care.

Using Federal Leverage to Improve Health Care Quality

In 2008, federal, state, and local governments will spend more than $1.1 trillion on health care, nearly three-fourths through Medicare and Medicaid. Governments as buyers have enormous leverage to promote high-quality care and vast quantities of data with which current practices could be analyzed. Those capacities are barely used.

Medicare has begun to introduce some reforms based on developments in commercial insurance. One is "disease management." Its goal is to improve compliance with recommended medical regimens among those with costly chronic diseases, such as diabetes, asthma, or congestive heart failure. Medicare ran a large experiment in which some patients were assigned randomly to receive extra disease management services and some were not. The experiment found that disease management improved some aspects of quality of care but did not lower spending.

A second Medicare innovation is "pay for performance," a program that adjusts what providers are paid according to patient outcomes or providers' adherence to certain specified procedures. Surprisingly, such practices are new to medicine, and progress has been slow for both substantive and political reasons. Among the substantive problems are that extra pay for providing certain beneficial procedures may shift resources from other services that are equally beneficial but unmeasured; the payment algorithm has to be updated as new information emerges, so that standards do not enshrine outmoded procedures; auditing physicians' performance is costly; and rewarding patient outcomes is prone to error since outcomes depend not only on the physician's actions, but also on the patient's underlying health, the severity of the particular case, and the patient's cooperation (for example, does the patient take prescribed drugs?). Politically sensitive and economically important issues include whether rewards are based on absolute or relative performance, whether superior care is rewarded or inferior care is punished, and how much money is at stake.

Another opportunity for improving quality of care resides in Medicare and Medicaid records, a treasure trove of data that could improve evaluation of providers' performance and the identification of effective treatments. Currently, those data are little used for two reasons. First, because they are intended to support the claims process, they lack key elements necessary for valid clinical analyses, such as patient diagnosis or the outcome of laboratory tests. Historically, data on Medicare beneficiaries enrolled in organized plans such as health maintenance organizations were incomplete. And no outpatient prescription drug data were available until 2006. Second, currently collected data that are generally available for analysis suppress certain information, especially beneficiary and provider information, in order to protect individual privacy. These omissions mean that Medicare data cannot be linked to clinical information from commercial insurers to obtain a more comprehensive picture of service use and provider performance. Meanwhile, Medicaid data are almost unused, in part because they reside in fifty states, and Congress has not authorized federal administrators to set standards to ensure their comparability and availability.

These qualifications do not mean that the massive amounts of data generated by Medicare and Medicaid are useless. Since more than $800 billion of public funds is being spent on these programs, it is vitally important to see that the data collected are supplemented from other sources and made available to analysts to improve the quality of care.

FULFILLING THE PROMISE OF HEALTH INFORMATION TECHNOLOGY

Many managerial reforms and a change in the culture of medical practice are necessary to achieve the promise of modern medicine. Health information technology (HIT) can greatly facilitate this process. When information on each patient is recorded in an electronic form that can be read easily by other physicians, the quality of care can be improved, duplicative tests can be forestalled, and harmful drug interactions can be detected or avoided. In addition, adopting a single computer-based system of recording medical procedures and charges can simplify billing, saving providers and patients time and money.

Implementing HIT faces major obstacles—technical, economic, and sociological. Without improved safeguards and data-handling practices, patient privacy is in jeopardy. Without easy-to-use interfaces that make appropriate parts of these large data sets available to key users—physicians and other health care personnel, payers, facility administrators, analysts, and patients themselves—the data will languish. Without changes in physicians' practice habits and the willingness to surrender at least some autonomy to a team, the potential of HIT will not be fully realized. The up-front costs of hardware, software, and implementation for such systems are large. For small physician practices, they can be unaffordable; but even if the hardware and software are free, some physicians refuse them.

The federal government has taken some steps to promote HIT and has established important principles for the development of these systems, notably functionality, interoperability, and security. A federal office to coordinate such efforts began operations in 2004. However, the executive order creating it explicitly excluded any additional money to support the effort. Some hospital systems have implemented programs to enforce standard protocols of care among affiliated physicians. The stakes are high in the expansion of these efforts and their eventual success, especially for the elderly and people with disabilities served by Medicare and Medicaid. Members of these groups are particularly likely to suffer from multiple conditions, and HIT is especially valuable in such cases. Federal financial support to accelerate the introduction of HIT is justified. In addition, federal legislation could remove obstacles to private investment and implementation of HIT. Both the Democratic and Republican nominees in the 2004 presidential campaign spoke glowingly of HIT's potential, but action so far has been meager.

MALPRACTICE REFORM

Elected officials have decried the malpractice system for years. Numerous bills have been introduced to change it, most of them misguided because they would not correct the system's real shortcomings. Malpractice insurance should compensate victims of medical negligence for injuries that they have suffered, operate at a reasonable administrative cost, and goad poorly performing practitioners to either improve their performance or stop practicing.

The current malpractice system performs poorly on all scores. Most victims of medical negligence—more than 90 percent according to careful studies—never receive any form of compensation. Negligent physicians can continue to practice for a long time with no or only slight financial penalty, because malpractice premiums respond incompletely and with considerable lags after negligence occurs. Administrative costs are high because compensation is typically awarded only after protracted and expensive litigation.

Finally, the system is inequitable. Lawyers typically charge plaintiffs nothing unless they prevail in the litigation. In that event, the winning lawyer may retain one-third or more of the settlement, plus expenses. Since compensation for lost wages, medical expenses, and other financial losses are the largest part of most settlements, people with little earning capacity—the elderly, the unskilled, or those who are out of the labor force—are unattractive clients. Judgments in their cases may not even cover litigation costs.

Juries sometimes award compensation for non-economic damages, so-called pain and suffering—a highly subjective undertaking. A relatively small number of highly publicized cases with multimillion-dollar judgments (many of which are reduced markedly in later, less well publicized proceedings) have provoked outrage regarding "runaway juries" and led to an exaggerated and inaccurate belief that malpractice is responsible for a large part of increasing medical expenditures.

The fear of litigation is widely thought to foster "defensive medicine"—care that is intended to insulate the provider from judgment in the event of a lawsuit but that does not produce significant medical benefit.

Precise measurement of how much is spent on such care is impossible, since even standard medical care often produces small benefits. And the care that physicians provide trying to protect their legal flanks may offer at least some benefit as well. Furthermore, physicians' worries about lawsuits are disproportionate to the risk, since only those in a few high-risk specialties—obstetrics, anesthesiology, and some surgical subspecialties—are likely to face malpractice litigation.

Against this background, several states have sought to rein in medical expenditures by capping non-economic damages. Repeated efforts have been made to enact federal legislation imposing similar limits but with mixed success. Should the next president support such legislation at the federal level? If enacted, would it help hold down health care spending? Would it do so in a desirable way? Would it correct the major failings of the current malpractice system? Are there better alternatives?

The starting point for answering these questions should be an understanding of trends in malpractice insurance and of the effects of caps. The belief that capping compensation will modestly lower premiums for malpractice insurance does seem to be correct.[4] Evidence of the strategy's impact on defensive medicine is less clear. However, contrary to common belief, the cost of malpractice insurance fell from 1986 through 2000 by an average of about 10 percent for all physicians and by larger proportions for the high-risk specialties of surgery, obstetrics-gynecology, and anesthesiology. Furthermore, caps, which apply to awards for pain and suffering, reduce potential awards to old and poor plaintiffs proportionally more than they reduce awards to high earners. Thus, caps would make the system even more unfair than it already is.

The principal problem with the current system is not that too much is being paid overall to compensate victims of medical negligence, however questionable some of the largest settlements may be. The problem is the reverse—that nothing is paid to more than 90 percent of the victims and that administrative costs are so high. The solution to both problems is to replace the system of malpractice litigation with simplified and streamlined dispute resolution. One such plan would provide federal grants to physicians, hospitals, and health systems that disclose errors to patients and offer compensation directly, perhaps with mediation by a third party. Patients would not give up the right to sue, but any admission of error by the provider in this arrangement would not be admissible in later litigation. Such a program could be accompanied by subsidies to encourage data reporting, quality improvement initiatives, introduction of modern information technology, and other measures. To ensure equitable access to compensation, some nations require that fees for plaintiffs' attorneys be based on time and expenses, with subsidies to make legal fees affordable for low-income complainants. A system of fixed compensation for specific injuries also could be instituted, similar to that used in workers' compensation programs, in order to reduce uncertainty and administrative costs.

CONCLUDING OBSERVATIONS

The U.S. government has a huge stake in health care. First, it has a fundamental interest in the health of the citizenry, especially those who would be unable to obtain care without assistance—the poor, the elderly, and people with disabilities. Second, the government pays for services through major programs, regulates many aspects of health care and professional practice, and promotes populationwide health measures through public health programs. Third, it supports an enormous research enterprise that promises great advances in clinical care and a more efficient system of service delivery.

But not all the news is good. This giant enterprise is enormously expensive, with health care spending the source of all projected government budget deficits. On the private side, employees see an ever-larger share of compensation diverted to pay for health insurance. Health care quality is deficient, yet the knowledge is available that could improve it. The United States simply is not getting as much as it could for its enormous investment in health care services. Formulating policy on health care financing, regulation, and research will be the most important domestic issues that the next president faces. No presidential candidate should be permitted the luxury of answering these questions with vague generalities.

ADDITIONAL RESOURCES

Aaron, Henry J., Jeanne M. Lambrew, with Patrick F. Healy. 2008. *Reforming Medicare: Options, Tradeoffs, and Opportunities.* Brookings.
Aaron, Henry J., and William B. Schwartz, eds. 2004. *Coping with Methuselah: The Impact of Molecular Biology on Medicine and Society.* Brookings.
Aaron, Henry J., William B. Schwartz, and Melissa Cox. 2005. *Can We Say No? The Challenge of Rationing Health Care.* Brookings.
Frank, Richard G., and Joseph P. Newhouse. 2007. "Mending the Medicare Prescription Drug Benefit: Improving Consumer Choices and Restructuring Purchasing."

Hamilton Project Discussion Paper. Brookings (April) (www.brookings.edu/papers/2007/04useconomics_frank.aspx).

Institute for Healthcare Improvement (for components of quality care) (www.ihi.org).

Kaiser Family Foundation. 2005. *Medicare Chartbook,* 3d ed. Menlo Park, Calif.: Henry J. Kaiser Family Foundation (www.kff.org/medicare/7284.cfm).

———. Various years. "State Health Facts" (www.statehealthfacts.org/).

Localio, A. Russell, and others. 1991. "Relation between Malpractice Claims and Adverse Events Due to Negligence: Results of the Harvard Medical Practice Study III." *New England Journal of Medicine* 325, no. 4 (July 25): 245–51.

McFadden, Daniel, Florian Heiss, and Joachim Winter. 2007. "Mind the Gap! Consumer Perceptions and Choices of Medicare Part D Prescription Drug Plans." Working Paper 13627. Cambridge, Mass.: National Bureau of Economic Research (November).

McGlynn, Elizabeth A., and others. 2003. "The Quality of Health Care Delivered to Adults in the United States." *New England Journal of Medicine* 348, no. 26 (June 26): 2635–645.

Mongan, James J., Robert E. Mechanic, and Thomas H. Lee. 2006. "Transforming U.S. Health Care: Policy Challenges Affecting the Integration and Improvement of Care." Health Policy 2006-02. *Health Policy Issues and Options Brief.* Brookings (December 15).

Rodwin, Marc A., Hak J. Chang, and Jeffrey Clausen. 2006. "Malpractice Premiums and Physicians' Income: Perceptions of a Crisis Conflict with Empirical Evidence." *Health Affairs* 25, no. 3 (May–June): 750–58.

NOTES

1. Because some adverse selection might occur at initial enrollment, net costs to the government might increase somewhat.

2. Medicare enrollees in forty-seven states can choose from among at least fifty stand-alone prescription drug plans. Drug plans can also apply utilization management tools to covered drugs, such as prior authorization, quantity limits, and step therapy (which requires that a patient be given the cheapest and safest drug before costlier and possibly riskier drugs are tried).

3. Some plans have provisions that aid consumers, for example, by providing limited coverage—usually of generic drugs—within the "doughnut hole"; other provisions hurt consumers, for example, by counting as out-of-pocket expenditures only those purchases of drugs that are included on a particular plan's formulary.

4. Economist Kenneth E. Thorpe reports that states that cap awards have premiums that are 17.1 percent lower than those of states that do not. See Kenneth E. Thorpe, "The Medical Malpractice 'Crisis': Recent Trends and the Impact of State Tort Reforms," *Health Affairs,* web exclusive (January 21, 2004): W4-20–W4-30 (http://content.healthaffairs.org/cgi/content/full/hlthaff.w4.20v1/DC1).

23

Slowing the Growth of Health Spending

We Need Mixed Strategies, and We Need to Start Now

JOSEPH R. ANTOS AND ALICE M. RIVLIN

SUMMARY ❯ Americans are deeply concerned about paying their mounting bills for health care. This is true whether they have private insurance or public (Medicare or Medicaid)—and certainly for the 46 million with no insurance at all. The federal government's health spending, primarily for Medicare and Medicaid, is clearly unsustainable. If current commitments are kept, other government services will have to be slashed or taxes increased drastically just to pay for these two programs. But the problem of rising health care costs is not confined to the federal budget; private health spending is rising just as quickly. Conventional strategies to slow federal health spending—like cutting Medicare and Medicaid benefits or restricting eligibility—will merely shift the financial burden of health care to other payers and swell the ranks of the uninsured. These efforts will not significantly slow the growth of total health spending.

Despite the recognized successes of U.S. health care, there are abundant opportunities for increasing efficiency and spending health care dollars more wisely. The federal government—and the new president—might take advantage of these opportunities, using federal programs to provide

This chapter is adapted from Alice M. Rivlin and Joseph R. Antos, *Restoring Fiscal Sanity 2007: The Health Spending Challenge*, chapter 2 (Brookings, 2007). The authors are indebted to Marni Schultz for extraordinary assistance.

leadership that would slow the growth of total health spending and move the whole health care system toward greater efficiency and effectiveness.

Specifically, the new president should adopt a broad agenda of reform, drawing from policies that

—use markets and regulations to make incremental reforms;

—continue to use Medicare and Medicaid to promote systemwide improvements through, for example, the adoption of clinical practice guidelines and disease management for costly chronic conditions;

—use their marketplace clout to improve price setting through carefully applied pay-for-performance strategies, competitive bidding, and direct price negotiations;

—encourage better system management through deployment of health information technology;

—promote consumerism in health care, to make individuals more aware and responsible for costly health coverage and care choices;

—adjust the open-ended entitlement provided by Medicare and Medicaid in ways that could shrink costs without sacrificing beneficiary health or shifting costs elsewhere. ❚

CONTEXT ❚ When people spend increasing amounts on video games or espresso drinks, no one suggests second-guessing them to slow spending down. Society relies on market prices to keep supply and demand in balance and ensure reasonably efficient production. But health care is different.

The Basic Problem: Third-Party Payment

Society does not accept the notion that people should be denied needed care just because they cannot pay. Moreover, illness often comes in costly, unpredictable episodes, such as a sudden heart attack. People want to be protected from sudden, involuntary bills that could bankrupt them.

These characteristics have led to third-party payment for most health services almost everywhere. Many countries have universal health coverage paid out of tax revenues. The United States has a complex system involving employer-based insurance subsidized through the income tax, other private insurance, and state and federal government programs covering seniors, the disabled, and many of the poor. In other words, most health bills for most people are paid by someone else, although about 16 percent of Americans are without health insurance.

When a third party—whether the government or a private insurer—is paying most of the cost, patients have little incentive to consider the cost of services or to find the most efficient provider. Providers, who typically are paid for each individual service rendered and who realize that their patients are not paying the bill, have little reason to economize. Thus third-party payment results in higher spending for health care than would have occurred if patients paid the full cost directly.

The effects of third-party payment on spending can be diminished by requiring that patients pay more of the cost of their care out of their own pockets. However, such payments may cause hardship, especially for the less affluent and for people on fixed incomes. They may keep people from seeking care when a condition is at an early stage, when it is less costly to treat.

Health plans sometimes try to limit direct access to services, usually by requiring patients to obtain a referral from a "gatekeeper" (usually a primary care physician) before obtaining costly specialist services. These limits help control spending, but they are unpopular with patients and providers.

Public programs provide health coverage to millions of people and improve the health status of seniors and the poor, but like private insurance, they also contribute substantially to the rapid growth of health spending. Subsidizing private insurance through the tax system (mostly because employers' premium contributions are excluded from employees' taxable income) has enabled millions of Americans to have health insurance. It also encourages the purchase of more generous insurance plans (with lower out-of-pocket costs paid by consumers), which blunts the consumer's sensitivity to health care prices and encourages greater use of services.

Despite its downsides, eliminating third-party payment is not a realistic or desirable option. The challenge is to mitigate its perverse incentives without doing more harm than good. ❯

DO WE GET OUR MONEY'S WORTH?

Analyzing variations in medical practice and outcomes can yield clues about the effectiveness and efficiency of care. Dr. Jack Wennberg and colleagues at the Center for Evaluative Clinical Sciences at Dartmouth Medical School have long studied Medicare data to uncover variations across regions, states, and providers in the resources used to treat the same diagnoses, as well as the outcomes achieved.

This research yields three robust results. First, variations in resource use are huge. Medicare spending for the average patient in Miami is about two and a half times what it is in Minneapolis. This is true even after controlling for health and demographic differences between the two populations. In the last two years of life, when costs tend to be relatively high, these enormous differences persist. For example, in New Jersey in recent years, Medicare spent on average $40,000 per patient in the last twenty-four months of life but only $25,000 in Ohio.

Second, resource use is sensitive to supply. In areas with more hospital beds per person, Medicare patients were more likely to be hospitalized, and in areas with more cardiologists per person, Medicare patients with heart disease had more cardiologist visits.

Third, and most important, more aggressive treatment and higher spending do not result in better patient outcomes. One study that followed Medicare patients with three specific diagnoses found that greater care intensity (that is, more services and costs) was associated with *increased* mortality rates. Moreover, both high- and low-cost areas underutilize effective preventive services, such as mammography or vaccination for pneumonia. These findings indicate that making the practices of the least efficient providers more like the most efficient would save significant resources, both in Medicare and in the rest of the health system. For example, a recent five-year study of large California hospitals found that Medicare spending per patient in the last two years of life ranged from $24,722 to $106,254—again, with no demonstrable difference in health status, quality of health care, or longevity. During the study period, Medicare could have saved $1.7 billion in the Los Angeles area alone, if the resource-intense hospital care there had matched the type of care provided in lower-cost areas of the state.

The challenge is moving from documenting inefficiency to actually reducing it. At present, providers often have inadequate information on what works best and for whom or fail to use the information available. Payment systems encourage greater resource use and reward excessive treatment, even when it results in preventable medical errors. If a patient acquires an infection in a hospital and has to be readmitted, Medicare will pay the costs of that second hospital stay.

Efforts are under way to design incentives for providers to collect and share information on effective treatments. Medicare, for example, now pays for certain treatments (such as implantable cardiac defibrillators) only provisionally, contingent on learning more about the success of this treatment among Medicare patients.

Despite the lack of clear evidence for much of what is done in medicine, the wealth of information on treatment options can be overwhelming, even for well-trained physicians trying to keep up with medical progress. Methods of helping physicians manage information overload include the following:

—Practice guidelines based on evidence

—Disease management and patient management methods that rely on evidence-based protocols and improved coordination among providers

—Improved Internet access to the latest scientific studies

—Computer-based decision support tools

Unfortunately, many physicians do not make the best use of such information tools for both cultural and business reasons. Computers are not always accessible—in examining rooms, for example—and can interfere with face-to-face interaction between physician and patient. Hand-held devices may reduce this problem, but the many older physicians are uncomfortable with the technology. Conventional practice often lags behind the latest evidence unless new findings are brought to the physician's attention.

Adhering to evidence-based standards also may be bad for business. Fee-for-service payment combined with low negotiated reimbursement rates from insurers rewards the use (and overuse) of health services. The patient, who is not paying much of the bill and is typically not knowledgeable about the options, is unlikely to recognize or object to treatment that does not meet evidence standards.

To improve the efficiency and effectiveness of health care, the knowledge base necessary for sound medical decisionmaking must be built and that knowledge must be made accessible and usable to patients, physicians, and payers. The financial incentives must be redirected toward more prudent use of care while also finding mechanisms that ensure that patients seek and receive the care they truly need.

TWO IMPEDIMENTS TO ADDRESSING
HEALTH SPENDING GROWTH

A first impediment to slowing the rapid growth of health spending is the notion, espoused by many policy analysts, that the United States cannot control the growth of health spending until it undertakes comprehensive reform of its complex and fragmented health system. We believe the opposite is more likely true. Comprehensive reform will take time and require major institutional and cultural changes. The nation cannot wait for comprehensive reform to address the problem of rising spending. Indeed, squeezing waste and inefficiency out of the system and designing mechanisms to make health spending more effective can set the stage for more fundamental reform.

A second impediment is the unrealistic hope that there is some simple remedy that will provide better health care at lower cost for everyone. Some believe that accelerating the adoption of information technology can greatly increase productivity in the health sector. Some pin their hopes on prevention and healthier lifestyles. Others argue that capping awards in medical malpractice cases could substantially reduce the cost of health care. Still others voice enthusiasm for "evidence-based medicine" and "pay for performance" and believe that aligning provider reimbursement with patient outcomes can result in higher quality at lower cost.

All of these prescriptions have merit—and we discuss them further below—but none is a silver bullet. Slowing the growth of health spending will require multiple policy interventions and persistent effort. Every-one—patient, provider, employer, taxpayer—will ultimately be involved in the difficult decisions necessary to slow the growth of spending to a sustainable rate.

REFORM STRATEGIES: THE OPTIONS

Perhaps the greatest impediment to realistic reform is the belief that a clear-cut choice must be made between two competing strategies for restraining health spending: market strategies and regulatory strategies. On the contrary, we believe that a blend of the two strategies is necessary for effective reform.

Market Strategies

Proponents of market strategies believe that if individuals had more direct responsibility for the cost of their care, they would weigh these costs and the value they receive more carefully. Providers would be forced to com-pete for consumer dollars on the basis of price, quality, and customer service. This heightened competition would cause health care providers to adopt more efficient practice styles. Prices for services would be established in the market, reflecting both supply and demand and providing incentives for continued medical innovation.

A modest step toward a market strategy involves giving consumers choices among competing health plans at different prices. For example, some analysts have suggested including other groups in the Federal Employees Health Benefits Program (FEHBP), which offers federal employees and retirees a wide choice of health plans. This approach may make consumers more cost-conscious when they choose plans, but it still leaves a third party (the plan) paying most of the bills.

A more aggressive approach would require consumers to pay out of pocket for most health expenditures, with insurance protecting them only from the catastrophic losses that could accompany a major illness or accident. Such consumer-driven health plans typically offer insurance with a high deductible plus a savings account intended to help people set aside funds to cover out-of-pocket costs. Congress embraced this concept in 2003 when it enacted health savings accounts (HSAs)—tax-favored accounts available to people with catastrophic coverage.

Health spending is concentrated—10 percent of the U.S. population accounts for 69 percent of the nation's health spending. Much of the spending for high-cost patients is above the deductible amount for a typical consumer-driven health plan and therefore unaffected by financial incentives. Other methods, such as care management for high-cost cases, may be more effective in limiting inappropriate spending in this group.

Market strategies, in theory, rely on decisions by informed consumers. At present, the information that people need to make sound health care decisions—reliable information on the cost, quality, and appropriateness of services—is largely unavailable. It is almost impossible to find out in advance the cost of a full episode of care, since services of multiple providers (physicians, hospitals, imaging and laboratory services, and so on) are typically billed separately. Mortality rates, hospital readmission rates, and other commonly available quality indicators are inadequate assessments of provider quality. Data comparing the effectiveness of alternative treatments are not readily available, and the typical consumer would need substantial medical knowledge or the advice of a disinterested, knowledgeable physician to interpret the studies that do exist. Insurers, providers, and government agencies are beginning to develop better information for consumers, but the average person is still poorly equipped to interpret complex price and quality information.

In short, market strategies hold promise, but the steps necessary to create a functioning health market are daunting.

Regulatory Strategies

Advocates of regulatory strategies argue that the nation has a social responsibility to ensure that everyone has access to good quality care that is delivered as efficiently as possible. We cannot rely upon private companies to provide that care without regulation, they say, since experience shows that insurers try to avoid enrolling people with serious health conditions and that drug companies charge substantially more than their costs of production. They believe that the considerable market power of government programs should be exercised on behalf of consumers and taxpayers.

There are risks to setting lower prices for health services than those that would have prevailed in an unregulated market, since health providers may try to make up for lower prices by increasing the volume of services. Moreover, if prices are held too low for too long, health providers and suppliers exit the market and innovation is stifled. For example, Medicaid's low reimbursement rates have made many providers unwilling to serve Medicaid-covered low-income people, and some providers limit the number of Medicare patients in their practices.

Proponents of regulation argue that just because regulation has sometimes been done badly does not mean it cannot be done well. They envision a system in which the government uses its power to ensure that health services are effective and delivered efficiently. This government-led regulation could involve analyzing data to establish best practices, promulgating practice guidelines, and refusing to pay for care that does not conform to those guidelines, as well as imposing caps on total health spending and devising rules for enforcing those caps. However, undertaking any of these steps requires considerable technical and political effort.

The More Feasible Option: A Blended Strategy

America's health system already is a hodgepodge of market and regulatory elements. Moving the current system toward greater efficiency as well as equity will take a blend of market-oriented and regulatory reforms. For example, aggressive implementation of pay for performance by both public and private payers could involve elements of both strategies. Better information and stronger financial incentives could be established to encourage consumers to seek out providers who offer the best value in terms of price, quality, and customer service. But reform must recognize that the largest decisions about what and where to buy are made by third-party payers and that regulations, as well as incentives, may be needed to guide those decisions.

Regulation and markets are facts of life in the health system. Reforms may nudge the system toward greater regulation or more competitive markets, but a wholesale shift in either direction is both unlikely and undesirable.

OPPORTUNITIES FOR FEDERAL LEADERSHIP

Because of the size and impact of federal health policies and programs, well-designed reforms in Washington can catalyze improvements in the whole health system. Of course, poorly conceived federal policy can make matters worse for everyone, so it is important to get the reforms right.

Medicare is the largest single purchaser of health care, and its policies directly affect virtually every health care provider. Medicare's record-keeping, coding, and billing practices are the industry norm. When Medicare introduces innovations in payment methods, such as prospective payment, they are widely adopted by private insurers too. For example, the Medicare prescription drug benefit has prompted health plans and providers to alter the way they manage both their Medicare and private business.

Innovative approaches are being tested by states seeking to improve the operation of their Medicaid programs—including Maine, Massachusetts, West Virginia, and California. Efforts to make other federal health programs more efficient—including the State Children's Health Insurance Program (SCHIP), the Veterans Health Administration (VHA), and the Defense Department's TRICARE program—could reduce the growth in federal outlays. The lessons learned from such initiatives could be applied more broadly. For example, more efficient practices in VHA already are influencing other systems.

Altering federal tax subsidies could have a major impact on employment-based private health insurance. Restructuring the tax preference by capping the amount that may be excluded from taxable income and providing a refundable tax credit for health insurance could better target those in need and minimize the adverse incentives that promote inefficiency in the health system.

Regulatory agencies—the Federal Trade Commission (FTC) and the Food and Drug Administration (FDA)—can shape competition in the health sector and determine how quickly new drugs and devices enter the market. Research agencies, such as the National Institutes of Health (NIH) and the Agency for Healthcare Research and Quality (AHRQ), contribute to the development of medical innovation and improvements in clinical practice and the delivery of health care. However, despite the large potential payoff of health systems research, including analysis to compare effectiveness of treatments, this field currently receives relatively little funding.

Federal action could play an important role in health reform in several key areas, including information development, price setting, improving care delivery, and encouraging competition. The policy options listed below represent a starting point, not an exhaustive survey of possible reforms.

Develop Information

All approaches to improving the efficiency of the health system and the quality of care depend on making reliable information readily available to providers, administrators, and consumers. Federal action can improve the knowledge base for clinical decisionmaking by developing comprehensive data on patient care and by sponsoring research on outcomes and effectiveness of care. It can make these data easier to collect, analyze, and disseminate by promoting health information technology (HIT).

Accelerate Development and Use of Health Information Technology

The health care sector lags behind many other segments of the U.S. economy in developing and deploying information technologies to serve the needs of clinicians, administrators, and patients. A great many national initiatives are already under way, and among their first priorities are the following:

—*Develop standards for interoperable HIT.* The development of information-exchange networks and adoption of standards for interoperable technology will enable data to be shared among physicians, hospitals, and patients, eventually eliminating less-efficient paper records and making patient information immediately available to those who need it, when they need it.

—*Provide incentives and financing for HIT adoption.* The costs of implementing HIT, or transforming an existing system to comply with standards, can be significant—especially for solo or small physician practices. The federal government could promote wider adoption through grants, tax incentives, or the reduction of legal barriers to private subsidies from insurers and hospital systems for physicians to purchase HIT.

—*Build on HIT activities already under way.* Use existing exemplary systems as a testing ground for improvements in HIT, including the development of fully interoperable systems accessible across sites of care, new hardware and software, and changes in work methods.

Promote Research on Outcomes and Effectiveness

—*Develop tools to analyze patient-level data across health plans.* Ideally, a fully wired health system could gather and analyze information from many sources on patients and their treatment. Until such a system develops, existing Medicare data can provide a rich source of patient information on which to base assessments of clinical outcomes and quality of care. Other insurers—including Medicaid, VHA, FEHBP, and private plans—could also contribute information for such analyses.

—*Promote research and disseminate results widely.* The federal government should increase its support for research on effectiveness through additional funding and by making data available to private researchers, health plans, and insurers for their own analyses. Additional research on cost-effectiveness and comparative effectiveness of various treatments could improve clinical decisionmaking and influence insurers' decisions on what services to cover.

Improve Health Care Delivery

Beyond developing better information on the effectiveness and quality of care of health services, additional steps can be taken to improve health care delivery.

Develop and Disseminate Practice Guidelines

—*Create evidence-based practice guidelines.* Clinical guidelines can promote appropriate, high-quality care by helping physicians incorporate the latest evidence into their treatment decisions. The federal government can use its data development activities to generate more comprehensive clinical guidelines in conjunction with medical groups.

—*Encourage use of guidelines in assessing provider performance.* Medicare and Medicaid could examine provider-specific patterns of service to identify outliers from local or national norms. Scorecards benchmarking providers' performance against average performance in their market could include incentives to improve performance. Giving providers information to compare their performance against that of their peers can be effective in improving adherence to guidelines.

Promote Care Management and Coordination

—*Support the development of effective care management models.* Better patient management—especially for such costly chronic diseases as diabetes—offers the promise of more effective treatment and possibly lower costs, but evidence on what works best is lacking. Medicare has several demonstration projects under way to test disease management for patients with chronic conditions and complex health needs.

—*Increase incentives for enrollment in managed care and disease management programs.* Medicaid has continued to use managed care methods to discourage unnecessary spending while maintaining reasonable access to care. Many states also use disease management programs. Such programs provide patients with education on managing their disease, actively monitor the patient's condition, and coordinate care and facilitate information sharing across providers.

—*Improve coordination of patient care.* Providers often do not have an easy way to share information that could reduce unnecessary or duplicative services and avoid medical errors. Changing financial incentives—such as introducing a case manager or directly rewarding the involvement of physicians and hospitals in joint efforts to manage patient care—could promote coordinated care. Another help is, again, using information technology that electronically delivers patients' complete medical records to each provider caring for them.

Support Other Improvements in Care Delivery

—*Improve coordination and delivery of end-of-life care.* Nearly one-quarter of all Medicare and Medicaid outlays is spent on care of patients in their last year of life, though such patients account for only 5 percent of the elderly population. Increasing the use of hospice care may help reduce these costs as well as improve quality. Greater adherence to evidence-based guidelines could minimize costs of treating severe disease and functional impairment. Better coordination is needed between acute and long-term care providers as well as between Medicare and Medicaid.

—*Encourage use of lower-cost delivery settings.* Visits to hospital emergency departments increased 26 percent during the past decade, with nearly one-third of those visits classified as nonurgent or semi-urgent. Contrary to popular opinion, Medicaid beneficiaries are more likely to use the emergency department than are the uninsured. Encouraging federal health program beneficiaries to use lower-cost sites of care—for example, by expanding hours at federally financed clinics—could reduce unnecessary emergency department visits.

—*Promote healthy behavior and disease prevention.* The poor health habits of average Americans add significantly to the cost of health care. While disease prevention strategies like immunization programs and environmental strategies like ensuring a clean water supply provide unequivocal benefits, it is unclear whether behavior change programs aimed at reducing smoking or obesity or increasing exercise can yield substantial cost savings. Beyond the difficulty of achieving wide-scale behavior change, even successful health promotion activities—such as smoking cessation programs—may not reduce health care spending in the long term. The government could provide additional support for studies of the cost-effectiveness of prevention and promotion efforts.

Improve Price Setting

The ways in which health care products and services are priced or reimbursed can determine the type of services that are provided, the quality of care, and the cost of that care.

—*Pay for performance.* Fee-for-service payments create incentives for providing more services, even if these will likely generate only minimal health improvements. Pay-for-performance (P4P) approaches are being developed to promote more effective care in a fee-for-service setting, although it will be challenging to implement them. Developing specific quality measures to identify differences in provider performance will be necessary to make this approach successful and sustainable. Medicare's size and regulatory authority give it the clout to advance P4P, but it must move carefully to avoid institutionalizing an inadequate payment formula.

—*Competitive bidding.* Bidding approaches require all sellers to submit their best offers in advance. This strategy can elicit prices that more accurately reflect local market conditions than a national price formula can. Bidding can reduce program costs, although the bidding process must be carefully designed to avoid driving out competition, which ultimately may lead to higher prices.

—*Direct price negotiation.* Medicare's decision to use bidding to set payments for Part D (the drug benefit), rather than taking advantage of its aggregate buying power to keep prices low, has been controversial. Outside Medicare—for example, Medicaid "best price" requirements and the Department of Veterans Affairs' Federal Supply Schedule—the federal government uses its market power and legal authority to extract below-market drug prices. This approach may achieve short-term savings, but over the longer term, it may cause suppliers to drop out of the market or discourage the entry of new products and services.

Promote Consumerism and Competition

Numerous policy changes are required to introduce effective competition and informed consumer and provider decisionmaking into the health care market.

—*Introduce premium support in Medicare.* Premium support would provide Medicare beneficiaries with a fixed subsidy for a basic set of benefits, while permitting beneficiaries to purchase more expansive insurance coverage if they are willing to pay the additional expense. Such a system operates in FEHBP, which provides federal employees and retirees with a wide choice of competing health plans. The government pays about three-quarters of the insurance premium, based on the plans' average bid, and enrollees pay the remainder. This arrangement limits the government's financial exposure and fosters competition among the plans that could result in greater efficiency.

—*Encourage states to test and implement consumer-oriented approaches in Medicaid.* Both Medicaid and SCHIP may provide premium assistance to beneficiaries who enroll in employer-sponsored insurance instead of the government program. Some states have implemented reforms that provide Medicaid beneficiaries with individual budgets for care, giving them more control over how that money is spent. Cash and Counseling programs, which give Medicaid beneficiaries who are eligible for personal care services a consumer-directed allowance in lieu of agency services, have improved patient satisfaction without increasing program costs. This model is being used in twenty-two states.

—*Promote use of high-deductible plans tied to tax-favored health savings accounts.* Increasing the deductibles in insurance plans makes beneficiaries more aware of the cost of routine care and generally lowers the insurance premium. In shifting to this type of health plan, employers often contribute to the HSA to help employees with their higher out-of-pocket costs. In 2005, FEHBP introduced the option of high-deductible plans with HSAs.[1] Medicare recently announced a new initiative to test account-based coverage. If employers adopt HSAs widely, future generations of seniors may want a similar option when they become eligible for Medicare.

Limit Health Outlays

Directly limiting outlays in Medicare and Medicaid (or limiting tax breaks for private health insurance) would impose fiscal pressure that could promote other health system reforms.

—*Convert Medicaid to a block grant.* States receive a federal matching grant that covers at least 50 percent of the cost of their Medicaid programs. This arrangement has enabled states to cover more beneficiaries for more health services, but it has also encouraged rapid spending increases. A block grant could be structured to reward states that achieve better health outcomes and lower-cost treatment. Block grants give the federal government budget predictability and a simple lever for controlling future spending. States would also have stronger incentives to develop ways to save money, since they could keep all the savings.

—*Modify the entitlement status of Medicare and Medicaid.* Current law ensures that Medicare and Medicaid will automatically finance all necessary health services covered by the programs without limit. Congress could alter this arrangement by requiring a periodic vote (perhaps every five or ten years) on overall program spending levels and future trends—in essence, a national referendum on the long-term financial promises made by the program.

—*Limit the tax exclusion for employer-provided health insurance.* Capping or limiting the tax exclusion for employer-sponsored insurance would encourage the purchase of less expansive coverage with greater cost-sharing requirements, promoting greater cost-consciousness on the part of consumers and providers. The policy also would yield additional federal revenue that could be used to increase insurance subsidies for low-income Americans.

Other Options

Beyond the major health entitlement programs, other government entities contribute to the legal, institutional, and scientific structure in which public and private health programs operate. The drug approval process and medical malpractice are examples of areas that could be modified to promote efficiency in the health system.

Change the Drug Approval Process

—Streamline the FDA approval process for new drugs and devices. The Food and Drug Administration is charged with protecting consumers from unsafe or ineffective drugs without unduly impeding the introduction of innovative products to the market. Increased postmarketing surveillance of new drugs would add to patient safety without imposing unreasonable delays on drug introduction. The FDA's Critical Path Initiative attempts to modernize the process through which basic scientific discoveries translate into new medical treatments, including implementing standards for clinical trial design and helping companies "fail faster" on drugs that eventually would not be approved.

—Speed the review of generic drugs. The FDA can promote price competition in the drug market by introducing close substitutes for brand-name products more quickly. Better funding for the FDA's Office of Generic Drug Approval could help alleviate the growing backlog of applications to bring new generic products to market. Advances in science and regulation would open the door to "follow-on" biologics—complex molecules that offer great promise for medical treatment. However, the benefits of price competition must be balanced against the need to maintain strong incentives for innovation in this emerging pharmaceutical field.

Reform the Malpractice Tort System

—Public attention periodically focuses on the rising cost of medical liability insurance premiums and concerns about patient safety. Although capping awards and limiting attorneys' fees would lower the cost of malpractice insurance, the impact on overall health costs would be modest. More attention should be placed on preventing medical errors and providing appropriate redress for injured patients. Structured payment rules and use of alternative methods for resolving malpractice claims—such as an administrative compensation system or specialized health courts— would make the system more equitable.

CONCLUDING OBSERVATIONS

The U.S. health care system accounted for 16 percent of GDP in 2005— almost $2 trillion a year and rising. Such a large industry naturally has powerful interests—of clinicians, health systems, health plans, drug and device manufacturers, employers, and even consumers themselves—and resistance to change, even in the face of a growing financial crisis, is great. Meanwhile, science moves forward, and what is possible today was un- thinkable a dozen years ago. A dozen years hence, many other "disruptive technologies"—that is, those that can fundamentally change a sector— may be in place.

Because the health sector is big, important, and rapidly changing, a sin- gle, go-for-broke health reform seems highly unlikely. Instead, we will find ourselves in the position of the man trying to build the bicycle while riding it—fixing one piece here through regulation, another one there through market reforms, and a third one by changing some aspect of the information environment. The trip may be bumpy, but like it or not, we must get on and ride.

ADDITIONAL RESOURCES

For information about the constellation of studies of geographic and inter-institutional differences in costs and outcomes of care, see Dartmouth Atlas Project, Center for the Evaluative Clinical Sciences (www.dartmouthatlas.org/).

Cunningham, Peter J. 2006. "Medicaid/SCHIP Cuts and Hospital Emergency Depart- ment Use." *Health Affairs* 25, no. 1 (January–February): 237–47.

Davis, Karen. 2004. "Consumer-Directed Health Care: Will It Improve Health System Performance?" *Health Services Research* 39, no. 4 (part 2, August): 1219–234.

Foster, Leslie, and others. 2003. "Improving the Quality of Medicaid Personal Assis- tance through Consumer Direction." *Health Affairs*, Data Watch: Medicaid web ex- clusive (March 26): W3-162–W3-175 (http://content.healthaffairs.org/cgi/content/ full/hlthaff.w3.162v1/DC1).

Milgate, Karen, and Sharon Bee Cheng. 2006. "Pay-for-Performance: The MedPAC Perspective." *Health Affairs* 25, no. 6 (March–April): 413–19:

Pauly, Mark V. 1968. "The Economics of Moral Hazard: Comment." *American Economic Review* 58, no. 3 (part 1, June): 531–37.

Penner, Rudolph G., and C. Eugene Steuerle. 2005. "A Radical Proposal for Escaping the Budget Vise." *National Budget Issues* 3 (June): 1–6 (Urban Institute).

———. 2007. *Stabilizing Future Fiscal Policy: It's Time to Pull the Trigger.* Washington: Urban Institute (August).

Struve, Catherine T. 2004. "Improving the Medical Malpractice Litigation Process." *Health Affairs* 23, no. 4 (July–August): 33–41.

NOTE

1. Other types of health accounts, including flexible savings accounts (FSAs) and health reimbursement arrangements (HRAs) are available through FEHBP and many private employers. See U.S. Office of Personnel Management, "Federal Employee Health Benefit Program: RI 70-1 for Federal Civilian Employees," 2006 (http://opm.gov/insure/06/guides/70-01).

24

Promoting Retirement Security

Make Saving Easier and More Rewarding

WILLIAM G. GALE

SUMMARY ❱ The past twenty-five years have brought a dramatic shift in our nation's pension system away from defined benefit plans and toward defined contribution accounts, such as 401(k)s and individual retirement accounts (IRAs). But many of our public policies have not been updated to reflect the increased responsibility placed on workers to prepare for their own retirement. The next president can improve and strengthen retirement security substantially through a series of common-sense reforms that would make the defined contribution pension system easier to navigate and more rewarding for American families:

—The most important change would be to *make saving easier* and less complicated. One way would be through automatic 401(k)s for workers at firms offering pensions and automatic IRAs for other workers.

—Another important move would be to *restructure tax incentives* for retirement saving. Existing incentives mostly subsidize asset shifting by higher-income households rather than encourage new saving by middle- and lower-income households. A simple 30 percent match for everyone would give moderate- and lower-income households—some 80 percent of households—a stronger incentive to save.

—Finally, *implicit taxes on retirement saving should be reduced*. These steep and confusing taxes are often imposed through means-tested benefit programs, such as the Food Stamp program, Medicaid, Supplemental Security Income, and cash welfare assistance.

This set of policies is much more promising than the alternative of simply raising contribution amounts or income limits on tax-preferred retirement saving. Such strategies merely perpetuate tax preferences for households that already are well prepared for retirement and undermine the public policy benefit from these tax incentives. ❯

CONTEXT ❯ The trend away from traditional, employer-managed retirement plans and toward saving arrangements directed and managed largely by employees themselves, such as 401(k)s and IRAs, is in many ways a good thing. Workers enjoy more freedom of choice and more control over their retirement planning. But for too many households, the 401(k) and IRA revolution has fallen short.

The most vivid manifestation of the shortcomings of today's private pension arrangements is the simple fact that many families approaching retirement age have little or no retirement savings.[1] In 2004, according to data from the Federal Reserve's Survey of Consumer Finances, half of all households headed by adults age fifty-five to fifty-nine had $15,000 or less in an employer-based 401(k)-type plan or tax-preferred savings account. Although the savings option is there, Americans do not take advantage of it for two principal reasons:

—The system is too complicated.

—Incentives to save for retirement are weak or nonexistent.

In the face of the difficult choices and limited encouragement presented by the current system, many people simply procrastinate and never save enough for retirement.

The primary policy tool used to encourage participation in employer-based retirement plans and IRAs is a set of deductions and exclusions from federal income tax. The immediate value of any tax deduction or exclusion, however, depends directly on the taxpayer's income tax bracket. For example, a couple with $6,000 in deductible IRA contributions saves $1,500 in tax if they are in the 25 percent marginal tax bracket but only $600 if they are in the 10 percent bracket.[2] Thus this approach provides the smallest benefits to the middle- and lower-income families who most need to save more in order to meet their basic needs in retirement. Furthermore, as a strategy for promoting national saving, the subsidies are poorly targeted. Higher-bracket households are disproportionately likely to respond by shifting existing assets from taxable to tax-preferred accounts. To the extent that such shifting occurs, the net result is that the pensions serve as a tax shelter rather than as a vehicle to increase saving. By contrast, middle- and lower-income households that participate in pensions are most likely to use the accounts to increase net saving. ❯

MAKING IT EASIER TO SAVE

To make it easier for households to save, policymakers should encourage greater adoption of automatic 401(k)s and create an automatic IRA.

Automating the 401(k)

401(k)-type plans typically leave it to the employee to choose whether to participate, how much to contribute, which investment vehicle offered by the employer to select, and when to pull the funds out of the plan and in what form. Workers are thus confronted with a series of complex decisions, each of which involves risk and requires a certain degree of financial expertise. Many workers shy away from making those decisions and simply do not choose. Those who do choose often select poorly.

To improve 401(k) participation, we should recognize the power of inertia in human behavior and enlist it to promote rather than hinder saving. Under an automatic 401(k), each of the key events in the process—enrollment, escalation, investment, and rollover—would be programmed to make contributing and investing easier and more effective. In each case, workers could always choose to override the defaults and opt out of the automatic design. Automatic retirement plans thus do not dictate choices any more than do conventional default options, which exclude workers unless they opt to participate. Instead, automatic retirement plans merely point workers in a pro-saving direction when they decline to make explicit choices on their own.

Research shows that these steps can be remarkably effective. For example, one of the strongest empirical findings from behavioral economics is that *automatic enrollment boosts the rate of plan participation substantially.*[3] Further, as figure 24-1 shows, automatic enrollment is particularly effective in boosting participation among groups that face the most difficulty in saving.

Figure 24-1. Effects of Automatic Enrollment on 401(k) Participation

Percent

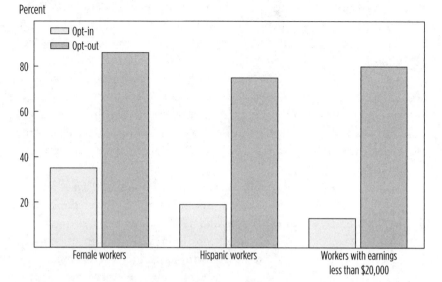

Source: Brigitte Madrian and Dennis Shea, "The Power of Suggestion: Inertia in 401(k) Participation and Savings Behavior," *Quarterly Journal of Economics* 116, no.4 (November 2001): 1160.

Automatic enrollment is a relatively new strategy, but a small and growing share of 401(k) plans today include this feature. According to a recent survey, 24 percent of 401(k) plans (and 41 percent of plans with at least 5,000 participants) have switched from the traditional "opt-in" to an "opt-out" arrangement.[4] In August 2006, President Bush signed pension legislation that goes a long way toward taking down the barriers to corporate adoption of the automatic 401(k). Now corporate America has the opportunity to automate more of its 401(k) plans.

Creating an Automatic IRA

Since, at any one time, only about half of the U.S. workforce is offered an employer-based pension, we also must make it easier for other workers to save. An "automatic IRA" would address this challenge.[5] As in the case of 401(k) plans, the automatic IRA's features would apply at each relevant step: enrollment, escalation, and investment. In the case of the IRA, rollover is not an issue, because these accounts would be held by the individual, rather than linked to an employer. As with the automatic 401(k), workers could choose to override the IRA defaults at any stage.

Under this proposal, firms that do not offer any type of automatic pension plan would be required to set up automatic payroll deduction IRAs for their workers. Firms that do offer 401(k) or other qualified plans also could set up these IRAs, but they would not be required to do so. Workers who did not opt out would have part of their paycheck flow into the "automatic IRA." The share of the paycheck flowing to the account would automatically escalate over time, unless the worker declined such increases. Legislators could provide a modest tax credit for start-up administrative costs at firms required to offer an automatic IRA. The IRA's funds would be automatically invested in a limited number of diversified funds.

The automatic IRA also could receive part of a household's income tax refund each year. For many households, and particularly for those with low or moderate incomes, the refund is the largest single payment received all year. Accordingly, the more than $200 billion in refunds issued annually presents a unique opportunity to increase personal saving. As of January 2007, taxpayers may split their refunds between designated accounts, which could include their automatic IRA. Allowing taxpayers to split their refunds could make saving simpler and, thus, more likely. Families also might be able to commit to depositing an increasing share of their *future* tax refunds to the automatic IRA. Families could always override this decision when the time came, but the default would be that, over time, a rising share of each year's tax refund would be deposited into the automatic IRA.

INCREASING THE INCENTIVE TO SAVE

Even though savings decisions can be heavily influenced by behavioral factors such as defaults, economic incentives are nonetheless important. In fact, the rate at which the government matches retirement savings contributions can have a significant effect. For example, a recent well-designed study found that households selected significantly higher IRA contributions when offered a higher match rate.[6]

Unfortunately, current tax incentives for retirement saving do not promote new saving among those most at risk of inadequate retirement security. To better target incentives to save, we should replace the existing tax deductions for contributions to retirement saving accounts with a government matching contribution into the account.[7] Unlike in the current system, workers' contributions to employer-based 401(k) accounts would no longer be excluded from taxation and contributions to IRAs would no longer be tax deductible. Furthermore, any employer contributions to a 401(k) plan would be treated as taxable income to the employee, just as current wages are. These increases in taxable income would be offset by making all qualified employer and employee contributions eligible for a government matching contribution. Earnings in 401(k)s and IRAs would continue to accrue tax free, and withdrawals from the accounts would continue to be taxed at regular income rates, as under current law. This proposal would be roughly revenue neutral for the federal government, according to estimates from the Tax Policy Center microsimulation model.

Advantages of this approach over the existing system are numerous. For any given dollar deposited into an account, the match rate would depend solely on savings relative to income (up to the contribution limits), not on the level of income itself. As a result, the matching system would provide every family with the same proportional benefit for saving (at least up to the contribution limits). Many investment advisers counsel people to save a certain percentage of their income, in order avoid a sharp decline in their living standard after retirement. Providing a government match based on the share of income saved promotes this consistent approach to saving.

As noted above, the government matching payment would be directly deposited into the retirement account. This strategy would make the matching funds more likely to be saved than are the funds represented by the current tax deduction. This form of the incentive may even induce additional household saving, since, possibly analogously, direct matches appear more effective than equivalent tax rebates at inducing people to contribute to charities, for example. A further incentive for keeping the matching funds in savings arises because when they are withdrawn from the account, they are subject to taxation, just as under an existing 401(k) or traditional IRA.

Compared with the current system, these proposed incentives would reduce the tax subsidy for saving by high-income households while raising it for lower- and middle-income individuals. A family with $30,000 in income receives no benefit under the existing system of tax deductions and exclusions (since the family does not have positive income tax liability), but under this proposal the family would receive $600 as a match for saving $2,000. In contrast, the overall benefit for a family with $500,000

in income and $20,000 of retirement contributions would decline from
$7,000 to $3,900. Still, roughly 80 percent of all households would enjoy
a stronger saving incentive under this proposal than under current law,
including all households with incomes below $30,000 and more than 40
percent of households with incomes between $75,000 and $100,000.

REDUCING IMPLICIT TAXES
ON RETIREMENT SAVING

Another way to increase incentives for middle- and low-income households to save is by removing penalties imposed on saving.[8] In particular,
the asset rules in means-tested benefit programs often penalize moderate-
and low-income families who have saved for retirement in 401(k)s or IRAs.
The major means-tested benefit programs, including the Food Stamp program, cash welfare assistance, and Medicaid, either require or allow states
to apply asset tests when determining eligibility, as does the Supplemental
Security Income (SSI) program for the elderly and people with disabilities.
Asset tests can force households that rely on these benefits—or might rely
on them in the future—to deplete retirement savings in order to qualify,
even when doing so involves a financial penalty. As a result, the asset tests
represent a substantial implicit tax on retirement saving.

These asset tests are one of the most glaring examples of how our
laws and regulations have failed to keep pace with the evolution in the
nation's pension system. Employer-sponsored defined benefit plans were
the norm when the rules were developed, and the plans generally were
not considered in asset tests. But at that time, defined contribution
accounts like 401(k)s and IRAs were not exempted, because they were
not viewed as primary pension vehicles. The failure to update these rules
means that many means-tested programs still exempt defined benefit
plans while counting 401(k)s and IRAs. Excluding these plans when
applying asset tests would be much more equitable and would remove a
significant barrier to increasing retirement saving among low-income
working households.

Furthermore, the rules governing the means-tested benefit programs are
complex, confusing, and often seemingly arbitrary as they apply to 401(k)s
and IRAs. As just one example, workers who roll their 401(k) over into an
IRA when they switch jobs, as many financial planners suggest they
should, could disqualify themselves from the Food Stamp program.

Table 24-1. 401(k) Participants Making the Maximum Contribution in 2000

Household income (AGI)	Total contributors (in thousands)	Percentage of total contributors	Percentage contributing the maximum
Less than $20,000	2,874	7.5	1
$20,000 to $40,000	8,881	23.2	2
$40,000 to $80,000	15,319	40.1	4
$80,000 to $120,000	6,589	17.2	11
$120,000 to $160,000	2,190	5.7	20
$160,000 or more	2,373	6.2	38
Total	38,226	100.0	7

Source: Author's calculations based on Congressional Budget Office, *Utilization of Tax Incentives for Retirement Saving: An Update* (February 2006), table 4.
AGI = adjusted gross income.

To not count saving in retirement accounts when applying the asset tests would allow low-income families to build retirement saving without having to forgo means-tested benefits at times when their incomes are low during their working years.

AVOIDING FURTHER TAX SUBSIDIES FOR ASSET SHIFTING

The commonsense reforms described above could significantly bolster retirement security for millions of Americans. However, some policymakers seem inclined to couple these proposals with a number of other provisions that would expand income and contribution limits on tax-preferred retirement accounts. Such proposals would have fundamentally different effects: rather than bolstering retirement security among middle- and lower-income workers, proposals to increase income and contribution limits would generate significant asset shifting and primarily benefit households already disproportionately well prepared for retirement. Policymakers should not be tempted to create substantial new tax subsidies for this type of asset shifting at the expense of sensible policies to bolster retirement security among middle- and lower-income households.

One common proposal would increase the maximum amount that can be saved on a tax-preferred basis, such as by raising the amount that can be contributed to an IRA or 401(k). But only a small fraction of households would be affected.[9] Table 24-1 shows that in 2000, only 7 percent of all 401(k) participants made the maximum allowed contribution but that the percentage who did so rose sharply with income. In short, rather than encouraging new saving, the expanded tax preference would mostly translate into subsidizing saving that would have occurred anyway and provide windfall gains to a few well-resourced households.

CONCLUDING OBSERVATIONS

Bolstering retirement security on top of Social Security need not be contentious and divisive. Over the past twenty-five years, the ways in which Americans save for retirement have changed, shifting more responsibility to workers, and our fiscal policies need to catch up. Given the known shortfalls in retirement saving among millions of American households, policies that improve retirement security are urgently needed. But these should not be accompanied by policies that merely encourage government-subsidized asset shifting among households that already tend to be adequately prepared for retirement. Instead, policymakers should focus on the groups most in need, making saving easier and increasing the incentive to save for middle- and low-income workers.

NOTES

1. For a broader discussion of these issues, see William G. Gale and Peter R. Orszag, "Private Pensions: Issues and Options," in *Agenda for the Nation,* edited by Henry J. Aaron, James M. Lindsay, and Pietro S. Nivola (Brookings, 2003), pp. 183–216; Peter R. Orszag, "Progressivity and Saving: Fixing the Nation's Upside-Down Incentives for Saving," testimony before the House Committee on Education and the Workforce, 108 Cong. 2 sess. (February 25, 2004); J. Mark Iwry, "Defined Benefit Plans and Their Role in the Private Pension System," testimony before the House Committee on Education and the Workforce, Subcommittee on Employer-Employee Relations, 108 Cong. 1 sess. (June 4, 2003). These and other related publications are available on the Retirement Security Project website (www.retirement securityproject.org).

2. Some of this difference may be recouped when the contributions are withdrawn and taxed, if families who are in lower tax brackets during their working years are also in lower tax brackets during retirement.

3. Brigitte Madrian and Dennis Shea, "The Power of Suggestion: Inertia in 401(k) Participation and Savings Behavior," *Quarterly Journal of Economics* 116 (November 2001): 1149–187; and James Choi and others, "Defined Contribution Pensions: Plan

Rules, Participant Decisions, and the Path of Least Resistance," in *Tax Policy and the Economy,* vol. 16, edited by James Poterba (MIT Press, 2002), pp. 67–113.

4. Profit Sharing/401(k) Council of America, *50th Annual Survey of Profit Sharing and 401(k) Plans* (Chicago: PSCA, 2007).

5. J. Mark Iwry and David C. John, *Pursuing Universal Retirement Security through Automatic IRAs* (Washington: Retirement Security Project, February 2006).

6. Esther Duflo and others, "Saving Incentives for Low- and Middle-Income Families: Evidence from a Field Experiment with H&R Block," *Quarterly Journal of Economics* 121 (November 2006): 1311–346.

7. William Gale, Jonathan Gruber, and Peter Orszag, "Improving Opportunities and Incentives for Saving by Middle- and Low-Income Households," Hamilton Project Discussion Paper (Brookings, April 2006).

8. Zoe Neuberger, Robert Greenstein, and Eileen P. Sweeney, *Protecting Low-Income Families' Retirement Savings: How Retirement Accounts Are Treated in Means-Tested Programs and Steps to Remove Barriers to Retirement Saving* (Washington: Retirement Security Project, June 2005).

9. See, for example, David Joulfaian and David Richardson, "Who Takes Advantage of Tax-Deferred Saving Programs? Evidence from Federal Income Tax Data" (Washington: Office of Tax Analysis, U.S. Treasury Department, 2001); Janette Kawachi, Karen E. Smith, and Eric J. Toder, "Making Maximum Use of Tax-Deferred Retirement Accounts," Working Paper (Washington: Urban Institute, May 2006); U.S. Government Accountability Office, *Private Pensions: Issues of Coverage and Increasing Contribution Limits for Defined Contribution Plans,* GAO-01-846 (GAO, September 2001). The GAO also found that 85 percent of those who would benefit from an increase in the 401(k) contribution limit earn more than $75,000. These figures reflect the effects of other changes included in the Economic Growth and Tax Relief Reconciliation Act of 2001 that have already taken effect, such as the elimination of the previous percentage cap on the amount of combined employer-employee contributions that can be made to defined contribution plans.

25

Fixing the Tax System

Support Fairer, Simpler, and More Adequate Taxation

WILLIAM G. GALE

SUMMARY ❱ A good tax system raises the revenues needed to finance government spending in a manner that is as simple, equitable, stable, and conducive to economic growth as possible. But the challenge for the next president will be to make reform work not just in the abstract, but in the real world, where special interests often rule the roost. The next president should support reforms that would tax all income once (only) at the full tax rate, simplify and streamline the tax code, and, of course, raise sufficient revenues. To achieve these goals, the package of specific reforms proposed in this paper would

—tax all new corporate investment income only once;

—remove all corporate subsidies in the tax code and strengthen corporate anti-sheltering provisions;

—integrate payroll and income taxes for individuals;

—introduce return-free filing for many taxpayers;

—consolidate and streamline tax subsidies for education, retirement, and families;

—eliminate or revise various tax deductions;

—create a value-added tax that would, eventually, raise 5 percent of the gross domestic product (GDP) in revenues. ❱

CONTEXT ❯ In the next few years, several factors will push tax issues to the forefront of policy discussions. First, under current law, almost all of the Bush administration's tax cuts will expire at the end of 2010. The loss in revenues from making the tax cuts permanent would be enormous—equal to several times the resources needed to repair Social Security—and economic growth would be unlikely to come anywhere close to covering that loss. As a result, the required spending reductions would be enormous, too. For example, if certain key programs—Social Security, Medicare, Medicaid, defense, homeland security, and net interest—were off-limits, all other federal spending would have to be cut by *almost half* to pay for permanent tax cuts.

A second factor is the rapid growth in the Alternative Minimum Tax (AMT), which will increase the inequity and complexity of the tax system. Tax filers pay the AMT when their AMT liability exceeds their regular income tax liability. Designed in the late 1960s and strengthened in 1986, the AMT operates parallel to the regular tax system and was originally intended to capture tax on excessive sheltering activity. The tax has evolved, however, so that it does not tax many shelters but does tax a variety of other things—like having children, being married, or paying state taxes—that most people do not consider shelters. Moreover, the number of taxpayers facing the AMT is slated to grow exponentially, from about 3.5 million today to 32 million by 2010, because the AMT is not indexed for inflation and because some temporary AMT tax cuts are about to expire.

A third issue—which may not require immediate action but should nevertheless help frame the current debate—is the expected increase in government spending over the next several decades. Since 1950, tax revenues have hovered between 16 and 20 percent of GDP. Under current projections, however, government spending will rise to about 29 percent of GDP by 2030.[1] The increase will be fueled mainly by increased entitlement spending for Social Security and especially Medicare and Medicaid. Unless candidates are willing to suggest truly massive cuts in such programs, they will have to come to terms with the need for an increase in revenues to above 20 percent of GDP.

Despite these pressures on the system, tax changes are not inevitable, and achieving meaningful reform—that is, with substantial design improvements—will require strong political leadership. ❯

WHY JUNKING THE INCOME TAX IS NOT THE ANSWER

Discarding the nation's existing Byzantine tax system and instituting "simple" flat-rate taxes has visceral appeal, and some candidates have endorsed reform proposals based on this approach. However, when real-world implementation issues are considered, each of these proposals has significant drawbacks. The three primary flat-rate reforms are the following:

—A national retail sales tax (NRST), under which a single tax rate would apply to all sales by businesses to households. Sales between businesses and between households would be untaxed.

—A value-added tax (VAT), requiring each business to pay tax on the sum of its total sales to consumers and to other businesses, less its purchases from other businesses, including investments. Thus, the increment in value of a product at each stage of production would be subject to tax. Cumulated over all stages of production, the tax base just equals the value of final sales by businesses to consumers—in theory, the same as with an NRST.

—The flat tax, originally developed by Hoover Institution scholars Robert Hall and Alvin Rabushka, is simply a two-part VAT: the business tax base would be exactly like the VAT except that businesses would also be allowed deductions for wage payments and pension contributions. Individuals would pay tax on wages and pension income that exceeded personal and dependent exemptions. Businesses and individuals would be taxed at a single flat rate.

These three models are all flat-rate, broad-based consumption taxes. Some people would like to use such taxes to replace our current graduated, narrowly based income tax. Advocates claim that such fundamental reforms could boost economic growth significantly, slash tax burdens, simplify compliance, and eliminate the IRS. Unfortunately, a more realistic assessment is less optimistic.

In order to replace almost all existing federal taxes and maintain government programs, a national retail sales tax would require markups at the cash register of *more than 40 percent,* not the 23 percent advertised by plan supporters.[2] This assumes there is little or no legal avoidance or illegal evasion of taxes. Experience in other countries, however, shows that a national retail sales tax would have difficulty controlling tax evasion if rates went much above 10 percent. Higher evasion, in turn, would require even higher tax rates to raise the necessary revenue.

The pure flat tax could theoretically replace the existing income and corporate tax with a rate of about 21 percent (and all federal taxes with a rate of about 32 percent) but could result in significant dislocation in the economy and declines in charitable contributions, real housing prices, and the number of households with health insurance. Businesses would find their tax liability varied dramatically from the current system and would no longer be based on profits. For example, Hall and Rabushka show that under their flat tax, General Motors' 1993 tax liability would have risen by a factor of twenty-five, from $110 million to $2.7 billion. In contrast, Intel's would have fallen by three-quarters.

More realistic versions of the flat tax—which would smooth out these problems by allowing transition relief; individual deductions for mortgage interest, charitable contributions, and state taxes; and business deductions for health insurance and taxes—would require flat tax rates of 30 percent or higher just to replace individual and corporate income taxes. In addition, under the flat tax, which has never been tried as a stand-alone system anywhere in the world, it appears that firms could re-label cash flows and shelter significant amounts of income, which would require even higher tax rates to make up the difference.

Junking the current system and moving to an NRST, VAT, or flat tax would provide massive tax cuts for the wealthiest households and increase the tax burden on low- and middle-income households. The so called X-tax is a variant of the flat tax that would introduce graduated taxation of earned income. The X-tax would be more progressive than the flat tax and would reduce, but not eliminate, the distributional disparities.

Many of the problems and trade-offs created by these types of tax reforms could be mitigated if they boosted economic growth dramatically. In their pure forms, the NRST and flat tax could have positive effects on economic growth, but when the taxes are subjected to the realistic considerations noted above, studies indicate that they would likely generate little if any net growth in the economy and actually could retard it.

FIVE ESSENTIAL REFORMS

The next administration can propose a number of reforms that would make taxes significantly simpler, fairer, more conducive to economic prosperity, and responsive to likely government spending increases.

Tax All Capital Income Once and Only Once
at the Full Income Tax Rate

The taxation of capital income—the return from saving—in the current system is, in plain terms, a mess. A family's saving is the difference between its income and what it spends on consumption. Thus, the difference between an income tax and a consumption tax hinges on the treatment of saving. The current tax system's treatment of saving has features of both types of tax. In some cases—notably the treatment of 401(k) plan investments—the system operates like a consumption tax; in others, it operates like an income tax—for example, the interest income on a savings account is subject to tax every year. Unfortunately, by combining features of an income and a consumption tax, the system creates the opportunity to shelter income.[3]

Now consider the complexities of corporate taxation. The issue of "double taxation" of corporate income has received some public attention. This occurs when earnings are taxed at the corporate level and then paid to individuals as dividends, when they are taxed again. But today, no corporate income is fully double taxed, since dividends are now taxed at only 15 percent. Corporate income can avoid taxes at the corporate level through shelters and at the individual level to the extent that the income accrues to nonprofits and pensions. As a result, only about a quarter of corporate income appears to be taxed at both the individual and corporate levels, whereas about one-quarter of corporate income is taxed at the individual level, but not the corporate level; one-quarter is taxed at the corporate level, but not the individual level; and one-quarter appears never to be taxed at all.

The bottom line is that capital income is taxed at greatly different rates depending on the organizational form, the type of activity in which the investment is deployed, the type of asset, the type of financing, and so on. This system is inequitable, inefficient, and complicated. Some analysts conclude that because taxpayers can use these conflicting rules to their advantage, the country collects little if any net revenue from capital income taxes. *The solution is to tax all capital income once and only once at the full income tax rate.* Reforming this part of the system would require policymakers to address several issues simultaneously:

—First, the integration of corporate and individual capital taxation should occur only for income stemming from new corporate investment.

There is no reason to give tax breaks on the income stemming from old investments; those tax breaks would be windfall gains.

—Second, individual-level taxation of corporate dividends and capital gains (on new investments) should be removed only if the full tax has been paid on the income at the corporate level. To the extent that corporate taxes were not paid, then corporate dividends and capital gains should be taxed at the *full* individual rate (not capped at 15 percent).

—Third, efforts to shut down corporate tax sheltering need to be beefed up substantially. This could include both increased enforcement as well as altered accounting procedures that require more conformity between income reported to shareholders (book income) and income reported to the IRS (taxable income).

—Fourth, a wholesale attack on corporate subsidies—for example, in agriculture, mining, oil, timber, and so on—would be a final, key element in this package.

If a new administration successfully promoted this entire package of changes, it could expect to increase net federal revenues from corporate and capital income.

Tax Labor Income Once and Only Once at the Full Income Tax Rate

Although much of the attention in tax policy debates is devoted to capital income taxes, wages and salaries represent the largest share of income for most people. Labor earnings are taxed under two separate systems: the personal income tax and the payroll tax. The liability for payroll taxes is, in legal terms, split equally between the employer and the employee. In practice, though, workers bear all or almost all of the burden of such taxes through reduced take-home wages. Payroll taxes are levied for Social Security contributions (12.4 percent of wages up to $102,000) and Medicare contributions (2.9 percent of wages without limit). Thus, net burdens are about 15 percent of wages up to the Social Security earnings limit and 3 percent on additional earnings. For about 70 percent of all households, and virtually all filers in the bottom 40 percent of the income distribution, these payroll tax burdens exceed income tax payments.

The payroll tax and the income tax could be integrated by providing a refundable income tax credit or abolishing the payroll tax on the first $5,000 of earnings or on all earnings, with the revenue loss made up by an across-the-board increase in income tax rates. Alternatively, the earnings ceiling on Social Security taxes could be raised or eliminated, or a tax on earnings above the Social Security earnings cap could be created, in which case an across-the-board reduction in the income tax rate could occur. Any of these changes would make the tax system more progressive and reduce the burden on low-income earners.

Rationalize the Structure of Deductions, Exclusions, and Credits

The tax system subsidizes literally scores of economic activities through a variety of mechanisms. Exclusions, exemptions, and deductions reduce taxable income on a dollar-for-dollar basis. As a result, a $1 deduction is worth more to a high-income household with a high income tax rate than it is to a low-income household with a low or zero income tax rate. By contrast, credits reduce tax liability directly, so that a $1 credit reduces each household's tax liability by a dollar. For very low-income households, credits that are "refundable" can generate a negative tax liability and can be paid back in cash, whereas "nonrefundable" credits merely reduce tax liability to zero. Clearly, nonrefundable credits are useless for households that do not have any tax liability to begin with. On the grounds of simplicity, equity, and possibly efficiency, credits that are aimed at meeting social policy objectives should be made refundable, so that they provide benefits to the households who need the funds most.

Expenses that truly reduce taxpayers' ability to pay taxes should be deductible in full, but very few of the currently allowable "itemized deductions" completely meet that standard. Although they are immensely popular and subsidize activities thought of as "good," for the most part they subsidize activity that would have occurred anyway as well as create numerous problems. They complicate tax filing and enforcement. They erode the tax base and are regressive, giving bigger benefits to high-income filers.

Finally, they hide subsidies that would be obvious if they were spending programs. Imagine that instead of a mortgage interest deduction, we had a program called "homeowner welfare," in which taxpayers earned a "welfare entitlement" equal to their annual mortgage interest payment times their tax rate. Anyone whose entitlement was below a certain threshold, say $6,000, would receive nothing. Anyone whose entitlement exceeded the threshold would receive the entitlement in cash. Such a program is not dissimilar to the way the mortgage interest deduction actually works.

The best solution would address each of the current deduction categories directly. *Charitable contributions* should be fully deductible; this preserves the largest incentive for giving for the highest-income households and ensures that those who give away all of their income would not owe tax. The *mortgage interest* deduction should be converted to a refundable, first-time home buyers' tax credit. This would generate revenue, improve homeownership rates, and eliminate incentives to buy ever-bigger houses with ever-bigger mortgages. Deductions for *state and local taxes* could be eliminated as part of Alternative Minimum Tax (AMT) reform; if the AMT is allowed to grow as under current law, very few taxpayers will have access to the state and local deduction anyway. Tax subsidies for *health insurance* should be handled in the context of a broader health care reform effort, but there is no question that they need to be restricted. Under the current system, in which health insurance payments are tax deductible, consumers do not face the full price of the health care benefits that they demand.

Simplify Taxes and Improve Administration

Although presidential candidates consistently say they would support a simpler tax system, every year taxes seem to become more complex. Some of the complexity is the by-product of using the tax system to achieve other policy goals, such as greater equity, but much complexity could be eliminated without making a serious dent in other objectives. As a prime example, return-free filing could be achieved for as many as 50 million taxpayers with relatively minor changes in the tax code. Return-free filing already exists in dozens of countries around the world and would eliminate the hassles of filing and compliance for the households least able to cope with them.

The number of households that could avoid filing would be further increased and other simplifications would occur if the personal exemption, the child credit, and the Earned Income Tax Credit were consolidated and if the standard deduction were increased. Increasing the standard deduction by the value of a personal exemption and reducing the number of personal exemptions by one would be revenue-neutral, and it would greatly reduce the number of people who must itemize. Similarly, education subsidies and retirement saving programs could be consolidated and streamlined.

The Alternative Minimum Tax should be abolished, if—and these are some big ifs—the anti–tax-sheltering provisions of the AMT are brought into the income tax rules, dividends and capital gains are taxed as described above, and the revenue from AMT repeal is made up by adjusting income tax rates upward. Alternatively, the AMT could be retained but reformed in a revenue-neutral manner that would both raise the AMT exemption substantially, to remove the middle class from the tax, and tax dividends and capital gains at regular tax rates, thus restoring the AMT's goal of closing shelters.

An intelligent tax reform also would equip the Internal Revenue Service with the resources it needs to enforce and administer the system. Many taxpayers simply do not pay taxes they actually owe. Providing the IRS with additional resources for enforcement generally would boost revenues and produce a fairer distribution of the tax burden.

Pay for Long-Term Government Spending

Given the increased government spending trends noted earlier, presidential candidates must give serious thought to the best ways to raise additional revenues over the next decade. Extracting another 5 to 10 percent of GDP in revenues out of the current individual and corporate income tax system—with its narrow base and ubiquitous deductions—would be extremely difficult, because the increases in tax rates that would be required would generate significant avoidance and evasion activities.

The need for higher revenue makes it even more important to reform the current system to keep tax rates as low as possible and the tax base as broad as possible. Doing so would increase the chances of raising significant new revenue from the individual and corporate income tax systems or payroll taxes if tax rates were increased in the future.

Alternatively, new revenue sources could be explored. The best bet here—and one for which there is very strong evidence that effective administration is possible—is a VAT, as a complement to the current system, not a replacement.[4] A 10 percent VAT could raise an additional 4 to 5 percent of GDP in revenue if the tax base were kept fairly broad. The great advantage of a VAT over a national retail sales tax is that the VAT is a proven collection system in force in more than 100 countries around the world. Exporters could follow established procedures for getting rebates at the border.

"Green" taxes—levies on pollution or resource extraction—also could be considered. Besides raising revenues, these taxes can contribute to a cleaner, healthier environment by providing price signals to those who pollute. They have foreign policy benefits as well, as they plausibly reduce U.S. demand for oil and dependence on oil-producing nations.

CONCLUDING OBSERVATIONS

Nobody likes to pay taxes. But the U.S. tax system does not have to be as complex and unfair as it currently is. Candidates should consider that the reforms proposed above would not only simplify the system from the tax-payer's point of view, they also would make taxes more equitable and—an important consideration—they would provide the long-term financial resources for the government spending that the public demands.

ADDITIONAL RESOURCES

Aaron, Henry J., and William G. Gale. 1996. "Introduction." In *Economic Effects of Fundamental Tax Reform,* edited by Henry J. Aaron and William G. Gale. Brookings.

Altig, David, and others. 2001. "Simulating Fundamental Tax Reform in the United States." *American Economic Review* 91: 574–95.

Bakija, Jon, and Joel Slemrod. 2004. *Taxing Ourselves: A Citizen's Guide to the Great Debate over Tax Reform.* 3d ed. MIT Press.

Batchelder, Lily L., Fred T. Goldberg Jr., and Peter R. Orszag. 2006. "Reforming Tax Incentives into Uniform Refundable Tax Credits." Policy Brief 156. Brookings (August).

Burman, Leonard E., William G. Gale, and Jeffrey Rohaly. 2003. "The Expanding Role of the Alternative Minimum Tax." *Journal of Economic Perspectives* 17: 173–86.

Goolsbee, Austan. 2006. "The 'Simple Return': Reducing America's Tax Burden through Return-Free Filing." Hamilton Project Discussion Paper 2006-04. Brookings (July).

Hall, Robert E., and Alvin Rabushka. 1995. *The Flat Tax.* Stanford, Calif.: Hoover Institution Press.

Hanson, Craig, and David Sandalow. 2006. "Greening the Tax Code." Tax Reform, Energy and the Environment Policy Brief 1. Brookings and the World Resources Institute (April).

Rivlin, Alice M., and Isabel Sawhill. 2005. *Restoring Fiscal Sanity 2005: Meeting the Long-Run Challenge.* Brookings.

NOTES

1. This estimate comes from the "alternative fiscal scenario," which represents "one interpretation of what it would mean to continue today's underlying fiscal policy." See Congressional Budget Office, *The Long-Term Budget Outlook* (December 2007).

2. The advocates of the sales tax made a simple logical error in calculating the required tax rate. When they estimated the government revenues that a sales tax would generate, they implicitly assumed that, relative to the current economy, consumer prices (what consumers pay, including taxes) would rise by the full amount of the sales tax. But when they estimated the amount of government spending that would be needed under a sales tax to maintain government programs, they implicitly assumed that consumer prices (including the sales tax) would remain unchanged from those in the current system. This inconsistency led to a systematic and substantial understatement of the required tax rate. See William G. Gale, "The National Retail Sales Tax: What Would the Rate Have to Be?" *Tax Notes* 107 (May 16, 2005): 889–911; President's Advisory Panel on Federal Tax Reform, *Final Report* (Washington: GPO, 2005) (www.taxreformpanel.gov/final-report/ [July 13, 2007]).

3. For example, if families borrow money by taking out a second mortgage, the interest payment is tax deductible. But if they use the money to invest in a 401(k) plan, the tax on the interest is deferred until withdrawal occurs. As a result, the effective tax rate on the investment is negative—investors can make money without risking any of their own capital simply by taking out a tax-deductible loan and investing in a tax-deferred asset.

4. Yale University law professor Michael Graetz also has proposed a VAT, but he would use the revenues gained to cut the income tax substantially—raising the exemption to about $100,000 and taxing income above that level at a flat 25 percent—and to halve the corporate tax rate. A significant concern with this proposal is that it leaves the government with virtually no options for funding what is likely to be a significant increase in future government spending. See Michael J. Graetz, "100 Million Unnecessary Returns: A Fresh Start for the U.S. Tax System," *Yale Law Journal* 112 (2004): 263–313.

26

Strengthening U.S. Information Technology

Keep America No. 1 on the Net

SEAN MALONEY AND CHRISTOPHER THOMAS

SUMMARY ❯ Leadership in information technology (IT) is the foundation for U.S. competitiveness and future economic well-being. The Internet is and will be the central medium of information technology today and for the next decade. It underpins large market opportunities for software, hardware, and Internet applications, and it enables a far broader set of industries to achieve greater transaction profitability, increase productivity, and create new markets—this is how the Internet and IT sparks growth.

America must stay no. 1 on the Net. The next president should endorse policies that enable American companies to remain the primary inventors and purveyors of Internet technology, that stimulate American entrepreneurs to continue to develop the best new Internet businesses, and that help American workers continue to receive the benefits of increased productivity and economic growth.

Retaining U.S. leadership is by no means ensured. It will require the next president to follow a well-documented path—investing in basic research and development, welcoming talented immigrants, making science and engineering education a priority, and encouraging expanded Internet availability.

Specifically, the next president should pursue the following objectives. The nation should

—recruit and retain 10,000 new mathematics and science teachers per year,

—double our annual number of engineering graduates,

—each year convince 1,000 or more of the nation's top engineering students to pursue doctoral studies,

—at least double the number of H1-B visas for highly skilled foreign workers to meet market demand.

By the end of the next two presidential terms

—regulators should "free the airwaves," so that 90 percent of Americans have broadband access, and 50 percent have wireless broadband access;

—the United States should double current federal funding for fundamental natural and physical sciences research to $40 billion annually.

These are not easy steps, but they are straightforward. The United States has all the ingredients for future Internet leadership—stellar research universities, a deep pool of financial risk capital, the largest domestic market in which to launch new technologies, and the greatest number of large technology companies that spawn new firms and new ideas. The policies of the next president will be a central catalyst to this leadership recipe. ❯

CONTEXT ❯ Technology leadership brings unique benefits to the U.S. economy. Information and telecommunications technology are fundamentally important drivers of economic growth.[1] They are substantial industries in their own right—for example, the U.S. semiconductor industry employs more than 250,000 skilled workers and accounts for 7 percent of GDP. A large proportion of the Fortune 500 includes IT companies, and twelve of the world's top 100 most valuable brands belong to U.S. IT companies, more than to any other industry.

However, IT has a broader and more powerful economic impact, because it enhances all aspects of the growth equation (capital input, labor input, and total productivity). It makes both capital and labor more efficient. But most important, IT enables the creation and distribution of new knowledge and breakthrough ideas more rapidly and completely, at little to no marginal cost. Increasing the generation and distribution rate of new knowledge is very powerful.

Technology investment has propelled U.S. economic growth for the last decade. In fact, IT investment contributed 20 percent of total U.S.

economic growth over the last five years, *not even counting* its impact on productivity outside the IT sector.[2] During that time frame, the United States generated more growth out of IT than did any other G-7 economy. If the United States had *not* invested in IT and telecommunications capital in the ten years from 1995 to 2004, the U.S. GDP would be roughly 9 percent smaller—that is, more than $1 trillion less. The well-publicized 2000–02 technology industry "bust" has proved to be a blip in a long upward trend of IT investment driving strong returns. ❱

THE RISE OF THE INTERNET

The massive uplift from IT investment since 1995 parallels the establishment of the global Internet and its accessibility via the World Wide Web. The long-term accumulated asset of distributed global computing was unlocked by the ability to connect it all together. Since the 1994 introduction of the Mosaic browser, which made the scattered data on the Internet accessible to the masses, the Internet and the web have grown very quickly. The number of Internet users worldwide has increased eighteenfold since 1997, to more than 1 billion. On a typical day, the average working American spends more time on the Internet than watching television. Figure 26-1 shows a similar growth trend for expenditures on the Internet compared with expenditures on all other media.

The rise of the Internet coincided with the rise of the great U.S. corporations of the last two decades. Nearly all of the major players of the supporting industries of the Internet reside in the United States. Google and Yahoo! were created to make the vast information on the Internet usable. Cisco Systems provides more than half of all Internet routers. Dell and Hewlett-Packard are the world's largest vendors of personal computers (PCs). Intel and AMD microprocessors power more than 95 percent of the PCs and servers on the Internet—and most of those computers run Microsoft's operating system.

The Internet is changing the world economy far beyond generating new IT equipment and software industries. Across numerous industries, physical transactions and physical products are being abstracted to virtual transactions that are then executed across the Internet. The Internet enables the one-to-one, one-to-many, and many-to-many mass processing of transactions between customers and businesses, maximizing marginal revenues and minimizing marginal costs for almost all types of commercial

Figure 26-1. The Internet Moves Up: Global Consumer Spending on Media

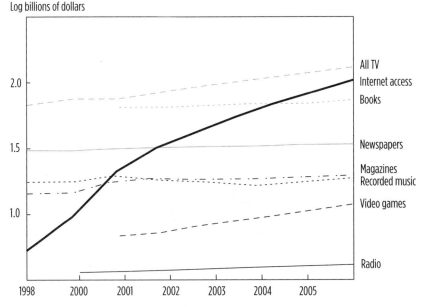

Source: PricewaterhouseCoopers, *Global Entertainment and Media Outlook: 2006–2010.*

interactions. Companies large and small (and often brand new) compete by knowing what, when, and how to best sell both digital and physical items while making the best trade-offs among production, inventory, and delivery costs. Large financial services companies are investing dramatically in connected computing power, because faster trades let them profit from fleeting market opportunities. Oil companies are analyzing massive amounts of underwater seismic data to increase the chances of hitting oil. Tiny "eBay entrepreneurs" by the hundreds of thousands run home-based retail businesses not possible before.

The Internet is rapidly changing the knowledge industries of news and entertainment. "Personalized" (versus mass) media now use the web to deliver customized information and news to millions through real-time subscription services or blogs. This demand trend marries the supply trend of user-generated content. Millions of individuals now create and share as much information over the Internet as they receive, with no printing costs, no editors, no producers, and no need for special equipment. More than 100 million video clips—the most popular of which are amateur videos—are downloaded each day. By the end of 2007, the installed base of digital cameras, camera phones, and camcorders that can create this homegrown content will reach 1 billion globally. Consumers now purchase their entertainment via highly personalized microtransactions—entertainment in thirty-second up to two-hour blocks, customizable by device, by song, by artist, by time, and by place.

Advertising is following viewers. Online advertising is growing 30 percent annually at the expense of television and print. Craigslist.org is the new alternative to local newspapers' traditional moneymaker—the classified ads. Search engines capture every click of a user's mouse, optimize the advertisements the user sees, and then sell that optimization to the highest bidder (who are advertisers).

What's Next for the Internet?

The Internet will advance as fast as the underlying technology allows. Rapid improvement in telecommunications and IT capability continues unabated—if anything, it is accelerating. Within the next two presidential terms, computer-based radios will have 250 times today's transmission capability, and semiconductor transistors will have 250 times today's number-crunching capability.[3]

Technology advancement at such a pace forces rapid industry evolution and destabilizes the structure of the technology industry (and of industries highly dependent on technology). The Internet, unlike any previous medium, is an open platform—anyone with an IP (Internet Protocol) address and a terminal can build a new Internet application, and at this moment, the next Google, Intel, MySpace, or Cisco is most likely a scribble in some graduate student's notebook.

THE INTEGRATION OF COMMUNICATIONS, COMPUTING, AND SENSING CAPABILITY

It will become difficult to characterize the Internet as the traditional model of a user, a PC, and a fixed broadband connection. Wireless Internet communications and computing capability will be embedded in an increasing array of phones, mobile computers, cameras, game consoles, home appliances, automobiles, clothing, and industrial equipment. These varied devices also will have sensing capabilities that will let them interact with the physical world. Phones will have global positioning system capability and will provide different services in different locations; UPS packages will have radio frequency identification transponders that will enable companies to optimize their supply chain through constant tracking of packages' status; home PCs will sense physical characteristics (blood sugar levels, heart rate, weight) to provide health and wellness data to both users and remote doctors. There are many more of these types of capabilities coming. These applications are possible today with customized technology—but the real impact will be when advancement lowers the cost and moves them to the mainstream.

GLOBALIZATION

In the 1990s there were hundreds of news stories describing how different countries were attempting to re-create Silicon Valley. These efforts are bringing results: Europe is home to global leaders in mobile telephony and telecommunications infrastructure; Korea and Japan have far higher broadband penetration than does the United States; China is investing heavily in local semiconductor companies, and its personal computer brand, Lenovo, recently bought IBM's PC division; and Taiwan, Inc., designs and manufactures nearly all the PCs today. Nearly all industrialized nations are doubling their investment in higher education in science and engineering and are promoting competitiveness in technology industries through tax credits and subsidies. And these countries are aiming at the crown jewels of the technology industry; the prime minister of India has commented often how advanced semiconductor manufacturing and process technology development (the hardest of the hard stuff) are central to India's future growth. China's focus is extreme. In the latest Chinese five-year economic plan, sixteen priority industries are slated to receive state focus and support (on a massive scale); five of those industries are the technology building blocks of the Internet.

THE FUTURE INTERNET: DEEPER, BROADER—AND MORE IMPORTANT

The Internet will remain the single most important "big thing" in the telecommunications and information technology industries for the next decade. Metcalfe's Law, which states that the value of a network rises as the square of the number of participants, indicates the massive value inherent in this singular network—and that the value increases exponentially each year as more users go online.

The demographics of usage indicate very high growth. For many young people, the Internet has become central to their social and cultural lives. At the same time, the emerging markets are getting online globally. Before the end of the next two presidential terms, more than 2 billion people will have instantaneous and permanent access to the collective knowledge of humankind via the Internet.

The Internet will be an even greater economic leveler. An online video website can be created for much less than $1 million. Amazon.com's recent effort to become an Internet utility that rents out its capabilities (bandwidth, server space, application hosting) will lower costs even further. The barriers to entry for starting an Internet-based business become smaller all the time.

Computing will become even more distributed—with processing power in far more objects and in the hands of far more people. Very small biotechnology companies will be able to use servers to test chemical characteristics of drugs at a scale far greater than the major pharmaceutical companies can do today in physical labs; the amateur astronomer will be able to do more detailed analyses of cosmic data than what NASA does today; and the smartest future students will be able to simulate nuclear explosions in their basements.

The Internet will go completely mobile, and just as mobile telephony has changed voice communications, the mobile Internet will greatly magnify the value and importance of the Internet. An always-on, always-available broadband Internet connection will have much greater meaning to users because it is much more useful—people want to know and do different things at different times and in different places.

The Internet will have real cultural effects. The most viewed Internet site currently is MySpace, a social networking site that connects people who never would have met otherwise. A quarter of single Americans have used an online dating service. There is some fear that these sites will cause societies to atomize—that people will spend too much time in their basements online. Yet the Internet is inherently a tool that expands, rather than contracts, social relationships.

PREPARING FOR TOMORROW

The above review leads to two conclusions: *we are only at the beginning of the Internet era—the biggest impact and the most groundbreaking innovations are yet to come, and IT leadership is of utmost importance to our nation's present and future economic success.* By leading at the beginning, the United States molded an Internet conducive to American technologies, American companies, American workers, and American users.

But the United States does not have any special right to be the global leader on the Net. The United States is currently benefiting from thirty, fifty, or even seventy years of educational, infrastructure, and basic research investment combined with a pragmatic business and political culture that encouraged innovation and the practical application of fundamental research. However, recent investments in this country have not matched this history. Ironically, the Internet's open nature makes it inherently easier for other countries to catch up—even if the United States were on the top of its game, other countries would be gaining.

Increases in foreign investment in and development of information technology are not bad for the U.S. economy. The IT industry benefits from economies of scale. Intel sells essentially the same set of microprocessors in more than 150 countries. Foreign companies purchase more than $500 billion annually in semiconductors, computers, servers, software, and fiber optics designed and produced in the United States. This begs several questions: Can the United States benefit just as much from the Internet era even if it is not the leader in its fundamental technologies? Can it be a "fast follower" as many other countries are today? Can U.S. companies simply use foreign-designed innovations? And can U.S. companies facing labor shortages find more skilled workers offshore easily? The nature of success in IT industries suggests that the answers to these questions are that we cannot.

In technology, the bulk of the profits and the prime market position are almost always held by those who first perfect or deploy a new technology solution—economies of scale and learning efficiencies make product leadership and being first-to-market of enormous benefit. This holds for Intel in the semiconductor market. *We believe this holds for countries as well.*

Product and time-to-market leadership are most likely to happen where one finds the best underlying technical infrastructure and the brightest technical workers. This fact is augmented by technology's powerful clustering effect and the dynamic IT industry structure. One successful company in one location prompts the creation of others. Supporting industries (venture capitalists, for example) then move in to drive greater investment, until an entire ecosystem is built around a certain geographic area—that is, innovation hot spots where start-ups flourish. A country's policies must support the growth of these small companies so that the country can grow the next giant. There were dozens of Silicon Valley search engine start-ups in the late 1990s—but only two have become major companies. The same math applied to personal computer companies in the 1980s.

A final argument for leadership in basic Internet technologies defies statistical analysis. The Internet is structured on an inherently American cultural model: open, egalitarian, participatory, dynamic, not kind to those who would hide or distort data—in short, a free marketplace of ideas, products, and services. Preserving this culture through continued U.S. predominance is an exceedingly powerful mandate.

Our fundamental recommendation is that the next president takes steps to ensure that America stays no. 1 on the Internet.

Secure the U.S. Leadership Position on the Internet

Keeping the United States in the forefront of IT innovation and development is a multifaceted goal that means that

—the United States leads in developing new fundamental and application technologies, in both the academic and commercial spheres;

—the United States is the best place to start new fundamental and applied technology companies;

—U.S. companies are the first to utilize and build upon new Internet technologies;

—the United States leads in extending Internet access to its people.

The next president can best achieve these goals by

—increasing U.S. investments in science and math education;

—developing an immigration policy that encourages the world's best and brightest to study, work, and live in the United States;

—substantially increasing the federal investment in basic research and development;

—investing more in, and encouraging the development of, our basic technology infrastructure, specifically broadband wireless technologies.

Strategies to ensure our continued IT leadership should involve public-private partnerships in education, research, and technology support. For example, the government can catalyze innovation and government policies can ensure a level playing field for investment, but the private sector can deliver the product.[4]

Restore U.S. Educational Leadership in Math, Science, and Engineering

Human brainpower is the raw material of technology advancement. Math and science are the foundational skills of technological success. U.S. companies were successful as the Internet took off because they tapped a diverse pool of talented, highly skilled workers built up over decades. This precious asset is seriously threatened, and although this paper will not address all of the reforms needed in the U.S. educational system, many specific shortcomings directly imperil U.S. leadership in technical education.

First, U.S. primary and secondary school students are falling increasingly behind their peers in other leading countries in math and science—at best we rank middle-of-the-pack. Our students' test scores are lower, and they are far less likely to have teachers with science and math backgrounds. Although U.S. students' scores on standardized tests have stabilized, we are standing still while other countries are advancing. Nearly all of the countries that are our primary competitors have defined, funded programs focused on improving math and science skills. Students who excel in these subjects are most likely to specialize in them in college; and as important, IT fluency and a grasp of the underlying technical concepts will be "table stakes" for nearly all the career opportunities that we will want our children to pursue.

Second, talented college undergraduates increasingly avoid technical disciplines, and our universities do not graduate enough engineers and scientists. Meanwhile, other countries have picked up the pace (table 26-1).

Engineers with advanced degrees have a disproportionate impact—they usually spark new ideas and breakthroughs. At the time of its initial public offering, Intel had only nine PhDs out of 342 employees. However, three of those nine were its two founders and its director of operations (Gordon Moore, Robert Noyce, and Andrew S. Grove).

Table 26-1. Bachelor Degrees Awarded in Engineering[a]

Country	Degrees per year (thousands)
China	220
EU-15	180
Japan	105
Russia	82
India	82
United States	**60**
South Korea	57
Taiwan	27
Mexico	24
Poland	22

Source: U.S. National Science Board, *Science and Engineering Indicators 2004* (Arlington, Va.: National Science Foundation, 2004), appendix table 2-33, as referenced in *Losing the Competitive Advantage? The Challenge for Science and Technology in the United States* (Washington: American Electronics Association, 2005) (www.aeanet.org/Publications/idjj_AeA_Competitiveness.asp).

a. The chart uses reported data from 2000 or the most recent year.

The United States still leads the world in the number of doctoral degrees per year in science and engineering. Our postgraduate programs in these two disciplines appear strong, with awarded degrees hitting an all-time high in 2005. Yet this total is up only 3 percent since 1996, while the IT industry has more than doubled. All of this growth in degrees is from foreign students—the absolute number of doctoral candidates with U.S. citizenship has actually *decreased* in the last five years.

The next president should advocate a decade-long strategy to improve math and science performance and increase capacity at every level of the U.S. educational system:

—The United States *should aim to recruit and retain 100,000 new math and science teachers* (10,000 per year) *as the foundation of our technical education programs.* The first step is to provide financial incentives for trained graduates to pursue this career, using four-year scholarships or student loan forgiveness of $5,000 annually.

—The government should work with private industry to fund *skills training for current teachers, with the goal of upgrading the skills of up to 500,000 teachers* by 2016.

—At the collegiate level, we must increase the number and quality of U.S. students who complete science and engineering degrees, *doubling the annual number of U.S. engineering graduates over the next decade,* by providing an additional 50,000 students per year with $15,000 annual scholarships for engineering and science study.

—At the graduate level, we should *recruit an additional 1,000 of the top U.S. engineering graduates per year to pursue doctoral work, using fellowships, scholarships, and federal research funds.*

A public relations campaign should support these initiatives and counter the perception that math and science workers are geeks and nerds, by making students aware of the financial facts of life: having in-demand technical skills leads to the well-paying jobs of the future.

Collectively, these programs would cost approximately $4 billion per year.[5] And clearly, while they would greatly benefit growth and development in the IT sector, they would be of enormous benefit to many other high-tech industries in the biosciences and energy development, among others.

Welcome Highly Trained Immigrants

In the past, the gap between the U.S. demand for technical workers and domestic supply has been filled by foreign nationals. In the current vigorous debate about U.S. immigration policy, the contributions of these workers are sometimes lost, even though their impact has been unequivocally positive. One out of every five scientists and engineers working in the United States in 2004 was foreign-born. Yet this situation poses nearly zero threat to the native-born workforce—unemployment in science and engineering has always been less than that of the general population and has *never* risen above 5 percent during the twenty-two years when it has been tracked.

However, just as domestic demand for highly skilled foreign workers is rising, the federal government has increased barriers to entry. The number of visas for these workers dropped to 65,000 after 9/11, down two-thirds since the late 1990s. Foreigners increasingly sense they are unwanted in America, and these potential Andy Groves or Vinod Khoslas are voting with their feet: foreign applications to U.S. graduate programs have fallen every year since 2001. Meanwhile, other countries are working hard to attract them. Japan has increased its foreign high-skilled workers by 10 percent since 1999, while relaxing its employment and residency requirements.

Immigrants are not just stopgap solutions to workforce holes—they also develop many new businesses. The largest U.S. companies founded by immigrants are all in the information technology fields. In a 2006 survey, the National Venture Capital Association learned that 47 percent of today's venture-financed start-ups were founded or cofounded by immigrants; and of all the U.S. publicly traded companies that *ever* received venture financing, *one out of four were founded by immigrants.*

The next president should lead efforts to roll out the welcome mat to highly skilled foreign workers and graduate students, through public statements and policy action. *These policies should increase the number of H1-B visas for highly skilled workers to meet market demand—to at least double the number today. At the same time, the student visa and H1-B visa approval process should be simplified and expedited, including rapidly minimizing the backlog of security background checks.*

Increase Investments in Science and Engineering Research

During the last ten years, the federal government has reduced its financial support for fundamental research and development that underpins Internet technologies. Public sector support is critical, because the federal government is the nation's primary funding mechanism for basic research. This makes economic sense—basic research has the longest lead time from breakthrough to commercialization, carries the greatest risk, and is least likely to receive private sector funding. The Internet would not exist if the National Science Foundation and the Defense Advanced Research Projects Agency had not created the first Internet that linked Department of Defense computers. The Web browser, fiber optics, routers, computer-aided design tools, and the computer mouse all started in federally funded labs.

The federal commitment to research and development funding is now at 0.75 percent of GDP—well below its pre-1990s peak of approximately 1.25 percent of GDP. The proportion of this funding applied to engineering, the physical sciences, math, and computer science has dropped considerably. Total government spending on space research, general technology, and the physical sciences will reach only $18 billion in 2006. *In stark terms, the United States is moving in the opposite direction of its global competitors.*

The new president should increase funding for fundamental natural, physical, and general sciences research to a total of $40 billion annually by the end of two presidential terms (an average annual increase of 10 percent from the current $20 billion level).

Strengthen the Internet's Physical Infrastructure

Leadership in Internet technologies depends on more than just a skilled workforce and research and development spending. The presence of a robust Internet infrastructure—and its use—is central. The more people who have high-performance personal computers, high bandwidth mobile telephones, and high-speed broadband connections, the greater the network effect and the greater the Internet's value. Companies in countries with the most advanced technology infrastructures can bring new, performance-hungry applications to market more quickly than can companies in less technologically advanced countries, thereby reaping the valuable first-mover advantage.

During the last five years, the United States has lagged behind other countries in technology infrastructure investment. The penetration of broadband Internet access—high-speed connections to the World Wide Web for homes and businesses—is a powerful indicator of infrastructure leadership. Sadly, we lag behind several countries in high-quality, affordable broadband access. (Japanese broadband users pay a tenth of what U.S. broadband subscribers pay, and they have far faster service.) In addition, with respect to mobile telephony, the United States has fallen behind other countries in advanced wireless technology. Although third-generation (3G) mobile telephony service has not delivered the performance and experience promised when it launched in 1999, it remains a solid step forward from existing 2G systems. First rolled out in East Asia, then Europe, 3G had no appreciable uptake in the United States until 2006.

Finally, the United States suffers from a substantial "digital divide"—high-income households are far more likely to have broadband Internet access than are the economically disadvantaged or rural residents (figure 26-2). Increasingly, this divide reinforces economic inequalities, because access to technology leads to more and better opportunities.

Encourage Broadband Wireless through Market-Driven Spectrum Regulation

Broadband wireless technologies are the most important of several solutions to digital access problems. Most broadband service customers today are connected to the Internet via wired connections, such as digital subscriber lines (DSL) or cable modem service. These technologies have been very successful in the United States, and growth was robust over the first

Figure 26-2. Broadband Internet Penetration, by Annual Family Income, 2006

Percent

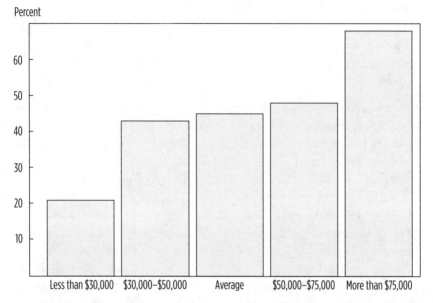

Source: John B. Horrigan, *Broadband Adoption 2006* (Washington: Pew Internet and American Life Project, May 2006) (www.pewinternet.org/pdfs/PIP-Broadband_trends2006.pdf).

decade of the Internet. However, geographic areas that do not have access to these technologies today most likely will never have it. Installing wired technologies in sparsely populated areas is simply too costly.

In the future, broadband wireless, which can be universal *and* mobile, will be the primary means for Internet communications. *U.S. policy should be designed to enable 50 percent of the population to have access to high-speed broadband wireless and 90 percent to have some form of high-speed broadband access by the end of the next two presidential terms.*

The United States has a significant opportunity to be the broadband wireless first mover—it can leapfrog other countries through emerging technologies. Wi-Fi uses unlicensed radio spectrum to deliver high-speed broadband over short distances in the home and office, and operators are experimenting with using Wi-Fi citywide. WiMAX delivers broadband access over a much wider area and can be used for fixed-location *and* mobile access. WiMAX can utilize both licensed and unlicensed spectrum and is inherently more efficient than existing 3G technologies.

Profitable deployment of these new technologies will require access to large, adjacent, and efficient blocks of the radio frequency spectrum—blocks not available to private enterprise today. Service providers will need to make substantial (at minimum $5 billion) investments over the next several years to achieve nationwide coverage. There must be a clear path to economic returns, or operators will not make this investment.

Federal agencies can accelerate deployment of broadband wireless by allowing private entities to use the spectrum bands best suited for broadband, giving providers the flexibility to deploy the most efficient technologies, and encouraging innovation and entrepreneurship by permitting more unlicensed operation in portions of the spectrum.

The United States has advantages already—it is one of the first countries to set a hard date for the transition from analog to digital television (scheduled for February 2009), which will free up 60 megahertz of spectrum that is ideal for broadband. The government should continue to make more spectrum available. *The National Telecommunications and Information Administration and the Federal Communications Commission should conduct a band-by-band analysis of the spectrum they regulate, identify any bands that are not being used efficiently, then allow market-based mechanisms to encourage more efficient use.* [6]

Finally, America should continue to move away from "command and control" spectrum management (whereby the government mandates specifically which technologies can be used in which spectrum bands), which locks in inefficient uses and technologies.

In particular, the new president should encourage the relevant agencies to provide operators with exclusive licenses that enable the technical and economic flexibility that will best promote market-driven competition and create largely unregulated, license-exempt, technology-neutral frequency bands to enable continued experimentation.

CONCLUDING OBSERVATIONS

The United States has the great advantage of incumbent leadership on the Internet—but that position is in peril. Yet our country's technology destiny can still be altered with the right policies, and there is reason to be optimistic. The Internet's future will benefit the innovative scientist, the risk-taking entrepreneur, and the pragmatic businessman. Americans thrive in these roles. America can become more competitive by becoming more American—more willing to welcome talent from abroad, more willing to invest in the future, more willing to promote engineering as sexy, and more willing to encourage scientific exploration.

The programs we advocate would require approximately $25 billion in new government spending annually (after eight years). The direct return from this funding is clear from past experience. Dozens of U.S. technology companies have market capitalizations exceeding $50 billion. Intel alone—one of many companies that benefits from government policy— employs approximately 50,000 U.S. workers, who receive compensation much higher than the national average, and it has paid nearly $30 billion in taxes over the last decade.

This is about more than simple economics. The Internet is an inherently decentralizing and democratizing medium that empowers the individual citizen, businessperson, and student. It allows and encourages the socialization and interaction of people across physical, demographic, and socioeconomic boundaries, encouraging an equality that resonates with the core American character. The Internet reinforces who we are and who we aspire to be. Finally, because it showcases core American ideals, it is an incredible tool of cultural "soft power" that is being embraced and embedded in economies around the world. For this reason as well, U.S. leadership in information and telecommunications technology is essential to our national interests. Our next president must commit strongly to keeping America no. 1 on the Net.

NOTES

1. This chapter uses the term *technology* in two senses: fundamental technology advances the basic capabilities of computing and communications (such as by increasing the storage capacity of a hard drive or the amount of data that can be sent over a fiber optic connection), and applied technology advances the use of those capabilities for a specific purpose (such as a new retail website or a network-linked manufacturing control program).

2. Dale Jorgenson and Khuong Vu, "Information Technology and the World Growth Resurgence" (Harvard University, Department of Economics) (http://post.economics. harvard.edu/faculty/jorgenson/papers/handbook.worldgrowthresurgence.palgrave.pdf).

3. *Moore's Law*: In 1965 Gordon Moore, who later founded Intel, predicted that the number of transistors that would be built on an integrated circuit would double

every two years—*an observation that has held true ever since*—while the cost of computing falls at the same rate. In ten to twelve years, this will give a basic personal computer the capability of today's supercomputer. *Cooper's Law*: Wireless networking technologies advance at a similar cadence, with carrying capacity doubling every two-and-a-half years for the past century, an observation made by Martin Cooper, an inventor of the portable phone.

4. Note that these recommendations do not explicitly propose sustaining America's market-leading risk capital industry, which is so central to new firm development, because this area currently is healthier than the others.

5. The calculation is as follows: $5,000 × 10,000 students × 4 years = $200 million; for engineering recruitment: $15,000 × 50,000 students × 4 years = $3 billion; for teacher training in math and science and for doctoral fellowships in engineering, including advertising, recruitment, and overhead, less than $1 billion.

6. See, for example, Technology CEO Council, *Freeing Our Unused Spectrum: Toward a 21st-Century Telecom Policy* (Washington, February 2006) (www.techceocouncil.org/documents/TCC-radiospectrumfinal3.pdf).

Contributors

HENRY J. AARON
Brookings Institution

HADY AMR
Brookings Institution

JOSEPH R. ANTOS
American Enterprise Institute

JEFFREY A. BADER
Brookings Institution

PETER BERKOWITZ
Hoover Institution

ROBERT BIXBY
The Concord Coalition

RICHARD C. BUSH III
Brookings Institution

ROBERT W. CRANDALL
Brookings Institution

KENNETH W. DAM
*Brookings Institution and
University of Chicago*

WILLIAM FRENZEL
Brookings Institution

WILLIAM G. GALE
Brookings Institution

MICHAEL GREEN
*Center for Strategic and
International Studies*

RON HASKINS
Brookings Institution

G. WILLIAM HOAGLAND
CIGNA Corporation

MARTIN S. INDYK
Brookings Institution

389

BRUCE KATZ
Brookings Institution

J. ROBERT KERREY
The Concord Coalition

AMY LIU
Brookings Institution

SEAN MALONEY
Intel Corporation

JOSEPH P. NEWHOUSE
Harvard University

MICHAEL E. O'HANLON
Brookings Institution

CARLOS PASCUAL
Brookings Institution

PETER G. PETERSON
The Concord Coalition

JOHN EDWARD PORTER
Hogan & Hartson
Washington, D.C.

HUGH B. PRICE
Brookings Institution

BRUCE RIEDEL
Brookings Institution

ALICE M. RIVLIN
Brookings Institution

PETER W. RODMAN
Brookings Institution

WARREN B. RUDMAN
The Concord Coalition

DAVID SANDALOW
Brookings Institution

ISABEL V. SAWHILL
Brookings Institution

JEREMY SHAPIRO
Brookings Institution

P. W. SINGER
Brookings Institution

REBECCA SOHMER
Brookings Institution, now at
Virginia Tech

CHARLES W. STENHOLM
Former Representative from Texas

CHRISTOPHER THOMAS
Intel Corporation

MARGERY AUSTIN TURNER
Urban Institute

TAMARA COFMAN WITTES
Brookings Institution

Index